AAT

INTERACTIVE TEXT

Foundation Units 22 - 23

Healthy workplace/Personal effectiveness

May 2001 edition

This Interactive Text for Unit 22 Health, Safety and Security and Unit 23 Achieving Personal Effectiveness is designed to be easy on the eye and easy to use.

- Clear language and presentation

- Lots of diagrams and practical examples – updated to reflect current best practice

- Numerous activities

New in this edition

In common with our other foundation material we have provided more activities and material to use in class

- More examples of Health & Safety policies

- Helpful re-organised material, to reflect changes at the Foundation level

- Updated coverage for topic areas such as health and safety, discrimination, data protection and grievance, to reflect recent legislation and Codes of Practice

- Practice Devolved Assessment material covering Unit 23

The text fully reflects the new standards for Units 22 and 23. It is up to date with developments in subject matter as at 1 May 2001.

BPP Publishing
May 2001

First edition 2000
Second edition May 2001

ISBN 0 7517 6506 6 (previous ISBN 0 7517 6210 5)

British Library Cataloguing-in-Publication Data
A catalogue record for this book
is available from the British Library

Published by

BPP Publishing Limited
Aldine House, Aldine Place
London W12 8AW

www.bpp.com

Printed in Great Britain by Ashford Colour Press

We are also grateful to the Lead Body for Accounting for permission to
reproduce extracts from the Standards of Competence for Accounting,
and to the AAT for permission to reproduce extracts from the mapping
and Guidance Notes.

	Page	Answers to activities

BPP
PUBLISHING

HOW TO USE THIS INTERACTIVE TEXT

Aims of this Interactive Text

> To provide the knowledge and practice to help you succeed in the devolved assessment for Foundation Unit 22 *Monitor and Maintain a Healthy, Safe and Secure Workplace* and Unit 23 *Achieving Personal Effectiveness.*

To pass the devolved assessments you need a thorough understanding in all areas covered by the standards of competence.

> **Interactive Text**
>
> This covers all you need to know for the devolved assessment for Unit 22 *Monitor and Maintain a Healthy, Safe and Secure Workplace* and Unit 23 *Achieving Personal Effectiveness.* Icons clearly mark key areas of the text. Numerous activities throughout the text help you practise what you have just learnt. This Interactive Text also covers certain information common to Foundation, such as the use of various communication formats and the basic structures and systems of organisations.

Recommended approach to this Interactive Text

(a) To achieve competence in Units 22 and 23 (and all the other units), you need to be able to do **everything** specified by the standards. Study the Interactive Text carefully and do not skip any of it.

(b) Learning is an **active** process. Do **all** the activities as you work through the Interactive Text so you can be sure you really understand what you have read.

(c) Before you take the devolved assessment, check that you still remember the material using the following quick revision plan for each chapter.

(i) Read through the chapter learning objectives. Are there any gaps in your knowledge? If so, study the section again.

(ii) Read and learn the key terms.

(iii) Look at the devolved assessment alerts. These show the sort of things that are likely to come up.

(iv) Read and learn the key learning points, which are a summary of the chapter.

(v) Do the quick quiz again. If you know what you're doing, it shouldn't take long.

This approach is only a suggestion. Your college may well adapt it to suit your needs.

Remember this is a **practical** course.

(a) Try to relate the material to your experience in the workplace or any other work experience you may have had.

(b) Try to make as many links as you can to your study of the other Units at Foundation level.

(c) Keep this text: (hopefully) you will find it invaluable in your everyday work too!

BPP PUBLISHING

FOUNDATION QUALIFICATION STRUCTURE

The competence-based Education and Training Scheme of the Association of Accounting Technicians is based on an analysis of the work of accounting staff in a wide range of industries and types of organisation. The Standards of Competence for Accounting which students are expected to meet are based on this analysis.

The Standards identify the key purpose of the accounting occupation, which is to operate, maintain and improve systems to record, plan, monitor and report on the financial activities of an organisation, and a number of key roles of the occupation. Each key role is subdivided into units of competence, which are further divided into elements of competences. By successfully completing assessments in specified units of competence, students can gain qualifications at NVQ/SVQ levels 2, 3 and 4, which correspond to the AAT Foundation, Intermediate and Technician stages of competence respectively.

Whether you are competent in a Unit is demonstrated by means of:

- *Either* a Central Assessment (set and marked by AAT assessors)

- *Or* a Devolved Assessment (where competence is judged by an Approved Assessment Centre to whom responsibility for this is devolved)

- Or *both* Central *and* Devolved Assessment

Below we set out the overall structure of the Foundation (NVQ/SVQ Level 2) stage, indicating how competence in each Unit is assessed. In the next section there is more detail about the Devolved Assessment for Unit 4.

All units are assessed by Devolved Assessment, and Unit 3 is also assessed by Central Assessment.

NVQ/SVQ Level 2 - Foundation (All units are mandatory)

Unit of competence

Elements of competence

Unit 1	Recording income and receipts

1.1	Process documents relating to goods and services supplied
1.2	Receive and record receipts

Unit 2	Making and recording payments

2.1	Process documents relating to goods and services received
2.2	Prepare authorised payments
2.3	Make and record payments

Unit 3	Preparing ledger balances and an initial trial balance

3.1	Balance bank transactions
3.2	Prepare ledger balances and control accounts
3.3	Draft an initial trial balance

Unit 4	Supplying information for management control

4.1	Code and extract information
4.2	Provide comparisons on costs and income

Unit 20	Working with information technology

20.1	Input, store and output data
20.2	Minimise risks to data held on a computer system

Unit 22	Monitor and maintain a healthy safe and secure workplace (ASC)

22.1	Monitor and maintain health and safety within the workplace
22.2	Monitor and maintain the security of the workplace

Unit 23	Achieving personal effectiveness

23.1	Plan and organise own work
23.2	Establish and maintain working relationships
23.3	Maintain accounting files and records

BPP PUBLISHING

UNITS 22 AND 23 STANDARDS OF COMPETENCE

The structure of the Standards for Units 22 and 23

The Unit commences with a statement of the **knowledge and understanding** which underpin competence in the Unit's elements.

The Unit of Competence is then divided into **elements of competence** describing activities which the individual should be able to perform.

Each element includes:

(a) **A** set of **performance criteria.** This defines what constitutes competent performance.

(b) **A range statement.** This defines the situations, contexts, methods etc in which competence should be displayed.

(c) **Evidence requirements.** These state that competence must be demonstrated consistently, over an appropriate time scale with evidence of performance being provided from the appropriate sources.

(d) **Sources of evidence.** These are suggestions of ways in which you can find evidence to demonstrate that competence. These fall under the headings: 'observed performance; work produced by the candidate; authenticated testimonies from relevant witnesses; personal account of competence; other sources of evidence.'

The elements of competence for Unit 22 and Unit 23 are set out below. Knowledge and understanding required for the unit as a whole are listed first, followed by the performance criteria and range statements for each element. Performance criteria are cross-referenced below to chapters in this Text.

Unit 22: Monitor and Maintain a Healthy, Safe and Secure Workplace

What is the unit about?

This unit is about the individual's ability to monitor the workplace to minimise risks to self and others and to maintain a healthy and safe working environment. This includes the identification and rectification, when authorised and competent, of potential hazards and emergencies and adherence to legal and other regulations relating to safe and healthy work practices. Also included is following set procedures for the security of the premises and its contents, identifying security risks and taking appropriate action.

Elements contained within this unit are:

Element: 22.1   Monitor and Maintain Health and Safety Within the Workplace

Element:22.2   Monitor and Maintain the Security of the Workplace

Knowledge and understanding

- Common forms of accident/health emergency (Element 22.1)

- Types and uses of fire and emergency equipment (Element 22.1)

- Hazards in the use of equipment (Element 22.1)

- Methods of minimising hazards in the work area (Element 22.1)

- Organisation's procedures for dealing with emergencies (Element 22.1)

- Own scope and limitations for dealing with emergencies (Element 22.1)

- Methods of reporting emergencies (Element 22.1 & 22.2)

- Relevant legal requirements (Element 22.1)

- Location of fire and emergency equipment (Element 22.1)

- Identification of potential security risks (Element 22.1)

- Organisation's security procedures (Element 22.1)

- Own scope and limitations for dealing with security risks (Element 22.1)

Element 22.1 Monitor and Maintain Health and Safety within the Workplace

Performance criteria	Chapters in this Text
1 Existing or potential hazards are put right if authorised	1
2 Hazards outsider own authority to put right are promptly and accurately reported to the appropriate person	1
3 Actions taken in dealing with emergencies conform to organisational requirements	1
4 Emergencies are reported and recorded accurately, completely and legibly in accordance with established procedures	1
5 Work practices are in accordance with organisational requirements	1
6 Working conditions which do not conform to organisational requirements are promptly and accurately reported to the appropriate person	1
7 Organising of work area minimises risk to self and others	1

Range statement

1 **Workplace:** all equipment, fixtures and fittings within own area of responsibility; all areas within the organisation

2 **Emergencies:** illness; accidents; fire; evacuation

3 **Organisational requirements:** instructions provided by the organisation to ensure compliance with legal requirements and codes of practice.

BPP PUBLISHING

Element 22.2 Monitor and Maintain the Security of the Workplace

Performance criteria		Chapters in this Text
1	Organisational security procedures are carried out correctly	2
2	Security risks are correctly identified	2
3	Identified security risks are out right or reported promptly to the appropriate person	2
4	Identified breaches of security are dealt with in accordance with organisational procedures	2
Range statement		
1	**Security systems:** personal identification; entry; exit; equipment	

Unit 23: Achieving personal effectiveness

What is the unit about?

This unit relates to the personal and organisational administration aspects of the accounting technician's role. At this level the individual is expected to organise their own work, establish good working relationships with colleagues, customers and suppliers, and to ensure all the relevant financial information is filed in accordance with organisational and legal requirements.

The first element requires the individual to use planning aids such as diaries, schedules and action plans, and to seek assistance where necessary to meet specific demands and deadlines. The second element relates to the individual developing good working relationships through responding to requests, meeting commitments and using appropriate communication methods. The final element is about the individual maintaining the filing and recording system in line with organisational and legal requirements.

Elements contained within this unit are:

Element: 23.1 Plan and Organise Own Work

Element:23.2 Establish and Maintain Working Relationships

Element 23.3 Maintain Accounting Files and Records

Knowledge and understanding

The business environment

- The different types of people: customers; peers; manager; other members of staff (Elements 23.1 & 23.2)

- Relevant legislation: copyright; data protection; equal opportunities (Element 23.2)

- The different types of documentation: incoming correspondence; copies of outgoing correspondence; financial records (Element 23.3)

- Sources of legal requirements: data protection; companies acts (Element 23.3)

Methods

- Prioritising and organising work (Element 23.1)

- Work planning and the use of planning and scheduling techniques and aids (Element 23.1)

- Time management (Element 23.1)

- Team working (Element 23.1)

- Work methods and practices (Element 23.1)

- Handling confidential information (Elements 23.1 & 23.2)

- Methods of establishing constructive relationships (Element 23.2)

- Seeking and exchanging information, advice and support (Element 23.2)

- Handling disagreements and conflict (Element 23.2)

- Using appropriate actions and different styles of approach in different situations (Element 23.2)

- Different communication methods and styles (Element 23.2)

- Types of communication difficulties and how to resolve them (Element 23.2)

- Employee responsibilities in complying with the relevant legislation (Element 23.2)

- Methods of classifying information: alphabetical; numerical; alphanumerical (Element 23.3)

- Sorting, handling and storing information (Element 23.3)

- The purpose of storing and retaining documents (Element 23.3)

The Organisation

- The organisational and departmental structure (Elements 23.1 & 23.2)

- Own work role and responsibilities (Element 23.1)

- Organisation's administrative procedures (Element 23.1)

- The customer base (Element 23.2)

- Organisational document retention policy (Element 23.3)

BPP PUBLISHING

Element 23.1 Plan and Organise Own Work

Performance criteria		Chapters in this Text
1	Routine and unexpected tasks are identified and prioritised according to organisational procedures	3, 4
2	Appropriate planning aids are used to plan and monitor work	3, 4
3	Where priorities change, work plans are changed accordingly	3, 4
4	Anticipated difficulties in meeting deadlines are promptly reported to the appropriate person	3, 4
5	Assistance is asked for, where necessary, to meet specific demands and deadlines	3, 4, 5

Range statement

1   **Planning aids:** diaries; schedules; action plans

Element 23.2 Establish and Maintain Working Relationships

Performance criteria		Chapters in this Text
1	Information is provided to internal and external customers in line with routine requirements and one off requests	8
2	The appropriate people are asked for any information, advice and resources that are required	5
3	Commitments to others are met within agreed timescales	5
4	Communication methods are appropriate to the individual situation	6
5	Any communication difficulties are acknowledged and action is taken to resolve them	6
6	Opportunities are taken to promote the image of the department and organisation to internal and external customers	5, 7
7	Confidentiality and data protection requirements are strictly followed	8, 9

Range statement

1   **Internal customers:** peers; manager; other members of staff

2   **External customers:** suppliers; customers; external agencies

3   **Communication methods:** written; verbal; electronic

Element 23.3 Maintain Accounting Files and Records

Performance criteria	Chapters in this Text
1 New documentation and records are put into the filing system in line with organisational procedures	8, 9
2 Item movements are monitored and recorded where necessary	8, 9
3 Documentation and records are kept according to organisational and legal requirements	8, 9
4 Out of date information is dealt with in accordance with organisational procedures	8, 9
5 Opportunities for improving filing systems are identified and brought to the attention of the appropriate person	8, 9

Range statement

1   **Documentation:** incoming correspondence; copies of outgoing correspondence; financial records

2   **System:** manual; computerised

3   **Legal requirements:** document retention; confidentiality

BPP PUBLISHING

ASSESSMENT STRATEGY

This unit is assessed by **devolved assessment**.

Devolved Assessment

Devolved assessment is a means of collecting evidence of your ability to carry out practical activities and to **operate effectively in the conditions of the workplace** to the standards required. Evidence may be collected at your place of work or at an Approved Assessment Centre by means of simulations of workplace activity, or by a combination of these methods.

If the Approved Assessment Centre is a **workplace** you may be observed carrying out accounting activities as part of your normal work routine. You should collect documentary evidence of the work you have done, or contributed, in an **accounting portfolio**. Evidence collected in a portfolio can be assessed in addition to observed performance or where it is not possible to assess by observation.

Where the Approved Assessment Centre is a **college or training organisation**, devolved assessment will be by means of a combination of the following.

(a)   Documentary evidence of activities carried out at the workplace, collected by you in an **accounting portfolio**

(b)   Realistic **simulations** of workplace activities; these simulations may take the form of case studies and in-tray exercises and involve the use of primary documents and reference sources

(c)   **Projects and assignments** designed to assess the Standards of Competence

If you are unable to provide workplace evidence, you will be able to complete the assessment requirements by the alternative methods listed above.

Part A

Unit 22
Health, safety and security

1 Health and safety at work

This chapter contains

1   Introduction: Why bother with health and safety?

2   Legal aspects of health and safety

3   Identifying and minimising hazards

4   Fire safety

5   Emergency procedures

6   Reporting procedures

Learning objectives

On completion of this chapter you will be able to:

- Put right existing or potential hazards, if authorised
- Report hazards outside your authority to the appropriate person
- Deal with emergencies in accordance with organisational requirements
- Report and record emergencies accurately, completely and legibly in accordance with established procedures
- Comply in all work practices with organisational requirements
- Report work conditions which do not conform to organisational requirements promptly and accurately to the appropriate person
- Organise your own work area to minimise risk to yourself and others
- Discuss common forms of accident/health emergency
- Describe types and uses of fire and emergency equipment
- Identify and know how to minimise potential hazards
- Outline the organisation's procedures for dealing with emergencies, and location and use of fire and emergency equipment
- Understand your own scope and limitations for dealing with emergencies
- Understand available methods of reporting emergencies
- Outline relevant legal requirements

Performance criteria

(1)   Existing or potential hazards are put right if authorised

(2)   Hazards outside own authority to put right are promptly and accurately reported to the appropriate person

(3)   Actions taken in dealing with emergencies conform to organisational requirements

(4)   Emergencies are reported and recorded accurately, completely and legibly in accordance with established procedures

(5)   Work practices are in accordance with organisational requirements

(6)   Working conditions, which do not conform to organisational requirements, are promptly and accurately reported to the appropriate person

(7)   Organising of work area minimised risk to self and others

Range statement

1   **Workplace:** all equipment, fixtures and fittings within own area of responsibility; all areas within the organisation

2   **Emergencies:** illness; accidents; fire; evacuation

3   **Organisational requirements:** instruction provided by the organisation to ensure compliance with legal requirements and codes of practice

Knowledge and understanding

- Common forms of accident/health emergency (Element 22.1)

- Types and uses of fire equipment (Element 22.1)

- Hazards in the use of equipment (Element 22.1)

- Methods of minimising hazards in the work area (Element 22.1)

- Organisation's procedures for dealing with emergencies (Element 22.1)

- Own scope and limitations for dealing with emergencies (Element 22.1)

- Methods of reporting emergencies (Element 22.1)

- Relevant legal requirements (Element 22.1)

- Location of fire and emergency equipment (Element 22.1)

- Identification of potential security risks (Element 22.1)

- Organisation's security procedures (Element 22.1)

- Own scope and limitations for dealing with security risks (Element 22.1)

1   INTRODUCTION: WHY BOTHER WITH HEALTH AND SAFETY?

1.1   You could probably make your own list of reasons for operating safely in the workplace.

(a)   Obviously, and most importantly, to protect yourself and others from **dangers** that might cause injury or sickness.

(b)   Sickness, accidents and injuries **cost money**.

(c)   Employees, as well as employers, have **legal obligations** to observe health and safety requirements. (We'll discuss these in Section 2 below.)

Risks in the office

1.2 You perhaps associate risk in the workplace with building sites or factories with heavy machinery or coal mines, but assuming you work in an **office** of some sort you need only look about you to find many potential **sources of injury** or **ill-health**.

- Slippery or uneven floors

- Frayed carpets

- Trailing electric leads, telephone cables and other wires

- Obstacles (boxes, files, books, open drawers) in gangways

- Standing on chairs (particularly swivel chairs) to reach high shelving

- Blocked staircases, for example where they are used for extra storage space

- Lifting heavy items without bending properly.

- Removing the safety guard on a machine to free a blockage or to make it run faster.

- Using chemicals without protective clothing or adequate ventilation.

- Taking inadequate work breaks, allowing excessive exposure or strain.

1.3 Sometimes none of these things are needed to cause an accident: it is very easy to do it without props! **Carelessness** or **foolishness** are major causes of accidents, and you need to remember that you are responsible for your own behaviour at work. Practical jokes and 'cutting corners' in work practices can have unforeseen consequences!

DEVOLVED ASSESSMENT ALERT

Don't think of health and safety as purely a legal or procedural matter! You need to be able to demonstrate an awareness of how everyday working practices, the working environment and the behaviour of people can put you and others at risk. (This unit is about the individual's ability to monitor the workplace to minimise risk to self and others and to maintain a healthy and safe working environment.)

Accidents and illness cost money

1.4 More than 700,000 people are injured at work in Britain every year, and the Health and Safety Executive estimate that the real **cost of work-related ill health, accidents and injury** equates to between five and ten percent of Britain's gross trading profit every year, an average of £170 - £360 per employed person.

Activity 1.1

What might be the cost to you, the employee, of a serious accident or illness at work?

1.5 **Costs to the employer**

- **Productive time lost** by the absent employee

- Productive time lost by **other employees** who (through choice or necessity) stop work at the time of, or following, the accident

- A proportion of the cost of employing **first aid and medical staff**

- The cost of **disruption** to operations at work

- The cost of any **damage to the equipment** or any cost associated with the subsequent **modification** of the equipment

- The cost of any **compensation payments or fines** resulting from legal action following an accident

- The costs associated with **increased insurance premiums**

- **Reduced output** from the injured employee on return to work

- The cost of possible **reduced morale**, increased absenteeism or increased labour turnover among employees

- The cost of **recruiting and training a replacement** for the absent employee

2 LEGAL ASPECTS OF HEALTH AND SAFETY

2.1 In the UK there are several Acts of Parliament applying to workplaces. The UK has also implemented six *EC directives* on various aspects of health and safety by issuing new **Regulations** and **Codes of Practice** under the **Health and Safety at Work Act 1974**. Regulations are legally enforceable, but Codes of Practice do not have to be followed to the letter. They are more like the Highway Code in the sense that failure to comply with them is *indicative* of failure of a legal duty in this context to provide a safe and healthy place of work. Some of the main provisions will be discussed in this section.

DEVOLVED ASSESSMENT ALERT

You are not expected to have a detailed knowledge of health and safety law, but you *do* need to be able to monitor and fulfil organisational procedures and instructions designed to ensure compliance with relevant legal requirements and codes of practice. The following background will help you to evaluate and fulfil these organisational requirements - but make sure you know exactly what your employer's health and safety rules and procedures are.

2.2 We need to look mainly at the **legal duties of the employer**. This is not so that you can police him or threaten him with prosecution, but simply so that you know what a safe and healthy workplace is supposed to be. Employers are obliged to designate specifically one or more competent workers to assist them in undertaking protective and preventative measures. If this topic interests you, you could consider putting yourself forward as such an assistant. Firstly, though, be aware that *you* have certain obligations.

Duties of employees regarding health and safety

2.3 You have a general **responsibility not to cause harm** to other people or property wherever you are - walking down the street, attending a lecture, working at your desk or sitting at home in front of the TV. You are guilty of a crime and/or a tort if you damage other people or property.

6

2.4 As an *employee*, you are obliged under the **Health and Safety at Work Act 1974** to:

- Take **reasonable care** to avoid injury to yourself and others
- **Co-operate** with your employer to help him comply with his legal obligations

2.5 Under the **Management of Health and Safety at Work Regulations 1992** you have the added responsibility to:

- Use all equipment, safety devices, etc, provided by your employer **properly** and in accordance with the instructions and training received

- **Inform** your employer, or another employee with specific responsibility for health and safety, of any perceived shortcoming in safety arrangements or any serious and immediate dangers to health and safety.

2.6 If an employee **flouts safety regulations** (whether or not an accident actually occurs) he can be prosecuted and fined up to £20,000 or, for very serious cases, he can be fined without limit or imprisoned. If he himself is injured he may be refused compensation because he brought the injuries upon himself. Even if the case does not go to court, the guilty employee may face disciplinary action by his employer.

Duties of employers: safety policy

2.7 The **Health and Safety at Work Act 1974** imposes specific duties upon employers to make sure that all systems (that is, work practices) are safe, that the work environment is safe and healthy (see below) and that plant and equipment is kept up to the necessary standard. Regulations issued under the authority of this Act require the employer to do the following.

(a) Produce a **written statement of his safety measures** and the means used to implement them. This statement should be brought to the notice of his employees. An employer who has less than five employees is exempt from this requirement.

(b) **Consult with safety representatives** appointed by recognised trade unions with a view to the effective maintenance of adequate safety measures.

(c) Appoint a **safety committee** if requested to do so by the safety representatives, to keep safety measures under review.

2.8 Under the **Management of Health and Safety at Work Regulations 1992** employers must:

(a) Carry out **risk assessment**, generally in writing, of all work hazards on a continuous basis

(b) Introduce **controls** to reduce risks

(c) Assess the **risks to anyone else** affected by their work activities

(d) **Share hazard and risk information** with other employers, including those on adjoining premises, other site occupiers and all subcontractors coming onto the premises

(e) Should revise **safety policies** in the light of the above, or initiate safety policies if none were in place previously

(f) **Identify employees who are especially at risk**

(g) Provide up-to-date and appropriate **training in safety matters**

(h) Provide **information** to employees (including temps) about health and safety

(i) Employ **competent safety and health advisers**

Activity 1.2

Consider the health and safety programme at your place of work (or study).

(a) How well *aware* are you of any rules, procedures and information regarding health and safety? (Who is responsible for *making* you more aware of such matters?)

(b) How well do the organisation's rules, procedures and information comply with the requirements of the Regulations?

2.9 EXAMPLE: A HEALTH AND SAFETY POLICY STATEMENT

The following is the Policy Statement released by the Department for Environment, Transport and the Regions (DETR), drawn from its staff InfoNet site.

Health and safety policy statement

"In my role as Permanent Secretary I am accountable to the Secretary of State for Departmental health and safety performance. I have overall responsibility to ensure that the Department has complete and comprehensive arrangements for health and safety issues.

This Health and Safety Policy Statement is to be observed by staff throughout the Department (including the Agencies and Government Offices). It reflects the importance I attach to the health, safety and welfare of all staff and others who may be affected by our activities. That includes contractors and visitors to our premises.

I expect all managers to give similar importance to these issues in their operational area and when determining local priorities, plans and resource allocation. I also recognise the valuable role played by Safety Representatives appointed by Trade Unions.

As the Department responsible (through sponsorship of the HSC and HSE) for health and safety policy within the UK, we will promote the highest standards of health and safety in our own work places. I will establish arrangements within the Department to deliver the following:

1 Objectives The Department will meet all current and proposed legal requirements in the Health and Safety at Work etc. Act 1974 and relevant subordinate legislation. This will be achieved through effective risk assessment and the implementation of appropriate measures for the prevention or control of risks at work. The Department will promote continuous improvement in health and safety performance to become an exemplar of good practice. Regular feedback on progress will be provided.

2 Systems The Department will put systems and procedures in place designed to ensure a safe system of work. As far as reasonably practicable, all equipment, vehicles, plant, premises, other work sites and work practices will be safe and free from any hazards to health and that employees, the public and others affected by our operations are not exposed to undue risk.

3 Communication/Co-operation The policy will be brought to the attention of all employees and contractors. Legally all employees must co-operate in establishing and maintaining safe and healthy working conditions and avoid any actions which may adversely affect the health, safety and welfare of themselves, their colleagues, contractors or visitors. Consultation on Departmental health and safety issues will be undertaken through the Departmental Whitley Council.

4   Monitoring and Auditing   The Department will monitor and audit health and safety management systems and performance. An annual report on health and safety will be produced reflecting the Department's progress, forward plans and innovative initiatives.

5   Review   The policy will be continuously reviewed. A full review, including related management arrangements and performance, will be held in three years time, or earlier, following any major change in health and safety legislation or our organisation.

The policy is fully endorsed by the Board and will be implemented by management throughout the Department. Roles and responsibilities will be clearly defined to ensure effective communication, provision of information, training, and systems for reporting to those with delegated responsibilities."

Duties of employers: the work environment

2.10   The **Offices, Shops and Railway Premises Act 1963** has a number of rules governing the environment in which employees work and these have been supplemented by the **Workplace (Health, Safety and Welfare) Regulations 1992**, under the EU Workplace Directive.

(a)   **Cleanliness**

Floors and steps must be cleaned at least once a week. Furniture and fittings must be kept clean. Rubbish must not be allowed to accumulate in work areas. This, of course, means not only paper but also food debris and so on.

(b)   **Overcrowding**

Each person should have at least 11 cubic metres of space, ignoring any parts of rooms more than 3.1 metres above the floor or with a headroom of less than 2.0 metres. This sounds like quite a lot of space, but it is not much more than the space occupied by your desk and chair and a passageway around it sufficient to allow you to get in and out.

(c)   **Ventilation**

There must be an adequate supply of fresh or purified air in circulation.

(d)   **Temperature**

A reasonable temperature must be maintained (except for brief periods). The minimum is 16°C where people are sitting down, or 13°C if they move about to do their work. A thermometer must be provided on each floor on permanent display.

(e)   **Lighting and windows**

There must be adequate natural or artificial light (preferably natural, if practicable). Windows must be kept clean inside and out and lighting equipment must be properly maintained. Windows should be made of safe materials and if they are openable it should be possible to do this safely.

(f)   **Toilets**

There must be enough suitable toilets and they must be properly ventilated and lit, kept clean and properly maintained. Broadly speaking, enough means a Gents and Ladies WC for every 15 to 20 employees.

(g) **Washing facilities**

These should be provided on the same scale as toilets. They should have clean hot and cold water, soap and towels or the equivalent.

(h) **Drinking water**

Adequate drinking water must be provided together with cups or a fountain.

(i) **Clothing**

There should be somewhere to hang up outdoor clothing and facilities for drying it. Facilities for changing clothing should be available where appropriate.

(j) **Seating**

Seats must be provided for rest periods, and, where work can or must be done sitting down, seats must be suitable in design, construction and dimensions.

(k) **Eating facilities**

Suitable facilities must be available for workers who eat in the workplace. Normally a desk in an office would be regarded as suitable.

(l) **Lifts**

Lifts must be safe. They must be examined by a competent engineer at least every 6 months.

(m) **Floors, passages and stairs**

These should be soundly constructed and maintained, without holes, slip-free, and kept free from obstruction. Stairs should have hand-rails; floor openings should be fenced round.

(n) **Traffic routes**

These should have regard to the safety of pedestrians and vehicles alike.

(o) **Doors and gates**

These should be suitably constructed and fitted with any necessary safety devices (especially sliding doors and powered doors and doors opening in either direction).

(p) **Escalators and travelators**

These should function safely and have readily accessible emergency stop devices.

(q) **Machinery and equipment**

All equipment should be properly maintained. Dangerous parts of machines should be fenced. No person under the age of 18 should be required to clean machinery if this would expose him to risk, and no person should be allowed to operate a machine specified as dangerous unless fully instructed of the dangers. Equipment is discussed in more detail below.

(r) **Heavy lifting**

People should not be required to lift, carry or move a load likely to cause injury. This is further discussed below.

(s) **Falls or falling objects**

These should be prevented by erecting effective physical safeguards (fences, safety nets, ground rails and so on).

(t) **Fire precautions**

Appropriate fire-fighting equipment should be provided and there must be an adequate means of escape. Business premises should generally have a valid fire certificate from the local fire authority (though this depends on the number of floors and the number of people). Fire exits should be clearly marked and escape routes kept unobstructed. Fire alarms should be provided and tested periodically and people working in the building should be familiar with the escape drill.

(u) **First-aid**

A firstaid box or cupboard under the charge of a responsible person should be provided for every 150 employees or fraction thereof (there should be two if there are 160 employees). Where there are more than 150 employees the responsible person should be trained in first aid and should be available to attend to accidents during working hours. Where there are more than 400 employees there should be a first aid room.

2.11   Even if you are **working at home,** you are still an employee and so your employer is required to provide you with a safe place of work, just as he has to for those employees working at his actual premises.

Duties of employers: first aid

2.12   The **Health and Safety (First Aid) Regulations 1981** require employers to provide adequate and appropriate equipment, facilities and personnel to enable first aid to be given to employees if they are injured or become ill at work. The minimum contents that should be found in a first aid box, for example, consist of dressings (plasters) and bandages of various sizes.

2.13   There are also certain items that should **not be kept in a first aid box**, including:

- Tablets
- Scissors
- Creams
- Tweezers
- Lotions
- Eyewashes
- Potions

These must not be offered or administered to employees even if requested.

2.14   This does not mean that you can't take a paracetamol tablet at work if you have a headache. However, it is **your responsibility** to provide yourself with what is appropriate. If you are allergic to a particular drug *you* are expected to have the sense not to take it.   .

Duties of employers: consultation with employees

2.15   Under the **Safety Representatives and Safety Committees Regulations 1977** and the **Health and Safety (Consultation with Employees) Regulations 1996,** employers must consult all of their employees on health and safety matters (such as the planning of health and safety training, any change in equipment or procedures which may substantially affect their health and safety at work or the health and safety consequences of introducing new technology). This involves giving information to employees *and* listening to and taking account of what they say before any health and safety decisions are taken.

BPP
PUBLISHING

Activity 1.3

A quick quiz! Under health and safety legislation there are certain requirements for workplace conditions. In your own words, briefly state the requirements under each of the following headings.

(a) Temperature   (e) Ventilation
(b) Eating facilities   (f) Equipment
(c) Room dimensions   (g) Sanitary conveniences
(d) Lighting

3 IDENTIFYING AND MINIMISING HAZARDS

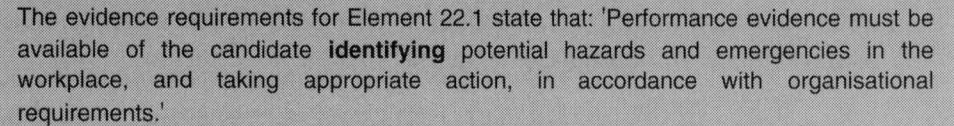

KEY TERMS

A **hazard** is a thing likely to cause injury, or a point of exposure to risk of accident, injury or loss.

3.1 In order to **minimise hazards** in the workplace, employers will need to assess the likely risk to the workforce from things such as the equipment and the machinery used by its employees and also the layout of the office in which the employees work.

DEVOLVED ASSESSMENT ALERT

The evidence requirements for Element 22.1 state that: 'Performance evidence must be available of the candidate **identifying** potential hazards and emergencies in the workplace, and taking appropriate action, in accordance with organisational requirements.'

Do not hesitate to check your workplace and work practices against the potential hazards described in this section.

Office equipment

3.2 You are expected to be able to use equipment as laid down in **operating instructions**. In practice you will probably be shown how to use office equipment like the photocopier, the fax machine and the computer printers in your first few days in a job. It is when you first encounter difficulties that you need to be careful.

3.3 It will not be long before you are the one using the photocopier when it runs out of paper or your print-out gets chewed up by the printer because the paper is not feeding through correctly. Obviously if you have not been shown what to do in these circumstances you should **ask somebody who knows**.

3.4 If you are likely to be using the equipment in question a good deal, **read the operating manual** and learn how to deal with routine problems.

Electrical equipment

3.5 Many of the items of equipment found in the workplace these days are electrical. The following adaptation from a photocopier instruction manual is designed to

demonstrate the kind of **precautions which should be taken when operating any electrical equipment**.

3.6 **General rules that apply when operating any electrical equipment**

(a) Never place **heavy objects** on the equipment, or subject it to shocks.

(b) **Insert the plug fully** into the electrical socket. Do not use damaged plugs or sockets.

(c) **Do not remove or open any covers** while using the equipment.

(d) If the equipment becomes **jammed**, follow the instruction manual for unjamming. Be sure to turn the equipment off if the information manual tells you to do so.

(e) Never **unplug or turn off** the equipment while it is in operation.

(f) When unplugging the power cord, do not pull on the cord. **Grasp the plug** and pull it out.

(g) If the plug or the socket get hot, **switch off at the socket,** pull out the plug and call a qualified electrician.

(h) Never bring any **magnetised object** near the equipment.

(i) Never use **inflammable aerosols or liquids** near the equipment.

(j) Never place a **vessel containing water** on the equipment.

(k) Be careful not to **drop paper clips, staples or other small objects** into the equipment.

(l) If the equipment produces smoke, becomes inordinately hot, or produces abnormal noises, turn it off, unplug it and then **call your local dealer** immediately.

(m) Turn the equipment off at the **end of the workday** or during a power blackout.

(n) **Do not plug the equipment into the same power outlet** being used for other electrical equipment.

(o) Watch out especially for **exposed wires**: stress points like the base of the plug and the point where the flex enters the equipment are particularly dangerous.

3.7 If the worst happens and someone receives an **electric shock** you should stop the current if possible by switching off at the wall or pulling out the plug. If this is not possible you should stand on a dry surface (a piece of wood or a newspaper is ideal) and knock the part of the victim's body clear of the source of the electricity using something non-conductive like a piece of wood, or a rolled up newspaper - *not* metal. Avoid anything wet and do not touch the person's body with your own until the current is switched off.

Activity 1.4

Your company has just purchased some laser printers manufactured in the USA to replace its old dot matrix printers. An extract from the manual is shown below. Read it carefully.

ⒷⓅⓅ
PUBLISHING

Laser safety

This printer is complied with 21 CFR Chapter 1 Subchapter J as a Class 1 laser product under the US Department of Health and Human Services (DHHS) Radiation Performance Standard according to the Radiation Control for Health and Safety Act 1968. This means that the printer does not produce hazardous laser radiation.

Since radiation emitted inside the printer is completely confined within protective housings and external covers, the laser beam cannot escape from the machine during any phase of user operation.

FCC Regulations

This equipment generates and uses radio frequency energy, and if not installed and used properly, that is, in strict accordance with the manufacturer's instructions, may cause interference to radio and television reception. It has been type-tested and found to comply with the limits for a Class B computing device in accordance with the specifications in Subpart J of Part 15 of the FCC rules, which are designed to provide reasonable protection against such interference in a residential installation.

DOC * regulations

This digital apparatus does not exceed the Class B limits for radio noise emissions from digital apparatus set out in Radio Interference Regulations of the Canadian Department of Communications.

* DOC: Canadian Department of Communications.

Regulations for United Kingdom

This equipment is approved under approval number NS/G/23/J/100003 for indirect connection to public telecommunication systems in the United Kingdom, ie when connected to the correct interface of a type approved apparatus in accordance with the instructions for use of that apparatus. If you are uncertain about the connection arrangement, seek the help of a qualified engineer.

For ozone emission

This printer meets the requirements for ozone emission of the applicable standard published by Underwriters' Laboratories, Inc (UL). Ozone is a colourless gas (O_3), a by-product of the electrophotographic process. Ozone is only discharged while the printer is printing, and it is emitted through the exhaust port on the rear, left side of the printer.

Caution

Those who are particularly sensitive to ozone odour may rarely feel sick if exposed to it excessively. To avoid this, make sure that the following measures are taken.

- Install the printer in a well ventilated room. (Ventilate about every hour or choose a large room.)
- Avoid using multiple laser printers simultaneously.
- Avoid facing the exhaust port directly towards the users.
- Replace a disposable ozone filter every 100,000 pages.
- Avoid using the printer without a filter.

Required

Frederick thinks lasers are dangerous and is therefore very worried about these new laser printers. How would you reassure him that the printer can be operated safely?

Mechanical equipment

3.8   Basic **office tools** also need care: devices designed to puncture or cut paper or plastic are just as good at making holes and gashes in flesh! Beware of guillotines, scissors, hole punches, binding machines, franking machines, letter openers and staplers. Anything, in fact, but especially anything with a point or a sharp edge or which works by impact, is capable of causing an injury if it is misused or even if it is left lying unguarded. Don't forget, also, that electricity and moving parts generate heat. A machine that is left ticking over all day may get *very* hot.

3.9 Be particularly careful with **personal effects** like necklaces, bracelets or other jewellery, and ties and scarves, all of which are inclined to get trapped in machines with moving parts. Long hair can also be a hazard: you may prefer to tie it back in some way if you feel it is particularly at risk because of machinery you use.

3.10 **Vibration White Finger** (VWF) is a painful condition which may be developed by regular users of hand-operated tools and machinery which produce high levels of vibration. The disease is estimated to affect around 20,000 people, with 1,400 new cases being reported each year. The risk of developing the condition can be reduced in a number of ways.

- Use the **right tool** for the job.
- Keep tools and machinery in **good working order** to minimise vibration.
- Avoid using machinery for long periods without a **break**.

> **DEVOLVED ASSESSMENT ALERT**
>
> 'Phasing work activities to minimise risk to self' is one of the cited sources of evidence for this element: it means pacing yourself and taking breaks, so far as you have authority to do so. Be aware of how your work patterns and hours can cause or minimise risks such as exposure to VDUs, VWF (discussed above), RSI (discussed below), tiredness and loss of concentration (which may lead to accidents) and so on.

Chemicals

3.11 Some items of equipment and machinery may need liquid or powder additives: beware of corrosive or toxic chemicals, flammable substances such as spirit or oil, and anything that gives off fumes. **Tippex** is harmful if it is inhaled or swallowed or comes into contact with your eyes. Sniffing **glue** or other solvents can be fatal.

3.12 Containers should be clearly labelled with their contents and warning signs as appropriate. If the **instructions** say wear protective gloves or wash off any splashes then do so!

3.13 The short-term effects of **breathing in harmful substances** can cause coughing, wheezing and shortness of breath. Long-term or high short-term exposure to substances like hay, wood dust and some glues can lead to chronic disablement from diseases like occupational asthma.

3.14 If skin comes into contact with substances such as shampoos, the sap from certain agricultural crops and cement, a serious and debilitating disease called **work-related dermatitis** can occur. Symptoms of the condition include redness, itching, scaling and blistering of the skin. The skin can crack and bleed and the dermatitis can spread all over the body. It can be painful enough to keep people off work or even force them to change jobs. The disease is most widespread among industries such as hairdressing, catering and cleaning.

3.15 Certain chemicals which are used in the workplace have the potential to cause cancer and it is estimated that about 6,000 deaths a year (of which 3,000 are caused by exposure to asbestos) are due to **work-related cancer**.

3.16 The **Control of Substances Hazardous to Health Regulations 1994** require employers to prevent or, if this is not possible, control employees' exposure to such substances.

3.17 If you or your organisation uses a harmful substance you should report any defects in **control measures** (such as local exhaust ventilation). Wear the respiratory protection that is provided and take care of it if you are likely to be breathing in a harmful substance. If you discover any material or dust which you suspect contains asbestos, stop any work that is being carried out and get advice. If you or your organisation uses asbestos material you should find out what precautions to take to protect health and make sure that they are followed.

Noise

3.18 As a general rule, if you have to shout to be clearly heard by someone two metres away then **noise** may well be a problem in your job. According to the Government, regular exposure to noise levels equivalent to the noise generated by a busy street over an eight-hour day is hazardous. Common sources of loud noise include pavement hammering, chainsaw work, sheet metal working and wood machinery. Poor maintenance, such as holes in compressed air lines and escaping steam, is also a cause of loud noise.

3.19 The **Noise at Work Regulations 1989** require workers to be protected from loud noise. Employers must therefore reduce noise levels as far as is reasonably practicable. If having done this the daily noise exposure level is equivalent to the noise of a heavy lorry, an employer must provide workers with ear protectors and mark the areas in which they should be worn.

3.20 **How to protect your hearing**

   (a) Use **noise control equipment** provided by your employer.

   (b) Tell your employer if something needs **repairing**.

   (c) Don't remove from a machine any **equipment supplied for controlling noise**.

   (d) Wear **ear protectors** provided and look after them; use them properly, keep them clean and replace damaged muffs.

Computer workstations and VDUs

3.21 Most office workers today use a computer.

3.22 If you have ever worked for a long period at a VDU you may personally have experienced some **discomfort**. Back ache, eye strain and stiffness or muscular problems of the neck, shoulders, arms or hands are frequent complaints.

KEY TERM

Repetitive Strain Injury or RSI is the common term for a condition that arises when you work for long periods at a VDU.

3.23 **Disorders seem to arise from poor equipment, environment and posture,** which lead to muscles being starved of oxygen, the build up of waste products in the body and the compression of nerves.

3.24 Workstations have to meet **stringent legal requirements**.

DEVOLVED ASSESSMENT ALERT

Two of the potential sources of evidence of your competence in this element is your observed behaviour in 'organising your own workstation to reduce hazards - reducing glare, positioning equipment, furniture and materials' and 'phasing your work activities to minimise risk to yourself - exposure to VDUs'. Take advantage of the following advice to make the most of the opportunities.

Activity 1.5

The provisions of the Health and Safety (Display Screen Equipment) Regulations 1992 and best practice are reflected in the following 'Self Assessment Form' issued by a government department

Use the form to:

(a) Assess your own workstation and practices;

(b) Determine what further training and/or information you may require to achieve bast practice in this area (we have not included the documentation which would be attached to the form for employees' guidance); and

(c) Suggest a specific action plan for improvement

BPP PUBLISHING

Health & Safety Risk Assessment for Display Screen Equipment (DSE)

Self-assessment Form

Name:	Grade:
Staff number:	Tel No:
Division:	Office Type - Cellular or Open Plan:
Location:	

Employment Status: (Please Tick) Permanent ☐ Casual ☐ Short term placement ☐ Agency ☐ Work experience ☐

What is the average time you spend each day using a display screen?   Hrs

How long have you been using a display Screen?   years.

Have you previously had any problems in using display screen equipment?   Yes/No **(Delete not applicable)**

If yes, please provide brief details:

Please provide brief details of any display screen related <u>health & safety training</u> you have received other than listed in section A below:

If you require any advice on completing this form please contact your health & safety co-ordinator or the Occupational Health & Safety Unit Help Desk, on

A. TRAINING BEFORE COMPLETING THIS FORM	YES (✓)	COMMENT
1. Please confirm that you have worked through the Postural Health Care (Computer based training) package located under the "Start" menu in windows NT. Put N/A in the comment column if this package is not available to you.	☐	
2. Please confirm you have read through the Best Practice for Display Screen Users (Attached below OHSU9) and incorporated the best practice at your display screen (where possible) before completing this assessment form.	☐	

Please do not proceed with this form until you have completed the actions in section A

B. DISPLAY SCREEN	YES	NO	COMMENT Add any further comments to explain your answe
3. Do you regularly use another display screen other than your main one? Note: If you use another display screen regularly, you complete a separate form for each display screen.	☐	☐	
4. Are the characters on the screen well defined, clearly formed and of adequate size and spacing to read them easily?	☐	☐	
5. Is the image on the screen stable and clear with no flicker?	☐	☐	
6. Can you adjust the brightness and contrast of the display to a comfortable setting easily?	☐	☐	
7. Can you swivel and tilt the screen easily to achieve a comfortable viewing position?	☐	☐	
8. Is the screen in a comfortable location on your desk?	☐	☐	
9. Is the screen at a comfortable height for you?	☐	☐	
10. Is the screen free from troublesome glare and reflections?	☐	☐	
11. Are the windows in your room fitted with adjustable coverings – blinds, curtains etc that you can adjust easily to prevent direct glare, and reflections on your screen?	☐	☐	
12. Are screen cleaning materials available if you require them?	☐	☐	

Health & Safety Risk Assessment for Display Screen Equipment (DSE)

C.	KEYBOARD/MOUSE	YES	NO	COMMENT
				Add any further comments to explain your answ
13.	Is the keyboard tiltable and separate from the screen so as to allow you comfortable working position?	☐	☐	
14.	Can the keyboard be easily read with no glare on the keys and all the symbols on the keys clearly legible?	☐	☐	
15.	Is there space in front of the keyboard for you to find support for your hands and arms for periods when you are not keying?	☐	☐	
16.	Is the mouse located on a flat surface or suitable mouse mat?	☐	☐	
17.	Do you know how to clean the mouse to ensure the pointer remains responsive?	☐	☐	
18.	Is your mouse located close to you and in a comfortable position for you which avoids stretching of the arm or poor postures to use it?	☐	☐	
19.	Do you know how to adjust the sensitivity of the mouse and how to change the button operation to suit your needs (i.e. for left or right-handed use).	☐	☐	
D.	**WORK STATION OR WORK SURFACE**			
20.	Having set up your (DSE) correctly *where possible* (Please see attached guidance OHSU 9) does the workstation / desk have sufficient space and legroom for you to comfortably carry out your range of duties?	☐	☐	
21.	Do you sit and face straight on to the display screen so no head turning or body twisting movements are required to look at the screen?	☐	☐	
22.	Are the items of equipment you use positioned in locations where you can reach and operate them easily?	☐	☐	
23.	Having adjusted the chair height correctly (see attached guidance OHSU 9) is the desk at a suitable height to allow a comfortable working position for your legs and arms?	☐	☐	
24.	Do you require a document holder? Note: these are particularly useful for work that involves frequent reference to hard copy documents.	☐	☐	
25.	If you already have a document holder, is it stable, adjustable and do you know how to position it correctly to avoid excessive head and eye movements? Please put N/A in the comment column if this question is not applicable to you.	☐	☐	
E.	**CHAIR**			
26.	Does your chair provide a comfortable working position and lumbar (lower back) support?	☐	☐	
27.	Is the chair in good working order, stable and suitable for easy freedom of movement?	☐	☐	
28.	Do you know how to fully adjust your chair in both height and tilt?	☐	☐	

BPP PUBLISHING

Health & Safety Risk Assessment for Display Screen Equipment (DSE)

	YES	NO	COMMENT Add any further comments to explain your answer
29. Having adjusted your chair and posture correctly, do you require a footrest to support your feet / legs in a comfortable position or to avoid excess pressure on the underside of your thighs? Please See guidance OHSU 9	☐	☐	
F. ENVIRONMENT			
30. Is the level of lighting satisfactory for all the tasks performed at the workstation?	☐	☐	
31. Is the noise emitted by equipment in your area at an acceptable level so as to enable you to concentrate and hold a normal conversation?	☐	☐	
32. Is your area free from hazards e.g. trailing cables, worn or improperly connected cables, broken or poorly positioned floor boxes?	☐	☐	
33. Is the equipment in your area positioned to avoid risk of injury or dislodging it?	☐	☐	
G. GENERAL			
34. Are you aware of your entitlement to free eyesight testing?	☐	☐	
35. Does your work pattern include regular changes of activity (i.e. reading, meetings, telephone calls etc) from using the display screen equipment and mouse?	☐	☐	
36. Can you control your own pace of work and take breaks when you need to?	☐	☐	
H. HEALTH			
37. Having read the best practice for display screen users (Attached OHSU 5) – are you currently experiencing any health symptoms which you believe may be related to using your DSE?	☐	☐	
38. Does the heat generated by the equipment in your area cause you discomfort or make the humidity a problem? (A typical sign of poor humidity would be dry or itching eyes).	☐	☐	
I. SOFTWARE			
39. Have you been trained to use the software/systems relevant to your work?	☐	☐	
40. Are the software / systems suitable to enable you to complete your tasks efficiently?	☐	☐	
41. Do the software / systems provide appropriate feedback i.e. error messages & suitable assistance i.e. (Help) facilities?	☐	☐	
J. ANY OTHER COMMENTS			

After completing Section J the user should sign and date here and forward the form to an Assessor or Health & Safety Co-ordinator to complete section K.

USER

Signature:

Name (Capitals):

Date:

Health & Safety Risk Assessment for Display Screen Equipment (DSE)

K. ASSESSMENT STAGE (All actions from the assessment should be detailed below by the assessor who should state who is responsible and indicate whether the action is urgent or routine in the 2nd column. The user should sign in the 3rd column as each action is completed).		
AGREED ACTION POINTS	ACTION BY (incl indication whether urgent or routine)	ACTION COMPLETED – USER'S NAME, SIGNATURE AND DATE

(The assessor should sign here to confirm the date when the assessment was carried out and that the actions have been entered above)

ASSESSOR

Signature: Name (Capitals):   Date:

L. SIGN OFF STAGE (Please sign below to confirm that all actions from the assessment have been completed)	
User	**Assessor, H&S Co-ordinator or Property Manager**
Signature:	Signature:
Name (Capitals)	Name (Capitals)
Date	Date

WHEN COMPLETED THIS DOCUMENT SHOULD BE FILED ON THE OFFICER'S PERSONNEL FILE OR LOCAL H&S FILE FOR AGENCY / WORK EXPERIENCE STAFF

3.25 The following diagram shows the recommended way of **sitting at a VDU** and of positioning the equipment.

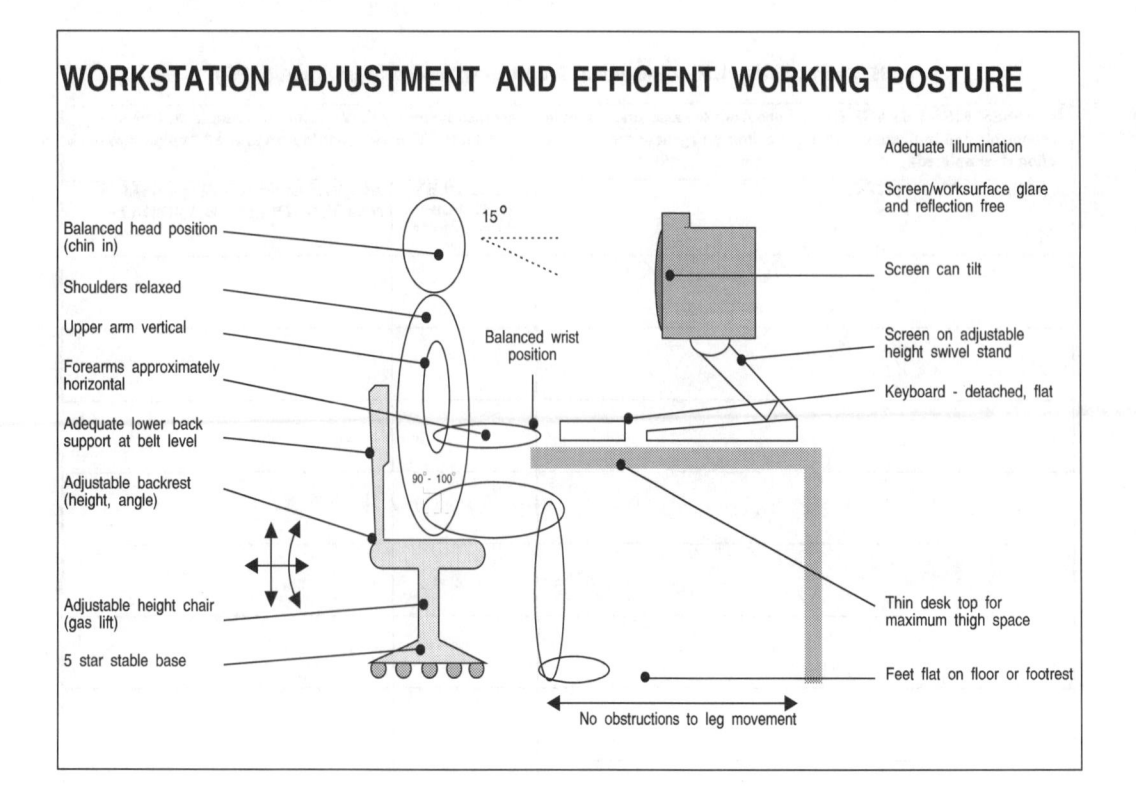

WORKSTATION ADJUSTMENT AND EFFICIENT WORKING POSTURE

Activity 1.6

You are normally quite fit but ever since you started working in your present office you have found that you have a slight backache when you wake up in the morning.

What sort of things might be causing your backache and what should you do to avoid straining your back in future?

Office layout

3.26 **Accidents** occur because people have to move about and do things within the office or factory environment. We will look briefly at hazards in the locations and methods by which people go about their work. This is to help you to recognise potential hazards in your own workplace, and understand when you or others may be at risk.

3.27 Office layout is determined by a number of considerations, such as **economy of space, efficiency** and **security**, but the **safety** of the occupants should not be forgotten. If there is insufficient **space** for people and equipment (and movement), there may be safety hazards, as movement is obstructed. Particular attention must be given to access to **emergency equipment** (such as fire extinguishers) and emergency exits, the ability to close **fire or security doors** and so on.

3.28 Proximity and accessibility

(a) Within each section, attention should be given to the **proximity** of people regularly working together (for example the manager and his/her secretary), and supervisors and those under their control.

(b) Attention should also be given to the **accessibility** of people **whose advice or services are required by the section as a whole** (such as supervisors, typists), and **equipment and facilities regularly used and shared by the section** (such as files, photocopier, coffee machine). A further consideration will be the **need for privacy or quiet** of some individuals (such as managers).

3.29 **Work flow between different departments** will depend on the layout of the premises as a whole. The same principles of **proximity** and **accessibility** ought to apply. So, for example, Purchasing and Accounts departments may be located for easy communication with each other; the mail room and office supplies may be centralised, and rest areas and toilets distributed for general use.

3.30 **Some common sense measures**

(a) Locate any design, drawing and planning activities in studio-type accommodation, with plenty of **natural light.**

(b) Locate activities involving the **movement** of heavy machinery, materials or goods as close to ground level and transport facilities as possible.

(c) Ensure that senior management offices and conference facilities are situated where **interruptions and noise** are minimal.

(d) Keep **dining, drinking, rest and recreation** areas (if any) separate from those where concentrated work is taking place.

Activity 1.7

What potential hazards would be minimised by the measures listed in paragraphs 3.27 and 3.28?

Your work area

3.31 In the light of the above look at **your own work area** - not just the desk you sit at but the corridors, passageways, staircases and so on that you use regularly as you go about your work.

	Suggested improvement
Do you often have to carry heavy files from one place to another?	Can you house often-used files in a cabinet within reach of your desk?
Do you have enough light for the work that you do?	Can you reorient your desk to take better advantage of natural light? Would a desk lamp help?
What's the temperature like?	Do you have access to the air control switch or thermostat? Could you get agreement for a temperature adjustment from other people in the same area?
Do you have difficulty getting objects safely from shelves?	Make sure that heavy or unstable objects are at the bottom. (The same applies to liquids or chemicals.) Ask about the availability of a stable 'step up' aid to reaching higher shelves: chairs and step ladders are not ideal.

	Suggested improvement
Are the things you need in easy reach?	Tidiness helps!
Is your chair comfortable and is your desk the right height?	If you often have backache or neckache, the height and contour of the chair probably need adjusting. Taking regular breaks and stretching or walking about are also recommended.

Each time you encounter an obstruction or potential hazard, **note it** - and come up with an **improvement plan**.

DEVOLVED ASSESSMENT ALERT

Remember that part of your competence is to demonstrate that you can spot potential hazards. Identifying – and *recording* your identification of – hazards in your own area is a great start!

Behaviour in work areas

Movement

3.32 You have known from painful experience since you were small that **sudden violent movements** in **confined spaces** are liable to cause damage. If you run past doorways, round blind corners or up or down stairways, if you throw objects across a room because you are too lazy to get up, if you wave your arms about, if you lean back on your chair too far, or if you stretch awkwardly to reach inaccessible files - if you do any of these things the chances are that *this time* you will come to no harm. But next time may be different. You are an accident waiting to happen. The same applies to **practical jokes** and '**clowning around**': it's all fun until someone loses an eye!

Alcohol and drugs

3.33 There may well be strict **drug and alcohol policies** in force in the workplace. Even if not, know your limit and recognise that any amount of alcohol is likely to impair your work performance and make you feel sleepy. It also lowers your concentration, awareness of risk, and reaction times: you are less safe when operating office equipment (let alone heavy machinery or motor vehicles!). The same may apply to prescription medications: be sensible about your capacity to work safely if you have taken drowsy-making painkillers or hayfever tablets. If in doubt, ask to be transferred to lower-risk duties, or consult your supervisor.

Smoking

3.34 Increasingly, firms are introducing a **non-smoking policy** in workplaces, often with the full support of staff, including smokers. There may be a complete ban or separate areas set aside for smokers during breaks. The health risk from **passive smoking** is well-publicised. There is also a fire risk, which may be magnified in offices where smoking is not normal and proper ashtrays and so on are not therefore available. Brent Council for example, has introduced a total ban, saying: 'Smoking is regarded as a fire hazard and a health risk'.

Activity 1.8

What are the policies of your workplace in regard to:

(a) Drugs and alcohol?
(b) Smoking?

If there is no formal policy statement: consider drafting one!

Heavy lifting

3.35 More than a quarter of accidents reported each year are associated with manual handling, back injuries being the most common. This activity is covered by the **Manual Handling Operations Regulations 1992**.

(a) Employers should **avoid the need for their employees to undertake any manual handling activities** which will involve the risk of their becoming injured, so far as this is reasonably practical.

(b) If such risks cannot be entirely avoided, employers should see to it that **information is available about the weight of each load** and the heavier side of any load whose centre or gravity is not positioned centrally.

(c) **Employees** then have a duty to take note of the information available and to make use of any equipment provided to help carry the load.

(d) Employees also have a duty to **inform their employer** of any injury or conditions that may affect their ability to undertake manual handling tasks.

Mental well-being

3.36 A hidden, but evidently very serious, source of potential hazard in the workplace is **Work-related stress**. Stress can be caused by a wide range of factors.

- Work overload; excessive work or pressure

- Work 'underload' - boredom, monotony and lack of meaning

- Poor management style: lack of clear instructions or targets, unpredictable moods and so on

- Lack of constructive relationships with colleagues: hostility, competition, 'cliques' and so on

- Insecurity, uncertainty; change over which the individual has no control

- Personality factors, such as emotional sensitivity, lack of flexibility, or perfectionism

- Non-work factors or circumstances: bereavement, illness, financial or relationship difficulties and so on

3.37 The **signs of harmful stress** include irritability and mood swings; sleeplessness; skin and digestive disorders and other physical symptoms; withdrawal; abuse of drugs or alcohol; apathy and low confidence; and changes in behaviour at work (eg unusually poor timekeeping or error rates).

Activity 1.9

Who would be the appropriate person to ask about **managing workplace stress** in your organisation (or outside it)? Selecting an appropriate communication method, request information on how to manage stress.

Risk assessment

3.38 The principal aim of the Health and Safety Executive is to ensure that health and safety risks from work activities are properly controlled. In order to do this, risks must be assessed:

Step 1	Look for hazards
Step 2	Decide who might be harmed, and how
Step 3	Evaluate risks arising and decide if existing precautions are adequate
Step 4	Record your findings
Step 5	Review your assessment periodically and revise as necessary

Good practice for everyone

3.39 The following is an article drawn from the Department of the Environment Transport and the Regions (DETR) InfoNET site. It illustrates both good health and safety practice *and* effective employee communication in this area. (You might consider turning it into a checklist for your own practice – and documentary evidence of your competence in this area.)

> This year sees the 25th anniversary of the main piece of H&S legislation in this country – the Health and Safety at Work Act 1974. The Health and Safety Executive (sponsored by this Department) are initiating a campaign to Revitalise Health and Safety for everyone as part of the anniversary.
>
> Here are **25 things you could do** to ensure high standards of Health and Safety for yourself and others in your work area. *(Please note reference to the WED Help desk would usually be building managers for non HQ buildings)*
>
> Report workplace faults or hazards promptly to the WED help desk.
>
> Report accidents and near misses promptly to the WED help desk.
>
> Check you know the main evacuation route(s) from your area and the procedures for when an alarm sounds and if you do not know ask the WED help desk who your fire warden is.
>
> If you are a Display Screen User ask your H&S co-ordinator for a risk assessment if you have not had one at your current workstation.
>
> Check your entitlement to a free eye test paid for by the Department – see the forms cabinet (Health & Safety section for details).
>
> Clean you computer screen regularly – the materials can be ordered through stationery. Do not put post-it notes on a computer screen or around it as they will mark the screen and also distract the eye whilst using the computer.
>
> Arrange for any unused or old items of IT or equipment to be removed from your area.
>
> Try to vary your duties to ensure you do not work at a computer for more than an hour at a time – it is advisable to have a 10 minute change of activity for every hour. Switch off all equipment at the end of the day where possible.

Look through the Computer based Training package on postural health and adjust your seating position and posture as necessary. If you do not have the package download it from the INFONET using the instructions at: Corporate/other corporate/H&S/training.

Try not to spend lunchtime doing intensive keyboard or reading work if your normal work consists of them – this will give your eyes a change to rest.

Keep your desk clear at the end of the day so it can be cleaned.

Ensure rubbish in the area is disposed of promptly by contacting the WED help desk.

Do not use dangerous machinery ie. shredders unless trained to do so.

Do not try to clear paper jams or faults with copiers, shredders or faxes unless you are fully conversant with the machine.

Do not tamper with or touch equipment with electrical faults – report them to the WED help desk.

Close all cabinet or pedestal drawers after use to avoid people colliding with them.

Report any broken floor boxes or tripping hazards to the WED help desk.

Do not overload electrical sockets. You should avoid connecting one extension lead to another.

If extension leads are used in most sockets ask the WED help desk for advice on safety.

Do not lift heavy or awkward items – call the porters instead or ask your H&S co-ordinator to arrange for a manual handling risk assessment.

Do not store items on top of cupboards.

If you are pregnant inform your manager so they can arrange for a H&S co-ordinator to carry out a risk assessment.

If you are a young worker (under 18 years of age) inform your manager so they can arrange for a H&S co-ordinator to carry out a risk assessment.

Comply with requests for H&S information particularly when asked to complete risk assessment forms.

Look through the good practice not for DSE users on the INFONET at:

Corporate/othercorporate/H&S/good practice.

Contacts: a list of health and safety co-ordinators, help desk, first aid officers and others follows.

If you are a manager of any **new or temporary staff** ensure they are briefed on the safe practices above and for the area they will be working in, the evacuation procedures and the numbers for the help desk to report building faults.

Crown Copyright © 2000

Activity 1.10

A scene from everyday office life is shown on the next page.

Note down anything that strikes you as being dangerous about this working environment.

BPP PUBLISHING

4   FIRE SAFETY

Safety procedures: fire

4.1   The general regulations relating to fire contained in the **Offices, Shops and Railway Premises Act 1963** were reinforced in the **Fire Precautions Act 1971**. (Specialised buildings are covered by other legislation such as the Fire Safety and Safety of Places of Sport Act 1987.) More recently, European legislation was implemented in the **Fire Precautions (Workplace) Regulations 1997**, which require employers to do the following.

(a)   Provide the appropriate number of **fire extinguishers** and other means for fighting fire.

(b)   Install **fire detectors** and **fire alarm systems** where necessary.

(c)   Take whatever measures are necessary for **fighting fire** (eg the drawing up of a suitable emergency plan of action) and nominate a sufficient number of workers to implement these measures and ensure that they are adequately trained and equipped to carry out their responsibilities.

(d)   Provide adequate **emergency routes and exits** for everyone to escape quickly and safely.

(e)   Ensure that **equipment and facilities provided to protect workers** from the dangers of fire are regularly maintained and any faults found are rectified as quickly as possible.

KEY TERM

Fire equipment and facilities include **fire doors, fire notices, fire alarms, fire extinguishers** and **sprinklers**.

Causes of fire

4.2 The main causes of fire in industry and commerce tend to be associated with **electrical appliances and installations**, and **smoking** is a major source of fires in business premises.

4.3 **Flammable materials** like clothing and some furniture are a danger, particularly in an office which is heated by electric bar fires. **Flammable substances** left in the wrong place can also be a problem, for example if an aerosol is left in direct sunlight.

Activity 1.11

As with identifying hazards in your own workstation, see if you are up to speed with fire safety in your office.

Area	Am I competent?
Do you know what to do if fire breaks out in your workplace?	
Would you recognise the sound of a smoke alarm or fire alarm for what it was?	
Where is the nearest fire extinguisher?	
How do you set off the fire alarm?	
Where is the nearest fire exit?	
Where is the meeting point in case of evacuation?	
Should you leave doors open or shut?	
Does anybody know at any given time when you are (or are not) in the building?	
Who is the Fire/Safety officer?	

4.4 The notices below provide some fire safety information, but it is more important that you take note of the **fire safety policy** within your own office.

BPP
PUBLISHING

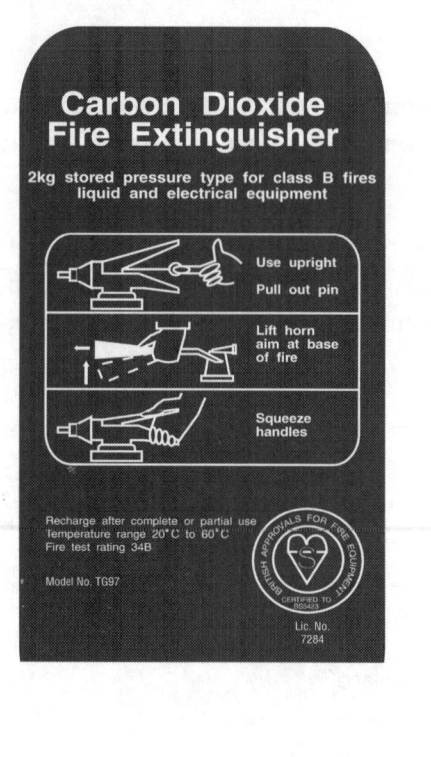

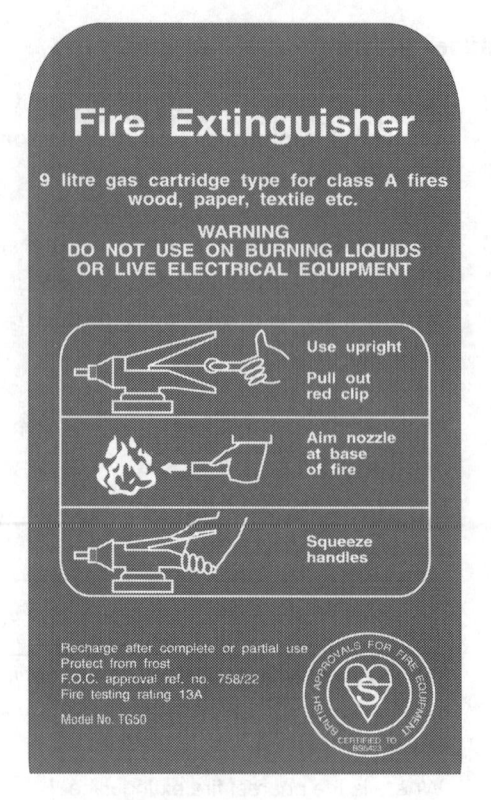

5   EMERGENCY PROCEDURES

Evacuation procedures

> **DEVOLVED ASSESSMENT ALERT**
>
> One of the potential sources of evidence of your competence in this Element is your being observed to take part in evacuation drills. Be aware of this: do not miss the opportunity! Do you know what to do in the event of an evacuation of your office? If not, make sure that you find out!

5.1   One of the most common reasons for evacuating staff from a building is the **outbreak of fire**. Other reasons include **bomb threats** and **unsafe buildings**.

5.2   Every organisation should have a set of procedures that should be followed when a building needs to be evacuated. Evacuations are generally conducted by a resident **safety officer** or **fire officer**. These officers usually have some sort of formal training by the local fire brigade or by the Health and Safety Executive, and are responsible for making sure that all persons known to be in a building at the time of evacuation can be accounted for.

Step 1   When requested to do so, everyone present in a building that is to be evacuated should leave as quickly as possible using the quickest and safest route.

Step 2   Employees should meet at a designated meeting place outside the building, and they should assist any visitors (or any others who do not know where to go) to the correct meeting place.

Step 3   Once all staff have gathered at their relevant meeting place, the appointed fire officer or safety officer accounts for the staff that he is responsible for by calling a register. (This register is picked up as he is leaving the building.)

Step 4   Each employee must make sure that he or she is familiar with the organisation's evacuation procedures and official meeting place. Each office or department should clearly display notices detailing what you should do when the building you work in is to be evacuated.

5.3   EXAMPLE: EVACUATION PROCEDURE

The following is taken from the health and safety procedures pages of the staff Intranet system (InfoNET) OF THE DETR (Department of Environment, Transport and the Region).

Fire evacuation procedure for staff

Ashdown House (V) has a two-stage fire alarm system, in addition there is a Voice Alarm System.

In any fire incident, this will automatically broadcast Alert and or Evacuation messages.

In the event of a detector or alarm being activated all floors of Ashdown House will be put into the Alert Status by the Voice Alarm System.

No action is required at this stage except to secure confidential papers, be prepared to evacuate the building.

BPP
PUBLISHING

When a second stage alarm is activated. The Voice Alarm System will broadcast the Evacuation message.

- Do not run down the stairs.
- Do not pass others.
- Do not turn back for any reason.
- Do not carry all your possessions with you.
- Do not lock any doors.
- On reaching the final exits from the building go to the assembly area, in

The Cathedral Piazza

Staff who are disabled and/or temporarily incapacitated, will be escorted to the fireman's lift where a member of the Security staff will rescue them. Your floor warden will have nominated an escort to remain with you until arrival in the assembly area.

The assembly area is a safe area. The instruction advising when Ashdown House is safe to re-enter will be given from the Cathedral Piazza.

Individual responsibility

Staff who feel that they may need assistance (on a permanent or temporary basis) in the event of an emergency or evacuation should notify their floor warden, and an escort will be nominated to assist.

Bomb evacuation procedure for staff

Should a threat be received advising there is a bomb in Ashdown House, or that the building may be under threat from an externally located bomb, the Voice Alarm System will be used as the method of communication to staff and visitors.

Listen clearly to all messages broadcast, there may be a change to the procedure, to suit the current situation ie a change in the evacuation route.

Other emergencies

5.4   Safety procedure in the case of emergencies will obviously depend upon what has happened. Quite often it will mean evacuating the building according to fire safety procedures as we have just seen, but in the case of, say, armed intruders it might mean ensuring that certain doors are locked. In **any emergency situation** you should do the following.

Step 1	Stay calm.
Step 2	Avoid personal danger.
Step 3	Call for help: contact the company's first-aider or security staff as appropriate or, if no-one is available, call the emergency services. (Check that you know who your first-aider, fire officer and security officer are, and how to contact each of them.)
Step 4	Help others to avoid danger if possible.
Step 5	In no circumstances move injured people unless it is more dangerous not to do so. Remove the source of danger instead, if possible.
Step 6	Do not attempt to administer first-aid yourself unless you are trained to do so.

Calling the emergency services

5.5   In the UK you can be put straight through to the **police,** the **fire brigade** or the nearest **ambulance station** by dialling 999. The operators are very well trained and will guide you through the procedure.

Step 1   Once you are through you will be asked which service you require and be transferred as appropriate.

Step 2   Your call will be traced automatically, in case it is cut off for some reason: you will hear your telephone number being given to the person who will deal with your call. The call is also tape recorded.

Step 3   You will be asked for details of the location of the incident, what has happened, the number and approximate age of any casualties and the extent of the injuries, if any.

Step 4   You should not hang up until after the person you are speaking to has done so (otherwise he may not have all the information he needs).

Step 5   If there is a casualty try if possible to ensure that he or she is not left alone. Send somebody else to make the call but insist that they come back and tell you that the call has been made.

6   REPORTING PROCEDURES

Reporting potential hazards

6.1   In the case of illness, accident and fire at work, '**prevention is better than cure**'. Don't wait to display your competence in emergencies! If you are aware of a practice at work that is unsafe or if you think that conditions are unhealthy report it at once to your supervisor. You may be told that this is a matter for the personnel department, say, or a special safety officer, in which case report the matter to him or her.

6.2   When companies recognise trade unions, the trade union is allowed to appoint **safety representatives** chosen from the company's employees. If no action is taken after your initial approach and your employer has a safety representative, you should report the matter to him or her. Failing that you can get in touch with a Health and Safety Executive Inspector or the environmental health officer of the local authority. (The latter usually deals with offices; the former deals mainly with industrial premises.)

6.3   Contacting a third party is obviously a last resort: a well-run company will have a **proper reporting system and control procedures** to make sure that any potential hazards are reported and action taken to eliminate them. **Find out what the procedure is in your organisation.**

Reporting accidents

6.4   You may have an accident yourself, or you may witness one and be asked to make a **report**. No matter how minor an accident may seem at the time there may be complications later. The reporting procedure should ensure that the 'facts' are recorded accurately at the time for possible future reference. It should also alert those responsible to the need for extra safety measures.

6.5   Let us assume that you have had an accident. This is what you should do.

BPP PUBLISHING

Step 1	Get firstaid **(from someone properly** qualified **to give it)!**
Step 2	Report the incident as soon as possible **to someone in authority. You may be asked to fill in a form.**
Step 3	**If your company employs more than 10 people, it should by law keep an** accident book. **See that your accident is accurately recorded in the book – in other words read the entry for yourself if it is made by someone else.**
Step 4	**If you are injured to the extent that you cannot immediately check the entry,** write to your employer **(or get somebody to write on your behalf) setting out your version of events.**
Step 5	**If anybody else witnessed the accident** get signed statements **from them and make sure that you know their names and addresses.**

Obviously, again, not all of these measures will be necessary for a small cut or bruise, but you should be aware of the need to protect your own interests and those of other potential victims, in the case of a serious accident.

6.6   The drawing below shows the format of a **typical accident book**. The one used by your organisation may be laid out differently, or it might consist of loose-leaf sheets.

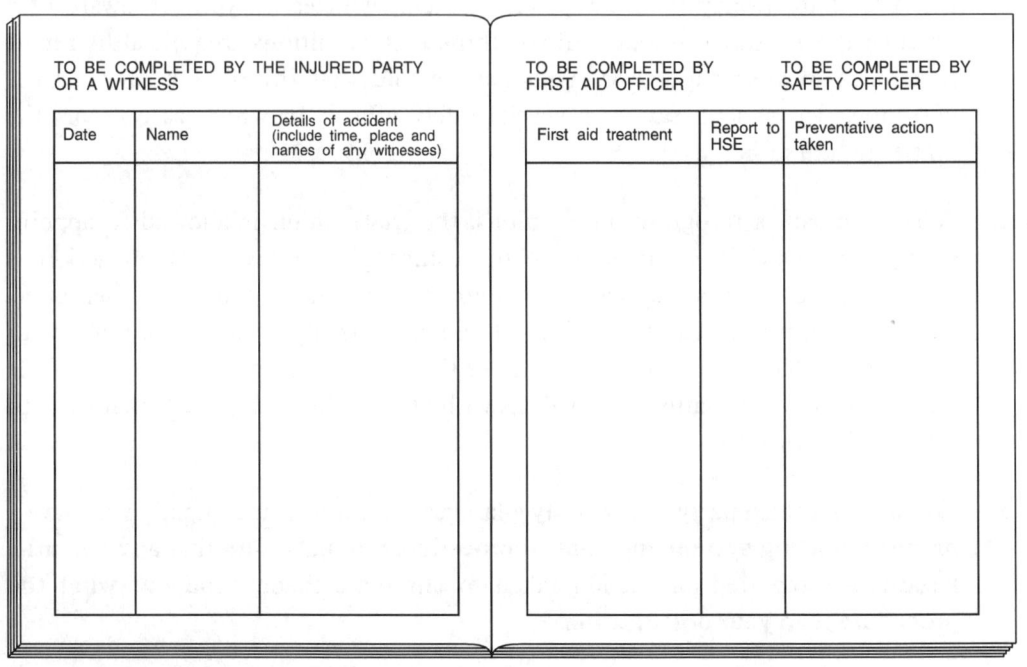

Notifiable accidents and diseases

6.7   **Certain accidents, dangerous occurrences** and **cases of disease** must be notified to:

- The **environmental health department** of the employer's local authority if the business is office based, retail or wholesale, warehousing, hotel and catering, sports or leisure, residential accommodation (excluding nursing homes) or concerned with places of worship

- The **Health and Safety Executive** for all other types of business.

6.8   The **Reporting of Injuries, Diseases and Dangerous Occurrences Regulations 1995 (RIDDOR 95)** require employers to do the following.

    (a)   **Notify the enforcing authority immediately** (for example, by telephone) if:

- **There is an accident** connected with work and either an employee or self-employed person working on the premises is **killed** or **suffers a major injury** (including as a result of physical violence) or a member of the public is killed or taken to hospital.

- There is a **dangerous occurrence**.

    (b)   **Send a completed accident report form to:**

- **Confirm** within ten days a telephone report of an accident or dangerous occurrence as described in (a) above

- **Notify**, within ten days of the accident, any injury which stops someone doing their normal job for more than three days

- **Report** certain work-related diseases

6.9   **RIDDOR** contains a long list of what constitutes a **major injury**, a **dangerous occurrence** or a **notifiable disease**.

KEY TERMS

- **Reportable major injuries** include things like fracture 'other than to fingers, thumbs or toes', amputation, temporary or permanent loss of sight and any other injury which results in the person being admitted to hospital for more than 24 hours.

- **Reportable dangerous occurrences** are 'near misses' that might well have caused major injuries. They include the collapse of a load bearing part of a lift, electrical short circuit or overload causing fire or explosion, the malfunction of breathing apparatus while in use or during testing immediately before use, and many others.

- **Reportable diseases** include certain poisonings, occupational asthma, asbestosis, hepatitis and many others.

6.10   The **standard form** for the notification of injuries and dangerous occurrences is reproduced on the next two pages.

6.11   RIDDOR stipulates that if there is an accident, or if there is an incident which could have resulted in an accident, the incident or accident should be **investigated**. The site of the incident/accident should therefore be left undisturbed unless the site is dangerous to others and it is important that you are aware that you should not clear up what could be vital evidence.

BPP PUBLISHING

Health and Safety at Work etc Act 1974
The Reporting of Injuries, Diseases and Dangerous Occurrences Regulations 1995

HSE
Health & Safety
Executive

Report of an injury or dangerous occurrence

Filling in this form
This form must be filled in by an employer or other responsible person.

Part A

About you
1 What is your full name?

2 What is your job title?

3 What is your telephone number?

About your organisation
4 What is the name of your organisation?

5 What is its address and postcode?

6 What type of work does your organisation do?

Part B

About the incident
1 On what date did the incident happen?

/   /

2 At what time did the incident happen?
(Please use the 24-hour clock eg 0600)

3 Did the incident happen at the above address?

Yes ☐   Go to question 4

No ☐   Where did the incident happen?

☐ elsewhere in your organisation - give the name, address and postcode

☐ at someone else's premises - give the name, address and postcode

☐ in a public place - give the details of where it happened

If you do not know the postcode, what is the name of the local authority?

4 In which department, or where on the premises, did the incident happen?

Part C

About the injured person
If you are reporting a dangerous occurrence, go to Part F.
If more than one person was injured in the same incident, please attach the details asked for in Part C and Part D for each injured person.

1 What is their full name?

2 What is their home address and postcode?

3 What is their home phone number?

4 How old are they?

5 Are they
☐ male?
☐ female?

6 What is their job title?

7 Was the injured person (tick only one box)
☐ one of your employees?

☐ on a training scheme? Give details:

☐ on work experience?

☐ employed by someone else? Give details of the employer:

☐ self-employed and at work?

☐ a member of the public?

Part D

About the injury
1 What was the injury? (eg fracture, laceration)

2 What part of the body was injured?

3 Was the injury (tick the one box that applies)

☐ a fatality?

☐ a major injury or condition? (see accompanying notes)

☐ an injury to an employee or self-employed person which prevented them doing their normal work for more than 3 days?

☐ an injury to a member of the public which meant they had to be taken from the scene of the accident to a hospital for treatment?

4 Did the injured person (tick all the boxes that apply)

☐ became unconscious?

☐ need resuscitation?

☐ remain in hospital for more than 24 hours?

☐ none of the above?

Part E

About the kind of accident

Please tick the one box that best describes what happened, then go to part G.

☐ Contact with moving machinery or material being machined

☐ Hit by a moving, flying or falling object

☐ Hit by a moving vehicle

☐ Hit by something fixed or stationary

☐ Injured while handling, lifting or carrying

☐ Slipped, tripped or fell on the same level

☐ Fell from a height
How high was the fall?

[_____ metres]

☐ Trapped by something collapsing

☐ Drowned or asphyxiated

☐ Exposed to, or in contact with, a harmful substance

☐ Exposed to fire

☐ Exposed to an explosion

☐ Contact with electricity or an electrical discharge

☐ Injured by an animal

☐ Physically assaulted by a person

☐ Another kind of accident (describe it in part G)

Part F

Dangerous occurrences

Enter the number of the dangerous occurrence you are reporting. (The numbers are given in the Regulations and in the notes which accompany this form.)

[_____]

Part G

Describing what happened

Give as much detail as you can. For instance
- the name of any substance involved
- the name and type of any machinery involved
- the events that led to the incident
- the part played by any people.

If it was a personal injury, give details of what the person was doing. Describe any action that has since been taken to prevent a similar incident. Use a separate piece of paper if you need to.

Part H

Your signature

[_____]

Date

[/ /]

Where to send the form
Please send it to the Enforcing Authority for the place where it happened. If you do not know the Enforcing Authority, send it to the nearest HSE office.

For official use

Client number [_____] Location number [_____] Event number [_____] ☐ INV REP ☐ Y ☐ N

BPP PUBLISHING

Activity 1.12

Look back at the scene from everyday office life in Activity 4.10.

Adopt the role of each of the three workers shown and, assuming that you have by now had one of the many accidents possible in this working environment, fill out a report in the Accident Book shown below.

Accident book

Full name, address and occupation of injured person (1)	Signature of injured person or other person making this entry* (2)	Date when entry made (3)	Date and time of accident (4)	Room/place in which accident happened (5)	Cause and nature of injury † (6)
1					
2					
3					
4					
5					
6					
7					
8					
9					
10					

* If the entry is made by some person acting on behalf of the employee, the address and occupation of that person must also be given
† State clearly the work or process being performed at the time of the accident

Key learning points

- When using **office equipment,** take care to ensure that operating instructions are followed carefully. As with equipment, **machinery** needs to be handled with care, especially those devices which are designed to puncture or cut things.

- The way in which an office is laid out is determined by economy of space, efficiency, security and also the **safety** of the employees. The **office layout** should also consider the movement of staff and the movement of documents (or **workflow**). Individual work areas and workstations should be organised in order to minimise hazards in the workplace.

- General rules regarding fire safety
  - There must be adequate means of escape
  - Doors out of the building must be able to be opened from the inside
  - Employees should be familiar with the fire alarm system
  - A fire alarm system must be present. It must be effective and regularly tested
  - Firefighting equipment must be easily available and in working order

- General rules for dealing with emergencies
  - Remain calm
  - Avoid personal danger
  - Call for help
  - Help others
  - Remove source of danger if possible
  - Administer first aid, only if you are trained to do so
  - Only move injured people if it is less dangerous to do so

- If you have an **accident** at work, here is what you should do.
  - Get first aid
  - Report the incident as soon as possible to someone in authority
  - Make sure your accident is recorded accurately in an accident book
  - Get the names and addresses of any witnesses and get signed statements from them

Quick quiz

1   What is Repetitive Strain Injury?

2   What are the main causes of fire in the workplace?

3   What are the main types of fire equipment and facilities maintained by employers?

4   What are the main reasons for evacuating a building?

5   Outline the steps involved in calling the emergency services.

6   What should you do if you have an accident at work?

7   What is 'RIDDOR'?

BPP
PUBLISHING

Answers to quick quiz

1   A condition that arises when you work for long periods at a VDU. Common complaints include back ache, eye strain and muscular problems.

2   Smoking, flammable substances left in the wrong place, electrical applications.

3   • Fire doors
     • Fire notices
     • Fire alarms
     • Fire extinguishers

4   • Fire
     • Security alert (eg bomb scare)
     • The building is deemed to be unsafe

5   • Dial 999 (in the UK)

     • State the emergency service that you require

     • Give details of the incident, location, what happened and details of any casualties (if any)

     • Do not hang up until you are sure that the person you are speaking to has all of the information that he needs

6   • Get first-aid

     • Report the accident as soon as possible

     • Check to see that your accident is recorded correctly in your organisation's accident book (if there are less than ten employees then your organisation is not required by law to hold such a book)

     • Get signed statements, and names and addresses from witnesses

7   The Reporting of Injuries, Diseases and Dangerous Occurrences Regulations (1995).

2 Security at work

This chapter contains

1   Introduction to security

2   Security risks

3   Security devices and procedures

4   Security of information

Learning objectives

On completion of this chapter you will be able to:

- Carry out organisational security procedures correctly

- Identify security risks correctly

- Put right, or report promptly to the appropropriate person, identified security risks

- Deal with identified breaches of security, in accordance with organisational procedures

- Outline the organisation's security and reporting procedures

- Understand your own scope and limitations in dealing with security risks

Performance criteria

(1)   Organisational security procedures are carried out correctly

(2)   Security risks are correctly identified

(3)   Identified security risks are put right or reported promptly at the appropriate person

(4)   Identified breaches of security are dealt with in accordance with organisational procedures

Range statement

1   **Security systems:** personal identification; entry; exit; equipment

BPP PUBLISHING

1 INTRODUCTION TO SECURITY

1.1 It is difficult to pin down the meaning of the word **security**. Basically it is used in the sense of defending things against people or events which might take them away or harm them. Think of 'job security' or 'financial security', or feeling 'secure' amongst your family and friends.

> ### KEY TERM
>
> **Security** involves measures taken to protect against theft, espionage, unauthorised access and so on.

1.2 In the context of Unit 22, we are concerned with the **security of the workplace**: the building where you work and the people and physical things in it. The security of **information** is also very important - especially its **confidentiality** - but this will be discussed in more detail later in this Text.

The principles of security

1.3 Effective security is a combination of first **delay** and then **alarm**.

Step 1 Delay **is achieved by having** several lines of defence before any vulnerable items can be reached.

(1) Outer doors **to its main building**

(2) **A** reception **area to greet guests but also to screen out unwanted intruders into the building.**

(3) Further doors **guarding rooms where valuable items such as computers are kept**

(4) Lockable drawers and cabinets **in which smaller items are kept**

Step 2 Raising the alarm, **once an intruder is identified, so that those responsible for dealing with the problem have time to get to the scene and take action.**

(1) Electronic devices

(2) Alertness and prompt actions

2 SECURITY RISKS

At-risk items/people

2.1 Security aims to prevent others from taking away or doing damage to things that belong to your organisation or people that work for it. What type of belongings or people are particularly **at risk**? Here are ten suggestions. Try to think of more that apply in your organisation.

- Cash and cheques
- Stocks
- Vehicles
- Moveable equipment such as computers
- Confidential files and documents (on paper or floppy disk)
- Ownership documents like share certificates, title deeds and so on

- Pass cards allowing access to the building, or secure parts of it
- Staff in the front line (security guards)
- Staff with custody of assets (eg counter staff in banks)
- Key personnel, who may be held to ransom.

Vulnerable points in premises and procedures

2.2 What are the most **exposed or vulnerable** areas of an organisation? Again, here are some suggestions, but think what others might apply in your own organisation.

(a) **Public or open areas**, such as entrances, hallways, parking areas, toilets, stairways and lifts - especially if these are unattended, or inadequately attended for the volume of traffic.

(b) **Points of entry and exit** - such as doors, windows, gates and lifts. By definition, these are points where 'outsiders' may attempt to gain access.

(c) **Isolated areas**, such as store rooms or back stairs, where there are not always people about.

(d) **Ill-lit areas**, such as car-parks or stair wells.

(e) **Reception areas**, since if an unauthorised person can talk, trick or slip his way past reception, he may be much harder to identify as a stranger, and locate within the premises, later.

(f) **Areas where at-risk objects are concentrated**, such as store rooms, computer rooms, offices, file stores and so on - especially if they are located near points of entry or exit, or busy public areas.

(g) **Points of transit or storage** outside the organisation's premises. Valuable items taken out of the office (for banking, delivery, work at home or whatever) are particularly vulnerable.

DEVOLVED ASSESSMENT ALERT

The evidence requirements for Element 22.2 include the following. 'Evidence is ... required of identifying security risks.' Without being paranoid about it, keep an eye out at work (and in simulations) for the two elements of at-risk items/people and vulnerable points in premises and procedures.

Activity 2.1

What security risk(s) can you identify in the following, and what could be done in each case to minimise the risk?

(a) There is one person on the reception desk in a busy entrance area, and she is dealing with five impatient people trying to get visitors' tags and directions, plus two couriers trying to deliver packages.

(b) It is very hot in the office, so the back door (at the end of the corridor by the storerooms) has been propped open to allow air to circulate.

(c) A visitor has been shown into your supervisor's office and asked to wait: he is early for an appointment, and your supervisor has not yet returned from lunch. Nobody else knew about the appointment. The visitor says he does not wish to be in the way, and shuts the office door.

3 SECURITY DEVICES AND PROCEDURES

Security devices for controlling access

3.1 **Controlling access** will usually involve a combination of devices and procedures for:

- **Controlling people's ability physically to open points of access**, such as gates, doors and windows

- **Identifying people** as authorised or unauthorised individuals for entry to the premises or particular areas.

3.2 **Methods of controlling access to a building**

(a) **Doors can be closed and locked**. For particularly sensitive areas extra-strong doors can be used.

(b) **Windows can be closed and locked**. Sensitive areas may also have strengthened glass or even bars across the windows.

(c) **Plastic cards** (like cashpoint cards) that have to be inserted into a device at a door are used in some organisations.

(d) **Combination locks in the form of electronic keypads**. Only people who are authorised to enter a particular area are told the combination number. This number triggers off a switch which unlocks the door. The code can be changed from time to time.

(e) **Video cameras** may survey the entrance so that the person who is responsible for opening the door to visitors can see who is waiting outside.

(f) **Entryphone system** can require the caller's to state their business before being allowed in.

(g) **Voice recognition**. A computer controlling the door lock responds only to those voices recorded on its files. This method is far from common, however.

(h) In the future we are likely to see systems that recognise visitors' **fingerprints**.

3.3 **Cabinets, cupboards** and **drawers** can also be protected by means of locks. Some items should always be kept in a **safe**, cash being the most obvious example. The more valuable the item, the stronger the safe should be. Most have **keys** and **combinations**. Some have **electronically-controlled time-locks**.

Security procedures

3.4 Most organisations of any size have to have some **formal security measures**, if only to satisfy their **insurers**. The extent of the measures will depend on the risks involved in the business.

DEVOLVED ASSESSMENT ALERT

The evidence requirements for Element 22.2 include the following. 'Performance evidence ... must be available of the candidate **following set procedures** for the security of the workplace and its contents.' Such evidence may be as simple as being observed using passwords, signing in and out as required, locking cabinets and so on. Don't take these routine things for granted!

3.5 If your organisation has a formal **security procedures manual** get hold of a copy and read it carefully. It is likely to have the following procedures.

Procedure for	Examples
Identifying regular staff	If the procedures state that you should wear your **identity badge** at all times, then you must do so, no matter how well known you are to the security staff.
	If the procedures state that you should **show your pass** to the security guard whenever you enter the building, you should do so, and you should not be allowed access if you do not do so.
	Likewise if you are required to **sign in and out**, don't forget to do so.
Vetting non staff members	If somebody is coming to visit you on business then you may be required to go down to reception and accompany them to the place where you work. If you have not met them before you may have to ask them to produce some further means of identification: a letter inviting them to a meeting or the like.
Non business visitors	Say a friend is meeting you for lunch. Some organisations will not let such visitors past reception at all. Others allow free access to non-sensitive areas. Make sure your friend does not unwittingly break the rules.
Protecting the building	A particular door may have to be kept locked at all times. It may be the individual's responsibility to ensure that all windows in his or her working area are closed and locked at the end of the day.
Protecting the organisation's assets	You might be expected to lock away items like calculators in your desk drawer at night, for example.
Protecting documents and information	Locking away files and ledgers, or not leaving your computer terminal in a state where it can be used by someone without the password, are typical of measures of this sort. Other aspects of your work may be sensitive, and there may even be a confidentiality clause in your contract of employment: check.
Protecting the procedures	It ought to go without saying that you should not reveal your computer password to others and there is no point in having doors or safes with combinations if the combination is given to anyone who asks for it. Likewise there should be procedures to control keys – such as a list of authorised keyholders and instructions about where keys should be kept. There is no point in locking doors if the keys are accessible to all. In fact, do not discuss your organisation's security procedures with *anyone* outside the organisation: if an outsider asks persistently about security, report this as suspicious.

BPP
PUBLISHING

Procedure for	Examples
Explaining what to do in the event of a breach of security	The names and numbers should be available of the people to ring, and of the information they will need to be told: location of the intruders, time of entry, how many there are, items missing or damaged, and so on.

3.6 In general, your employer has **no right to search** employees or visitors **without their consent**. However, some contracts of employment include a clause giving the employer this right, in contexts where 'pilfering' of stock, components or files is a particular risk or problem.

3.7 The right to **search visitors** can be secured simply by displaying a notice informing them (before they enter the premises) that they are liable to be searched. (This is often the approach of retail outlets, to deter shoplifting.)

Activity 2.2

Choose any one area of security (personal identification, entry and exit, security equipment, data security, breach of security and so on) and design a notice or poster, suitable for posting on a departmental noticeboard, outlining the procedure **and/or** communicating its importance to staff.

(If your notice accurately and effectively communicates a real procedure or procedures in your office, consider seeking authorisation to post it on a noticeboard - and keep a copy for your portfolio.)

The scope and limitations of your responsibility

3.8 There will obviously be a limit to the responsibility that *you*, as an accounts assistant, have for the security of your organisation, its premises, belongings and staff. Find out exactly what your **responsibilities** are in this respect and where they stop. Most probably they will stop with your:

- **Following the rules** that affect your behaviour directly
- **Notifying the appropriate person** if you become aware of a security problem. (Who is the appropriate person in your organisation? Make sure you know.)

3.9 There is no need to report every person who stops in the street outside. Use your discretion, otherwise you will not be listened to when you do have a serious point to make.

3.10 **Tact** is very important. Some people can be offended if you question who they are: but most should understand that you are only doing your job.

3.11 **So what can you do to help?**

(a) If you see a door or cabinet gaping open and know that it should be locked, **lock it**.

(b) If you see anybody who is definitely acting suspiciously, **report it**.

(c) Make sure that **new recruits** to your department know what procedures they are supposed to follow.

(d) Don't allow **others** to allow you to breach security. Even if the person on reception knows you so well that he doesn't need to see your pass, there is no harm in showing it to him anyway. It reminds him of part of *his* job, and helps him to do it more effectively when strangers enter the building.

(e) Be aware that **things are changing** in your organisation all the time. A development that affects your work directly may not have been thought about by others from the security angle: a new procedure for handling cash, say, or moving the safe over to a desk by a ground floor window while the decorators are in.

(f) If you are going **out** to meet a client or supplier, make sure somebody in the office knows: where you are going, who *exactly* you are going to meet, what time you will be back and (if possible) a contact phone number. Be careful when meeting a new client or supplier for the first time off your premises; make sure your office knows exactly who the person is, where they come from, and what the purpose of the meeting is.

(g) **Don't be a hero,** if you find yourself in a dangerous situation. Your organisation can replace its belongings: **the safety of people comes first**.

DEVOLVED ASSESSMENT ALERT

The evidence requirements for Element 22.2 include "taking appropriate action (to deal with security risks) within the limits of your own authority". If you have keys to a filing cabinet, or the password to a computer, *you* are responsible for using them. If a stranger is acting suspiciously in the hallway, or is not wearing an identity card, what are you authorised to do? If in doubt, know exactly to whom you would *report* a suspected breach of security (or an actual breach, such as a theft).

Activity 2.3

In answering the following questions you should explain what your own organisation's security procedure is, if it covers the scenario described. If not, state what you think would be the best course or courses of action.

(a) A man with a case full of tools has opened up your office photocopier and spent about five minutes peering into it and tinkering with it. Nobody seems to know who called the engineer in, or whether there was a fault in any case.

Eventually the man tells you that the photocopier cannot be repaired on site and will have to be taken away. He calls in an assistant who has been waiting in a van outside and the two of them start to wheel the copier away You are the most senior person in your department at the moment because your boss is on holiday.

What should you do before you allow the men to take away the photocopier?

(b) Your security pass has the most appalling photograph of you that has ever been seen. You are meant to wear it on your lapel at all times but you are getting fed up with the jokes and comments about the 'accounts assistant from hell' and so on.

Given that you are well known to the security staff and to others in the organisation with whom you have to deal, is there any reason why you should not just keep your pass in your pocket?

(c) You are minding the reception desk and the telephone rings. A highly abusive person comes on the line and starts to make threats of physical violence against the MD of your company who is mentioned by name and accurate physical description.

What should you do?

(d) The chief cashier has an accident in the cashier's office, a secure part of the building to which no unauthorised access is allowed. You are the only other person present in the cashier's office. The chief cashier needs medical attention.

What should you do?

(e) You work in a small building society which keeps all of its mortgage documents in a strong room (the 'Deeds Room') in the basement. You are required to work in the Deeds Room for about two hours.

What security and safety issues arise here?

4 SECURITY OF INFORMATION

4.1 We will be discussing security of information, or **confidentiality,** in detail in Part B of this Interactive Text, when we deal with the storage and handling of information.

> ### KEY TERM
>
> **Confidentiality** is the keeping of information, given 'in confidence' to particular parties, between those parties; not disclosing information to those not authorised to have access to it.

4.2 **Information** is an item at risk of security breach. It can be damaged, lost or stolen in the same way that equipment and valuables can. People may seek to sabotage or steal information from organisations for

- Monetary/sale value
- Competitive advantage
- Pure nuisance value

4.3 **Organisations seek to protect the confidentiality of certain types of information.**

(a) Information integral to the business's **standing and competitive advantage** - for example, unique product formulae, designs and prototypes, marketing plans and some financial information.

(b) **Personal and private** information relating to employees and customers - for example, grievance, disciplinary and salary details; customer credit ratings. (Some such information is protected by law.)

(c) **Information related to the security of the organisation** - for example, details of access codes, computer passwords, banking/delivery schedules.

(d) Information **integral to the outcome of dealings,** which would be affected by public knowledge - for example, legal or financial details of intended mergers, takeovers, redundancies.

4.4 Extending the principles of premises security to 'sensitive' information, you should consider the following - and any special rules and procedures set by your organisation.

(a) Do not leave **paper files** or **computer disks** where they are generally accessible (preferably, lock them away).

(b) **Lock** secure safes, boxes and filing cabinets when you have finished with them.

(c) Use **passwords,** where advised, to secure computers and computer files.

(d) **Do not share passwords,** combinations or keys with unauthorised people.

(e) Do not copy, transmit or send confidential information without **authorisation** and appropriate security measures.

(f) Select **appropriate communication channels** and media for confidentiality. (There is a big difference between a memo posted on a staff noticeboard, or a conversation in an open office, and a sealed letter or memo clearly marked 'Private and Confidential' or 'For addressee's eyes only'!) **Remember that e-mail is neither secure nor confidential.**

(g) **Avoid 'careless talk' or gossip** about sensitive work-related matters with, or in the hearing of, unauthorised people. (This includes mobile phone conversations in public!)

(h) **Respect the privacy of others** - and assertively request them to respect yours.

Key learning points

- Security is a combination of **delaying** unauthorised access and sounding the **alarm** promptly when a breach of security has been identified.

- **Access** - entry and exit - points must be controlled, as **vulnerable areas** of any premises.

- Attention should be given to the protection of **people, confidential information** and the **assets and resources** of the organisation (including money, tools and equipment).

- A wide variety of **security devices and procedures** may be in place in a given organisation. These should be (a) clear to all employees involved and (b) regarded as confidential.

Quick quiz

1 List five items that might be at risk of being stolen from an office.

2 Outline a three-step procedure for identifying authorised staff at work.

3 What measures can help keep security procedures secure?

4 Give two examples of how another person could lead you into a breach of security.

5 List three ways of keeping information secure.

Answers to quick quiz

1 Cash, cheques, stock, vehicles, computers, fax machines, files (and so on).

2 Showing an entry pass to the security guard at reception; wearing an identity badge at all times; signing in and out of the building.

3 Don't reveal passwords or combinations. Control access to keys. Don't describe procedures to outsiders.

4 A guard or receptionist not requiring you to show your pass. Someone asking to borrow your keys for unspecified purposes.

5 Computer passwords. Locked file cabinets. Avoiding careless talk.

50

Part B

Unit 23
Achieving personal effectiveness

3 Managing a workload

This chapter contains

1   Business organisations

2   Organisational structure

3   Administrative systems and procedures

4   Work roles and responsibilities

5   Personal time management

6   Priorities and deadlines

7   Resources

Learning objectives

On completion of this chapter you will be able to:

- Identify and prioritise routine and unexpected tasks according to organisational procedures

- Report anticipated difficulties in meeting deadlines to the appropriate person

- Seek assistance, where necessary, to meet demands and deadlines

- Demonstrate awareness of the organisational and departmental structure

- Demonstrate awareness of organisational systems and procedures

- Outline your own work role and responsibilities

- Demonstrate knowledge of techniques for time management and prioritising and organising work

Performance criteria

(1) Routine and unexpected tasks are identified and prioritised according to organisational procedures

(2) Appropriate planning aids are used to plan and monitor work

(3) Where priorities change, work plans are changed accordingly

(4) Anticipated difficulties in meeting deadlines are promptly reported to the appropriate person

(5) Assistance is asked for, where necessary, to meet specific demands and deadlines

Range statement

1   **Planning aids:** diaries; schedules; action plans

Knowledge and understanding

- The different types of people: customers, peers, managers, other members of staff

Methods

- Prioritising and organising work (Element 23.1)

- Work planning and the use of planning and scheduling techniques and aids (Element 23.1)

- Time management (Element 23.1)

- Team working (Element 23.1)

- Work methods and practice (Element 23.1)

- Handling confidential information

- The organisational and departmental structure

- Organisation's administrative procedures

- Own work role and responsibilities

1   BUSINESS ORGANISATIONS

KEY TERM

Organisations are social arrangements for the controlled performance of collective goals.

1.1   An organisation is a **social arrangement:** that is, it is **made up of people,** banded together to carry out the **various tasks** that will enable them to achieve their **shared goals** and objectives.

Banding together in an organisation offers:

(a) Greater ability for people and organisations to achieve their goals, because they can share ideas, and pool their resources

(b) The **satisfaction of each person's need** for information, support and relationships with other people

1.2 Each organisation has **collective goals**, or shared objectives, over and above the goals of the people within it. The goals of a **business organisation**, might include:

(a) **Profitability** (an excess of income over expenditure)

(b) **Market standing** (being a leader in the market, in relation to the competition, and/or having a good reputation as a service provider)

(c) **Productivity** (efficient use of resources in supplying goods and services)

(d) **Innovation** (new product development or technological advance)

(e) **Public responsibility** (involvement in community affairs, or simply compliance with regulations on pollution or safety and so on)

1.3 A **business organisation** is responsible to its **owners** and other interested parties (sometimes called **stakeholders**) for the **achievement** of its goals. It needs to find reliable and systematic ways of ensuring that the following occurs.

(a) People within it **understand the collective goals.**

(b) **Resources** are **obtained** and used to reach goals without undue risk, disruption or waste.

(c) It can **assess** whether, or to what extent, it has reached its goals - and if not, why not, and what can be done.

The social arrangements and activities of the organisation must be formalised to provide **controlled performance**.

KEY TERM

Control is the overall process whereby **goals and standards** are **defined**, and performance is **monitored, measured** against the goals and **adjusted**, if necessary, to ensure that goals are being accomplished.

1.4 A **formal organisation** is deliberately constructed to fulfil specific goals. It is characterised by:

(a) An **organisational structure** which allocates authority, responsibility and resources for performing particular tasks to particular individuals or groups, with clear lines of communication between them

(b) **Administrative systems and procedures** which formalise and standardise the flow of information and other resources around and through the organisation.

We will look at these aspects in Sections 2 and 3 of this chapter.

DEVOLVED ASSESSMENT ALERT

You will be assessed on your knowledge and understanding of how your own organisation (or a simulated organisational situation) works. So now is the time to start thinking about it. At each point of 'theory' throughout this Interactive Text, ask yourself: 'How do *we* do that?'.

1.5   Because the organisation is made up of people, there is also an **informal organisation** (eg groups of friends) within every formal one, consisting of the networks or relationships of individuals and groups. People exchange information informally, by-passing formal 'channels'.

Activity 3.1

You will find a constant tension in your studies and working life between the demands of organisation policies, systems and procedures on the one hand, and the demands of people and working relationships on the other. Organisations do not always do things the way the individuals who work within, or come into contact with, them would like. To start thinking about this, list at least **two** ways in which:

(a)   The office 'grapevine' (informal information exchange between people), and
(b)   Informal, non-procedural ways of doing things

could be:

(a)   Helpful for the formal organisation; and
(b)   Unhelpful for the formal organisation.

1.6   An organisation is a **system**, which takes in 'inputs' or resources from the environment in which it operates, and converts them into 'outputs' which flow back into that environment.

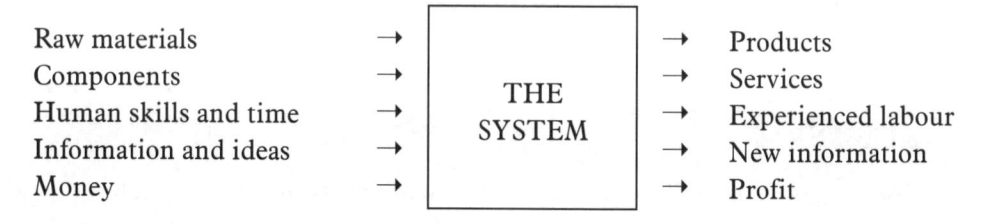

Raw materials → | THE SYSTEM | → Products
Components → | | → Services
Human skills and time → | | → Experienced labour
Information and ideas → | | → New information
Money → | | → Profit

2   ORGANISATION STRUCTURE

2.1   Organisations vary in **size** (that is, the number of people they employ). Think of the respective needs of a local newsagent and a government department, for example: **large organisations** involve **lots of people** doing lots of **different things** to complete **more (or more complex) tasks** and transactions. This requires **co-ordination**.

KEY TERM

Co-ordination is the harmonisation of the activities of individuals and groups within the organisation, reconciling differences in approach, timing and resource requirements in the pursuit of overall objectives.

2.2   The most important factor in co-ordination is a coherent **organisation structure**. The formal structure of an organisation is a **framework** intended to accomplish certain objectives; think about **your** organisation's objectives and structure. It many have a marketing department, finance department and so on. Your college may have different faculties.

Objective of organisation structure	Reason	Your organisation
To **link individuals** in an established network of relationships	So that authority, responsibility and communications can be controlled.	There will be individuals in certain roles in your organisation who you have to deal with regularly in order to do your job. Can you identify them?
To group together the **tasks** required to fulfil the objectives of the organisation as a whole, and to allocate them to suitable individuals or groups	This must be appropriate – it may be done on the basis of **function** (sales, production, accounting and so on), **geographical area** (regional sales territories, for example), **product** or **product type**.	What departments exist in your organisation? Why?
To allocate to individuals or groups the **authority** they require to perform their functions, as well as the **responsibility to account** for their performance to their superiors	This creates a hierarchy or **chain of command**, whereby **authority** flows downwards from senior management (a chief executive, managing director or board of directors) to each level of the organisation, and your **accountability** flows back up.	Can you identify the levels of authority in your own department? Who is your immediate superior, to whom you are responsible for your work? To whom is that person accountable?
To **co-ordinate** the objectives and activities of separate units	So that overall aims are achieved without gaps or overlaps in the flow of work.	What other departments or areas of the organisation do you have to liase with regularly?
To **enable the flow** of work, information and other resources through the organisation, via clear lines of co-operation and communication	So that all the different parts of the organisation are able to meet their objectives.	Where do you get the information and resources you require to do your job? To whom do you supply information and resources in return?

KEY TERMS

Authority is a person's right to do something, or to get others to do it.

Responsibility is the liability of a person to be called to account for the way he has exercised the authority given to him: an obligation to do something, or to get others to do it.

Delegation is the process by which individual A gives individual (or team) B the authority to do something (which falls within the scope of A's own authority). Delegation passes authority down the 'chain of command': note that the delegator remains *responsible* for the results of his delegation.

2.3 An **organisation chart** is often used to depict the structure of an organisation. We will use some organisation charts to illustrate the most common ways in which people and activities are grouped together in business organisations.

2.4 EXAMPLE: ORGANISATION STRUCTURE

Say you have an organisation which manufactures and sells a range of cars and buses in Asia and Europe, with a central committee of senior executives based in the UK. There are a number of functions to be performed, including sales and marketing, production, and finance and administration. There are a number of ways the business could be structured.

(a) In a **geographical** structure, responsibility for the organisation's activities is allocated on the basis of the areas or territories in which they are carried out. The Asia divisional manager, for example, would be responsible for all activities relating to all products in Asia.

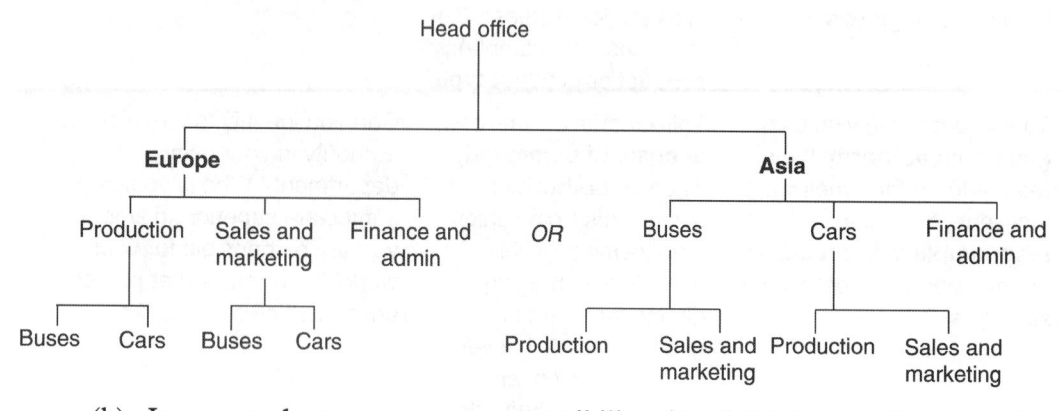

(b) In a **product** structure, responsibility is divided according to the organisation's products and their markets. The Buses divisional manager, for example, would be responsible for all activities related to buses, worldwide.

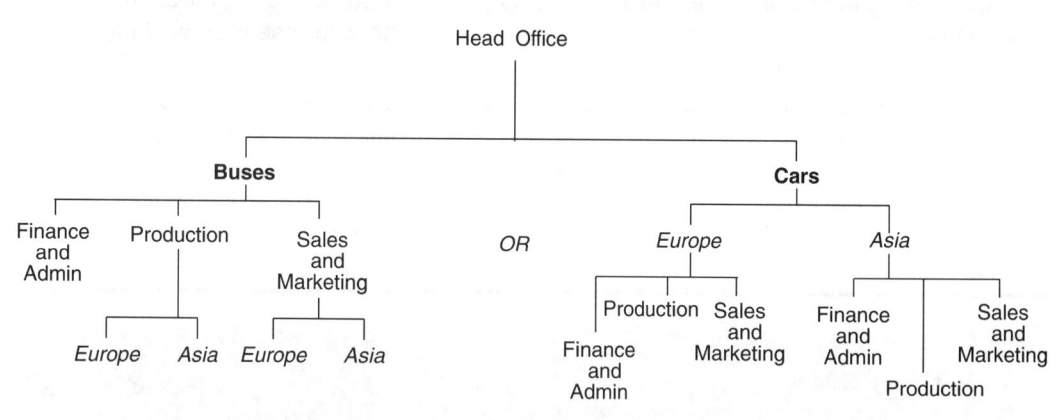

(c) In a **functional** structure, responsibility is allocated to specialised functions. The production divisional manager, for example, would be responsible for production activity on all products, worldwide.

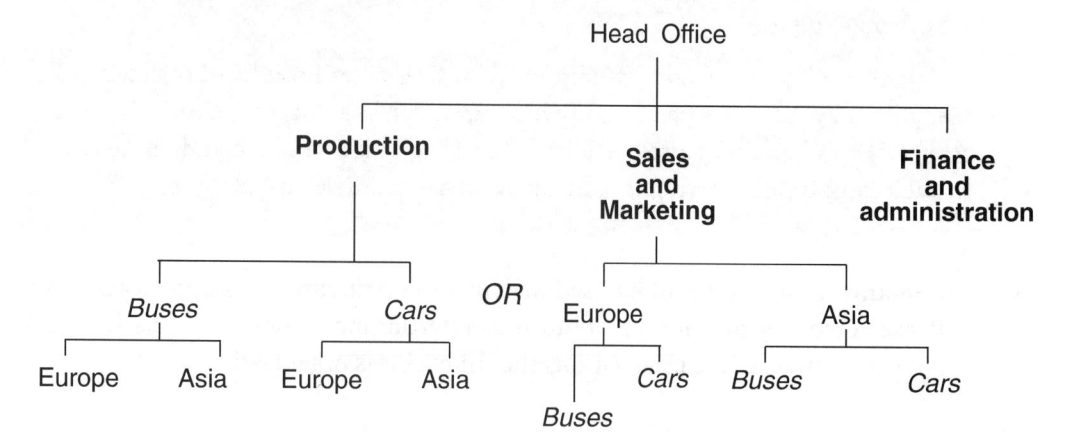

(d) In a **matrix structure**, multi-functional teams are created. An employee involved in production of buses (we will show this hypothetical employee on the chart below to clarify) would report both to his production department manager and to the buses product manager. (This would enable him to exchange information and co-ordinate his efforts with the sales, marketing, finance and administration people also involved with buses.)

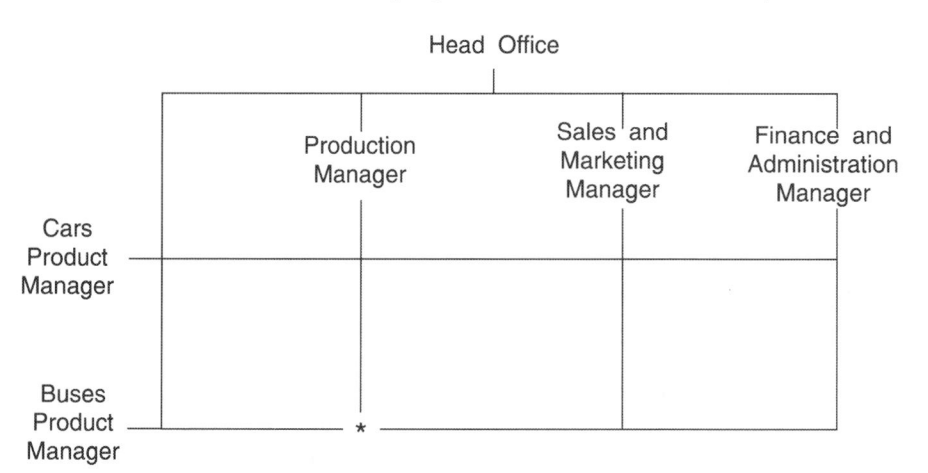

2.5 Consider the effect of the structure of the organisation affects its **accounting system,** in terms of how information is:

(a) **Collected**, and by whom

(b) **Sent** up and down the organisation hierarchy, and across the boundaries between different units

(c) **Processed and presented,** to suit the needs of users

Activity 3.2

(a) Match up each of the following activities with the person in the organisation you think would be responsible for carrying out the activity: write the appropriate number in the box next to the activity.

	Activity			*Person in organisation*
(i)	Delivering goods to customers		1	Purchasing manager
(ii)	Preparing cheques for suppliers		2	Accounts administrator
(iii)	Recording credit sales		3	Sales administrator
(iv)	Bank reconciliations		4	Distribution manager
(v)	Dealing with customers' enquiries		5	Factory supervisor
(vi)	Negotiating discounts with suppliers			
(vii)	Calculating wages due to production staff			

(b) For each activity, consider with which other person in the organisation (if anybody) that person might have to communicate (orally or in writing) in order to do the activity. Explain why, briefly.

Activity 3.3

Hamlet plc is a multinational company with operations in the UK and Denmark. The company's head office is in the UK. The company manufactures Yoricks and Ophelias. The following information is relevant to March 20X6.

	£'000
Head office costs	150
UK sales of Yoricks	1,000
UK sales of Ophelias	500
Denmark sales of Yoricks	1,500
Denmark sales of Ophelias	600
UK production costs of Yoricks	300
	£'000
UK production costs of Ophelias	130
Denmark production costs of Yoricks	375
Denmark production costs of Ophelias	150
UK marketing costs of Yoricks	100
UK marketing costs of Ophelias	70
Denmark marketing costs of Yoricks	200
Denmark marketing costs of Ophelias	80
UK finance and admin costs	75
Denmark finance and admin costs	105

Tasks

Every month, head office requires a summary of Hamlet plc's activities. On the assumption that the accounting system reflects the management of the organisation, prepare a summary of this information for head office on the basis that the organisation has:

(a) A functional structure
(b) A product-divisional structure
(c) A geographical structure

DEVOLVED ASSESSMENT ALERT

Several of the performance criteria for Units 22 and 23 require you to supply information 'to the appropriate person', and to know whether a particular action is within or outside 'your authority'. You therefore need a firm grasp of the scope and limits of your authority and responsibility in a given situation, and to whom you should report matters that are outside your authority. Obviously, you know who your immediate superior is - but do you know who is responsible for fire safety? Or first aid in the office? Or customer complaints? Or suspected breaches of security? In order to be aware of this, you need to be aware of the structure of your organisation and department.

2.6 **Know what is and is not within your authority and responsibility to do**.

Activity 3.4

(a) Draw an organisation chart, in any way that seems suitable to you, of your organisation. (If it is very large and complex, focus on the company or division of which your department is a part.)

(b) Draw a detailed organisation chart, in any way that seems suitable to you, of your department. Show its sections, and the job titles and names (if you know them) of individuals. (If it is a very large and complex department, focus on the individuals with whom you regularly have to deal: peers, superiors and subordinates.)

---

3 ADMINISTRATIVE SYSTEMS AND PROCEDURES

3.1 The other crucial mechanism of co-ordination is **administrative systems and procedures**. Individuals in an organisation cannot simply do their own thing in their own way in their own time: standard, predictable and dependable methods help everyone to work together to a common purpose and timetable.

> **KEY TERM**
>
> A **system** is a pre-determined logical plan or process for doing something.

3.2 An **administrative system** structures the relationship between tasks, procedures, data and resources to ensure a consistent, efficient and effective flow of information in and around an organisation. Examples include communication systems, management information systems, filing systems - and, of course, accounting systems.

> **KEY TERM**
>
> A **procedure** is a standard sequence of steps or operations necessary to perform an activity. (A recipe to cook a meal is a type of procedure.)

3.3 **Administrative procedures** basically 'programmed' activities relating to the flow of business information. Here is an example of such a procedure.

- All cash receipts are entered in the cash book
- At the end of the day, the totals are added up
- The addition is checked
- The totals in the cash book is posted into the main accounting records

Many such procedures, as simple consequences of instructions, can be **programmed into software and executed by computer.**

3.4 Procedures may also incorporate **rules**. If a procedure is 'the way it is done', a rule is 'the way it *must* be done (in order to be done right)'. Examples of rules are as follows.

(a) No computer disk should be loaded on to the organisation's computer system from an outside source without first being checked for viruses.

(b) The fire alarm and all fire extinguishers must be checked on a regular basis.

(c) Financial information must not be disclosed to unauthorised persons.

3.5 Large and well-established organisations will have a wide range of systems, procedures and rules in place.

- **Routine business transactions** and information flows (eg completing ledger accounts, stock control, issuing sales/delivery/invoice documentation and so on)

- **Internal running of the business** (eg safety precautions, reporting procedures, payroll preparation, recruitment and selection and so on)

- **Non-routine matters**, or contingencies, where pre-determined plans will minimise disruption and risk (eg in the event of emergency, disciplinary or grievance proceedings, the need for redundancies and so on).

3.6 Note that the work methods, practices and procedures of your department and organisation arise from:

BPP PUBLISHING

(a) The nature and logic of the **task**: what needs to be done, in what order and in what manner, in order for the purpose of the task to be fulfilled

(b) The requirements of the **law, regulations** and **Codes of Practice** established to ensure that tasks are completed safely, fairly and in accordance with the rights of individuals and society

(c) The requirements of **organisational policy**, formulated to reflect the organisation's values and intentions in regard to the task, the law, its objectives and so on

(d) **Formal instructions** from people in positions of authority. Where there are no set policy, procedure or legal constraints, a manager can to an extent dictate how things are done

(e) **Informal 'ground rules'** or **customs,** developed over time by the work group or the organisational culture: 'the way we do things round here'.

KEY TERM

Organisational culture is the shared assumptions, values and beliefs of the organisation's members; its collective self-image; its sense of 'the way we do things around here'; its general 'style'.

DEVOLVED ASSESSMENT ALERT

Don't forget that two key phrases in the Performance Criteria are:

- 'in accordance with organisational procedures'; and
- 'in line with legal requirements'.

Familiarise yourself with both, within the area of your responsibilities.

Activity 3.5

Give some examples of procedures affecting your work that arise from each of the influences listed in paragraph 3.6 above.

3.7 Many organisations have a **procedures manual** which is a useful source of information - and a point of reference in case of dispute. This should contain information on:

- The organisation's structure, products and services, with relevant guidelines
- Accounting and reporting systems
- Health and safety procedures
- Disciplinary and grievance procedures

3.8 Make sure that you are aware of any such formal guidelines provided by your organisation, as well as:

- **Instructions** given by your supervisor, colleagues and trainers
- Posted **notices**
- **Manuals and handbooks** accompanying equipment and machinery

and so on. If you are in any doubt, do not hesitate to ask questions – or to notify appropriate officials of any procedures needing improvement!

3.9 The **accounting system** of an organisation is simply one of its administrative systems. It is bound up with all the others, because it both:

(a) Monitors the flow of **money** (a vital resource) *within* the organisation and *between* the organisation and its environment; and

(b) Provides **information** about what and how the organisation is doing.

3.10 Every Unit in the Accounting NVQ/SVQ is essentially about the systems and procedures devised for accounting work.

4 WORK ROLES AND RESPONSIBILITIES

4.1 In Section 1 above we said that formal organisations are characterised by:

(a) An **organisational structure** which allocates authority, responsibility and resources for performing particular functions and tasks to particular individuals or groups, with clear lines of communication between them

(b) **Administrative systems and procedures** which formalise and standardise the flow of information and other resources around and through the organisation.

4.2 The **work role and responsibilities of an individual** must be seen in this context. You can only determine:

- What your **job and tasks** are

- What is **the scope and limitation of your authority and responsibility** to carry out that job and tasks

in the light of organisational and departmental arrangements for:

- The formal **delegation of authority**

- The specification of the tasks and areas of accountability

- Standardised plans, procedures and practices which define competent performance in the job

4.3 We will be discussing roles, authority and working with others in the context of **interpersonal relationships** in Chapter 5 of this Interactive Text. In this chapter, we simply want to call your attention to those aspects which **influence your ability to organise and manage your own workload**.

Job descriptions

4.4 Certain tasks need to be done in order for the department and organisation to meet their objectives. Those tasks must be allocated to particular job positions or individuals for the purposes of effective planning and control.

KEY TERM

A **job description** is a concise statement of the tasks, responsibilities and relationships involved in a given job.

4.5 **Contents of a job description**

(a) **Job title** and department and job code number. The person to whom the job holder is responsible. Possibly, the grading of the job.

(b) **Job summary** - showing in a few paragraphs the major functions and tools, machinery and special equipment used. Possibly also a small organisation chart.

(c) **Job content** - list of the sequence of operations and main duties that constitute the job, noting main levels of difficulty.

(d) The extent (and limits) of the jobholder's **authority and responsibility.**

(e) **Relation of job to other closely associated jobs**, including superior and subordinate positions and liaison required with other departments.

(f) Working hours, basis of pay and benefits, and conditions of employment, including location, special pressures, social isolation, physical conditions, or health hazards.

(g) Opportunities for training, transfer and promotion.

(h) Possibly, also, objectives and expected results, which will be compared against actual performance during employee appraisal - although this may be done as a separate exercise, as part of the appraisal process.

(i) The names and positions of the people/person who has;

- Prepared the job description
- Agreed the job description

(j) Date of preparation.

4.6 A highly simplified example might be as follows.

MIDWEST BANK PLC

1   *Job title:*   Clerk (Grade 2)

2   *Branch:*   All branches and administrative offices

3   *Job summary:*   To provide clerical support to activities within the bank

4   *Job content:*   Typical duties will include:

         (a)   cashier's duties;
         (b)   processing of branch clearing;
         (c)   processing of standing orders;
         (d)   support to branch management.

5   *Reporting structure:*

Administrative officer/assistant manager

Supervisor (Grade 3)

Clerk (Grade 2)

6   *Experience/Education:* experience not required, minimum 3 GCSEs or equivalent

7   *Training to be provided:* initial on-the-job training plus regular formal courses and training

8   *Hours:* 38 hours per week

9   *Objectives and appraisal:* Annual appraisal in line with objectives above

10 *Salary:* refer to separate standard salary structure

Job description prepared by: Head office personnel department

---

4.7   **Know what tasks you are expected to perform and in what context**.

Activity 3.6

(a)   If a job description exists for your position, obtain a copy: ask your supervisor, or the personnel department, if you do not have ready access to one. Read it through carefully, and consider whether it is an up-to-date, accurate and full description of what you actually do in your job. Compare it to the Standards for the Accounting NVQ/SVQ (including the ones reproduced at the front of this Interactive Text) Draft your own version of your job description, in the light of this appraisal. (You may like to discuss it with your supervisor!)

(b)   If a job description does not exist for your position, draft one!

Working with others

4.8   Your work role and responsibilities cannot be considered in isolation from organisational objectives and structures. Nor can they be considered in isolation from **other people**.

(a)   Where you are working in a department, section or team, you will have **joint objectives and goals,** which require you to pool your resources, information and efforts.

(b)   Your individual role will almost certainly involve **co-ordinating** your objectives and goals with those of other individuals and departments.

4.9   Why is **co-ordination** important?

(a)   The organisation is a collection of individuals and groups, each with their own interests and goals; these must be given a unified, common direction if the organisation as a whole is to achieve its objectives.

(b)   The organisation's activities involve a variety of people, tasks, resources and technologies which will have to be at the right place, at the right time, working in the right way, if smooth operations are to be maintained.

(c)   Some activities of the organisation will be dependent on the successful and timely completion of other activities: individuals need to ensure that they are aware of the requirements, plans and deadlines of others.

4.10   **Symptoms of poor co-ordination**

(a)   **Complaints** from clients, customers and other external parties, indicating that products and services are not being delivered on time, or that different units of the organisation are giving out different information.

(b)   **Work flow problems** within the organisation, with alternating overloads and waiting periods, as work arrives unplanned, or later than planned, from other units.

(c)   **Persistent conflict** within and between departments, especially the placing of blame for problems, and 'empire-building' and power games instead of teamworking and co-operation.

(d)   **Appeals to rules and red tape** in an attempt to give the appearance of integrated activity.

4.11   Some **solutions to co-ordination problems**

(a)   Systematic planning and control, allowing the plans and schedules of each unit to be integrated with those of other units

(b)   Direct supervision of the work to ensure that instructions are clear and effective, performance is monitored and controlled and so on;

(c)   Creating co-ordinating mechanisms in the organisation structure: multi-disciplinary teams, liaison or communication officers and committees;

(d)   The standardisation of work processes, targets, quality standards and so on.

4.12   Two of the most important **tools of effective co-ordination**, however, are to an extent within your individual control.

(a)   **Communication** is essential, ensuring that:

- The inter-relationships of different activities and plans is understood;

- Any variation from the plan, or difficulty meeting the deadline, are notified to other people likely to be affected by it;

- Task-related information is shared among those who can use it.

(b)   **Co-operation** must be worked at, and **conflict** controlled, so that individuals and teams take each other's needs into consideration, and do not compete, hoard valuable information and so on.

These matters will be discussed further in Chapter 5.

Activity 3.7

Select any three tasks from your job description (see Activity 3.6 above). For each, draw a flow-chart to show:

(a) where the instruction/authority, information, materials and other components of the same task come from in order to reach your desk;

(b) where the output from the task goes once it leaves your desk;

(c) any points (marked with an asterisk, say) where potential problems may occur: where the other individuals or units involved in the process have different methods or timescales to yours, perhaps;

(d) any points (marked in red, say) where problems actually tend to occur: where components you need to do your job reach you late, perhaps, or where you are put under pressure in order to meet your deadlines.

4.13 **Know how your work affects, and is affected by, other people**.

5 PERSONAL TIME MANAGEMENT

5.1 **Time is a resource, like money, information, materials and so on.** You have a fixed and limited amount of it, and various demands in your work (and non-work) life compete for a share of it. If you work in an organisation, your 'time is money': you will be paid for it, or for what you accomplish with it.

5.2 Time, like any other resource, needs to be managed, if it is to be used efficiently (without waste) and effectively (productively).

5.3 **Principles of good time management**

- Goals
- Action plans
- Priorities
- Focus
- Urgency
- Organisation

5.4 To be a truly effective time manager you must apply these principles to your personal life with the same enthusiasm that you apply them to your job - in fact, this is one aspect of the 'priorities' principle, as we shall see.

Goals

5.5 If you have no idea what it is you are supposed to accomplish, or only a vague idea, all the time in the world will not be long enough to get it done. Nor is there any way of telling whether you have done it or not. To be useful, goals need to be 'SMART':

- **S**pecific
- **M**easurable
- **A**ttainable
- **R**ealistic and
- **T**ime-bounded

5.6 This needs little explanation.

    (a) In work terms you could probably set **specific goals** by reference to your job description: 'prepare and despatch invoices for all goods sold'; 'issue monthly statements'; 'monitor slow paying customers' and so on.

    (b) However, **measurable** and **time-bounded goals** are very important for **effective time management**. If you say 'My goal is to see that invoices are issued and despatched for all goods sold *on the day of sale*' you have a very clear and specific idea of what it is that you have to achieve and whether you are achieving it or not.

5.7 **The same applies to personal goals**. 'I'd like a promotion' is just a wish. 'I aim to be promoted to General Manager by the end of my first year' is a goal, but not a realistic or attainable one. 'I aim to be promoted to supervisor of my section by the end of next year' gives you something to aim at.

5.8 **Set SMART goals for all aspects of your work, large and small**. It may seem silly at first to set yourself a goal of, say, always answering the phone before the third ring, but by the end of the first day you will have impressed everybody you speak to with your prompt service, besides having the personal satisfaction of having achieved something that you set out to do.

Action plans

5.9 Now you must make **written action plans that set out how you intend to achieve your goals**: the timescale, the deadlines, the tasks involved, the people to see or write to, the resources required, how one plan fits in with (or conflicts with) another and so on. These need not be lengthy or formal plans: start with **notes, lists** or **flowcharts** that will help you to capture and clarify your ideas and intentions.

5.10 Work planning will be considered in detail in Chapter 7.

Priorities

5.11 **Now you can set priorities from your plan.** You do this by **deciding which tasks are the most important** - what is the most valuable use of your time at that very moment.

5.12 Which task would you do if you only had time to do one task? That is your first priority. Then imagine that it will turn out that you have enough time to do one more thing before you have to leave. What would you do next? That is your second priority. Continue in this vein until you have identified three or four top priorities. Then get on with them, in order. Anything else is a waste of time that could be used in a more valuable way.

Focus: one thing at a time

5.13 Work on **one thing at a time** until it is finished.

5.14 If a task cannot be completely finished in one 'session', complete everything that it is in your power to complete at that time and use a **follow-up system** to make sure that it is not forgotten in the future. Correspondence, in particular, will involve varying periods of delay between question and answer, action and response.

5.15 **Make sure that everything that you need is available before you start work.** If not, you may not be able to do the task yet, but one of the things on your list will be to order supplies of the necessary forms or stationery, or to obtain the required information or do whatever it is that is holding you up.

5.16 **Before you start a task clear away everything from your desk that you do not need for that particular task.** Put irrelevant things where you will be able to retrieve them instantly when you come to deal with the tasks that you need them for. If they are not needed by anyone throw them away. It is quite hard to discipline yourself to do this because it might take some time initially and you might feel that that time could be spent doing other things. However, once tidy working becomes a habit, it will take no time at all, because your desk will always be either clear or have on it only the things you are using at that precise moment. Moreover, one of the best ways of helping yourself to concentrate and handle things one at a time is to remove less important distractions.

5.17 In accounts work it is not always easy to have a tidy desk. It is not untypical to be working with voluminous A3-sized computer print-out folders, with one for every day of the week. The office furniture in most offices is not really designed for this. This does not, however, alter the basic principle of single handling and tidy working. (And anyway, there may be a solution: would it be possible to print out reports in a smaller font size or on thinner paper to make physical handling easier?)

Urgency: do it now!

5.18 **Do not put off large, difficult or unpleasant tasks simply because they are large, difficult or unpleasant.** If you put it off, today's routine will be tomorrow's emergency: worse, today's emergency will be even more of an emergency tomorrow. Do it now!

5.19 **Think for a moment about how you behave when you know something is very urgent.** If you oversleep, you leap out of bed the moment you wake up. If you suddenly find out that a report has to go out last post today rather than tomorrow afternoon, then you get on with it at once. We are saying that you should **develop the ability to treat everything that you have to do in this way**. Procrastination is a natural tendency - fewer than 2% of people are reckoned to have a true sense of urgency - but procrastination really is the thief of time.

Organisation

5.20 Apart from working to plans, checklists or schedules (discussed in Chapter 7), your work organisation might be improved by the following.

(a) **An ABCD method on in-tray management.** When a task of piece of paper comes into your in-tray or 'to do' list, you should never merely look at it and put it back for later. This would mean you would handle it more than once – usually over and over again, if it is a trivial or unpleasant item! Resolve to take one of the following approaches

Act on the item immediately

Bin it, if you are sure it is worthless, irrelevant and unnecessary

Create a definite plan for coming back to the item: get it on your schedule or timetable

Delegate it to someone else

(b) **Organise your work in batches** of jobs requiring the same activities, files, equipment and so on. Group your filing tasks or word processing tasks, for example, and do them in a session, rather than having to travel to and fro or compete for equipment time for each separate task.

(c) **Take advantage of your natural work patterns**. Self-discipline is aided by developing regular hours or days for certain tasks, like dealing with correspondence first thing, or filing at the end of the day. If you are able to plan your own schedules, you might also take into account your personal patterns of energy, concentration, alertness etc. Large or complex tasks might be undertaken in the mornings before you get tired, or perhaps late at night with fewer distractions, while Friday afternoon is usually not a good time to start a demanding task in the office...

Activity 3.8

Which of the following apply in your case and which do not? Add explanatory notes where applicable.

	True	False	**Explanatory notes**
I work with a tidy desk.			
All my drawers, shelves and cabinets are tidy.			
Items that I use frequently are always ready to hand.			
Whenever I have finished with a file or a book I put it back where it belongs immediately.			
I write everything down and never forget anything.			
I work on one task at a time until it is finished.			
I do daily tasks daily except in very exceptional circumstances, in which case I catch up the next day.			
Every routine task that I do is done at a regular time each day.			
I never pick up a piece of paper without taking action on it (writing a reply, filing it, binning it, whatever).			
I organise my work into batches and do all of one type of work at the same time.			
I never run out of stationery that takes a while to obtain: I keep an eye on this and order in advance.			

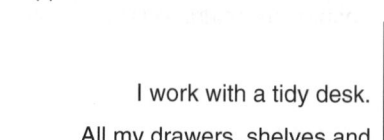

	True	False	Explanatory notes
My routine work could easily be taken over by someone else if I were unavoidably absent because I keep proper notes of what I am doing.			
I try to anticipate likely work and I ask my boss what is expected of me over the next week or so, so that I can plan out my work.			
I am able to estimate how long any task will take fairly accurately.			
I never miss deadlines.			
I do not panic under pressure.			

6 PRIORITIES AND DEADLINES

6.1 **Some jobs are entirely routine, and can be performed one step at a time**, but for most people some kind of **planning** and **judgement** will be required. For example, the most junior typist may have a large inflow and outflow of varying typing tasks, some of which are **more important or urgent** (requiring extra care or speed) than others.

6.2 Further up the organisation structure there will be greater responsibility for the execution of a wider range of tasks: a manager may have any number of matters calling for his/her attention at one time, and **will have to decide what to do first,** what to delegate and so on.

> **KEY TERMS**
>
> **Prioritising** basically involves arranging all the tasks which may face an individual at the same time (this week, or today) in order of **'preference'**. Because of the individual's responsibility to the organisation, this will not just be what he would 'like' to get done (or do first), but what will be most valuable to the attainment of his immediate or long-term goals.

High priority work

6.3 A piece of work will be **high priority** in the following circumstances.

(a) **If it has to be completed by a deadline.** The closer the deadline, the more urgent the work will be. A report which is to be typed for a board meeting the following day will take precedence in planning the day's work over the preparation of an agenda to be circulated in a week's time: **routine work comes lowest on the list,** as it can usually be 'caught up with' later if necessary.

(b) **If other tasks depend on it**: if the preparation of a sales invoice, or notes for a meeting, depends on a particular file, the first task may be to send a request for it to the file registry. Work can't start unless the file is there. Begin at the beginning!

(c) **If other people depend on it.** An item being given low priority by one individual or department - for example, retrieval or reproduction of a particular document - may hold up the activities of others.

(d) **If it is important.** There may be a clash of priorities between two urgent tasks, in which case relative consequences should be considered: if an important decision or action rests on a task (for example, a report for senior management, or correction of an error in a large customer order) then that task should take precedence over, say, the preparation of notes for a meeting, or processing a smaller order.

KEY TERM

A **deadline** is the latest date or time by which a task must be completed in order for its objective to be fulfilled.

Activity 3.9

Devise a mnemonic, using the letters 'P-R-I-O-R-I-T-Y', that will help you remember when a piece of work is high priority.

6.4 **Routine priorities,** or **regular peak times** include:

- Preparation of the weekly payroll
- Monthly issue of account statements
- Year end accounts preparation

6.5 They can be planned ahead of time, and other tasks postponed or redistributed around them.

6.6 **'Non-routine' priorities** occur when unexpected demands are made: events 'crop up', perhaps at short notice, or errors are discovered and require corrective action. If these are also **important** (as well as 'sudden') they should be regarded as high priority.

DEVOLVED ASSESSMENT ALERT

The evidence requirements for Element 23.1 include: evidence of performance ... of ... changing plans in line with organisational priorities.' You could demonstrate this by being observed assessing priorities, or by any notes and plans you make in the process.

Priority and urgency

6.7 Just because a task is **urgent** (that is, its deadline is close), it does not necessarily mean it is **high priority.** A task may be urgent but **unimportant,** compared to a task which has a more distant deadline.

On the other hand, as we noted earlier, you should **treat all important tasks as if they were urgent.**

Deadlines

6.8 The important points about deadlines are:

- They have been set for a reason
- They get closer!

6.9 **Reasons to avoid missing a deadline**

(a) **Delay on your part delays other people** from getting on with their work, and creates a bad impression of you and the organisation you work for.

(b) If you are late in producing a piece of work then you will tend to hurry it as the deadline draws near or passes, and its **quality will suffer**.

(c) You will have **less time to do your next piece of work.** That too will be late or below standard.

(d) You may get a **reputation** as someone who misses deadlines, and may not be trusted with responsibility in future.

6.10 On the other hand, there may be a problem if you find that you get a reputation as being someone who always **beats his or her deadlines**: you may find that you end up with a much larger workload than slower colleagues. This will have to be discussed with your superior: perhaps you are ready for more responsibility!

How to meet your deadlines: basic principles

6.11 **Different people approach their work in different ways**. You may like to get the easy tasks out of the way first. On the other hand you may prefer to get the difficult bits out of the way first.

6.12 As soon as possible after you are allocated a task and a deadline **think it through** (with a colleague if necessary)**from beginning to end.**

6.13 Then you can **plan out how you are going to achieve it in the time specified**: if you set aside one day for gathering information, say, two days for inputting and processing, and one day for analysing and preparing the results for presentation, you would comfortably meet a Friday deadline for a task allocated on Monday morning. **This planning stage is the time to renegotiate the deadline if it appears that the work cannot be done in the time that has been allocated.**

6.14 Your plan should **indicate what input, if any, you will need from others**. Before you do anything else, make sure that others are aware of the deadline you are working to and how their work fits in with your overall plan.

6.15 **Batch together any tasks that are similar and routine and do them all in one go**. For example you may have to write to those buyers of a certain product who share a certain characteristic. It is likely to be more efficient to identify all of the customers with the characteristic first, and then to write to them all, rather than writing to each customer as you come across his case.

6.16 **Monitor your progress constantly**. Something may take far longer than you anticipated: how will this affect your ability to complete the task on time?

Difficulties meeting deadlines

6.17 **As soon as you know** or can anticipate that a deadline is likely to be missed **tell the person who is relying on you** and explain why.

(a) If you are being delayed because you are **awaiting input from others**, the person you report to may have the authority to hurry them along.

(b) If **unforeseen difficulties** have arisen, your manager may be able to arrange for your workload to be shared, to make sure that the job comes in on time.

(c) If you are late because you have **not worked hard enough** you will naturally be reluctant to explain this to your superior. Own up earlier rather than later, while there is still a chance of salvaging the situation.

DEVOLVED ASSESSMENT ALERT

This may seem embarrassing and avoidable - but remember that it is actually a performance criterion: 23.1.4. One of the recommended sources of evidence is being observed **requesting assistance** when unable to meet specific workloads or deadlines!

Activity 3.10

A quick quiz!

(a) Why are deadlines important?
(b) Explain briefly how you can organise your work so that you meet your deadlines.

7 RESOURCES

7.1 Whenever people work, they are using **resources**, including:

- Their own time, which is paid for
- The time of colleagues, bosses and subordinates
- Information
- Materials
- Equipment, such as telephones, typewriters and computers
- Other items which cost money - such as electricity
- Money

7.2 Part of managing your workload is being responsible about **obtaining, organising and maintaining** the resources you use in the course of your work. What do you need? Have you got an adequate supply of the right type and quality, and in

suitable condition? How do you know when you need to replace an item, without disrupting your work? What is the procedure for doing so?

7.3   The following are some of the major resources which you may be required to manage in the course of your work.

Information resources

7.4   **Technical information** includes: reference books and other information regarding the products or services provided by your firm; information about the way in which procedures are performed or equipment used; information about laws and regulations relevant to your work.

7.5   **Organisational information** is information about the organisation. Examples include:

- **Manuals of instructions, procedures or best practice**
- **Staff planning charts**
- **Forms and reports** used by the organisation

7.6   **Personal information** is whatever relates to *you* as an individual.

- Diaries
- Copies of expenses
- Timesheets
- Appraisals and other reports about you
- Your portfolio of evidence of competence

7.7   You should have all the information that you need to do your work readily to hand.

(a)   **Make sure your manual of best practice is kept up to date.**

(b)   Make sure that you have current editions of things like **tax tables, accounting standards** or other such publications that you need to do your work. (Is your copy of your company's brochure the one that customers are using? Perhaps you need to keep copies of old brochures just in case.)

7.8   It is useful to keep at work a copy of any **personal documents** that you may occasionally need to refer to, such as your contract of employment, and a list of **personal details** (eg doctor, bank details) that you may need. Your personal life goes on even when you are at work.

Physical resources

7.9   **Pens** and **paper** are still basic 'tools' of the office worker. Make sure you have enough.

7.10   The paper obtained for an accountancy office usually includes **analysis sheets**, to help with the preparation of analysis columns by hand. Most offices also keep supplies of **notepads** (memo pads, telephone message pads, Post-It notes and so on).

7.11   You will also need things to keep paper together - **paperclips, staples, glue, sellotape** and so on - and things to help with filing of paper, like **hole punches**.

7.12 **Where accounting records are 'manual', special stationery needs to be provided** - for example a **cash book**. Where transactions are controlled by the use of **vouchers** or authorisation forms (such as journal vouchers, petty cash vouchers and authorisations to obtain cash from the cashier) a sufficient supply of the forms should be available at all times. Official forms, like **PAYE documentation**, may be needed urgently and may only be available from one source, so you should be particularly careful to maintain supplies of these.

7.13 If you work in a computerised environment you will also need a supply of **floppy disks**, **suitable paper** and **cartridges** for printers, **screen cleaning materials**, **mouse mats** and so on.

Activity 3.11

What other resources do you regularly use and 'have charge of' in the sense that you need to maintain them in good condition and/or monitor and maintain a regular supply of them? Use our categories in paragraph 5.1 to remind you, if you need to.

Activity 3.12

(a) Draw a diagram that shows how you currently *organise* your workspace (desk, personal storage furniture, in-trays and so on), and show how your work flows across it. When you get a piece of work to do, where does it arrive on your desk? Where do you keep it while it is waiting to be done? What area of the desk do you actually process the work on? Where is the work put when it is finished?

(b) Compare notes with your next door neighbour in the office (or in class) and ask him or her to comment on how they think your work area and workflow could be better organised.

(c) Put any good ideas that emerge from this exercise into practice at work.

Key learning points

- Organisations need a **structure** so that their activities can be co-ordinated. An organisation might have a geographical structure, a product division structure, a functional structure or a matrix structure.

- Organisations lay down **systems, procedures** and **rules** to ensure that tasks are performed in a standard way.

- **Work roles and responsibilities** are determined by organisational and departmental structure, job descriptions, the requirements of co-ordination and set policies, procedures and practices.

- **Effective workload organisation** involves deciding when and in what order to do your work, and making sure you have all the information and physical resources that you need.

- Effective **time management** involves goals, action plans, priorities, focus, urgency and organisation.

- **Prioritising** tasks involves ordering tasks in order of preference or **priority.**

- **High priority work** may need to be completed by a given deadline, other tasks may be dependent upon it, other people may depend on it, and more often than not, it will be important.

- **Routine priorities** can be planned ahead of time, whereas **non-routine priorities** occur when unexpected demands are made.

- **Deadlines** must never be missed. They are important because failure to meet them creates a bad impression of you and your organisation, the quality of your work may suffer as deadlines approach (too soon), and your next piece of work is likely to suffer as you'll have less time to do it in.

- Effective workflow organisation also involves making sure that you have sufficient **resources**. Resources include time, information, materials, equipment.

Quick quiz

1   Define the term 'organisation'.

2   List five possible objectives of a business organisation.

3   List five resources or inputs to the organisational system.

4   What objectives should an organisation's structure achieve?

5   What is a matrix structure?

6   Define (a) a rule and (b) a procedure.

7   What sources of information about relevant procedures might you consult?

8   What influences determine work methods, practices and procedures?

9   What should be contained in a job description?

10   List four symptoms of poor co-ordination.

11   What is 'organisation culture'?

12   List six elements of effective time management.

13   What makes a piece of work 'high priority'?

14   What is the first thing you should do if you are likely to miss a deadline?

15   What is involved in 'managing resources' required for your work?

Answers to quick quiz

1   An organisation is a social arrangement for the controlled performance of collective goals.

2   Business objectives include:

- Profitability
- Market share or standing
- Productivity
- Innovation
- Public responsibility

3   Business inputs include:

- Raw materials
- Components
- Human skills and time
- Information and ideas

- Money/finance

4   Linking in individuals in an established network of relationships; grouping together necessary tasks, and allocating them; allocating authority and ensuring accountability; co-ordinating separate units and facilitating co-operation and communication.

5   A matrix structure creates dual (for example, functional/product) responsibility for activities.

6   (a)   A rule is something which 'must' be done.
     (b)   A procedure is a sequence of operations defining 'how' something is done.

7   Procedures may be outlined in: organisation manuals; equipment manuals; written or verbal instructions; workplace notices.

8   Nature and logic of the task; requirements of law/regulation; requirements of organisational policy; formal instructions; informal customs.

9   Job title/department/responsibility relationships; job summary; job content; scope and limits of authority; relationship with other positions; working hours and conditions; objectives and target results; preparation data.

10   Complaints from customers; workflow problems within the organisation; conflict in and between departments; appeals to bureaucracy.

11   Culture is the shared values and beliefs in an organisation which create its collective self-image, general style and character.

12   Goals; action plans; priorities; focus; urgency; organisation.

13   Deadlines; other tasks depend on it; other people depend on it; importance.

14   Tell the person who is relying on you to complete your task.

15   Obtaining resources; monitoring and maintaining an available supply of resources; maintaining the condition of resources; organising resources for efficient use.

4 Work planning and control

This chapter contains

1   Introduction to work planning and control

2   Scheduling

3   Planning aids

4   Monitoring and follow-up

Learning objectives

On completion of this chapter you will be able to:

- Use appropriate planning aids to plan and monitor work

- Change work plans where priorities change

- Understand the process of work planning and the use of planning and scheduling techniques and aids

Performance criteria

(1)   Routine and unexpected tasks are identified and prioritised according to organisational procedures

(2)   Appropriate planning aids are used to plan and monitor work

(3)   Where priorities change, work plans are changed accordingly

(4)   Anticipated difficulties in meeting deadlines are promptly reported to the appropriate person

(5)   Assistance is asked for, where necessary, to meet specific demands and deadlines

Range

1   **Planning aids:** diaries; schedules; action plans

Knowledge and understanding

- The different types of people: customers, peers, managers, other members of staff

> **Methods**
>
> - Prioritising and organising work (Element 23.1)
>
> - Work planning and the use of planning and scheduling techniques and aids (Element 23.1)
>
> - Time management (Element 23.1)
>
> - Team working (Element 23.1)
>
> - Work methods and practice (Element 23.1)
>
> - Handling confidential information
>
> - The organisational and departmental structure
>
> - Own work role and responsibilities

1 INTRODUCTION TO WORK PLANNING AND CONTROL

> ### KEY TERMS
>
> **Planning** is the process of deciding what the 'ends' of an activity should be (objective-setting) and determining the most appropriate 'means' of achieving those ends.
>
> **Organising** is the process of establishing a framework within which plans can be carried out: determining structures and systems (such as those discussed in Chapter 6) for co-ordinating the human and other resources required.
>
> **Control** is the process of monitoring performance to check whether plans have been carried out as expected, and - if not - doing something about it.

Planning and control

1.1 Planning and control at a managerial or organisational level are essential for the following reasons.

(a) **Uncertainty**. The future cannot be foreseen with certainty. Nevertheless, plans and structures give some direction and predictability to the work of the organisation.

(b) **The need for co-ordination**.

- Sub units of the organisation know what it is they need to achieve, and when.

- Work 'flows' from one process (or department) to another without hold-ups or clashes, and without idle time or overwork for staff and machinery.

- The resources required for a task are available where and when they are required.

- Required work is being done by somebody – but not being duplicated by others, with a waste of effort.

- All of the above are achieved in such a way that products/services of the required quality are available to customers at the right place, at the right price and at the right time.

1.2 Planning involves decisions about:

- **What** to do
- **How** to do it
- **When** to do it and
- **Who** should do it (this is also the area covered by 'organising').

Such questions are relevant at all levels of organisational activity.

1.3 **Planning** is the process of deciding what should be done. **Control** is the process of checking whether it **has** been done, and if not, doing something about it. The combined processes of planning and control are known as a **control cycle**.

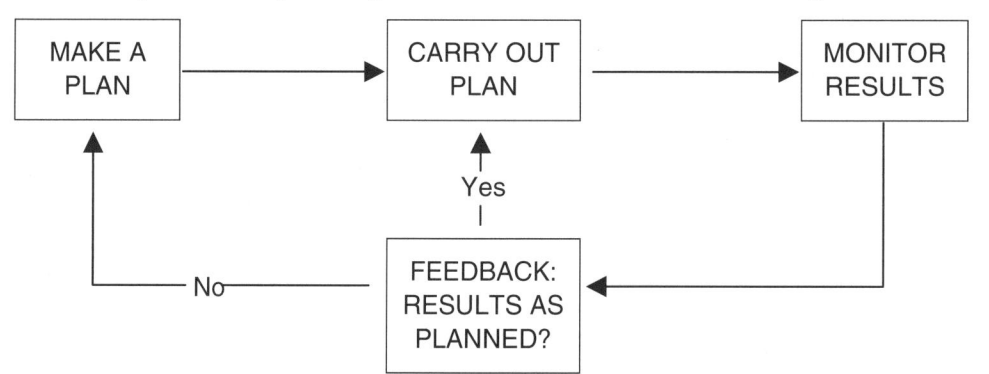

1.4 In more detail, the control cycle - which applies to your individual work planning as much as to the strategic planning of the organisation - has six basic stages.

Step 1	Making a plan: deciding what to do and identifying the desired results
Step 2	**Carrying out the plan**
Step 3	**Monitoring and measuring actual results achieved**
Step 4	**Comparing feedback on actual results against the plans**
Step 5	**Evaluating the comparison, and deciding whether further action is necessary to ensure the plan is achieved**
Step 6	**Implementing corrective action where necessary**

Individual work planning

1.5 **Work planning at an individual level involves:**

- Scheduling **routine tasks** so that they will be completed at appropriate times

- **Handling high priority tasks and deadlines**; that is, working into the routine urgent tasks which interrupt the usual level of working

- **Adapting to changes and unexpected demands**; that is, being prepared for emergencies, as far as possible

- **Meeting performance standards** for working

- **Co-ordinating** your own efforts with those of others

1.6   **Basic steps in work planning**

    (a) **The establishment of priorities**: considering tasks in order of importance for the objective concerned. (This was discussed in Chapter 3.)

    (b) **Scheduling or timetabling tasks**. (This is discussed in Section 2 below.)

    (c) Establishing **checks** and **controls** to ensure that priority deadlines are being met and that routine tasks are still achieving their objectives. (This is discussed in Section 3 below.)

Activity 4.1

(a) What is the most important single task that you have to do at work?

Write it down here.

_____

_____

_____

_____

(b) Make a list of all the routine tasks that you carry out at work on a regular basis. How often do you do each one and how long does each one take, on average?

Task	How often do you do it?	How long does it take?
_____	_____	_____
_____	_____	_____
_____	_____	_____
_____	_____	_____
_____	_____	_____
_____	_____	_____
_____	_____	_____
_____	_____	_____
_____	_____	_____
_____	_____	_____
_____	_____	_____
_____	_____	_____
_____	_____	_____

(c) How long do you spend each day doing routine things? You should be able to work this out from the list you have made.

Planning for uncertainty

1.7   Before we go on to discuss planning techniques, it is important to realise that **plans do not give you control over the future.**

    (a) **You can only anticipate what is likely to happen in future,** based on what has happened in the past, and any trends or tendencies that you can see in the pattern of past events.

(b) **Unexpected, uncontrollable events happen**. Computers break down, suppliers go bust, transport strikes shut down operations for a day and so on.

1.8 **Contingencies** are unexpected and uncontrollable events which do not feature in the main plan of the organisation. Contingency plans are those which are prepared in advance to deal with a situation that *may* (or may not) arise.

1.9 Remember that planning is part of the **control system**: plans may constantly have to be adjusted in order to correct or improve performance.

DEVOLVED ASSESSMENT ALERT

You are required to demonstrate competence not only in **making** plans, but in **changing** them as priorities change. Flexibility is key.

1.10 Planning of work should therefore cover the following.

(a) **Routine**: regular volumes of work achieved by established procedures to regular time scales.

(b) **Scheduled peaks**: workloads will be higher at predictable 'busy periods', for example for retailers at Christmas, or for auditors at the end of the financial year.

(c) **Unscheduled peaks and emergencies**: a special conference, a new product launch or a marketing drive are all outside the normal cycle of peaks and troughs in an organisation's activities, but plans could still be made to accommodate the extra work.

2 SCHEDULING

2.1 There are three basic stages to the scheduling of work.

- **Loading**
- **Sequencing**
- **Scheduling**

(In practice the term **scheduling** is often used to describe all of these stages.)

Loading

KEY TERM

Loading is the allocation of tasks to people or machines.

2.2 In accounting work, tasks are generally allocated to **people** - a single person or a team. The allocation will depend upon a number of factors.

(a) The **precise skills** required to do a job.

(b) The availability or unavailability of skilled people to do the work.

(c) The **demand for commonly used facilities**: computers, fax machine or photocopier, say.

2.3 **Your supervisor will generally decide whether you have the right skills to do a job.** You may also be involved in this decision, however.

2.4 It is **your responsibility to speak up at the outset if you are being asked to do too much**, or if you don't have enough to do.

2.5 **Accounting work also uses machines and equipment of various kinds.** Your organisation may have a **booking system** for the use of computer time or printer time, and if so this is something that you will have to build into your plan. Think about what time you will need *before* you start a task and book your time slot in advance. Be as realistic as you can: if you book some time and you have not finished the preparatory work when the time arrives, you will lose your slot.

2.6 Perhaps more usually in a modern office, with networked PCs, it will be a matter of coming to informal arrangements with your colleagues. 'Is that a long print-run, or can I send this document to that printer?' 'Are you just doing a few copies or shall I come back later?' This is all part of the give and take of everyday office life. Don't be selfish, but don't be a pushover if you have some really urgent work to get done.

Sequencing

KEY TERM

Sequencing is the determination of the order in which tasks should be completed.

2.7 We have already discussed prioritising on the basis of urgency, importance, workflow and so on. If issues of **urgency** (or **'least slack time'**) or **importance** (or **'high priority'**) are not involved, here are some other possible criteria for sequencing tasks.

(a) **Arrival time**. This is the first come, first served basis that you encounter all the time, in the bank, or whenever you ring somebody, for example. The order in which things are done are determined by the things themselves.

(b) **Most nearly finished**. This is not very scientific, but it recognises that great frustration can be caused by interrupting a job just before it is completed.

(c) **Shortest queue at next operation**. For example, seeing that the typist is about to run out of work, you might draft some letters before making the lengthy series of phone calls that you are due to make.

(d) **Least changeover cost**. For example if you have too much to do and are about to go on holiday, you should finish off all the things that it will be difficult for someone else to take over while you are away.

(e) **Shortest task first, then next shortest, and so on**. This is not very scientific, but it gets lots of things out of the way quickly.

(f) **Longest job first, then next longest, and so on**. Again this is not very scientific, but it gets the most daunting task out of the way rather than letting it hang about becoming ever more daunting.

Scheduling

> **KEY TERM**
>
> **Activity scheduling** provides a list of activities, in the order in which they must be completed: we have called this task sequencing.
>
> **Time scheduling** adds to this the timescale or start and end times/dates for each activity.

2.8 Determining the time that it will take to do a task is easy if it is a **routine task** that you have done a thousand times before. Simply keep a note of how long it takes you, on average.

2.9 With **non-routine tasks**, particularly substantial ones, it can be far more difficult to determine how long to allow. You can ask someone with more experience than you, or you might be able to break the new task down into smaller stages whose duration you can more easily estimate. The important thing is to be realistic.

2.10 Time schedules can be determined by different methods.

(a) **Forward scheduling** can be used, starting with a given start time/date and working through estimated times for each stage of the task (allowing for some which may be undertaken simultaneously, by more than one person or machine) to the estimated **completion** time/date. This method can be used, for example, when completing routine accounting tasks.

(b) **Reverse scheduling** is where you start with a **completion** time/date or deadline, and work **backwards** through estimated times for each stage of the task, determining **start times** for each stage – and for the task as a whole – which will enable you to meet the deadline. This method can be used to meet deadlines, for example, for a report to be prepared, for office relocation, and many other projects which have a set completion date.

2.11 Once scheduling is completed, **detailed work programmes can be designed** for jobs which are carried out over a period of time: ie some tasks will have to be started well before the deadline, others may be commenced immediately before, others will be done on the day itself.

Activity 4.2

Georgette works in the correspondence department of a large building society. She has made a list of all the tasks that she has to do today.

(a) Read and deal with first post
(b) Finish filing yesterday's work
(c) Attend staff meeting at 2.30pm
(d) Chase up replies to previous correspondence
(e) Read and deal with afternoon post
(f) Try to complete work outstanding from earlier days
(g) File today's work

How should Georgette organise her day?

2.12 Various aids to **scheduling** - and to **monitoring progress against schedule** - are available, and we will discuss these now.

3 PLANNING AIDS

Lists

3.1 Lists are a useful way of identifying and remembering what needs to be done, and of monitoring how far you've got. You should work from a list of 'Things to do' all the time. If you don't do this already, try this approach once and you will be hooked. What's more, your daily productivity will shoot up.

(a) **Plan the whole of the coming week**. It is best to do this when you are free from the pressures and distractions of actually being at work.

(b) **Make a list every day before you start work**. Again, it is probably best to do this the night before, so long as you don't forget to take your list into work with you the next day.

(c) **On the day itself refuse to do anything that is not on your list**. Every new task that arises has to be added to your list.

(d) **Every time you finish something on your list, cross it off**. This is the really satisfying part of making lists!

(e) **At the end of the day take all the items that are still on the list and transfer them to your list for the next day**. Don't skip this part and just staple today's unfinished list to tomorrow's unstarted one. The physical act of writing tasks down on paper is an important part of the process. They will not be channelled through your mind if you just look at them.

3.2 You will find that when you make out a list of things to do many of the things that have been nagging at the back of your mind don't seem that important or daunting. The items do not need to be in any particular order at this stage: **the important thing is that you list down everything that you have to do.**

3.3 **Do not rely on your memory**, even if you think your memory is a fantastically good one. It is highly unlikely to be infallible, and in any case you are not just creating a memory-jogger: the idea is that you should be able to see at a glance *all* the things you have to do so that you can get them into perspective.

Activity 4.3

Make a list **now** of everything you have to do for the rest of the day today **or** the whole day tomorrow.

Checklists

3.4 A checklist, or 'tick chart', is simply a list which allows for ticking or 'checking' off each task as it is completed (instead of crossing out). Again, it may or may not reflect the order in which you actually perform the tasks. You may simply have a column to put ticks against each task, or you may want to have a space for times/dates on which you started or finished the activity, or even for stages of the activity (for example, where a particular document is at a given date) – or elements of all of these.

3.5 As an example, here is a checklist for an accounts manager preparing deadlines for sending a number of job advertisements to press.

Ad	Due date	Writer	Designer	Photographer	Film	Print	Proofed	Sent?
Times	3/9	21/8	22/8	24/8	30/8	-	2/9	√
Standard	3/9	22/8	23/8	26/8	30/8	-	2/9	√
A5 classified	7/9	29/8	30/8	-	-	-	4/9	√
Leaflet A	12/9	10/8	12/8	15/8	-	2/9		
Leaflet B	13/9	2/9	3/9		-			

Activity 4.4

Suppose you are the accounts manager's assistant. She has fallen ill on the 5th September, and has asked you to take over the ad and leaflet production. 'I've left you my work checklist,' she says. 'You can work from that.' You find on her desk the checklist given as our example above.

(a) What can you tell from the checklist?

(b) What does this suggest about the usefulness of checklists?

(c) What tasks that you (as a real person, now) have to perform might benefit from the same approach?

Action plans

3.6 **Action plans** set out a programme of work or action, including time scheduling. Our example of a checklist above was a kind of action plan.

The following is another example, for the writing of a report.

	Activity	Days before due date	Target date	Date begun	Date completed
1	Request files	6	3/9		
2	Draft report	5	4/9		
3	Type report	3	6/9		
4	Approve report	1	8/9		
5	Signature	1	8/9		
6	Courier	0	9/9		

Precedence networks

3.7 If you are having trouble converting your list or checklist into a workable **sequence** of actions, a fairly simple approach to working it out is to 'map' it, using what is called a **precedence network**. A simple precedence network shows which

activities need to be completed before others. The squares or 'nodes' denote activities, and the arrows show logical progression and precedence.

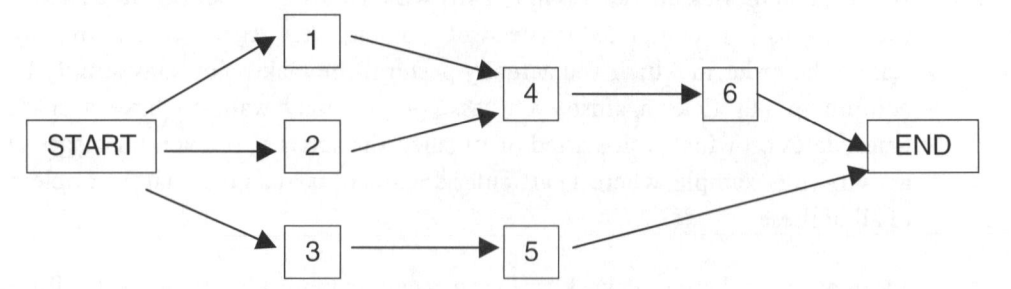

3.8 Consider the network above as a plan for going away on holiday, say.

Activity 1 = Reserving your holiday place by phone

Activity 2 = Booking travel insurance

Activity 3 = Renewing your passport

Activity 4 = Sending in a completed booking form. (This follows a reservation and requires details of insurance cover.)

Activity 5 = Obtaining a travel visa. (This can't be done until you have a valid passport.)

Activity 6 = Collection of tickets (for which you need to have made a written booking).

And you're off! The advantage of such a method is that (unlike a checklist) it allows you to show where a number of activities need to be done at roughly the same time (like activities 1, 2 and 3 above).

Activity 4.5

Choose any task you have to complete in the coming week.

(a) Brainstorm a list of the activities it will require, in no particular order.

(b) Put your list into the order in which you will (roughly) have to do the activities.

(c) Convert your checklist into a precedence network. (You could draw one large enough to write the activity into each node box, instead of numbering and listing the activities.)

Timetables and diaries

3.9 The information and dairies for your action plan could be formatted as a timetable or diary entry. You may already be using such methods to timetable your studies – and/or your social life! Timetables and diaries are designed to:

(a) remind you of key times and dates;

(b) remind you to make necessary advance preparations; and

(c) help you allocate your time effectively – no 25-hour days or clashing appointments.

Activity 4.6

Here is a timetable/diary page for the week of the 3rd to 9th September. Enter the schedule given in paragraph 3.5 as an action plan, as you would do a class timetable or appointments diary. Consider how you would highlight the due date.

SATURDAY 3	WEDNESDAY 7
SUNDAY 4	THURSDAY 8
MONDAY 5	FRIDAY 9
TUESDAY 6	Week commencing 3 SEPTEMBER S S M T W T F 3 4 5 6 7 8 9

3.10 A variation on the diary system is the more sophisticated **personal organiser**.

3.11 **Benefits of a personal organiser system**

(a) **You can store names, addresses, telephone numbers** and other basic information so that it is readily accessible, wherever you are.

(b) **You can set down tasks, goals and task priorities**, using a goal planning or 'do today' framework. It will also act as a **schedule** and **checklist** to ensure that you complete all tasks at the right time.

(c) **You will record appointments, day-to-day and in the longer term** if required. This will not only help to ensure that you do not forget them but will help you to plan ahead so that:

- You do not waste unnecessary time and energy travelling back and forth when you could fit in several tasks at the same time

- You can prepare, and have to hand any files or other information required;

- You can see where peak and slack periods fall, for planning other tasks.

(d) **You can take notes of ideas, meetings and plans** in a single, convenient format. (Portable electronic organisers also have 'notepad' facilities, albeit limited.) Keeping everything together - in flexible loose-leaf or (electronically) accessible format - will keep personal 'files' organised.

(e) **You will follow up tasks**. Uncompleted work, future action required, expected results or replies can be scheduled for the appropriate time as a memory jog.

3.12 **Potential problems of the system**

(a) The system requires a **time commitment** in itself. You may spend so much time filling in the sections of the personal organiser or using all of its functions (if it is electronic) that you lose work time.

(b) Just having a personal organiser is no guarantee of being suddenly organised. **Time management involves techniques which may only be acquired through training.**

(c) It is easy to grow very **dependent** on a personal organiser, to the point where its loss or destruction creates total chaos.

Activity 4.7

On the following page is shown an extract from the diary kept by your boss, Cynthia Cillie, who has just had an accident and who will therefore be off work for some time.

You will be standing in for Cynthia while she is away.

What will you have to do over the next week and what further information do you need?

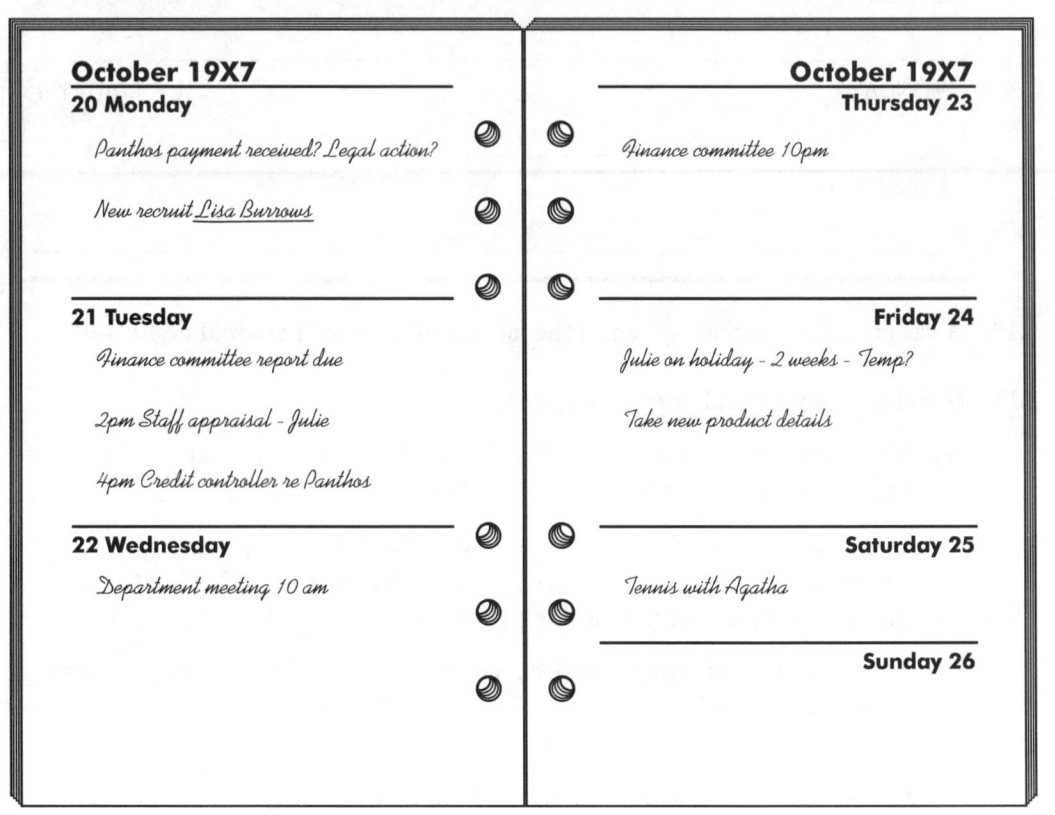

October 19X7

20 Monday

Panthos payment received? Legal action?

New recruit Lisa Burrows

21 Tuesday

Finance committee report due

2pm Staff appraisal - Julie

4pm Credit controller re Panthos

22 Wednesday

Department meeting 10 am

October 19X7

Thursday 23

Finance committee 10pm

Friday 24

Julie on holiday - 2 weeks - Temp?

Take new product details

Saturday 25

Tennis with Agatha

Sunday 26

Charts

3.13 Longer-term schedules may be more conveniently read using charts, peg-boards or year-planners. These can be used to show:

- The length of time to be taken for scheduled events or activities;
- The relationship between events or tasks;
- The relationship between planned and actual task duration or output.

Bar charts

3.14 The following is a simple example, which you may have seen used, of a year planner: in this case, a general plan for a fashion retail outlet.

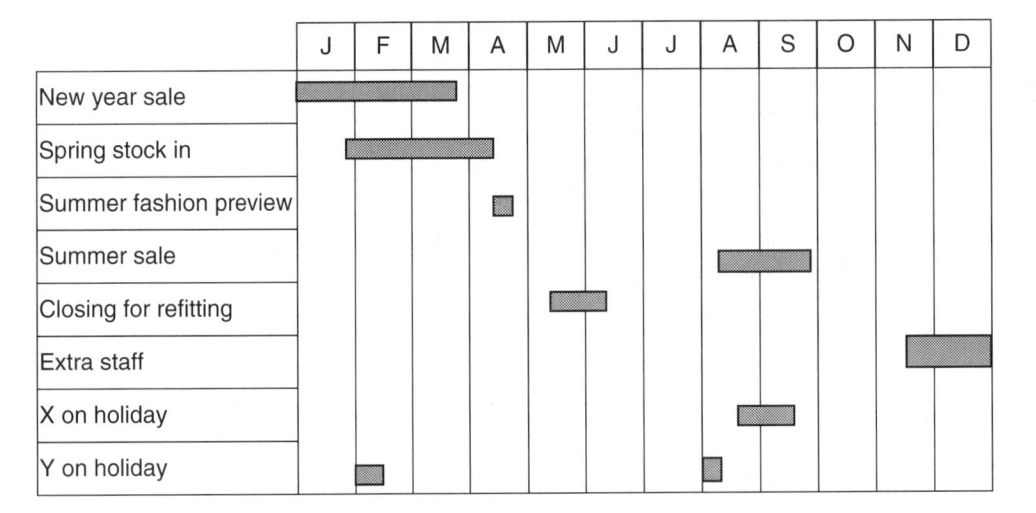

	J	F	M	A	M	J	J	A	S	O	N	D
New year sale												
Spring stock in												
Summer fashion preview												
Summer sale												
Closing for refitting												
Extra staff												
X on holiday												
Y on holiday												

Gantt charts

3.15 Another widely-used form of chart, which is used to show **progress** as well as schedule, is the Gantt chart.

A Gantt chart is like the horizontal bar chart used above, but each division of space represents both an amount of **time** and an amount of **work** to be done in that time. Lines or bars drawn across the space indicate how much work is scheduled to be done and/or how much work has actually been done: the more work, the longer the line or bar.

3.16 The advantage of such a chart is that you can see the relationship between time spent and amount done or produced. You can compare amounts produced in one week or month, say, with those in another (by the relative lengths of the bar or line). You can, similarly, compare amounts scheduled to be done with those actually done.

3.17 The following information, about planned work and actual progress, is set out in a Gantt chart.

Day	Daily schedule (units)	Cumulative schedule (units)	Work done in the day (units)	Cumulative work done (units)
Mon	100	100	75	75
Tues	125	225	100	175
Wed	150	375	150	325
Thu	150	525	180	505
Fri	150	675	75	580

Daily schedule and work actually done

Monday	Tuesday	Wednesday	Thursday	Friday
┄┄►100	┄┄►125	┄┄►150	┄┄► 150	┄┄►150
──► 75	──► 100	──►150	──► 180	──► 75

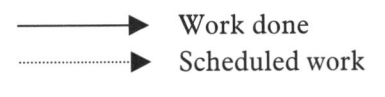

── ► Work done
┄┄ ► Scheduled work

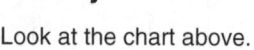

Activity 4.8

Look at the chart above.

(a) What information is clearly shown by the chart? (Is it more obvious how production is doing on the chart than on the tabulated data from which it was drawn?)

(b) What further Gantt chart might be helpful for the manager of this work, which can be drawn from the data given?

(c) Draw the Gantt chart you have suggested.

(d) What information is most usefully provided by this new chart?

4 MONITORING AND FOLLOW-UP

4.1 As we noted in paragraphs 1.3 and 1.4 of this chapter, monitoring and evaluating performance, and taking corrective or follow-up action where necessary, is an essential part of the planning and control cycle.

4.2 The organisation will have systems in place for areas such as budgetary control, inventory control, quality control and other forms of management control (which you should have encountered in your studies for other Units).

4.3 On an individual level, **control over work** must be maintained to ensure that jobs do in fact reach completion, and if those jobs involve various tasks over varying periods, planning will be necessary to keep track of future events, deadlines, results and so on.

4.4 Systems which provide for this are called **bring forward** or **bring up** systems. Anything which needs action at a later date (and therefore may get forgotten) should be processed in this way, for example:

- Checking on progress of an operation;
- Checking completion when the deadline is reached;
- Checking payments when they fall due;
- Retrieving files relevant to future discussions, meetings, correspondence.

4.5 Checklists are useful, as we suggested earlier, for monitoring what has been done and what hasn't. Diary systems may also be used.

4.6 Some **computer-based schedule/diary systems** (including Microsoft Outlook) issue **alert messages** when the scheduled event or completion time approaches. These may be visual (diary entries highlighted) and/or audible (a warning bell or bleep).

Activity 4.9

Alison's section is divided into teams of three people, a senior, Alison, an intermediate, Kathryn, and a junior, Margaret. Everybody has a steady stream of their own work to be getting on with but the section also engages in special work to get specific jobs done.

On Friday afternoon Alison's team is allocated some special work which the section leader wants completed by Tuesday week, although Friday week is the latest date by which it must be completed.

Alison has divided the work up into the following steps.

	Job	Experience level	Time required
1	Information extraction	Junior	2 days
2	Information analysis	Senior	1 day
3	Data entry	Junior	2 days
4	Interpretation of results	Senior	1 day
5	Liaison with production department	Senior	1 day
6	Correspondence	Intermediate	1 day

Senior and intermediate staff are able to do the work of lower levels although this is to be avoided where possible, especially because it does not save time. Junior and intermediate staff gain new experience by doing work at the next level up. This doubles the time normally required for the work and the work is then subject to review by a person at the next level which takes an additional half day. Staff development is encouraged. None of the tasks can be done before the previous task is complete, and sharing individual tasks generally proves to be inefficient.

Alison's team members are available as follows over the next two weeks.

M	T	W	T	F
—		—		
			—	—
—	—			

M	T	W	T	F
	—	—	—	

The dashes indicate days when the team member is committed to working on other matters.

Tasks

(a) Plan how the special work can best be achieved by Alison's team in the time available.

(b) What is the first matter that Alison should attend to, so as to be sure that the plan can be implemented?

(c) Margaret seems to be showing signs of developing flu. Should Alison take any action?

Key learning points

- **Planning** is the process of deciding what should be done, by whom, when and how.

- Plans are the basis of the **control cycle** and **control systems** of the organisation, through which performance is monitored, measured against the plan and adjusted where necessary.

- Work planning includes the following basic steps

  ○ Establishing priorities

  ○ Loading: allocation of tasks

  ○ Sequencing of tasks

  ○ Scheduling: estimating the time taken to complete a task and working forwards or backwards to determine start and target finish times

- Planning and scheduling aids include: lists and checklists, precedence networks, action plans, timetables, diaries or personal organisers and charts.

- Follow-up systems are required to signal when checks should be made to ensure that performance is proceeding according to plan.

Quick quiz

1   How does planning contribute to the flow of work?

2   What is a contingency plan?

3   Distinguish between forward and reverse scheduling?

4   What does a 'precedence network' show?

5   What kind of help does a diary offer a planner?

6   What does a Gantt chart show?

7   What is a 'bring forward' system? Give two examples.

Answers to quick quiz

1   Planning tries to avoid hold-ups or clashes and idle time or overwork for people or machines.

2   Planning in advance to deal with a situation which may (or may not) arise.

3   Forward scheduling estimates task duration forward from a given start time/date. Reverse scheduling works backwards from a given completion time/date.

4   The order in which tasks need to be completed, especially where they depend on each other.

5   It records appointments, deadlines and reminders, and can be used both for planning and for monitoring progress and triggering checks and controls.

6   It shows an amount of time, the amount of work to be done in that time, and the amount actually done.

7   A reminder system. Examples include: checklists, diary or file-insert reminder entries, computer 'alert' messages.

5 Working with others

This chapter contains

1   Introduction: what are working relationships?

2   Roles and relationships at work

3   Interpersonal skills

4   Working effectively in teams

5   Handling disagreements and conflict

6   The internal customer

Learning objectives

On completion of this chapter you will be able to:

- Ask appropriate people for any information, advice and resources that are required

- Meet commitments to others within agreed timescales

- Take opportunities to promote the image of the department and organisation to internal customers

- Appreciate the different types of people involved in working relationships

- Outline your responsibilities in complying with legislation

- Consider methods of establishing constructive relationships, handling disagreements and conflict, and seeking and exchanging information, advice and support

- Appreciate the need to use appropriate actions and styles of approach in different situations

Performance criteria

(1) Information is provided to internal and external customers in line with routine requirements and one off requests

(2) The appropriate people are asked for any information, advice and resources that are required

(3) Commitments to others are met within agreed timescales

(4) Communication methods are appropriate to the individual situation

(5) Any communication difficulties are acknowledged and action taken to resolve them

(6) Opportunities are taken to promote the image of the department and organisation to internal and external customers

(7) Confidentiality and data protection requirements are strictly followed

Range statement

1 **Internal customers:** peers; manager; other members of staff

2 **External customers:** suppliers; customers; external agencies

3 **Communication methods:** written; verbal; electronic

Knowledge and understanding

- The different types of people: customers, peers, managers, other members of staff

- Relevant legislation

- Handling confidential information

- Methods of establishing constructive relationships

- Seeking and exchanging information, advice and support

- Handling disagreements and conflict

- Using appropriate actions and different styles of approach in different situations

- Different communication methods and styles

- Types of communication difficulties and how to resolve them

- Employee responsibilities in complying with the relevant legislation

- The organisational and departmental structure

- The customer base

1 INTRODUCTION: WHAT ARE WORKING RELATIONSHIPS?

1.1 How might you describe a 'good working relationship'?

(a) **Good working**

A good working relationship allows or facilitates work **transactions,** the completion of **tasks** and the fulfilment of **objectives.**

(b) **Good ... relationships**

A good working relationship allows or facilitates ongoing and mutually satisfying **interpersonal relations.**

1.2 Elements in (a) might include prompt and willing service, co-operation and co-ordination, communication, expertise, teamworking skills and mutual reward or benefit.

1.3 Elements in (b) might include politeness, friendliness, trust, openness, the ability to resolve conflict and respect.

1.4 A working relationship can be established with **anyone with whom** you come into contact for the fulfilment of a transaction or task: colleagues, suppliers, customers or clients.

1.5 In this chapter, we will look at working relationships **within the accounts department** and between the accounts department and the rest of the organisation. In Chapter 7, we go on to consider relationships with customers and visitors, suppliers of services and finally the wider business and social community.

1.6 Many of the **general principles** of building relationships are discussed in this chapter. Interpersonal skills, conflict management and team roles and dynamics will be relevant to customer and supplier relationships too.

1.7 First of all, it is important to recognise that any group of people at work has relationships, roles and communication, even if they are not deliberately planned or developed. **You cannot not have relationships - although you can have unconstructive ones**. You cannot *not* adopt a role - although you may adopt a passive or destructive one. You cannot not communicate - although you can convey reluctance to communicate.

Activity 5.1

Complete the following questionnaire honestly.

There is somebody at work who is given far more challenging tasks than I am even though we are at the same level	True/False
I get on well with all or most of my colleagues	True/False
I actively dislike some of my colleagues	True/False
I am less inclined to co-operate with colleagues if I don't get on with them on a personal level	True/False
I think my boss treats me fairly	True/False
I think my boss is sometimes unfair without meaning to be	True/False
My loyalties lie with my colleagues rather than with my organisation	True/False
If one of my colleagues annoys or upsets me I always let them know how I feel about it	True/False
Little rivalries, jealousies and slights at work tend to get exaggerated because nobody will discuss them openly	True/False
If a serious difficulty arose in a working relationship with a colleague I would be prepared to take the matter to a higher authority	True/False
I always try to deal with problems in working relationships myself before taking the matter any further	True/False
I will bully my subordinates when I get more responsibility – it's all part of the training	True/False

I take an interest in my colleagues on a personal level, although I don't pry into their affairs	True/False
I apologise if I ever lose my temper with a colleague	True/False
When somebody else has done a good job for me or helped me I always praise them or thank them	True/False
Sometimes I forget to do things that I promised to do for colleagues; sometimes I just don't bother	True/False
I welcome positive criticism	True/False
I am bad at taking criticism	True/False
There is somebody at work that I don't talk to because none of my friends seem to like him/her	True/False
I make no effort to establish a rapport with more senior colleagues because they make no effort with me	True/False

DEVOLVED ASSESSMENT ALERT

The evidence requirements for Element 23.2 require consistent evidence 'of relationships with at least two types of ... internal ... customers being established.' These two types might be peers/colleagues, your supervisor or manager, or other members of staff - perhaps from other departments - that you liase with in the course of work, sit with on committees and so on. We suggest how such relationships may be formed and maintained in these chapters - but you actually have to **do it** - and **be seen to be doing it!**

2 ROLES AND RELATIONSHIPS AT WORK

Roles

2.1 **Roles** are sometimes described as 'parts' that people 'play' (like actors) or 'hats' that people 'wear'. These are ways of saying that:

- People adopt different roles in different circumstances

- Roles define 'who a person is' in these circumstances and in relation to others

- Roles have certain signs or characteristics associated with them, so that a style of behaviour is expected of a person in a given role

2.2 In the accounts department, you adopt your '**work role**', as opposed to your role as student, member of a family, sports enthusiast (or whatever). Within your work role may be more specific roles, such as payroll clerk, assistant to your superior, colleague to your peers, and so on - depending what function you are performing and what other people in that context (your 'role set') require and expect from you.

2.3 An important skill in working with others is being able to identify:

- What roles other people are in, and what your role should be in relation to them; and

- The behaviours and role signs expected of you in a given role.

This will help you to **avoid inappropriate behaviours** such as over-familiarity in a professional context, lack of leadership in an authority role or insubordination in a subordinate role, discussing matters irrelevant to the situation in hand, dressing inappropriately for the context and so on.

Structural relationships

2.4 Roles exist **in relation to each other**. In the work environment, there are three basic relationships between roles.

- **Subordinate role.** You work for and report to others.
- **Equal or peer role.** You work with others towards a shared goal.
- **Authority role.** Other people work for and report to you.

These are essentially relationships of **power, authority** and **influence**. Within this structure, there are also **functional** relationships.

2.5 Authority and functional relationships are built into the formal structure, communication and procedures of the organisation. Its **culture** dictates the way in which these relationships are regarded and expressed. Some organisations (or departments within them) are laid-back, informal and democratic, and some are formal and strictly hierarchical. You will need to judge the appropriate **relational style** in your own department and organisation.

2.6 Structural relationships shape two key aspects of working with others.

(a) **The scope and limits of authority**

Each person and team needs to know what areas they have authority over, and how far that authority extends. For example, you may have responsibility for making payments for certain purchases and amounts, but refer non-routine or larger payments for authorisation by your boss.

(b) **Co-ordination and communication**

Since your work objectives will be achieved for or through other people, you need to ensure an efficient flow of work, resources and information towards overall objectives. Your plans and schedules need to dovetail with those of other individuals and teams with whom your work is linked.

2.7 **Politics** flows from **authority relationships** in an organisation.

KEY TERM

Politics are activities concerned with the acquisition of power and the exercising of influence in relation to others.

Organisations are political systems in that they comprise individuals and groups who:

- Have their own **agendas**, priorities and goals
- Compete for their share of the organisation's **limited resources**, power and influence
- Form **cliques**, alliances, **pressure groups** and blocking groups centred around values and objectives which may be opposed by others

Interpersonal relationships

2.8 Overlaid on structural factors in relationships, there are interpersonal or human factors: individual **personalities**; interpersonal skills; whether people have rapport; personal **differences, attitudes and values**; **perceptions** (and misperceptions); **communication** and communication barriers; **group** behaviour.

2.9   When we talk about **building relationships,** we are mainly talking about developing **rapport, trust and effective communication,** which, although complicated by structural factors and politics, are essentially interpersonal skills.

Contractual and legal relationships

2.10   Some aspects of work relationships are covered by **contract, law and regulation.**

2.11   You have a general duty, for example, of **faithful duty to your employer** under your contract of employment. You also have specific responsibilities, under **health and safety legislation,** to work in such a way as to avoid injury to yourself and others (as discussed in Chapter 1).

2.12   Similarly, there are laws and regulations covering how your employer should treat you, including disciplinary situations, dismissal and redundancy, grievance handling, health and safety, working terms and conditions (pay, holiday entitlements) and so on.

Discrimination at work

2.13   Among the formal aspects of work relationships, you should be aware that you have responsibilities under **equal opportunities legislation** not to **discriminate** or show prejudice against people on grounds such as sex, race or disability. As a civilised human being in the business community, you should choose not to discriminate against any individual or group on any grounds. This applies to how you deal with colleagues, potential colleagues and members of the public.

> **KEY TERM**
>
> **Discrimination** is giving less favourable terms or treatment to a particular individual or group because of some characteristic that they are assumed to have, or some category to which they are assumed to belong.

2.14   The main **legal provisions** against **discrimination** are contained in:

   (a)   The **Sex Discrimination Acts 1975 and 1986,** outlawing certain types of discrimination on the grounds of sex or marital status (that is, whether the person is single, married or divorced)

   (b)   The **Race Relations Acts 1976 and 1996,** outlawing certain types of discrimination on grounds of colour, race, nationality or ethnic origin

   (c)   The **Disability Discrimination Act 1995,** outlawing certain types of discrimination on grounds of physical or mental disability

2.15   There are **two types of discrimination** under the Acts.

   (a)   **Direct discrimination** occurs when one interested group is treated less favourably than another. If you were serving a queue of people and decided not to serve anyone who was Welsh until last then you would be guilty of direct discrimination.

   (b)   **Indirect discrimination** occurs when requirements or conditions are imposed, with which a substantial proportion of the interested group could not comply, to their detriment. If you were serving a queue of people and

gave priority to those who could say 'Happy Christmas' to you in Welsh, you would be guilty of indirect discrimination.

2.16 Along with women, disabled people and ethnic minorities, there are other groups who are frequently discriminated against at work. Enlightened employers are forming their own policies about this.

(a) It is not currently illegal to discriminate on the grounds of **sexual orientation** (usually, against gays and lesbians) but some organisations have implemented policies which, for example, extend allowances given to married couples to gay and lesbian partners.

(b) It is not currently illegal to discriminate on the grounds of **age,** but 'ageism' has recently been highlighted as an undesirable feature of employment practice.

In October 2000, the EU member states agreed a directive (known a 'Article 13') which will outlaw discrimination on the grounds of sexual orientation and religion (by 2003) and on the grounds of age (by 2006).

2.17 You should consult the equal opportunities and anti-discrimination policies of your organisation with regard to the following.

Area of discrimination	Action to take
Recruitment and selection	If you are asked to draft a job advertisement, for example, you must not suggest a preference for a particular group – unless there is a very specific, legally-justifiable reason (such as requiring a black male to play the part of Othello, in Shakespeare's play). Similarly in interviews, the same questions should be asked of all groups of applicants. (You cannot, for example, ask only the women about their plans to have children.) Selection must be based on **suitability for the job.**
Training and promotion opportunities	All groups must be given equal access: it is even permissible to *encourage* previously disadvantaged groups to apply for training opportunities.
Redundancy and dismissal	You cannot select people to be made redundant on the basis of sex or race. Nor can you, for example, dismiss a woman because she is pregnant and requires maternity leave.
Positive initiatives	Active moves are permissible to encourage people from disadvantaged groups to apply for jobs, training and promotions and to make it more possible for them to succeed. Examples may include: (a) using ethnic languages in job advertisements; (b) offering assertiveness or management skills training to minority groups (often women); (c) offering child care allowances or facilities, to help women combine careers with child-rearing responsibilities; (d) awareness training or counselling for managers, to encourage them to think more about equal opportunities; (e) altering premises for ease of access to wheelchair users.

Such policies inform you of **your rights in the workplace**, as well as **your responsibilities to others**.

2.18 Another current issue in the workplace is **sexual harassment**, which has been ruled to be unlawful sexual discrimination.

> **KEY TERM**
>
> **Sexual harassment** is defined (in a 1991 EU Code of Conduct) as:
>
> - Unwanted conduct of a sexual nature, or other conduct based on sex, affecting the dignity of women and men at work
>
> - Unwelcome physical, verbal or non-verbal conduct
>
> - Conduct that denigrates, ridicules, is intimidatory or physically abusive of an employee because of his or her sex such as derogatory or degrading abuse or insults which are gender-related, and offensive comments about appearance or dress.

2.19 Your organisation may have policies about sexual harassment and procedures to manage it, including:

- Clear communication of the nature and **unacceptability** of sexual harassment

- Ways for victims to **report** the abuse, confidentially and to a colleague of the same sex

- **Complaint investigation procedures**, also with guaranteed confidentiality and right of reply

- **Counselling** for victims (and perpetrator)

- **Disciplinary action** for proven offences

Activity 5.2

Give five examples of conduct you would consider to be sexual harassment (assuming that it was **unwanted** by the person at whom it was directed).

Working with anybody

2.20 **Key individuals**, with whom you need to manage your relationships with particular care, include those who have authority over you and your work (your team leader or manager); people who have access to expertise, information or resources that you require (the librarian, say, or Information Technology Support Officer); and people on whom you depend for co-operation in order to complete your tasks.

2.21 Having said this, it is also important not to neglect or destroy relationships with non-key players. Relationships are the currency of co-operation favours and unexpected opportunities. Without people like receptionists, telephonists, post room staff, maintenance and security staff, your job would be a lot harder! These people are at the very least entitled to:

- Respect
- Courtesy
- Co-operation, or willingness to let them do their jobs;
- Fairness; and
- Safe working conditions.

3 INTERPERSONAL SKILLS

> **KEY TERM**
>
> **Interpersonal skills** are skills used in establishing and maintaining relationships between people. They are essentially communication skills, used in an interactive situation such as a face-to-face or telephone discussion.

3.1 There are a number of key interpersonal skills.

- Build **rapport**, or a sense of relationship, with another person
- **Persuade** or **influence** another person
- Gain the **trust**, **confidence** and **co-operation** of another person
- **Resolve conflict or disagreements**
- **Give** and **elicit information** effectively

3.2 Obviously, these are not things you can really learn in a book. You need to develop your communication skills, and to practise applying and adjusting them in every interaction that you encounter, until you consistently get the results you want.

3.3 We will look briefly at each of the areas (a) - (d) listed in paragraph 3.1 above: they are the building blocks of relationships. Communication will be discussed separately and in detail, in Chapter 6.

Building rapport

> **KEY TERM**
>
> **Rapport** is the process of establishing and maintaining a relationship of mutual trust, understanding and responsiveness between two or more people.

3.4 **Rapport** is the sense of 'being in tune with' another person, or 'getting on' with them. Building rapport is like building a bridge to the other person: creating a point of understanding and contact, on which meaningful communication and relationship can be based. So how is it achieved?

(a) **Matching, or mirroring**, the other person's non-verbal signals: posture, gestures, eye contact and volume and pace of speaking.

(b) Demonstrating **respect and understanding** for the other person's viewpoint, emotions or culture, by:

    (i) Talking about **topics of interest** to the other person, seeking to find mutual interests and shared values and beliefs

    (ii)   Using a **vocabulary** the other person shares

    (iii)   **Empathising** with the person's feelings

    (iv)   Wearing **clothes** and adopting **manners** which will not alienate the other person

    (v)   Appreciating the person's views, even if not agreeing with them

Influence

3.5   Lee Bryce (*The Influential Woman*) suggests two main types of influencing strategy.

'Push'	'Pull'

1. Identify the problem/opportunity and propose your solution.
2. Invite reactions.
3. Check that you understand each other's arguments.
4. Deal with objections:
   - by persuasion (if you want commitment)
   - by authority (if you only need compliance)
5. Agree on the outcome and action plan.
	1. State your view of the problem/opportunity.
	2. Clarify how the other person sees the situation.
	3. Work towards agreement on the nature of the problem/opportunity.
	4. Look for solutions, using as many of the other person's ideas as possible.
	5. Come to joint agreement on outcome and action plan.

• Directive • Effective where you are clear about problem/solution • Quick decisions where authority works to secure compliance, or where decision routine • Can appear authoritarian	• Supportive/collaborative • Effective where consensus, input desired • Slower decisions, but secures commitment • Can appear weak

3.6   The 'right' style will depend on your personality and the other person's, the work situation and relationship, the urgency of the decision, the importance of the other person's commitment to the solution, the organisation and culture. Develop and widen your repertoire!

Trust and co-operation

3.7   Rapport and influencing skills can be used to facilitate initial and occasional encounters. In order to **develop a relationship,** further investment is required.

3.8   Cultivating a relationship is a bit like cultivating a garden: it requires regular time, effort, nourishment and creativity, even at work, where you might think that sharing an office all day would be sufficient!

Keep in contact	Communicate regularly
Be dependable	Trust is built on trustworthiness: don't let people down, break promises or violate confidentiality.
Demonstrate shared values/interests/tastes	Keep rapport by taking opportunities to talk about or enjoy mutual pursuits or concerns; to express agreement or solidarity; to swap relevant information.
Showing willing	Offer or agree to give information, collaboration, help or support whenever appropriate: this builds up a credit bank of co-operation.
Make creative connections	These keep you in the other people's minds by showing that they are in yours (giving birthday cards is just one example).
Utilise social and informal opportunities	Lunch breaks, after-hours activities, even a quiet chat over the coffee machine, are designed to allow colleagues to get to know and trust each other as people, building a relationship that will benefit co-ordination and communication at work.
Avoid or mend conflict	Unresolved personality clashes, hostilities and rivalries ruin working relationships.
Show respect	for other people's personal beliefs and values, as well as for their professional competence and expertise, and their goals and objectives.
Maintain appropriate roles	However friendly you get with people outside work, or in informal situations, remember to behave appropriately when they have their professional 'hat' on in business contexts.
Maintain a 'net balance' of benefit	Do not exploit the relationship: if you gain benefits from it, make sure that the other person makes more or less equal gains over time.

3.9 Most work interactions or conversations are work-related. However, be aware of the range of purposes for which interpersonal discussions at work are quite valid.

Purpose	Role of discussion
Teambuilding	Conversation – on any topic – helps to establish and maintain relationships, and this is important to the organisation as well as to individuals. Discussions about the organisation and its objectives, or the work of people in other departments, can help to build a sense of belonging and loyalty.
Help and advice	It is important for you to ask for help with any difficulties you are having meeting a deadline or coping with your work-load. This affects your work performance. However, other types of difficulty and uncertainty also affect your work performance: tiredness, sickness, worry, bereavement, conflict, family problems or whatever. You spend most of your waking hours with people at work: do not be shy of **seeking advice and support** from them. (Some organisations have a **counsellor** available to help employees sort out problems. To whom in your workplace might it be appropriate for you to talk?)

BPP PUBLISHING

Purpose	Role of discussion
Support and encouragement	People need a balance of support (which makes them feel secure) and challenge (which makes them want to learn, try new things and take on new responsibilities). This benefits a work organisation, because it needs people who will develop and take on more responsible roles. Do not think it an inappropriate use of work time (within reason) to seek feedback on your performance, to get your competence evidence together, to ask for learning opportunities, or to find out what you need to do to progress in your organisation. (Some organisations appoint **mentors** or 'guides' for employees: someone higher or more established in the organisation who can coach, advise and challenge the junior person. Whom might you ask to take on such a role in your working life?)
Friendship	You shouldn't turn your workplace into a social club, but you spend most of your waking hours with your work colleagues: they will play a big part in whether you enjoy your work and feel good about yourself, or whether you live in constant stress and discontent. Don't forget: this too will affect your work performance! So allow yourself (within the bounds of the organisation's 'house style' for interpersonal conduct) to be friendly, as well as efficient.

Activity 5.3

Using the following grid, monitor all the various conversations or interactions you have at work in the course of one day. For each one, put a tick in the appropriate column.

	Technical/ work-related with colleagues	*Technical/ work-related with customers/ clients/ enquirers*	*Organisa-tional/team/ 'membership'*	*Asking for help or advice*	*Getting support/ encourage-ment/ challenge*	*Non work-related: just friendly/ courteous*
During work time						
During breaks/ lunch/after work etc						
	Total:	Total:	Total:	Total:	Total:	Total:

3.10 Remember to consider whether the **location** and **timing** of interpersonal contacts are:

- Appropriate to the nature of the discussion (formal/informal; work-related or social; confidential or open)

- Convenient for all parties involved (including the employer, who is paying for your time).

Activity 5.4

Consider the following subjects which are routinely discussed in many organisations.

(a)   Annual pay review (individuals)

(b)   Candidates for redundancy (managers)

(c)   The department's Christmas party (everybody)

(d)   Plans for new office location (everybody)

(e)   Current year's sales (sales and marketing team)

(f)   Most ideal candidate interviewed for new position in the accounts department (personnel department)

Required

For each of the above subjects, state the most appropriate locations for carrying out such discussions.

4   WORKING EFFECTIVELY IN TEAMS

KEY TERM

A **team** is a small number of people with *complementary skills* who are committed to a *common* purpose, performance goals and approach for which they hold themselves basically accountable.

4.1   The basic work unit of organisations has traditionally been the **functional department** (such as Accounting or Sales). In more recent times, businesses have adopted smaller, more flexible and responsive units: **teams.**

4.2   **Teamworking** allows work to be shared among a group, so that it gets done more quickly and with a sharing of skills and information, while allowing people to keep sight of the 'whole' task. Teams are particularly effective for **increasing communication**, generating new ideas and evaluating ideas from different view points, for example in:

- **Brainstorming groups**, generating creative ideas for problem-solving;

- **Quality circles**, which draw people together from different disciplines to share ideas about quality issues;

- **Project teams**, set up to handle particular tasks or projects;

- **Study and discussion groups**, explaining issues from different points of view;

- **team briefings**, where information and instructions are presented.

4.2   **Belbin** drew up a list of the most effective character-mix in a team. This involves eight necessary **roles** which should ideally be balanced and evenly 'spread' in the team.

Member	Role
Co-ordinator	Presides and co-ordinates; balanced, disciplined, good at working through others.
Member	Role
Shaper	Highly strung, dominant, extrovert, passionate about the task itself, a spur to action.
Plant	Introverted, but intellectually dominant and imaginative; source of ideas and proposals but with disadvantages of introversion.
Monitor-evaluator	Analytically (rather than creatively) intelligent; dissects ideas, spots flaws; possibly aloof, tactless - but necessary.
Resource-investigator	Popular, sociable, extrovert, relaxed; source of new contacts, but not an originator; needs to be made use of.
Implementer	Practical organiser, turning ideas into tasks; scheduling, planning and so on; trustworthy and efficient, but not excited; not a leader, but an administrator.
Team worker	Most concerned with team maintenance - supportive, understanding, diplomatic; popular but uncompetitive – contribution noticed only in absence.
Finisher	Chivvies the team to meet deadlines, attend to details; urgency and follow-through important, though not always popular.

The **specialist** joins the team to offer expert advice when needed: legal experts, tax consultants and so on.

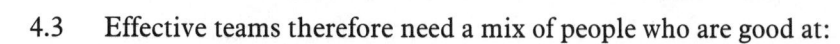

Activity 5.5

What teams are you currently a member of? What makes them feel like 'teams', rather than just groups of people? See if you can identify which of Belbin's team roles are fulfilled in your team, and where there are gaps which need to be filled.

4.3 Effective teams therefore need a mix of people who are good at:

- Getting things done
- Getting along with other people

Contributing to the team

4.4 Consultants Neil Rackham and Terry Morgan have developed a helpful categorisation of the types of **contribution** people can make to team discussion and decision-making.

Category	Behaviour	Example
Proposing	Putting forward suggestions, new concepts or courses of action.	'Why don't we look at a flexi-time system for the marketing support staff?'
Building	Extending or developing someone else's proposal.	'Yes. We could have a daily or weekly hours allowance, apart from a core period in the middle of the day.'
Supporting	Supporting another person or his/her proposal.	'Yes, I agree, flexi-time would be worth looking at.'
Seeking information	Asking for more facts, opinions or clarification.	'What exactly do you mean by 'flexi-time'?'
Category	Behaviour	Example
Giving information	Offering facts, opinions or clarification.	'There's a helpful outline of flexi-time in this article.'
Disagreeing	Offering criticism or alternative factors or opinions which contradict a person's proposals or opinions.	'I don't think we can take the risk of not having any staff here at certain periods of the day.'
Attacking	Attempting to undermine another person or their position: more emotive than disagreeing.	'In fact, I don't think you've thought this through at all.'
Defending	Arguing for one's own point of view.	'Actually, I've given this a lot of thought, and I think it makes sense.'
Blocking/difficulty stating	Putting obstacles in the way of a proposal, without offering any alternatives.	'What if the other teams get jealous? It would only cause conflict.'
Open behaviour	Risking ridicule and loss of status by being honest about feelings and opinions.	'I think some of us are afraid that flexi-time will show up how little work they really do in a day.'
Shutting-out behaviour	Interrupting or overriding others; taking over.	'Nonsense. Let's move onto something else - we've had enough of this discussion.'
Bringing-in behaviour	Involving another member; encouraging contribution.	'Actually, I'd like to hear what Fred has to say. Go on, Fred.'
Testing understanding	Checking whether points have been understood.	'So flexitime could work over a day or a week; have I got that right?'
Summarising	Drawing together or summing up previous discussion.	'We've now heard two sides to the flexi-time issue: on the one hand, flexibility; on the other side possible risk. Now ...'

BPP PUBLISHING

4.5 Each type of behaviour may be appropriate in the right situation at the right time. A team may be low on some types of contribution, and it may be up to the team leader to encourage, or deliberately adopt, desirable behaviours (such as bringing-in, supporting or seeking information) in order to provide balance.

Factors in team performance

4.6 **Some of the factors affecting the performance of teams**

(a) **Co-operation and conflict resolution.** Since teams are made up of a number of individuals, it is important that they all get on and work well with each other.

(b) **Clearly defined goals and responsibilities**. In order for a team to work well, it must have clearly defined goals, and each team member should have clearly defined (or jointly agreed) responsibilities. Teams should be **briefed** on a regular basis so that they know what is expected of them.

(c) **Clear and regular feedback.** The team must be given information of progress and results so that it can learn, correct or adjust its performance – or celebrate.

(d) **Group motivation.** As with individuals, if teams are encouraged to work hard, and rewarded for doing so, then this is likely to have a positive effect on performance. Teams should be rewarded and recognised as teams – not on an individual basis, which encourages intra-team competition.

(e) **Communication.** In general, the greater the communication between team members and team leaders, the greater the more effective the performance.

Activity 5.6

Why might the following be effective as team-building exercises?

(a) Sending a project team (involved in the design of electronic systems for racing cars) on a recreational day out 'karting'.

(b) Sending a project team on an 'Outward Bound' style course, walking in the mountains from A to B, through various obstacles (rivers to cross and so on).

(c) Sending two sales teams on a day out playing 'War Games', each being an opposing combat team trying to capture the other's flag, armed with paint guns.

(d) Sending a project team on a conference at a venue away from work, with a brief to review the past year and come up with a 'vision' for the next year.

These are actually commonly-used techniques. If you are interested, you might locate an activity centre or company near you which offers outdoor pursuits, war games or corporate entertainment and ask them about team-building exercises and the effect they have on people.

5 HANDLING DISAGREEMENTS AND CONFLICT

KEY TERMS

- **Co-operation** is working or acting together.

- **Conflict** is the clash or opposition of opposing 'forces', which may include the interests, opinions or beliefs of individuals or groups. Conflict often arises at work from competition for scarce resources and power, the incompatible goals and priorities of individuals and teams, lack of communication, and incompatibility of individual or team personalities or styles of working.

How conflicts and disagreements arise

5.1 **Conflicts** arise when an individual, group, or department becomes stressed or frustrated by another individual, group or department. **Disagreements** arise when one individual, group or department does not agree, or does not share the same opinions as another individual, group or department.

DEVOLVED ASSESSMENT ALERT

One potential source of evidence of your competence for Element 23.2 is being observed 'co-operating with other staff on work activities'. **Not** co-operating with other staff, because of disagreement or conflict, will be unhelpful performance evidence while the ability to **resolve difficulties** is likely to be a powerful indicator of competence in this area.

5.2 Conflicts and disagreements may arise in the following situations.

(a) **Relationships**. If individuals, groups or departments have a bad working relationship with each other, there is an increased possibility of conflicts and disagreements developing.

(b) **Poor communication**. For example, if a colleague fails to pass on an important piece of information to you, this could create a certain amount of bad feeling, and lead to future conflicts and disagreements between you.

(c) **Scarce resources**. When individuals or departments are competing for the same resources, and conflicts and disagreements will follow. Resources which are limited might include things such as time, tables, chairs, paper, books, printers, office space and so on.

(d) **Personality.** Sometimes there might just be a 'clash of personalities', which as you probably know is one of the most common reasons for conflicts and disagreements to arise.

Managing conflicts and disagreements

5.3 **The ways in which conflicts and disagreements might be managed**

(a) **Discussion** of the conflict/disagreement should be encouraged in order that the parties involved are encouraged to talk through their problems and reach a satisfactory conclusion.

(b) **Compromise**. In order that a satisfactory conclusion may be reached for any conflict or disagreement, it might be necessary for the parties involved to reach a compromise.

(c) **Personalities**. Where individual personalities are the major source of conflict, managers should try to structure their departments and the responsibilities of individuals in such a way as to minimise conflicts, or even contact.

The win-win model

5.4   One useful model of conflict resolution is the **win-win model**. This states that there are three basic ways in which a conflict or disagreement can be worked out.

Method	Frequency	Explanation
Win-lose	This is quite common.	**One party gets what (s)he wants at the expense of the other party**: for example, Department A gets the new photocopier, while Department B keeps the old one (since there were insufficient resources to buy two new ones). However well-justified such a solution is (Department A needed the facilities on the new photocopier more than Department B), there is often lingering resentment on the part of the 'losing' party, which may begin to damage work relations.
Lose-lose	This sounds like a senseless outcome, but actually **compromise** comes into this category. It is thus very common.	**Neither party gets what (s)he really wanted**: for example, since Department A and B cannot both have a new photocopier, it is decided that neither department should have one. However 'logical' such a solution is, there is often resentment and dissatisfaction on *both* sides. (Personal arguments where neither party gives ground and both end up storming off or not talking are also lose-lose: the parties may not have lost the argument, but they lose the relationship ...) Even positive compromises only result in half-satisfied needs.
Win-win	This may not be common, but working towards it often brings out the best solution.	**Both parties get as close as possible to what they really want**. How can this be achieved?

5.5   It is critical to the **win-win approach** to discover **what both parties really want -** as opposed to what they **think**:

(a)   They want (because they have not considered any other options)
(b)   They can *get away with*; or
(c)   They need in order to *avoid an outcome they fear*.

5.6   Department B may want the new photocopier because they have never found out how to use all the features (which do the same things) on the old photocopier; because they just want to have the same equipment as Department A; or because they fear that if they do not have the new photocopier, their work will be slower and less professionally presented, and they may be reprimanded (or worse) by management.

5.7 The important questions in working towards win-win are:

- What do you want this *for*? and
- What do you think will happen if you *don't* get it?

5.8 **These questions get to the heart of what people really need and want.**

5.9 In our photocopier example, Department A says it needs the new photocopier to make colour copies (which the old copier does not do), while Department B says it needs the new copier to make *clearer* copies (because the copies on the old machine are a bit blurred). Now there are options to explore. It may be that the old copier just needs *fixing*, in order for Department B to get what it really wants. Department A will still end up getting the new copier - but Department B has in the process been consulted and had its needs met.

5.10 EXAMPLE: THE WIN-WIN APPROACH

Two men are fighting over an orange. There is only one orange, and both men want it.

- If one man gets the orange and the other does not, this is a **win-lose** solution.

- If they cut the orange in half and share it (or agree that neither will have the orange), this is a **lose-lose** solution - despite the compromise.

- If they talk about what they each need the orange *for*, and one says 'I want to make orange juice' and the other says 'I want the skin of the orange to make candied peel', there are further options to explore (like peeling the orange) and the potential for both men to get exactly what they wanted. This is a **win-win** approach.

5.11 **Win-win** is not always possible: it is **working towards it** that counts. The result can be mutual respect and co-operation, enhanced communication, more creative problem-solving and - at best - **satisfied needs all round.**

Activity 5.7

Suggest a (i) win-lose, (ii) compromise and (iii) win-win solution in the following scenarios.

(a) Two of your team members are arguing over who gets the desk by the window: they both want it.

(b) You and a colleague both need access to the same file at the same time. You both need it to compile reports for your managers, for the following morning. It is now 3.00pm, and each of you will need it for two hours to do the work.

(c) Manager A is insisting on buying new computers for her department before the budgetary period ends. Manager B cannot understand why, since the old computers are quite adequate. She will moreover be severely inconvenienced by such a move, since her own systems will have to be upgraded as well in order to remain compatible with department A (the two departments constantly share data files). Manager B protests, and conflict erupts.

Formal grievance procedures

> **KEY TERM**
>
> A **grievance** occurs when an individual thinks that he or she is being wrongly treated by their colleagues or supervisor, that is, when business relationships break down. The individual may consider that he or she is being picked on, being given an unfair workload, unfairly appraised in the annual report or unfairly blocked for promotion, or discriminated against. When an individual has a grievance he or she should be able to pursue it and ask to have the problem resolved.

5.12 Grievances usually arise because of **difficulties in working relationships**. They will not go away if they are not discussed: those with the ability to resolve the grievance will not know what is wrong unless it is brought out into the open.

5.13 The best way to resolve such difficulties is by **direct discussion between the parties involved**.

5.14 EXAMPLE: DIFFICULTY

Suppose that Jane feels that Susan, her boss, treats her like an idiot. The best time to discuss this will clearly *not* be immediately after Susan has chastised her for doing something stupid. Tempers will be running high and neither party will be entirely rational. Jane should wait until she has done a job well and then say 'Look, I know I make silly mistakes sometimes, but do you think you could try not to make me look foolish in front of my colleagues? That just gets me flustered and then I make even more mistakes.' Hopefully Susan will be prepared to modify her behaviour.

5.15 If one-to-one discussion does not work a more formal approach will be needed. A typical **grievance procedure** provides for the following steps.

Step 1	**The grievance should be carefully explained** to the aggrieved individual's immediate boss (**unless he is the subject of the complaint, in which case it will be the next level up**). **Employees have the right to be accompanied by a colleague or representative to such an interview, if they feel they need support or a witness.**
Step 2	**If the immediate boss or other person cannot resolve the matter, or an employee is otherwise dissatisfied with the first interview, the case should be** referred to the next level of management (**and if necessary, in some cases, to an even higher authority**).
Step 3	**Cases referred to a higher manager should also be** reported to the personnel department, **for the assistance/advice of a personnel manager in resolving the problem.**

5.16 All complaints should be thoroughly investigated, so if you do find that you have to go through a formal grievance procedure it is important that **you are honest and fair**. Records should be kept of all interviews and actions taken – and these should be confidential.

Activity 5.8

Check what the grievance procedures are in your organisation! If there is nothing set out in your job description or procedures manual, ask the Personnel Department. (If you are asking your boss or a colleague, remember to say that this is for information purposes only!)

This is a useful exercise under 'asking the appropriate people for any information required' (Element 23.2).

5.17 A Code of Practice by the Advisory Conciliation and Arbitration Service (ACAS) in September 2000 underlines the importance of all workers being made aware of grievance procedures and all supervisors, managers and worker representatives being trained in their use. The Code suggests that, wherever possible, workers should be given a copy of the procedures, or access to the information (eg in a personal handbook or intranet site) and should have the detail explained to them, ideally as part of the induction process when they join the organisation.

6 THE INTERNAL CUSTOMER

The internal customer

6.1 What is an internal customer?

(a) Any unit of the organisation whose task contributes to the task of other units (whether as part of a process or in an advisory or service relationship) can be regarded as a **supplier of a service** like any other supplier used by the organisation.

(b) **Customer choice** operates **within** the organisation as well as in the external market environment.

(c) The unit's objective thus becomes the efficient and effective identification and satisfaction of customer needs, wants and expectations within the organisation as well as outside it.

(d) The unit must 'create, build and maintain mutually beneficial exchanges and relationships' within the organisation, as well as outside. In other words, customer relations is important internally, too. The 'exchanges' sought may be co-operation in fulfilling each other's objectives, or two-way flows of information.

Activity 5.9

Who are the internal customers of the accounting function? What are their needs/expectations?

Interdepartmental relations

6.2 'In principle, business functions should mesh harmoniously to achieve the overall objectives of the firm. In practice, departmental interfaces are often characterised by deep rivalries and misunderstandings.'

BPP PUBLISHING

6.3 The following paragraphs suggest some brief guidelines for working with individuals and teams from other departments (in addition to the relationship-building skills we have already covered).

Networking

6.4 The more you have contact with people in other functions, learn what they do and show that you appreciate their problems and capabilities, the more likely you are to develop co-operative relationships.

(a) Attend organisation-wide and interdepartmental events and meetings.

(b) Join quality circles and other multi-disciplinary teams and committees that focus on joint objectives.

(c) Use your contacts in other departments to arrange visits and briefings so you learn about each other's functions.

Internal 'public relations'

DEVOLVED ASSESSMENT ALERT

Note that one of the performance criteria for Element 23.2 is to take opportunities to 'promote the image of the department and organisation to internal ... customers' (as well as external ones).

6.5 We will be discussing 'public relations', and how you represent your department and organisation in the business environment in Chapter 7 on Dealing with (External) Customers. However, be aware that you **represent** the Accounts Department when you deal with people or tasks, or issue communications, **on its behalf** - and even when people simply **identify** you (and your behaviour, dress, speech and so on) with the Accounts Department because they know you work there. You need to consider what creates a positive impression.

Key learning points

- A **good working relationship** is one that allows the purpose of transactions to be fulfilled without either party being deterred from entering into further transactions.

- Relationships in work organisations are structural (based on authority and function), interpersonal (or human) and contractual/legal.

- People adopt a number of different roles and relate to each other in these roles (as well as interpersonally). The three main **role situations** within organisations are as follows.

  ○ Subordinate
  ○ Equal/peer
  ○ Authority

- **Discrimination** on grounds of sex, race and disability is illegal in the workplace, and should be covered by clear organisational policies.

- Interpersonal skills for building and maintaining relationships include: rapport building, influencing, building trust and co-operation and managing conflict.

- Teams are particularly useful when the sharing or testing of ideas is required. There are many different roles and styles of contributing in teamworking.

- The main ways of managing conflicts and disagreements are as follows.

  ○ **Understanding** the problem
  ○ Encouraging those parties involved to **discuss the problem**
  ○ Reaching a **compromise**
  ○ Considering the **personalities** involved
  ○ Using the **win-win** model

- Interdepartmental conflict stems from clashes of emphasis, as well as politics. The internal customer concept, networking and internal 'public relations' can help the accounts department reintegrate its activities with those of other departments.

Quick quiz

1   How can an awareness of 'role sets' and 'role signs' help you to work with others?

2   Why is there 'organisational politics'?

3   Give four examples of legal, contractual or policy provisions governing interpersonal behaviour at work.

4   If you had a personal problem that was affecting your work, who should you discuss it with in the first instance?

5   What are the advantages and disadvantages of the 'push' and 'pull' strategies of influencing?

6   List five steps you can take to cultivate relationships.

7   List Belbin's team roles.

8   (a)   What are the possible outcomes of a conflict, according to the 'win-win' model?
    (b)   What are the two most important questions in the 'win-win' model?

9   What is the internal customer concept?

Answers to quick quiz

1   'Role set' are the people relating to you in a particular role: their expectations of how a person in your role should behave towards them are a guide to 'appropriate' behaviour in a given situation. 'Role signs' are the signals people give indicating what role they are in: they help you to know whether to deal with them professionally or personally, formally or informally and so on.

2   Politics arise from authority relationships; competition for power, resources and influence; the agendas and priorities of different people.

3   Examples include: non-discrimination, sexual harassment, faithful duty to the employer, safe and healthy working, employment protection legislation, discipline and grievance procedures.

4   If it were purely a personal problem, a friend or counsellor might be the person to talk to. Since it is affecting your work, however, you should approach your immediate supervisor or manager - although if the problem is very sensitive, you need to find a superior you can trust (perhaps a personnel manager or superior whom you know personally).

5   'Push' is quick and effective where the solution is clear-cut, but can appear authoritarian and lose genuine commitment.

       'Pull' is supportive/collaborative and secures genuine commitment, but tends to be slower and can appear weak.

6   Keep in contact; be dependable; demonstrate shared values/interests; use social opportunities; avoid or mend conflict. (A full list can be found in paragraph 3.8.)

7   Co-ordinator, Shaper, Plant, Monitor-evaluator, Resource, Implementor, Team investigator/worker, Finisher.

8   (a)   Win-lose, lose-lose, win-win.
       (b)   What do you want it for? What do you fear will happen if you don't get it?

9   'Internal customer' implies that any unit of the organisation which contributes to the task of other units can be regarded as a supplier of a service, like any external supplier. The service unit must therefore regard the other units as customers, whose needs, wants and expectations must be satisfied.

6 Communication

This chapter contains

1 Introduction: what is communication?

2 Written communication

3 Oral communication

4 Visual communication

5 Non-verbal communication

6 Appropriate communication methods

7 Resolving communication difficulties

Learning objectives

On completion of this chapter you will be able to:

- Use communication methods appropriate to the individual situation

- Acknowledge any communication difficulties and take action to resolve them

- Understand the communication needs of different types of people in the business environment

- Appreciate and use different communication methods and styles

- Understand various types of communication difficulties and how to resolve them

Performance criteria

(1) Information is provided to internal and external customers in line with routine requirements and one off requests

(2) The appropriate people are asked for any information, advice and resources that are required

(3) Commitments to others are met within agreed timescales

(4) Communication methods are appropriate to the individual situation

(5) Any communication difficulties are acknowledged and action taken to resolve them

(6) Opportunities are taken to promote the image of the department and organisation to internal and external customers

(7) Confidentiality and data protection requirements are strictly followed

BPP PUBLISHING

Range statement

1 **Internal customers:** peers; manager; other members of staff

2 **External customers:** suppliers; customers; external agencies

3 **Communication methods:** written; verbal; electronic

Knowledge and understanding

- The different types of people: customers, peers, managers, other members of staff

- Relevant legislation

- Handling confidential information

- Methods of establishing constructive relationships

- Seeking and exchanging information, advice and support

- Handling disagreements and conflict

- Using appropriate actions and different styles of approach in different situations

- Different communication methods and styles

- Types of communication difficulties and how to resolve them

- Employee responsibilities in complying with the relevant legislation

- The organisational and departmental structure

- The customer base

1   WHAT IS COMMUNICATION?

KEY TERM

Communication is the transmission or exchange of information.

1.1   This is a very basic definition. The following paragraphs indicate on the one hand what a complicated activity communication is, and on the other, how fundamental communication is to everything that we do.

Activity 6.1

There are many different sorts of communication. Think about all the 'messages' you receive before you even start work for the day. List as many types of communication as you can.

1.2   Communication is so basic to our lives that you may never have thought about what is actually going on when we communicate. There is no need to go too deeply into the theory, but in the remainder of this section we shall think briefly about **why we communicate** and **what has to happen for effective communication to take place**.

Why we communicate

1.3   Sometimes we engage in communication for its own sake, without any specific purpose. **Communication is the basis of our relationships with other people**, as we saw in Chapter 5.

1.4   At other times the aim of communication is to get something done.

    (a)   In organisations the people in authority can **command, instruct** or **request** their subordinates to **carry out actions**.

    (b)   People communicate their **needs and requirements**: they may need to ask a superior, a colleague in another department or a customer for information, resources or help.

    (c)   People **exchange information, ideas, attitudes and beliefs**, in order to make decisions and solve problems.

DEVOLVED ASSESSMENT ALERT

Drafting routine business communications (particularly letters and memos) **within deadlines** and **in appropriate forms** are essential skills which cross over several elements of competence, and embrace many performance criteria, within wide range statements. Some of these skills are incorporated in the **Assessment** tasks for Units 1 - 4, where they are tested in the relevant accounting contexts. **Get as much practice in actual and simulated tasks as you can**. Attempt all the activities in this chapter. There are also many activities in other BPP Interactive Texts and Kits.

The communication model

1.5   **Effective communication** is a **two-way process,** often shown as a 'cycle'. Signals or messages are sent by the communicator and received by the other party who sends back some form of confirmation that the message has been received and understood.

1.6   The process of communication might be modelled as follows.

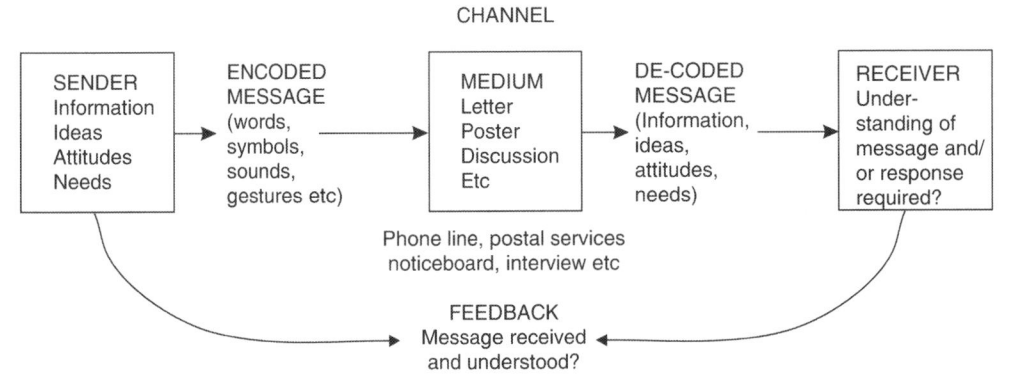

1.7   We use the terms **encoding** and **decoding** because words are only symbols or stand-ins for your ideas or intentions in communicating. Nor does communication involve only words. A **gesture** might have done equally well in the example given. In other situations **pictures, symbols** or **numbers** will be the most appropriate 'code' to use. **The important thing is that both parties understand the code.**

Feedback

1.8 **Feedback** is the reaction of the receiver which indicates to the sender that the message has (or has not) been received and enables him to assess whether it has been understood and correctly interpreted.

1.9 Feedback can range from a **smile** or a **nod** to a **blank look** or a **shrug**, or from the desired action being taken to no action or the wrong action being taken.

Activity 6.2

Give five examples each of what you would interpret as:

(a) negative feedback (a sign that your message was not having its desired effect); and
(b) positive feedback (a sign that your message was received and understood).

1.10 It is the **responsibility of the communicator** to adjust his message, in response to feedback, until he is satisfied that it has been understood. In a sense, the meaning of a communication is only what the other person understands by it. If you want a **result** from your communication (as opposed to just 'getting it off your chest'), it is up to you to make sure that you have communicated effectively.

Communication methods

1.11 We will now look at the four main types of communication:

- Written communication
- Oral communication
- Visual communication and
- Non-verbal communication.

2 WRITTEN COMMUNICATION

The letter

2.1 The letter is a very **flexible and versatile medium of communication**. It can be used for many different purposes.

- Request, supply and confirm information and instructions
- Offer and accept goods and services
- Convey and acknowledge satisfaction and dissatisfaction

2.2 The letter is also a **'high profile' medium of communication**. It is in many cases the first - or only - contact between organisations or the individuals who represent them. The content and style of the message must be finely tuned to get the desired result (action or acknowledgement from the recipient).

2.3 In order to be an effective letter-writer, you will therefore need to master the following.

(a) **Display**. You will waste all your good ideas unless you put them on paper in a clear, correct and attractive manner.

(b) **Style and tone in written English**. The content should be clearly and correctly expressed, and adapted to its purpose and recipient.

We can provide a good deal of guidance, but ultimately you will have to be sensitive to what is required in each given situation.

Standard elements

2.4   The modern business letter contains various **standard elements,** and you will
       need to know what these are and where they are located on the page. Here is a
       skeleton format and a full example. (Later we shall see some alternative layouts.)

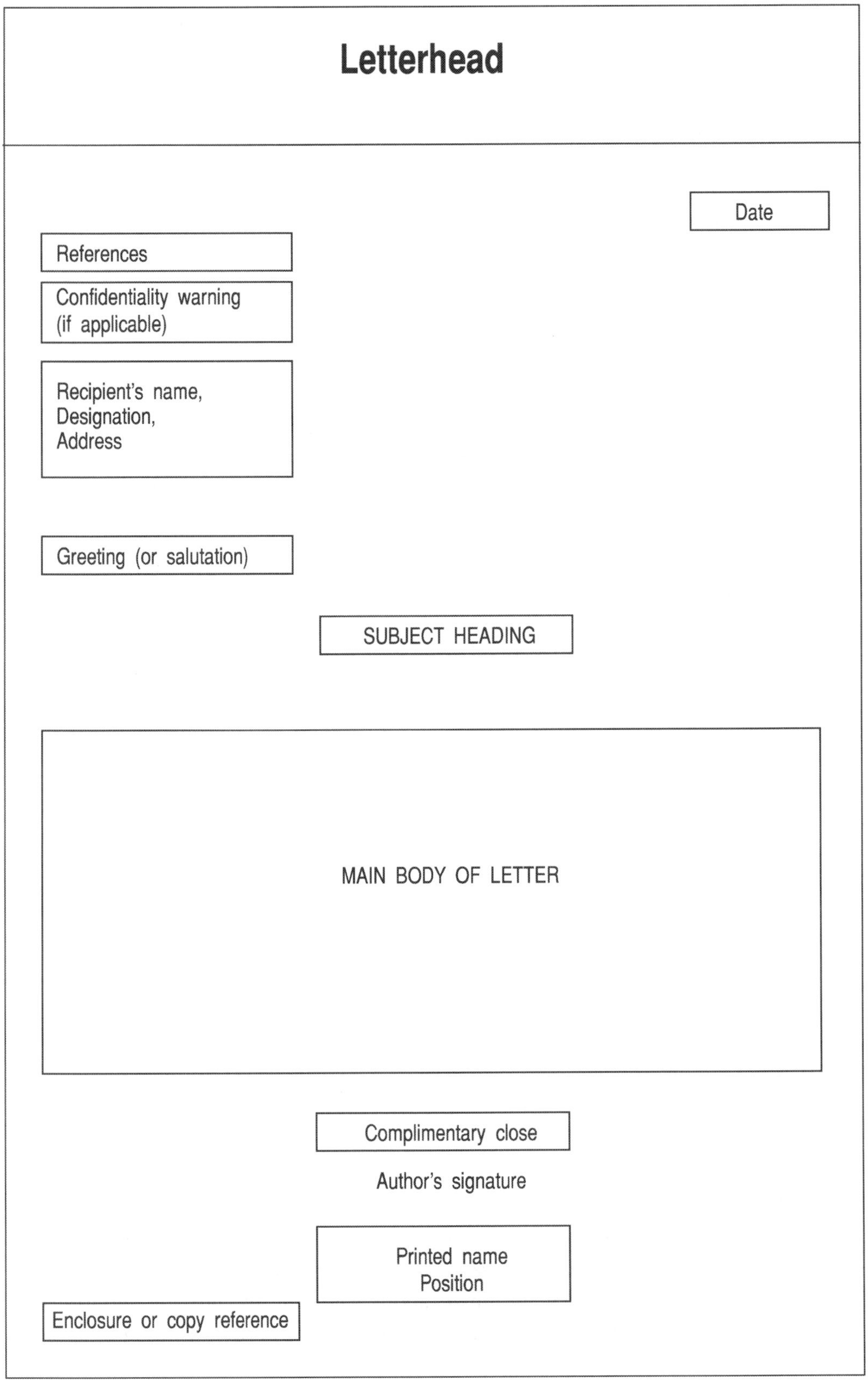

Letterhead

Date

References

Confidentiality warning (if applicable)

Recipient's name, Designation, Address

Greeting (or salutation)

SUBJECT HEADING

MAIN BODY OF LETTER

Complimentary close

Author's signature

Printed name Position

Enclosure or copy reference

BPP PUBLISHING

Hi-Tech Office Equipment Ltd

Micro House, High St, Newtown, Middlesex NT3 0PN
Telephone: Newtown (01789) 1234 Fax: (01789) 5678

Directors:	Registered Office:
I. Teck (Managing)	Micro House, High St, Newtown
M. Ployer	Middx NT3 0PN
D. Rechtor	Registered No 123 4 56 789
N. Other	Registered in England

Our Ref: IW/cw
Your Ref: JB/nn

7th June, 2000

Private & Confidential

J. M. Bloggs, Esq.,
Adminstrator,
Toubai Forze Timber Yard,
Wood Lane Industrial Estate,
SUSSEX SX1 4PW

Dear Mr. Bloggs,

WORD PROCESSING EQUIPMENT

Thank you for your letter of 3rd June 2000, in which you request further details of Hi-Tech's range of personal computers with word processing software packages. I am delighted to hear that our earlier discussions were of some help to you.

Please find enclosed our list of hardware and software with current prices. I have also included our leaflet entitled 'Desktop', which outlines some of the options for word processing on PCs: I trust this will answer your questions and give you an idea of the exciting possibilities.

I would also take this opportunity to remind you that two of your old printers are currently under maintenance contract with us, and that both of them become due for routine servicing within the next month. Perhaps you would contact my secretary to arrange a convenient date for our engineer to call at your offices.

I look forward to hearing from you, when you have thought about the word processing option. If you have any queries or need further information on accessories do not hesitate to let me know.

Yours sincerely,

I. M. Wright
SALES MANAGER

Enc.

House style

2.5   Peculiarities of layout and presentation do tend to vary from organisation to organisation, so you should be prepared to adapt to the accepted practice of your workplace. This is known as **house style**. Keep an eye out for variations or particular details in any correspondence you receive yourself at work or at home.

2.6 There are however, some general rules. Convention dictates, for example that the following greetings and closes be used together.

Greeting	Close	Context
Dear Sir/Madam/Sirs (*Name not used*)	Yours faithfully	Formal situations Recipient not personally known Recipient senior in years, position
Dear Dr/Mr/Mrs/Miss Cake Dear Sir Keith/Lady Jane Dear Lord Nelson (*Name used*)	Yours sincerely	Friendly (or would-be friendly, eg for selling or conciliatory letters) Established relationships
Dear Joe/Josephine	Yours sincerely	Close, informal relationships
My dear Joe/Josephine	Kind regards	More various, because more
etc.	Best wishes	Personal
	Affectionately	

2.7 If an assistant or secretary is signing a letter on behalf of the writer, the writer's name is preceded by 'For' (or its equivalent from legal terminology 'pp.' which stands for **per procurationem**).

> For   I. Sellwell,
>   Sales Manager

2.8 If you are putting something other than the letter in the same envelope, such as a cheque, price list or leaflet, you must call the reader's attention to it in the letter: refer to it as having been **enclosed**. To make sure that the reader or the person opening the mail does not overlook (and possibly discard) your enclosure in the envelope, **put a clear 'signal' at the foot of the letter**. For example, you may use: Enc. (or Encs. for more than one item).

2.9 If a duplicate of a letter has been sent to an interested third party, it is **courteous to acknowledge the fact to the letter's recipient** with a similar footnote:

Copies to (3rd party names) *or* cc: (3rd party names)

2.10 The second sheet, and all subsequent sheets, of a letter will be on plain (un-headed) paper. In case they should get detached or confused, therefore, **continuation sheets** are headed as follows.

Name of recipient, page number in letter, date.

Open or closed punctuation

2.11 In the example given earlier you may have looked at the various elements outside the main body of the letter and thought them rather 'cluttered' by punctuation, what with full stops for abbreviations, commas after each item or line and so on: this is called '**closed punctuation**'.

2.12 The alternative, which is quicker to type and plainer on the page, is '**open punctuation**'. This involves omitting all punctuation from the elements outside the main body of the letter.

(a) No comma is necessary in the date, after each line of the name/address block, after the salutation and complimentary close.

(b) Full stops are omitted from abbreviations, initials etc.

Note, however, that the main body of the letter should be fully punctuated as usual. In general books use open punctuation and most subsequent examples of letters in this text do likewise, now that you have seen 'closed' in action.

Alternative layouts

2.13 The overall impact of a business letter depends on how it first meets the reader's eye - not just the designer letterhead and good quality print, but the clarity and elegance of the layout of text on the page. Simplicity and attractiveness are general guidelines to good layout, and there are two main styles currently in use.

FULLY BLOCKED style is the easiest to type and therefore increases the typist's productivity. Everything starts at the left-hand margin. This style is becoming increasingly common.

Date _____
Ref: _____
Recipient _____
_____
_____

Dear _____

SUBJECT

Main body _____
_____

_____
_____
_____
_____

Yours _____

Name _____

Date _____
Ref: _____
Recipient _____
_____
_____

Dear _____

— SUBJECT —

Main body _____
_____

_____
_____
_____

Yours _____

Name _____

SEMI-BLOCKED style is much like fully blocked, but selected elements are moved over for balance. The *date* is against the right hand margin: the *complimentary close* starts from the centre: the *subject header* may be centralised.

DEVOLVED ASSESSMENT ALERT

We describe common conventions and guidelines - but it is essential for you to use this information to identify (and utilise) the particular styles, formats and features of letters (and other communications) which are **approved or conventional in your own organisation**. Start to analyse every communication you receive in this way.

Activity 6.3

The following is taken word for word from a business letter.

Scrooples & Co Ltd, 93 Brindle Close, Bolton, Lancashire, BL2 9AJ Telephone: 01101 222333 Fax: 01101 444555 Freda M Smethwick 8 Cornel Mansions Mapesbury Avenue Bolton Lancashire. BN19 4PJ 4 August 2000 Dear Freda <u>Post of receptionist</u> We have now completed our selection procedure for the post of receptionist and sadly I have to tell you that your application has not been successful on this occasion. I do hope that this will not be too much of a disappointment to you, and I would like to thank you for the interest that you have shown in Scrooples & Co. With best wishes for your success in finding suitable employment. Yours sincerely Nora Scroople Nora Scroople Personnel Manager Scrooples & Co Ltd Directors: Nora M Scroople BA; Dora M Scroople ACA; Thora M Scroople Registered office: 93 Brindle Close, Bolton, Lancashire BN2 9AJ. Registered in England, number 19191919

Required

Show how the letter should actually have been laid out on the page.

Letter content

2.14 The broad structure of all letters should be the same. A letter should have a **beginning,** a **middle** and an **end.** Look back at the sample letter from HiTech Office Equipment Ltd as you read the following paragraphs.

2.15 Don't dive straight in with the detailed point of your message, since the reader will not be as familiar with its context as you are. **Tell the reader what the context of the message is**: it may be a response to a previous communication from him, continuing a sequence of letters; it may be a response to other events (if you are complaining about something); you may be making initial contact (if you are introducing yourself for example, or advertising goods).

2.16 You would usually put the following in your opening paragraph.

- A straightforward (brief) **explanation** of why you are writing.

- An **acknowledgement of receipt** of any **previous correspondence,** together with its date and nature

- Important **details of the circumstances** leading to the letter (names, dates)

2.17 The middle paragraph(s) should then be used to set out the letter's message, which will **elaborate or move forward from the introductory paragraph**. This section will contain the substance of your response to a previous message, details of the matter in hand, or the information you wish to communicate.

2.18 **If you are making several points, start a new paragraph with each,** so that the reader can 'digest' each part of your message in turn. You should organise your material so that points are in some sort of logical order.

(a) **Chronological order** for narrating/explaining a sequence of actions or events (X happened and then Y happened)

(b) **Order of cause and effect** to explain that X happened (cause) and so Y happened (effect)

(c) **Topical order** to keep together points which are related to the same topic

(d) **Order of importance**

Putting the most important first gains attention, lesser details following: putting the major point last has more persuasive impact.

2.19 Your letter will not be effective unless it has the desired result of creating understanding or initiating action. Unless your message has been very brief and simple, it is a good idea to **draw together the points you have made in a brief summary** which will recall and put into perspective your main ideas.

2.20 If you are not just writing to inform, but want some action or response from the reader, the closing paragraph is the place to make clear exactly what you expect from him. The conclusion is the last item, apart from the complimentary close, that the reader will take in: it will be clearest in his mind when the letter is finished.

Activity 6.4

Your organisation supplied goods to the value of £1,445 to B & T Fashions Ltd (account code BTFASH) on 5 October 2000. Payment has not yet been received. Thirty days credit is allowed by your firm's normal terms of trade. Payment of the invoice is considered to be due on 7 November 2000. Your usual contact at B & T Fashions is named Peter Bruce.

You are required to write extracts from the following letters in the format shown below.

10 November 2000	First reminder enclosing a copy statement.
17 November 2000	Second reminder
24 November 2000	Third reminder, suspending further delivery of goods.
1 December 2000	Fourth reminder stating your organisation's reluctant intention to refer the matter to debt collectors if payment is not received within seven days.
10 December 19X6	A letter instructing the customer that the matter has been referred to your organisation's debt collectors.

The format to use is as follows.

> Date
>
> Dear
>
> **Subject**
>
> Letter
>
> Yours faithfully/sincerely

Activity 6.5

You work in a bank. Your manager has passed you the following letter and wants you to draft a reply for typing.

- *1st letter rec'd 29.6.00*
- *DD paid 6.7.00.*
- *Apologise + recredit a/c*
- *Recovery from LBG actioned*

Sum Wat Pora
9 Blackheath Way
Greenwich
London SE10 2AL

The Manager
Portland Bank plc
40 Greenwich High Street
London SE10 4QW

6 August 2000

Dear Sir,

Account no. 0139742 - S Wat Pora Esq

I wrote to you on 27 June 2000 instructing you to cancel the monthly direct debit from the above account in favour of the London Borough of Greenwich with immediate effect.

Upon receiving my bank statement for July 2000 I find that my instructions were not carried out.

I should be grateful if you would rectify this matter at your earliest convenience.

Yours faithfully

Sum Wat Pora

Sum Wat Pora

Memoranda (memos)

KEY TERM

The **memorandum** or 'memo' performs internally the same function as a letter does in external communication by an organisation. It can be used for reports, brief messages or 'notes' and any kind of internal communication that is more easily or clearly conveyed in writing (rather than face-to-face or on the telephone).

2.21 A memorandum may be sent **upwards, downwards** or **sideways** in the organisation's hierarchy. It may be sent from one individual to another, from one

department to another, from one individual to a department or larger body of staff.

Format

2.22 Memorandum format will vary slightly according to the **degree of formality** required and the organisation's policy on matters like filing and authorisation of memoranda by their writer. **Follow the conventions of house style in your own organisation**. A typical format, including all the required elements, is illustrated below - but get hold of your own organisation's memo pad (or computer template for memos) and start using that, if you do not already do so.

Organisation's name (optional)

MEMORANDUM

To: (recipient's name or designation)   **Ref:** (for filing)

From: (author's name or designation)   **Date:** (in full)

Subject: (main theme of message)

The message of the memorandum is set out like that of a letter: good English in spaced paragraphs. Note that no inside address, salutation or complimentary close are required.

Signed: (optional) author signs/initials

Copies to: (recipient(s) of copies)

Enc.: to indicate accompanying material, if any

Forrest Fire Extinguishers Ltd

MEMORANDUM

To: All Staff   **Ref:** PANC/mp

From: P A N Cake, Managing Director   **Date:** 13 January 2000

Subject: Overtime arrangements for January/February

I would like to remind you that thanks to Pancake Day on and around the 12th February, we can expect the usual increased demand for small extinguishers. I am afraid this will involve substantial overtime hours for everyone.

In order to make this as easy as possible, the works canteen will be open all evening for snacks and hot drinks. The works van will also be available in case of transport difficulties late at night.

I realise that this period puts pressure on production and administrative staff alike, but I would appreciate your co-operation in working as many hours of overtime as you feel able.

Copies to: All staff

Content

2.23 The following general guidelines should be followed when drafting notes and memoranda.

Section	Contents
Subject heading	General theme.
Opening paragraph or sentence	The reason for writing and the context of the message, including appropriate details.
Substance of message	Set out logically and clearly: this may be less formal than a letter, so you can use numbered points.
Closing paragraph or sentence	State clearly what is required of the recipient in response.

2.24 As with writing a letter, the most important factor to remember is your **recipient**. Since you are communicating within an organisation, you may now be writing to a fellow-specialist, and be able to use technical language and complex ideas. Think first, however: a memo to all staff might cover a vast range of fields and abilities, from security guard to accountant to engineer. If you are writing to more than one person, you will have to find 'middle ground' so that they can all understand your message, without being baffled by technicality or patronised by simplicity!

2.25 Your style will also vary according to your **position in the organisation relative to the recipient** of your memo.

(a) If you are reporting to, or making a suggestion to, someone **higher in the hierarchy** than yourself, your tone will have to be appropriately formal, businesslike and tactful.

(b) If you are dashing off a hand-written note on a memo pad to a **colleague** with whom you enjoy an informal working relationship, you can be as direct, familiar and friendly as you like.

(c) If you are instructing or disciplining **more junior personnel**, you will have to retain a certain formality for the sake of authority; a more persuasive and less formal tone might be appropriate if you are congratulating, motivating or making a request.

Activity 6.6

Here is a memo in the same condition as the letter in Activity 6.3.

> MEMO To: All staff Ref: US/JBS/4. From: Nora Scroople, Personnel Manager Date: 4 August 2000 Subject: Post of receptionist Please note that Laura M Scroople will be starting work with us on Monday next. I trust you will all make her very welcome.

Required

Show how the above memo could actually be laid out.

Activity 6.7

You were made responsible for ordering stationery in X Department a month ago. The system requires anybody who notices that stationery stocks are running low or are exhausted to fill in a standard requisition form and pass it to you in room 32. This is clearly stated in a notice on the door of the stationery cupboard. You have not received any requisition forms during your month in office but you have frequently been interrupted in your work by heads popping round the door making remarks like 'Why aren't there any yellow highlighters in the cupboard?' and 'Who is it that does the stationery then?'

This is annoying and you have decided to send a memo to all staff in your department reminding them of the system.

Required

Draft the memo, using your own name.

Activity 6.8

You sent the following order to your stationery suppliers some time ago.

| From: | **NEEDHAM BADDELY LTD** | | | Purchase order No: | *01573* |

To: *Pens and Paper Ltd*
31 Margin Alley
North Hinchsey

Date: *13 May 2000*

VAT REG: *6 721 3941*

Please supply the following

Your product reference	Item	Qty	Your list price £ p	Total (exc. VAT) £ p
TM/172	*Message pads (pk 10)*	*5*	*7.28*	*36.40*
HP4/013	*Highlighters (yellow, pk 4)*	*10*	*3.80*	*38.00*
BB/274	*Black biros (pk 50)*	*2*	*6.09*	*12.18*
PC/009	*Paperclips (pk 1000)*	*10*	*1.56*	*15.60*
GS/421	*Glue sticks (pk 25)*	*2*	*20.25*	*40.50*
E/66	*Erasers (pk 10)*	*10*	*5.87*	*58.70*
Total Discounts and special offers Net				*201.38*
Comments	*Urgent order*			

The only delivery note you have received since this order was sent is shown below.

017643

PENS AND PAPER LIMITED
31 Margin Alley
North Hinchsey

DELIVER TO: DATE: 17 May 2000

Needham Baddely Ltd
Skid Row
Wantage

Reference	Qty	Description	Check
TM / 172	5	Message pads	✓
HPY / 013	10	Highlighters	✗
BB / 274	2	Biros	✓
PC / 009	10	Paperclips	✓
GS / 421	2	Glue sticks	✓
E / 66	10	Erasers	✓

Customer signature

Received in good condition ....*J B Paying*........................

Queries to: William H Smythe

In your post today you received a brochure from Lou Sleaf (Stationery Supplies) Ltd. You also received the following slip which you have put on your orders folder together with seven similar requests received in the past two weeks. You phoned your suppliers last week about this matter and were promised immediate action. The person dealing with your order was not available when you phoned today.

STATIONERY REQUISITION

Please order the following stock item:

Description: Yellow highlighters _____

Reference (if known): ? _____

Name (please print): M. Fassize _____

Date: 13 June 2000 _____

Required

Take whatever action you think is necessary. Use your own name if you intend to communicate in writing.

E-mail messages

2.26 E-mail has become a popular alternative to paper- and delivery-based messages such as letters and memos. If you have access to e-mail facilities at home or at work, you will know how they work from a technical point of view. (**From a message point of view,** you should regard an e-mail message as the equivalent of an **informal note,** a **formal letter,** an **internal memo** - or **whatever your purpose in writing.**)

2.27 The 'Compose a Message' facility of e-mail usually sets up a **message format** for you much like standard memorandum stationery. You need to fill in the address (which in this case includes the identity of the addressee), subject, copy and enclosure (or 'attachment') details, just as you would in a memo.

2.28 For the body of your message, follow the style dictated by the purpose and intended recipient of the communication, as with any written message. You may, however, want to make your written style:

(a) **Briefer or more concise** (particularly if you are composing the message 'on line'). For informal messages, this may include abbreviations ('eg' for 'for example'; 'pls' for 'please'; 'asap' for 'as soon as possible' and so on) which you might not otherwise use.

(b) **More straightforward.** E-mails can seem very dry and abrupt, and are not good media for humour or ambiguity. This is why 'smiley faces' and other symbols are often used to signal clearly when the writer means something humorously or not literally. Likewise, capital letters are - by convention - the e-mail equivalent of SHOUTING, and should be used with caution.

2.29 Because email is very informal, people forget that email is often **stored** and can have a **legal impact**.

3 ORAL COMMUNICATION

3.1 Oral communication is communication 'by mouth'. It is sometimes also called **'verbal' communication**: communication in words.

3.2 Oral or verbal communication is the most basic and generally used way of sending a message to another person: think of all the people you talk to in a day, in person or on the phone.

DEVOLVED ASSESSMENT ALERT

'Verbal communication methods' are specified in the Range Statement for Element 23.2. That means that you need to be able to seek and offer information, meet commitments, promote the image of the department and organisation - and all the other performance criteria - via verbal means where appropriate.

Obviously, this is not something you can learn from a book. You need to develop your 'live' communication skills, and to practise applying and adjusting them in every interaction that you encounter, until you consistently get the results you want.

3.3 The same stages apply in oral communication as in written: **a message is conceived, encoded, transmitted, decoded, interpreted and acknowledged.** In face to face oral communication, however, you are sending and receiving messages

at the same time, or very close together: you **switch rapidly** between speaking and listening. All the time your relationship with the other person, (your tone of voice your expressions and gestures) are modifying, qualifying or confirming the messages you are sending and your response to messages received.

3.4 This cannot be a hit and miss affair. Just as much as if you were writing a letter, you must consciously judge in advance what effect your message (and the way it is expressed) will have on its recipient. The process is immensely complex and subtle, so even if you have had time to plan your message and delivery meticulously (which you usually will not), look for **feedback**: continually assess how your messages are being received in practice.

3.5 You must therefore acquire and practise **speaking and listening skills**.

Speaking involves	Listening involves
Articulation	Concentration
Structuring the message	Interpretation of tone
Style and tone	Visual signals (gestures, facial expressions)
Delivery	
Sensitivity to recipient(s)	Offering feedback

Speaking skills

3.6 We rarely pay attention to our own **articulation** and **pronunciation** until we have encountered a real problem.

Listen to other people speaking. What judgements do you make about them?

3.7 **Clear articulation** is vital: not because it is associated with a particular region, section of society or level of education, but because you want to be understood immediately and unambiguously by *any other person*, in order to get a response that you require. Be **considerate** to the recipient of your message: don't use or pronounce words in a way that he or she will not understand, and don't speak too quickly. If you are satisfied that your speech is clear, unambiguous and not mannered just for the sake of it: fine.

3.8 If you are articulating clearly, you will be much more audible, but you will also have to consider how to **project your voice**. Speaking softly or even at a normal **volume** will be ineffective in a large room with a high ceiling and heavy curtains.

3.9 **Intonation** affects *how* your message reaches its recipient, as much as volume affects *whether* it does. Be aware of how the placing of **emphasis** on different words alters the meaning of a sentence: the stress *implies* something to the listener. How does your voice sound? Cheery? Gloomy? Disapproving? Encouraging? Affectionate? Enthusiastic? Indifferent? Hostile? Stay alert: if your voice is not **expressive**, you may come across as bored or indifferent.

3.10 **Pace and pauses** are further elements in fluent but clear delivery. Don't garble your words or string together long breathless sentences. Avoid excessive use of 'um' or 'er' and phrases like 'sort of' and 'I mean'.

Listening skills

3.11 Many studies have been made on how the average white-collar worker spends his/her day: statistics suggest that around 45% of the time taken up by communication is spent on listening! All that time is wasted if the worker is not an effective listener.

3.12 **Effective listening** means **showing an interest**. This helps you to do a number of things.

(a) Get all the **information** you require for decisions and actions.

(b) **Motivate** the speaker to communicate positively to you, and give all that they have to offer.

(c) **Understand** the other person's ideas, attitudes and nature and improve relationships.

(d) Appreciate the other person's position in a disagreement, for **constructive discussion and problem-solving**.

3.13 **Brief hints on being a good listener.**

What to do	How to do it
Be ready	Get your attitude right at the start, and decide to listen. You might even be able to do some background research so that you have established a context for the message you intend to receive.
Be interested	Don't try to soak up a message like a sponge: make it interesting for yourself by asking questions: how is this information relevant to me and how can I use it?
Be patient	Try to hold yourself back from interrupting if you disagree with someone, and don't compete to get your view in before the speaker has properly finished. Wait until a suitable opening (ie while your point is still relevant to the immediate discussion, but not while the speaker is just drawing a breath between phrases). Don't be so preoccupied with how you're going to respond that you forget to listen to what is said in the meantime.
Keep your mind on the job	Concentrate. It is very easy to switch off as attention wanders or you get tired. Don't get side-tracked by irrelevancies in the message: co-operate with the speaker in getting to the point of what he is trying to say.
Give feedback	For example, try an interested and attentive look, a nod, a murmur of agreement or query ('Yes... Really?'). If there are opportunities, use some verbal means of checking that you have understood the message correctly: ask questions, referring to the speaker's words in a way that demonstrates your interpretation of them ('You said earlier that...' 'You implied that...'). The speaker can then correct you if you have missed or misinterpreted something.

3.14 You may be interested to glance at the results of a Gallup poll in which American adults were asked how they felt about others' **talking habits**. How many of these habits do you have or do you notice in other people? You may learn some home truths if you look through the list with some friends after a drink or two, and try to put names to habits!

Talking habit	Extremely annoyed	Not annoyed	Don't know
	%	%	%
Interrupting while others are talking	88	11	1
Swearing	84	15	1
Mumbling or talking too softly	80	20	0
Talking too loudly	73	26	1
Monotonous, boring voice	73	26	1
Using filler words such as 'and um', 'like um' and 'you know'	69	29	2
A nasal whine	67	29	4
Taking too fast	66	34	0
Using poor grammar or mispronouncing words	63	36	1
A high-pitched voice	61	37	2
A foreign accent or a regional dialect	24	75	1

Activity 6.9

Practise your skills by interviewing some friends. Ask them (a) what talking habits annoy them, and (b) how they respond (extremely annoyed, not annoyed, don't know) to the habits listed in the Gallup poll.

Part (a) allows you to practise listening, encouraging and clarifying while your friends talk in their own way. Part (b) allows you to practise your questioning, defining and leading skills.

The telephone

3.15 Oral communication does not need to be done face to face. The **telephone** offers the same advantages of exchange, flexibility and feedback as face-to- face oral communication, but because it cuts out the need for travel it is less time-consuming and costly. It is still probably the most used item of office equipment.

3.16 We will discuss the **use of telephones** in Chapter 7, since it is a major part of communicating with people outside the organisation.

4 VISUAL COMMUNICATION

4.1 The visual element can be used to add interest and immediate appeal to written communication by using **layout, colour, spacing, different typefaces, symbolic logos** and so on.

4.2 'A picture paints a thousand words' is an old proverb with a certain truth: a simple **visual presentation** of data has more impact and immediacy than a table or block of text that is uniform to the eye and may contain superfluous elements. You should, however, remember that a visual image is only effective if the **assumptions** behind it and the **'key'** to its use are shared by sender and receiver alike. Symbols which you take for granted may be obscure to someone else with different training, knowledge or experience.

4.3 Graphs and charts can be complex and highly technical, so they should, like any other medium of communication, be **adapted** to suit the understanding and information needs of the intended recipient: they should be simplified and explained as necessary, and include only as much data as can clearly be presented and assimilated.

Tables

> **KEY TERM**
>
> **Tables** are a simple way of presenting numerical information. Figures are displayed, and can be compared with each other: relevant totals, subtotals, percentages can also be presented as a summary for analysis.

4.4 A table is **two-dimensional** (rows and columns): so it can only show two variables: a sales chart for a year, for example, might have rows for products, and columns for each month of the year.

SALES FIGURES FOR 20--													
Product	*Jan*	*Feb*	*Mar*	*Apr*	*May*	*Jun*	*Jul*	*Aug*	*Sep*	*Oct*	*Nov*	*Dec*	*Total £'000*
A													
B													
C													
D													
Total													

4.5 You are likely to be presenting data in tabular form very often; in doing so, be aware of the following guidelines.

(a) The table should have a **clear title**.

(b) All columns should be **clearly labelled**.

(c) Where appropriate, there should be **clear sub-totals** and a right-hand **total column** for comparison.

(d) A **total figure** is often also advisable at the bottom of each column of figures for comparison.

(e) Tables should not be packed with too much data so that the information presented is difficult to read.

Charts

> **KEY TERM**
>
> A simple **bar chart** is a chart consisting of one or more bars, in which the length of each bar indicates the magnitude of the corresponding data item.

4.6 The **bar chart** is one of the most common methods of presenting data in a visual display. It is a chart in which data is shown in the form of a **bar** (two dimensional, or three dimensional for extra impact), and is used to **demonstrate and compare**

amounts or numbers of things. The bars are the same in width but variable in height and are read off a vertical scale as you would read water levels or a thermometer. A horizontal presentation is also possible.

4.7 A simple bar chart is a visually appealing way of:

* **Showing the actual magnitude of an item** (amount of money, hours, sales or whatever)

* **Comparing magnitudes**, according to the relative lengths of the bars on the chart

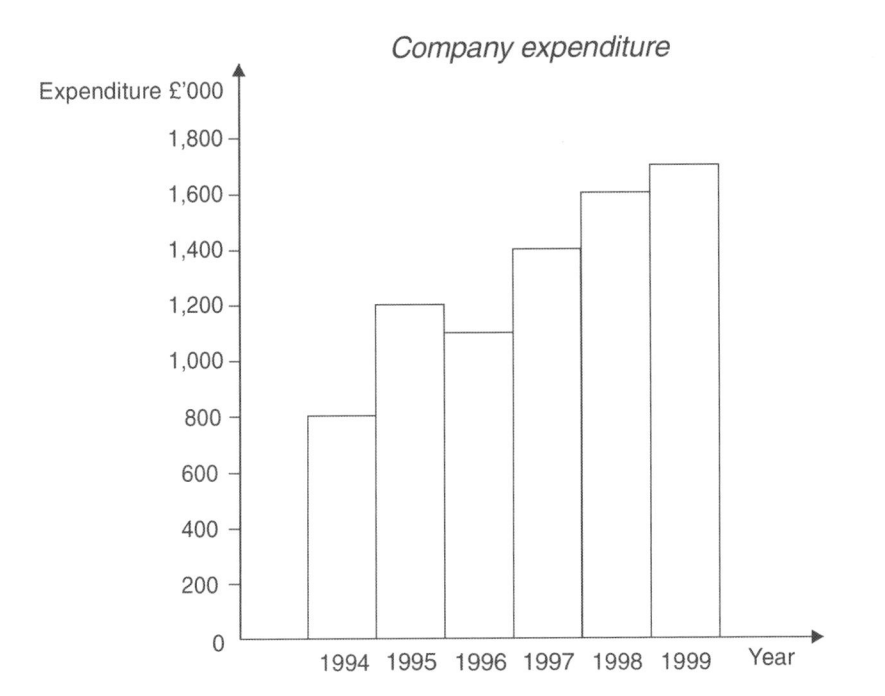

4.8 A more **complex bar chart**, showing the composition of the data in each bar, may be as follows.

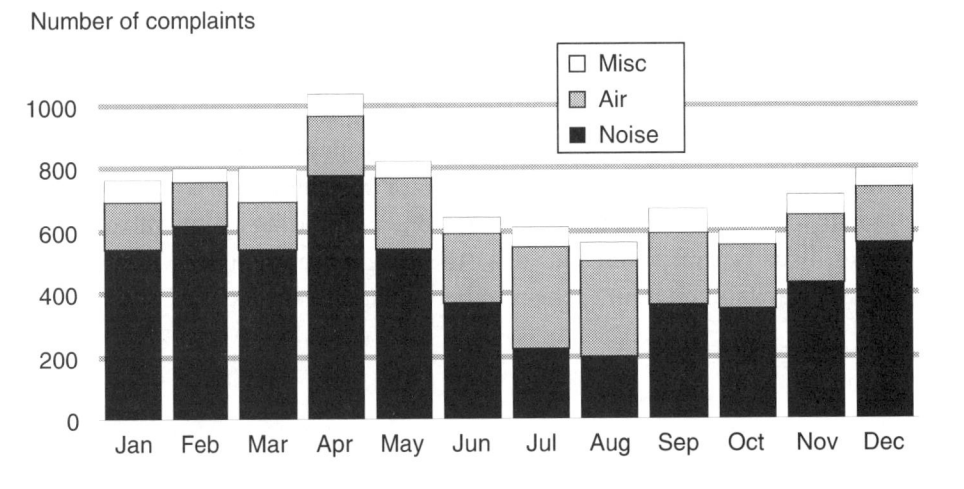

4.9 **Pie charts** are visually effective where the number of components is small enough to keep the chart simple, and where the difference in the size of the components is great enough for the eye to judge without too much supporting information.

KEY TERM

A **pie chart** is used to show pictorially the relative sizes of component elements of a total value or amount. It is called a pie chart because it is circular in shape like a pie (from a bird's eye view), which is then cut into 'slices' which represent a component part of the total.

The whole 'pie' = 360° (the number of degrees in a circle) = 100% of whatever you are showing. An element which is 50% of your total would therefore occupy a segment of 180°, and so on.

Breakdown of air and noise pollution complaints, 1996

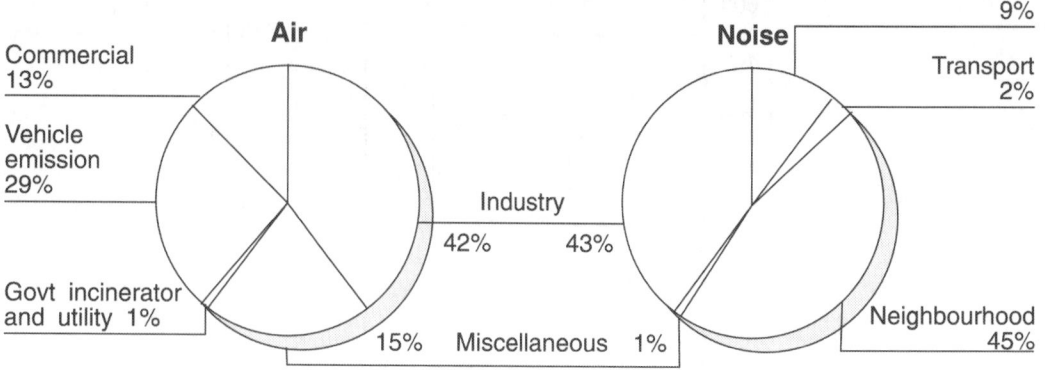

Graphs

KEY TERM

A **graph** is a form of visual display. A graph shows, by means of either a straight line or a curve, the relationship between two numbers (called variables).

4.10 **Line graphs** are often used in commercial contexts, to display a wide variety of information. They are particularly useful for **demonstrating trends**: the progress of events or the fluctuation over time of variables such as profits, prices, sales totals, customer complaints. This is done by plotting points of information on a grid, usually something like this (the y axis represents the number or variable which varies in relation to the number or variable on the x axis).

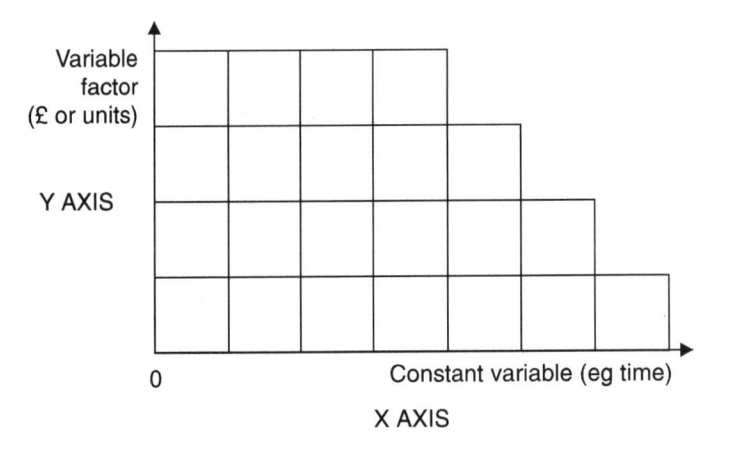

4.11 The points on this graph would be joined by a **line** which thus reflects the 'ups and downs' of the y axis variable, over a period of time. Two or three such lines may comfortably be drawn on a spacious graph before it gets too overcrowded, allowing several trends (for example the performance of several competing products over a period of time) to be compared.

4.12 It is easy to see the trend of share prices in the following graph, for example.

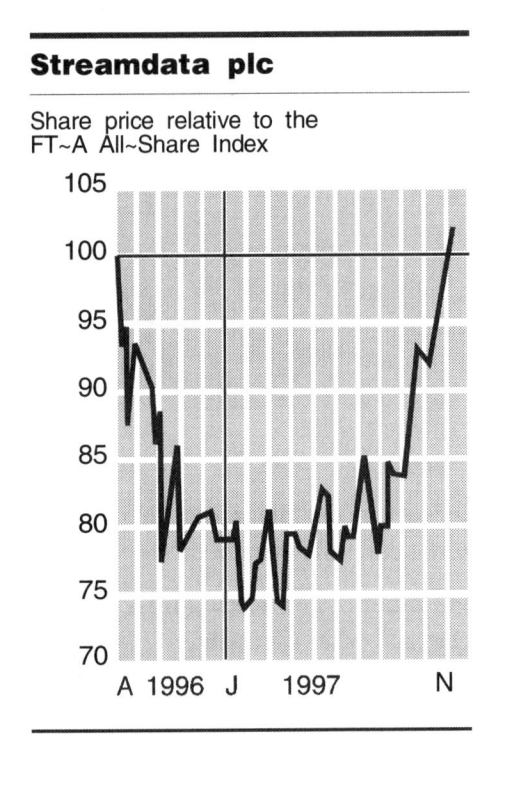

Activity 6.10

The table below shows a company's sales figures for 2000.

Product	Jan £'000	Feb £'000	Mar £'000	Apr £'000	May £'000	Jun £'000	Jul £'000	Aug £'000	Sep £'000	Oct £'000	Nov £'000	Dec £'000	Total £'000
T470	800	725	725	400	415	405	410	605	590	700	845	900	
S332	210	210	180	170	175	160	195	200	195	210	220	230	
V017	480	510	510	510	520	515	510	385	420	475	460	465	
J979	25	50	60	95	125	140	145	145	165	180	190	190	
B525	615	600	505	430	445	430	485	560	650	700	695	610	
Z124	370	360	370	385	370	350	380	375	375	360	325	355	

Required

Add up the columns and rows and then (making your presentation as simple or elaborate as you wish) construct the following.

(a)   A graph of the year's sales

(b)   A bar chart of the year's sales

(c)   A pie chart, showing whatever information you think is most appropriate to be shown in this form

(d)   Which method did you find most effective in presenting this information?

Flow charts

KEY TERM

Flow charts are a type of graphic which can be useful for presenting a summary of fairly complicated information in an easily digestible form and to indicate links and interrelationships between the different components (a bit like a family tree).

4.13   If you are using flow charts remember the following points.

(a)   **Take care in laying out the diagrams**: they can easily end up looking 'lop-sided' if they are not carefully designed.

(b)   Try to keep the **number of connecting lines to a minimum**. Avoid lines that have to jump over each other if possible.

(c)   Keep the narrative elements **brief and simple**.

4.14 EXAMPLE: FLOW CHART

Flow chart showing information flows

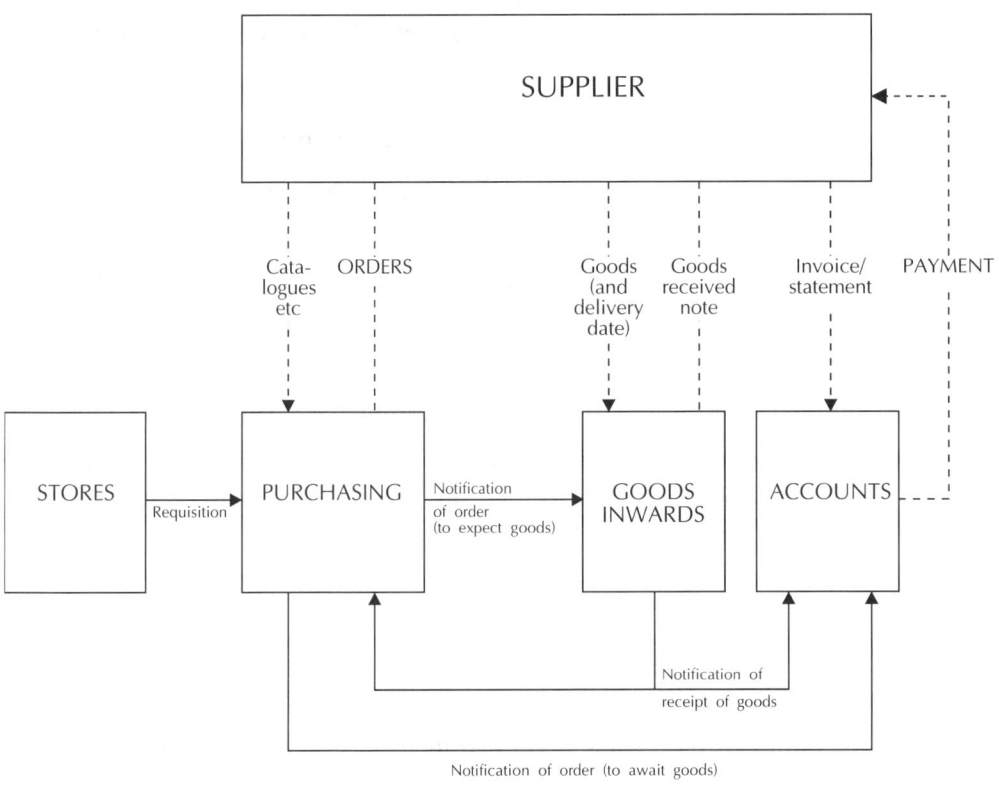

internal information flow
external information flow

Activity 6.11

(a) Redraft the 'cycle' model shown above as a **flow-chart** showing the steps in communication. (A useful practice of your visual communication skills: see Chapter 3 if you need a refresher.)

(b) Consider the communication exchange: 'What's the time, please?' 'It's half past three' - between you and a colleague. Draw a parallel flowchart to show how this exchange corresponds to the steps of your communication flow chart.

---

5 NON-VERBAL COMMUNICATION

KEY TERM

Non-verbal communication is, as its name implies, communication without words, or other than by words.

5.1 We convey more than half our meaning by means of **body language**. We may use it *deliberately*:

- **Instead of words**, for example storming out of a room, or pointing something out

- **To confirm or add to the meaning of our words**, for example nodding and saying 'yes', or pointing something out and saying 'look!'

5.2 We may also **unconsciously be confirming or even undermining our spoken messages** by our non-verbal ones, for example banging the table to reinforce a point; making a grim expression belying an assertion that 'Really - everything's fine'; a shaking hand revealing the truth behind 'Oh, I'm quietly confident, you know'.

5.3 We can fruitfully **control and *use* non-verbal communication**.

   (a) It can provide appropriate **'physical' feedback** to the sender of a message (a yawn, applause, a clenched fist, fidgeting).

   (b) It can **create a desired impression** (smart dress, no fidgets, a firm handshake).

   (c) It can establish a **desired atmosphere or conditions** (a friendly smile, informal dress, attentive posture, a respectful distance).

   (d) It can **reinforce** our spoken messages with appropriate indications of how our interest, seriousness and feelings are engaged (emphatic gesture, sparkling eyes, disapproving frown).

5.4 Learning to **recognise non-verbal messages** is also very useful.

   (a) We are able to receive **feedback** from a listener and modify the message accordingly.

   (b) We can recognise people's **real feelings** when their words are constrained by formal courtesies (for example an excited look, a nervous tic, close affectionate proximity).

   (c) It allows us to recognise **existing or potential personal problems** (the angry silence, the indifferent shrug, absenteeism or lateness at work, refusal to look someone in the eye).

   (d) It lets us 'read' situations in order to **modify our own communication and response strategy**. Is the potential customer convinced? (Go ahead.) Is the boss irritated at having to wait for his tea? (Reassure - and hurry.) Is the complainer on the point of hysteria? (Be soothing.)

5.5 **What is it that we see and interpret** when we say 'He looked upset', 'I could tell he was nervous', or 'She didn't say anything, but I could tell she was pleased'?

Sign	Meaning and interpretation
Facial expression	The eyebrows, eyes, nose, lips and mouth, jaw and head position all contribute to the expression on someone's face: lips can be tight or slack, eyes narrowed or widened, the eyebrows lowered or raised, the whole face moving or still, pale or flushed.
Gestures	People make gestures unconsciously: jabbing a finger in the air for emphasis, tapping the fingers when impatient. They also make conscious gestures - and not only impolite ones: a finger against the lips for silence, a jerk of the head to indicate a direction, a shrug to indicate indifference.

Sign	Meaning and interpretation
Movement	Watch how people move, at what pace, and to what effect. Someone who walks briskly conveys determination; someone who shuffles along, laziness or depression; someone who can never sit still, nervousness or impatience.
Positioning	You will probably find you sit closer to the people you like and trust, face them directly, or even lean towards them. You may keep a 'respectful' distance between yourself and someone with whom you have a more formal relationship.
Contact	Shaking hands is acceptable for transmitting greeting in most contexts but, for example, nudging or prodding for emphasis, or clapping on the back, implies familiarity and ease.
Posture	Consider the way you sit and stand. Lounge, hunch or sit/stand up straight and you convey relaxation, negativity or alertness. Lean forward when you listen to someone, and you transmit interest: lean well back and you convey weariness or boredom.
Sounds	A sceptical grunt, a sympathetic murmur and a delighted whoop are particularly useful non-verbal feedback signals.

Cultural differences

5.6 Gestures may mean **different things in different cultures**. In some countries it is considered very rude to point or speak with one's hands in one's pockets. You can cause great offence by using your left hand or crossing your legs. In Greece a nod of the head means 'No' and shaking your head means 'Yes' which could be very embarrassing! Watch out! People do make allowances for such differences, but you should consult a book of etiquette if you are visiting another country and important matters hang on the impression you make.

Activity 6.12

How might you interpret (or use) the following non-verbal cues?

(a) A clenched fist
(b) Stroking the chin slowly, with furrowed brow
(c) Head in hands
(d) Sitting elbow on knee, chin resting on fist
(e) Tapping toes
(f) Turning or leaning away from another person while talking
(g) A sigh, whole facial muscles relax and mouth smiles
(h) A sigh, while body sags and face 'falls'
(i) Eyebrows raised

---

6   APPROPRIATE COMMUNICATION METHODS

6.1 Communication will only be effective if the message is transmitted to the intended recipient **in a suitable format** and **through a suitable medium and channel**.

6.2 A number of factors need to be considered before the most appropriate method is selected.

Time	How long will be needed to prepare the message, and how long will it take to transmit it in the chosen form? This must be weighed against the urgency with which the message must be sent.
	Time of day must be considered when trying to communicate with overseas countries in different times zones.
Complexity	What medium will enable the message to be most readily understood? If detailed or highly technical information is to be exchanged or where a message has many interdependent parts, oral communication is not appropriate.
Distance	How far is the message required to travel? Must it be transmitted to an office on a different floor of the building, or across town, or to the other end of the country ?
Written record	A written record may be needed as proof, confirming a transaction, or for legal purposes, or as an aid to memory. It can be duplicated and sent to many recipients. It can be stored and later retrieved for reference and analysis as required.
Interaction	Sometimes instant feedback is needed for effective communication, for example when you are questioning a customer to find out his precise requirements ('small, medium or large?', 'green, red or blue?').
Degree of confidentiality	Telephone calls may be overheard; faxed messages can be read by whoever is standing by the fax machine; internal memos may be read by colleagues or by internal mail staff; highly personal letters may be read by the recipient's secretary.
The recipient	It may be necessary to be reserved and tactful, warm and friendly, or impersonal, depending upon the desired effect on the recipient. If you are trying to impress them, a high quality document may be needed.
Cost	Cost must be considered in relation to all of the above factors. The aim is to achieve the best possible result at the least possible expense.

Activity 6.13

(a) Why would it be inappropriate to read out a set of draft accounts to a client over the telephone?

(b) Would it be appropriate to read out the profit figure shown in the draft accounts?

(c) If you worked for an organisation employing sixty people what would be the most appropriate method of telling them that it was your birthday on Friday and the drinks were on you?

(d) Suppose there were 600 people in your organisation: what would be the most effective way of ensuring that they all received a piece of information?

(e) Somebody has just written to you inviting you to a meeting but not mentioning where it is going to be held. The meeting is in five days time. Should you write asking for the additional information or should you telephone?

Activity 6.14

What do you think are the **advantages** and **disadvantages** of **oral/verbal communication** in a business context, in comparison with **written communication**? Present your argument in any way you would find helpful. (Might it be worth filing as evidence of your awareness of how different communication methods are appropriate to different situations?)

7   RESOLVING COMMUNICATION DIFFICULTIES

Communication difficulties

7.1   **Reasons why communication may be ineffective.** (Draw up your own list before looking at our answers below.)

(a)   **Failure to communicate.** Even 'tactful' or 'thoughtful' silences are open to misinterpretation.

(b)   **Pointless communication.** Sending a message that is meaningless, irrelevant or unsuitable to the purpose and recipient of the communication.

(c)   **Unsuitable language.** An Accounting Technician should realise that not everybody understands the technical jargon used in finance and accounting.

(d)   **Physical noise**: other people talking in the room or the clatter of a computer printer can prevent a message from being heard, or heard clearly.

(e)   **Technical noise: faulty communication channels**. If you relay your message across a crackling telephone line, or you write it down using illegible handwriting, or if the fax machine breaks down the message will not be communicated effectively.

(f)   **Social noise: relationships** and **differences of perception**. If the relationship between the sender and receiver of a message is not good this will affect the ease and effectiveness with which it is sent and the willingness with which it is received and understood.

(g)   **Emotional noise: lack of attention**: a carefully prepared and presented message may still fail if the receiver is not interested or has other things on his mind, or is in the grip of strong distracting emotions which affect his ability to hear clearly.

(h)   **Too much information**: if the sender includes large quantities of (irrelevant) information the important items may be obscured, or there may simply be too much to take in.

(i)   **Too little information**: a vital point may be omitted which renders the whole communication ineffective (for example a closing date for applications).

(j)   **Faults in feedback**: if you fail to offer or seek feedback you will never know whether you have understood or have been understood correctly.

(k)   **Lack of skill** in communicating clearly, by appropriate methods and so on.

(l)   **Failure to take into account non-verbal signals.**

BPP
PUBLISHING

Activity 6.15

What communication problems are suggested by the following?

(a) [On the noticeboard] 'P Brown. Your complaint about the behaviour of your colleague S Simms is being looked into. Manager.'

(b) 'Prima facie, I would postulate statutory negligence, as per para 22 Sec three et seq. Nil desperandum.' 'Eh?'

(c) 'Smith – you've been scratching your head and frowning like mad ever since I started the briefing half an hour ago. I've tried to ignore it, but have you got fleas or something?'

(d) 'Sorry, this line's terrible – how many? how much? – what was that? NO, it's OK: I'll remember it all. We'll deliver on Monday – no, MONDAY: no, M-O-N ...'

(e) Date: 11 March. Report on communication: 463 pages. Please read for staff meeting: 12 March.

(f) 'Look. Nobody pays you to think: leave that to us professionals. Just do your job.'

7.2 **Additional problems in a work situation**

(a) Hostility or **resentment of subordinates towards management,** resulting in deliberate attempts to sabotage communication.

(b) Subordinates otherwise giving superiors **incorrect or incomplete information** (eg to protect a colleague, to avoid bothering the superior or to avoid giving 'bad news').

(c) People from **different levels** in the hierarchy, jobs or specialisms, being on a **different wavelength**: with different perceptions, attitudes, technical vocabulary and so on.

(d) **Lack of opportunity,** formal or informal, for subordinates to say what they think or feel.

(e) Employees simply **not taking an interest** in organisational matters which do not affect them personally.

(f) An **organisation culture** which shares information only on a functional or 'need to know' basis: common in bureaucracies.

(g) **Organisational politics** and conflict: since 'knowledge is power' people may be reluctant to share information with each other.

Improving communication

7.3 Communication problems fall into three broad categories.

- There may be a **bad formal communication system** hindering or discouraging the exchange of information.

- **Noise or distortion** may be causing misunderstanding about the content and meaning of messages.

- **Interpersonal differences** may be causing a break-down in communications.

7.4 Some interpersonal communication difficulties can therefore be overcome by:

- Encouraging people to be aware of the problems
- Training people in communication techniques
- Creating a trusting and communicative organisation culture

Activity 6.16

Indicate the most effective way in which the following situations should be communicated.

(a) Spare parts needed urgently.

(b) A message from the managing director to all staff.

(c) Fred Bloggs has been absent five times in the past month and his manager intends taking action.

(d) You need information quickly from another department.

(e) You have to explain a complicated operation to a group.

Activity 6.17

How might the barriers to communication listed in paragraph 7.1 be overcome? (There is nothing tricky or technical about this, nor is there one right answer. Just think through the problem: what could you do?)

Key learning points

- Communication is the **transmission and exchange of information**. It is fundamental to working relationships, transactions and information flow.

- Communication is a **two-way process**. **Feedback** is the signal returned from the recipient of the message to the sender, indicating whether (and how accurately) the message has been received.

- All letters should have a **beginning** (the opening paragraph), a **middle** (where the message is developed) and an **end** (the closing paragraph).

- **Memoranda** are used internally within an organisation, and perform the same function that a letter does in external communication by an organisation. They are generally structured as follows.

  ○ To/From/Date
  ○ Subject heading
  ○ Opening paragraph or sentence
  ○ Substance of message

  ○ Closing paragraph or sentence

- **Oral communication** is the least formal, most common way of communicating. It includes face-to-face and telephone discussions.

- Methods of visual communication include **charts** (for presenting data), **graphs** (for presenting trends and other information) and **tables** (for presenting numerical information).

- Elements in **non-verbal communication** include the following.

  ° Facial expression
  ° Gesture
  ° Movement
  ° Positioning and contact
  ° Posture
  ° Sounds

- In order to select the **most appropriate method of communication**, the following factors should be considered.

  ° Time
  ° Complexity
  ° Distance
  ° Written record
  ° Interaction
  ° Degree of confidentiality
  ° The recipient
  ° Cost

- Communication may be **ineffective** due to the following reasons.

  ° Non-communication
  ° Irrelevance
  ° Inappropriate language
  ° Physical noise
  ° Faulty communication channels
  ° Relationships and perceptions
  ° Lack of attention
  ° Too much information
  ° Too little information
  ° Faults in feedback
  ° Poor communication skills

Quick quiz

1   What are the standard elements contained in a business letter?

2   How do you sign off a letter in which the recipient is greeted 'Dear Sir'?

3   What is the main difference between letters and memoranda?

4   What are the two main methods of communicating by speech?

5   In what ways does face-to-face communication differ from other methods of communication?

6   As far as body language is concerned, how might the following actions be interpreted?

    (a)   clenched fist
    (b)   drumming fingers on the table
    (c)   stroking the chin

7   What is the best method of communicating bad news to someone?

8   If you wished to circulate a message to all of the staff in your department as quickly as possible, what would be the most suitable method of communication?

9   What are the main reasons for ineffective communication in organisations?

Answers to quick quiz

1   • Letterhead
    • Reference
    • Date
    • Recipient name and address
    • Greeting/salutation
    • Subject
    • Substance
    • Complimentary close
    • Signature
    • Author name and title

2   Yours faithfully

3   Letters are generally used as a form of external communication with another organisation, whereas memoranda are a form of communication used within an organisation between one individual and another, one department and another and so on.

4   By using the telephone, and by speaking face-to-face.

5   With face-to-face communication, messages are constantly being sent and received as you switch rapidly between speaking and listening. Good speaking *and* listening skills are therefore essential.

6   (a)   Anger
    (b)   Boredom
    (c)   Deep in thought

7   Face-to-face communication

8   Via e-mail (if available), face-to-face if it is a small department or perhaps by pinning a notice on the noticeboard.

9   See paragraphs 7.1, 7.2.

BPP PUBLISHING

7 Dealing with external customers

This chapter contains

Learning objectives

On completion of this chapter you will be able to:

- Provide information in line with routine requirements and one-off requests

- Ask the appropriate people for any information, advice and resources that are required

- Meet commitments to others within agreed deadlines

- Use communication methods appropriate to the situation and resolve any difficulties

- Take opportunities to promote the image of the department and organisation

- Follow confidentiality and data protection requirements

- Understand the organisation's customer base and the different people involved with the organisation

- Consider appropriate actions and styles of approach in different situations

- understand the source of, and your responsbilities in complying with, legal requirements for data handling

BPP
PUBLISHING

Performance criteria

(1) Information is provided to internal and external customers in line with routine requirements and one off requests

(2) The appropriate people are asked for any information, advice and resources that are required

(3) Commitments to others are met within agreed timescales

(4) Communication methods are appropriate to the individual situation

(5) Any communication difficulties are acknowledged and action taken to resolve them

(6) Opportunities are taken to promote the image of the department and organisation to internal and external customers

(7) Confidentiality and data protection requirements are strictly followed

Range statement

1 **Internal customers:** peers; manager; other members of staff

2 **External customers:** suppliers; customers; external agencies

3 **Communication methods:** written; verbal; electronic

Knowledge and understanding

- The different types of people: customers, peers, managers, other members of staff

- Relevant legislation

- Handling confidential information

- Methods of establishing constructive relationships

- Seeking and exchanging information, advice and support

- Handling disagreements and conflict

- Using appropriate actions and different styles of approach in different situations

- Different communication methods and styles

- Types of communication difficulties and how to resolve them

- Employee responsibilities in complying with the relevant legislation

- The organisational and departmental structure

- The customer base

1 INTRODUCTION: CUSTOMER CARE AND PUBLIC RELATIONS

Who is 'the customer'?

1.1 Customers are not just the people who buy the products or services of an organisation, or the 'end-users' of the products or services: the people 'out there'. In a sense, any individual or organisation that sources information, services, products or business relations from you is a customer.

1.2 The Range Statement for Unit 23 encourages you to consider the following **external customers**.

(a) **Customers**: buyers or end-users of the organisation's products and services. They may be direct customers of Accounts Department activity: prompt and accurate invoicing, credit control, payment recording and so on. As customers of the organisation as a whole, they are in any case crucial to its survival and success.

(b) **Suppliers**: people from whom the organisation sources goods and services. They are direct 'customers' of Accounts Department activity: accurate order information and prompt payment of invoices, for example.

(c) **External agencies**: organisations who purchase or are entitled to various services and outputs (mainly information). Some of these will be direct customers of the Accounts Department, from whom they require various reports and returns, which must be correct, complete and produced on demand. Again, members of these agencies are also potential customers/consumers of the organisation's products or services.

Activity 7.1

Give four examples of reports which might be required by external agency customers from the Accounts Department.

1.3 Do remember too that, as we discussed in Chapter 5, people *inside* your organisation are also your customers. **Internal customers** include your boss (to whom you supply information and work), your colleagues (to whom you provide help and information and workflow) and other departments (especially if you are in an administrative service department like accounts). Treat your internal customers with the same respect as you would an external customer: they, too, can go elsewhere if they do not like the service you give them!

DEVOLVED ASSESSMENT ALERT

The evidence requirements for Element 23.2 include 'relationships with at least two types of ... external customers being established'. If you think 'customer service' isn't your job, you will at least have to make it your job to this extent! Remember that suppliers and external agencies, as well as clients, are potential 'customers'.

Customer care

1.4 Business organisations are increasingly recognising that:

- Customers have an ever-widening **choice** of products and services available to them; and

- **Service** (including sales service, delivery, after-sales service and enquiry handling) is of major importance in winning and retaining customers.

1.5 If your organisation has a Customer Services Department, or the marketing department occasionally runs Customer Care Programmes, you might be forgiven for thinking that customer care is simply not your job.

KEY TERM

Customer care is 'the management and identification of 'moments of truth', with the aim of achieving customer satisfaction' (Thomas, 1986).

1.6 **'Moments of truth' in customer satisfaction**

(a) Reception when visiting or telephoning the organisation (especially for the first time

(b) The handling of **enquiries**

(c) The giving of information

(d) The handling of **complaints** or queries about products or services received (or not received)

(e) Encounters between customers and the **administrative functions** (receiving or querying invoices, say); often dreaded as 'red tape'

(f) After-sales **follow-up** and service

As an accounts assistant, you may be involved in any one of these customer care functions with external or internal customers.

Activity 7.2

Give an example of how you might have to perform each of the customer care functions listed in paragraph 1.6.

Public relations

1.7 In addition to 'moments of truth', there is the general **image** of the department and organisation to consider. Like customer care, public relations or **PR** is often thought of as the job of a specific department (which usually deals with the media and press, sponsorship, events and so on). But **public relations is everyone's job. Customer care is everybody's job**.

1.8 You need to be able to recognise situations in which you **represent** your department/organisation, because in those situations your behaviour, attitudes and messages have PR consequences for the organisation.

KEY TERM

The word **represent** means:

- to stand as an equivalent or substitute for someone/something
- to portray or act as a picture or expression of someone/something
- to exemplify or typify the characteristics of someone/something
- to act out the part of someone/something.

Activity 7.3

Before you read further, brainstorm your own list of situations in which you might represent an organisation, individually or in a group. (A group brainstorming session allows you to practise a range of interpersonal, planning and creative skills.) Go through your list and give examples of how you could create a positive or negative image in each situation. If you are in a group, role-play any examples that sound interesting: let observers and participants comment on the PR impact of different behaviours.

1.9 The following table suggests some of the contexts in which you might represent your organisation. (They would apply equally to internal communications in which you represent your department.)

Context	Example	Affects image of...
You **exercise authority** delegated to you by the organisation	You discipline or instruct a subordinate	Organisation's attitude to employees
	You make a contract with a supplier	Organisation's integrity/professionalism
You **issue communications** on behalf of the organisation/department	You write or approve an invoice, letter, memo and so on	The organisation's professionalism and attitude to whatever the topic of the message.
You **identify yourself** as a member of the organisation/department	You sign your name to a communication on company letterhead, or answer the telephone with the company name	Whatever what you say or do implies about the organisation/department. (Its attitudes are identified with yours.)
	You present a business card	
	You tell someone informally whom you work for	
You are **associated in people's minds** with the organisation/department	You handle a customer complaint	The organisation's attitude to customers/quality
	You give a presentation	The organisation's expertise
	You are on the organisation's stand at an exhibition	The organisation's expertise/service
		'Accountants' in general!

1.10 So how can you **promote or manage the department's or organisation's image** in these circumstances?

- **Awareness** that you are projecting an image.
- **Integrity**
- **Professionalism**
- **Discretion**
- **Good news spreading**

Awareness

1. 11   Be aware of the **attitude** implied by words, behaviour and work outputs. Do you (and those who work for and with you) convey a positive attitude towards;

- Your **work** and the organisation you work for?

- The **products and services** of the organisation?

- The **customer**, supplier, distributor or colleague you are dealing with, and towards the relationship between you?

- **Yourself**, your rights and responsibilities?

1.12   Consider what you would assume about the attitude of someone who missed deadlines, issued financial statements with errors, failed to return telephone calls, worked in an untidy or unhygienic environment, or spoke disrespectfully to you or about you. Consider what you would assume about the organisation that person represented.

1.13   Be aware of the **outward image** you and your environment and output present. Consider what impression is created by non-verbal communications such as:

- Untidy, unclean or inappropriate dress
- A slouching posture, or standing inappropriately close to someone

Company cultures and contexts differ widely, and there should always be room for individuality. You need to work out what the formal and informal rules are across a range of circumstances.

Integrity

1.14   **Illegal, dishonest or unethical behaviour** (not to mention its legal consequences) creates powerful negative PR, in the business and wider community - and within the organisation itself.

(a)   **Abide by law and regulation in the areas of your responsibility**.

(b)   **Abide by the terms of contracts.** (Remember that letters and verbal agreements as well as legal documents may constitute a binding arrangement.)

(c)   **Keep your promises.** Promises may not be legally binding, but going back on them repeatedly destroys trust, breaks relationships and loses co-operation.

(d)   **Strive to be fair**, socially responsible and respectful of cultural differences (especially when dealing with overseas colleagues or contacts).

Professionalism

1.15   What is understood by the term 'professionalism' will depend on the context and culture of the organisation.

(a)   **Courtesy.** This is a bare minimum requirement of all business communication.

(b)   **Expertise.** Professionalism implies a level of competence which justifies financial remuneration. Incompetence is bad PR. Work out what range and standard of performance people are reasonably entitled to expect from you, and ensure that you can achieve it.

(c) **Efficiency.** Transactions take time, and invariably cost someone money. Professionals place a value on their time, energy, money and other resources, and recognise that others do the same. Be organised, prompt to appointments, and deadline- and budget-conscious.

Activity 7.4

Imagine that your manager has asked you to give a presentation to Accounts Staff entitled: 'Conveying Professionalism: Everyday PR'. Prepare a visual aid which illustrates the main points of your presentation. (If you are in a study group, you may even take the opportunity to give this presentation: useful experience for your portfolio.)

Discretion

1.16 When you represent the department or organisation, even informally, to people outside it, you have to be aware of the need for discretion. 'Leaks' of information can be used for **good** or **bad** PR.

(a) Some information from within the organisation will be covered by laws or agreements of **confidentiality**. You may be required by contract, for example, not to disclose financial information. Personal details of employees are confidential under the **Data Protection Act**. (This will be discussed later in this chapter.)

(b) Another category of sensitive information is anything negative that you know about the department or organisation.

1.17 On the other hand, **swapping and spreading good news** about departmental and organisational successes and positive attributes is good image production. Be ready to contribute when issuing communications or dealing informally with people.

2 RECEIVING AND ASSISTING VISITORS

2.1 We have already covered some general rules on dealing with people, such as **effective oral communication, non-discrimination** and **courtesy.** These should of course be applied when dealing with anybody with whom you came into contact in the course of business.

Greeting people

2.2 First impressions are vital: if you do not get it right first time you may never deal effectively with that person. (You may never be given the opportunity to deal with them again.)

(a) **Smile**. Forget about your own troubles and concentrate on the matter in hand: a fellow human being, who needs you to help him. (If you are greeting somebody on the telephone, smile with your voice.)

(b) **Make eye contact**. Don't gaze intently into people's eyes - in some cultures, this is threatening and uncomfortable - but don't keep looking down or away, otherwise they will think that you are not interested in them and they may not trust you.

(c) If the visitor offers to **shake hands** with you, never decline the offer. Don't be limp-wristed, but don't break the person's hand or try to remove his arm at the shoulder! A firm clasp held for a few seconds indicates confidence and self-assurance. Whether you offer to shake hands *first* is really a matter for you to decide. If you do not do so naturally, you are unlikely to do it effectively.

2.3 If you are greeting somebody you know you must **gauge the formality** or otherwise of your greeting according to your relationship to date. **Do not be overly familiar,** but make sure that you use their name once or twice (their first name if the relationship has developed that far), since there is nothing more likely to win and keep somebody's attention than hearing their own name.

2.4 Remember that pleasantries ('How are you?', 'Did you have a good journey?') are useful in establishing rapport, but do not waste time in getting down to business. (If clients are inclined to gossip do not cut them dead, but say 'Well, what can I do for you today?' at the earliest opportunity.) Be aware that other people may be trying to contact you or may be waiting for you to contact them. Arrange your priorities according to the urgency of the work, not how well you get on with X Ltd's purchasing staff.

2.5 Standard **reception procedures** which should be carried out when receiving all visitors. These may be summarised as follows.

- Greet the visitor politely
- Sign in
- Notify the person that he has come to see that the visitor has arrived
- Stay with the visitor until he is collected, *or* (if the visitor is known),
- Direct the visitor to the office of the person he has come to see

2.6 Here are some further guidelines.

(a) **Don't keep visitors waiting unnecessarily.** They should be made comfortable whilst waiting, and offered refreshments and something to read.

(b) **Greet visitors by their name** (if known) and with a handshake. Apologise if you have been unavoidably held up.

(c) If dealing with **sensitive or personal matters,** do not speak loudly in public, or wait until you are behind closed doors before beginning such discussions.

(d) **Direct visitors** to the office or interview room where the meeting is to be held. This should be done as clearly as possible.

(e) **Attempt to put visitors at ease** if they appear to be at all uncomfortable while waiting.

(f) **Maintain a courteous and interested tone** during all dealings with external visitors.

(g) If you have to take a **phone call** whilst waiting with a visitor, or whilst in a meeting with one, keep it very brief (in most cases it is best to promise to call the caller back). This ensures both politeness and confidentiality.

Signing-in visitors

2.7 You will generally want to know three things about any visitor to your organisation (not necessarily in this order).

(a) Their name

(b) If appropriate, the name and department of the person they have come to see

(c) The purpose of their visit

2.8 **It is always useful to get a record of any visitor's name and some way of contacting them.** Even if they have come to the wrong place, or you have to send them away empty-handed, you might want or need to get in touch with them again. They may accidentally leave something on your premises, or you may have reason to mention the enquiry to a colleague who thinks he knows a way of helping them that you did not think of. This is why visitors should always be requested to sign-in when they arrive, and sign-out when they leave.

2.9 Signing-in and signing-out are also important procedures in terms of **security** (see Chapter 5) as it is always important that if anyone is wandering around your organisation, there is someone who is aware of it.

2.10 If, for some reason, the building you work in needs to be evacuated in case of fire or some other emergency, it is vital that everyone who was in the building is accounted for. Without a record of visitors who have signed-in on entering the building, there would be no way of knowing whether anyone might be trapped in a building that is on fire.

Internal visitors

2.11 It is important to remember that **all visitors** may be required to sign-in when entering an organisation or department. If, for example, an internal visitor (unexpected) just pops in to your department to see someone, it is important to stick to the procedures.

ASSESSMENT ALERT

An added benefit of maintaining accurate and complete records of visits is that they represent 'work products' in evidence of your competence in Unit 23.2.

Activity 7.5

Consider the following scenario in the head office of Baddley & Co Bank.

MRS WEAVER: [*Timidly, glancing at her watch*] Um...excuse me...that young man knows that I've arrived, doesn't he?

RECEPTIONIST: [*Not looking up*] Oh yes. He said he'll be along in a minute.

[*Several minutes pass by*]

PETER: [*Ambling out of the reception area and winking at the receptionist.*] Ah. Mrs...um. I see you've found some magazines! Would you like to finish reading that?

MRS WEAVER: [*Putting down* Banking World *and looking rather frightened.*] Hello. I had an appointment to see a Mr Benton. I hope I'm...

PETER: That's me - you can call me Peter. Mrs... [*flicks through file*] Weaver, ah yes, that's right - problems with loan repayments. Would you like to come this way?

[*PETER walks quickly down the corridor, pausing half way down to check that MRS WEAVER is following.*]

PETER: [*In doorway, to three junior staff in suits, smoking and laughing*] Could you clear out for ten minutes, please guys: I've got an F104.

[*MRS WEAVER arrives in the room. The three 'guys' pick up their papers, put out their cigarettes and leave. PETER leans his head out of the door before closing it and makes an inaudible remark which is greeted with loud laughter.*]

PETER: Well Mrs Weaver. Weaver fish is it? [*leans forward and leers*]. How can we help you?

MRS WEAVER: Well actually *you* wrote to me and asked me to come in and see you. I'm sorry.

[*The phone rings.*]

PETER: Oh, put him through. John! How are you? How's business?... Yes I did ring you, its about that ten grand you were after. I just wanted to say, no problem mate. Yes, I thought you'd be pleased. How's Caroline? [*Lengthy silence while PETER listens to the person on the other end of the line.*] I'm sorry... I had no idea, mate. So it's completely... um... there's no chance of you getting back together? ... Well, give it time, you know what they say. Look, I've got to go - I'll see you Friday, OK? Bye.

[*Peter now looks down at the file on the table and leafs through it for some time.*]

Now then, Mrs Weaver. You borrowed £2,000, when was it ... nearly four years ago. Monthly repayments...£60-ish. Three months arrears!

We're a *caring* bank, Mrs Weaver, but we do like people to keep up with their repayments. Is there a problem?

MRS WEAVER: Well, I suppose it was because my husband lost his job and there was no money in our joint account. It was you who wouldn't do the transfers, actually.

PETER: Um... it depends on your... er... overdraft facility. But...um...I take it your husband's trying to find another job?

MRS WEAVER: Well he will do, but we're going on holiday actually - his redundancy money was held up but it's just come through [*scrabbles in her handbag.*] I've got some cash here. I was going to pay off the arrears and settle the loan, if I'm allowed to do that. I don't want to break the rules.

PETER: [*Completely thrown.*] Um... yes, of course. I'll take you down to the front office and we'll work out what the outstanding amount is. [*Trying to recover.*] Well that is good news - I wish all our customers were like you! Was it...er...how...if it's a large sum we....

MRS WEAVER: Oh I'm not sure. My husband's dealing with all that - he just gives me pocket money [*She waves a large bundle of notes and smiles very sweetly*].

Required

(a) Peter clearly does not deal with Mrs Weaver very well. What criticisms would you make of his handling of this case?

(b) Write a brief note of what transpired at the interview for Mrs Weaver's file.

General guidelines for assisting visitors

2.12 There is a balance between what you can reasonably be expected to know about your organisation and knowing the **limits within which you are able to deal with enquiries**.

Activity 7.6

Your company is having an 'open evening' for its clients, partly as a public relations exercise and partly to demonstrate the full range of its services. A pleasant venue has been hired and there will be a buffet meal and drinks. Your manager would like you to attend because you are frequently the first point of contact with clients on the telephone. You will not be paid to attend. You had arranged to see some friends that evening, but this could be postponed.

Who will gain if you attend the open evening and in what ways?

2.13 There are many positive things that you can do to provide a good service to visitors.

(a) Be **polite**, interested, warm and friendly, but not over-familiar or disrespectful.

(b) Be as **helpful** as you can within the bounds of your responsibilities.

(c) If you cannot help but somebody else in your organisation can, then **put the customer in touch with that person** as soon as possible (there is more on this below).

(d) Make your customers trust you by **doing what you say you will do** promptly and efficiently.

(e) **Do not promise to do something that you do not have the ability or authority to do.**

(f) **Do not criticise your own organisation** in response to complaints or difficulties, whatever your personal feelings about it. You will only make things worse by whinging to outsiders.

(g) **If you make a mistake, apologise and put it right straight away.** Be aware that what may seem a minor, unimportant slip to you may have seriously inconvenienced or distressed your customer.

Dealing with 'difficult' customers

2.14 You will encounter **awkward or aggressive people** no matter how hard you try to please them or how well you do your own job. Some people seem to like complaining over the smallest thing; some people are arrogant bullies; some are simply having a bad day and your organisation's slip is the last straw.

2.15 In many ways dealing with customers who are upset or angry is like dealing with difficult colleagues. Here are some guidelines.

(a) **Be calm and polite.** If you speak in a fairly low, slow tone of voice, and keep your body fairly still (even if you are speaking to them on the phone), you can usually calm the other person down.

(b) **Listen** to what they have to say, and let them know you are listening (nod in face-to-face encounters; say 'yes' or 'I see' on the phone.

(c) Deal with **the problem, not the person** - and get the complainers to do the same.

(d) Use a **win-win approach** to show your willingness to be constructive and creative in getting the complainer what he wants if at all possible.

(e) **Do not grovel, apologise or give way too readily** however. The customer might have a valid complaint - or might not. Listen, be sympathetic but firm, and say that you will make sure that the complaint is investigated immediately.

(f) **Follow through** on any investigation or action you promise, and keep the person informed of progress and outcomes.

2.16 There may be an organisational policy for dealing with difficult people, for example handing over people who start to get difficult to a **more senior person**. If so, follow the rules in your organisation.

3 RESPONDING TO INFORMATION REQUESTS

3.1 A visitor or caller may request:

(a) **Personal information** (the Personnel department asking for your assessment details or National Insurance number, say)

(b) **Technical information** (a manager wanting a Budget update, or advice on costing methods, say)

(c) **Information about transactions** which you have performed or which are within your authority to perform.

3.2 This information may come from:

- Your own knowledge
- Your personal files
- Departmental transaction files; or
- The procedural/technical manuals or other library sources of the department.

Good information

3.3 **Good information** should be:

- Relevant
- Accurate
- Confidence –inspiring or reliable
- Timely
- Communicated by appropriate methods
- Cost effective

Let us look at these qualities in more detail.

Relevant

3.4 Information should be relevant to the **sender's purposes** and/or the **user's needs**. For the communicator, this means the following.

Communicator's tasks	Reasons
Identifying the user	Information must be suited to and sent to the right person - the one who needs it to do his job.
Defining the purpose	Information is effective only when it helps a user to act or make a decision. If you ask someone the way to the nearest train station, you do not expect or need to be told that the weather is fine, or even that there is a very interesting train station in another town some miles away. If you are asked to supply information for a particular purpose (as assumed by Element 24.2) - make sure you find out what that purpose is!
Judging the volume of information required	Information must be **complete** enough for its purpose, not omitting any necessary item. However, it should be no greater in volume than the user will find helpful or be able to take in. In other words, it should be **sufficient**.

3.5 Consider information as **the answer to a particular enquiry or problem,** anything else being strictly 'icing on the cake', and you will not fall into the trap of irrelevance.

Accurate

3.6 Information should be **accurate** within the user's needs.

(a) Information should be 'accurate' in the sense of '**correct**': downright falsehood and error are fatal to effective communication of any sort.

(b) It may, however, be impossible - or at least very time-consuming and expensive - to gather, process and assimilate information that is minutely **detailed**. An approximation or an average figure is often sufficient for our needs.

Confidence-inspiring, or reliable

3.7 Information should not give the user reason to mistrust, disbelieve or ignore it, for example because it is **out-of-date, badly presented** or taken from an **unreliable source.** Sources of information should be **reviewed regularly** in order to ensure that information is always up-to-date. Out-of-date information will not give the user any reason to have confidence in the information source that he is using.

3.8 It may help if the information is readily **verifiable**. If the user is faced with a situation where an important action or decision depends on an item of information, he should be able to check the facts.

Timely

3.9 Information must be made available within the time period which makes it useful: it must be in the **right place at the right time**. A beautifully researched and presented report will be of no value if it arrives on a manager's desk too late to influence his decision on the matter in hand. If you are asked for information for a particular purpose, make sure you **know exactly when it is required** (and by whom).

Appropriately communicated

3.10 Information will lose its value if it is not clearly communicated to the user **in a suitable format** and **through a suitable medium** (as discussed in Chapter 9). For example, your words and symbols should be familiar or they should be explained to the user; the layout of text and graphics should be easy to read; a telephone call may not be appropriate for complex or confidential matters, or those requiring written records (such as legal documents).

Cost-effective

3.11 Good information should **only cost as much as it is worth**. Gathering, storing, retrieving and communicating an item of information may require expense of time, energy and resources: if the expense is greater than the potential value of the item, re-consider whether the information is necessary to such a degree of accuracy or completeness - or even necessary at all.

Giving information to enquirers

3.12 If a visitor or caller requests **information about the products or services of the organisation**, you may well have the information to hand, although the degree of knowledge you need to have will depend on the nature of your involvement and the complexity of the organisation's activity.

3.13 The **degree of knowledge you need to possess** depends upon what kind of product or service your organisation provides and what the nature of your involvement is. Be sure, though, that you can given an answer to the following questions.

(a) **What does your organisation do?** What does your own department do, and what other departments are there?

(b) Does your organisation supply to other businesses, to domestic clients or to both? Does it export its product or services?

(c) Is there a brochure describing your organisation's products/services? There may be many such brochures - are you aware of all of them?

(d) What new products or services are going to be introduced? Are the old versions to be discontinued?

(e) Do you know where your organisation's branches are, in relation to major towns?

(f) Is your organisation part of a larger group or does it have smaller subsidiaries? What are their names and what do they do?

(g) Who are your organisation's major competitors? How are your organisation's products/services different from theirs?

(h) If you did not know the answer to a question about your organisation, who could help you or deal with the query?

3.14 Learn as much as you can about your organisation's business: it will make you more effective in your job and it will help if you are aiming for promotion or a transfer to another department.

3.15 If you **do not know the answer** to any enquiry, you have three options.

(a) You can simply say, 'I don't know'. (Rude and not exactly confidence-inspiring for the enquirer.)

(b) You can say, 'I don't know, but I will find out for you'.

(c) You can direct the enquirer to someone else who knows more.

3.16 **Asking other people** is an acceptable option. Recognise your own limits and get help. You should have a telephone list of departments and individual colleagues you can consult. Use your common sense as to:

- Who is the most appropriate person to consult.

- When and how to consult them.

3.17 Also, while you are conducting your information search, remember to **keep the enquirer informed**. ('I'm just calling the production department. I won't be a moment.')

3.18 The only drawback to asking others is where the information is **highly technical**. It may be time-consuming for you to ask the question and get the answer, which may then be difficult for you to understand and even more difficult for you to convey to the enquirer - and you may have to go back with even more questions.

3.19 **Referring the enquirer direct to the expert** is thus a legitimate option.

3.20 There are three ways of doing this.

(a) Directing the enquirer (in person or by phone) to the **appropriate department**, having explained the situation briefly first.

(b) **Calling the appropriate department** to arrange an appointment (immediate or later) for the enquirer.

(c) Taking an enquiry message, with the enquirer's details, so that the appropriate department can prepare a response and telephone the enquirer at a mutually convenient time.

To whom should you give information?

3.21 Whether or not you give **information** about transactions, or even about your organisation's products or services in response to unsolicited queries depends very much upon the nature of the transaction, product and service, and the identity of the caller (who may, or may not, be entitled to the information). The information may or may not be:

(a) Relevant to the enquirer's needs;

(b) Confidential, or sensitive, and therefore not for general dissemination.

3.22 In cases where the transaction/product/service is more limited in its availability or more sensitive in its nature, the organisation may require certain **formal checks** to be carried out to verify an enquirer's **identity** and **eligibility** to receive information.

(a) Some companies operate a policy of replying **only in writing** to requests for information that could be sensitive.

(b) Banks, for example, will not tell you your own bank balance unless you have agreed some **password** known only to you and them in advance.

3.23 **Less formal checks** are carried out all the time, sometimes even unintentionally.

(a) If a known client rings up and asks for certain information about his account and you agree to ring back with the details, you are verifying that the caller was who he said he was simply by ringing the number you have on record.

(b) You may get calls or written requests that your instinct tells you do not ring true - the address may be too suburban for a business-related product, say, or the amount ordered may be improbably large.

(c) You can carry out informal identity checks by looking people up in trade directories or Yellow Pages.

Confidentiality

3.24 The information you give out will also be limited by the principles and procedures of **confidentiality**. You do not expect the staff of your bank to discuss your personal financial circumstances with anybody who happens to walk into the branch.

(a) **Do not discuss the detailed affairs of one client with another**.

(b) If you are asked for the **names of some of your other customers** - for example if a potential customer wants a second opinion on the worth of your products - make sure you get permission from the other customers to use them as **references**.

(c) **Within your organisation use the 'need to know' principle**. If people in other departments do not need to be given all of the information that you possess about a particular client, do not give it to them.

(d) **Be careful about discussing clients with colleagues** who work in the same capacity as you.

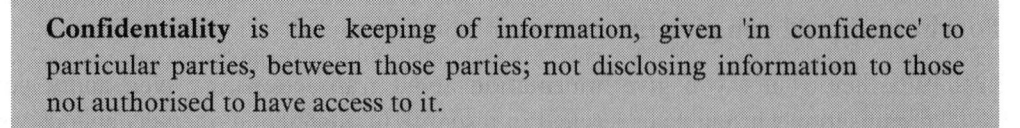

KEY TERM

Confidentiality is the keeping of information, given 'in confidence' to particular parties, between those parties; not disclosing information to those not authorised to have access to it.

3.25 Do not forget that the **affairs of your own organisation are confidential**. Do not gossip about your organisation to clients, or malign your colleagues. There may be some information on one of your customer's files that you would never dream of disclosing to him - a note of an internal meeting discussing whether to continue to do business with him, for example. In many cases it may not be so obvious what you should and should not reveal. If in any doubt refer the matter to your superior.

What if the information is not available?

3.26 Sometimes you will **not be able to provide the information that a customer wants**. This may be for a number of reasons: for example when a new product is

about to be launched and information is not yet available, or if you run out of brochures.

3.27 The lack of information may not be a worry to you, but again you must **appreciate your customer's position**.

(a) **Apologise** that you cannot yet meet his needs. There is no need to grovel, but do not be offhand.

(b) Explain **when** you will be able to supply the information required.

(c) **Keep the customer informed of developments**, especially if there is likely to be a long delay, or if unexpected delays occur.

(d) If possible **provide some alternative**. You might get permission to pass out information that is only available internally as a rule. An old brochure or price list might be more useful than no information at all, so long as you explain that an up-to-date one will be sent as soon as possible (and see that it is sent).

DEVOLVED ASSESSMENT ALERT

It may actually be helpful to you if enquirers leave details of information they require, for you to forward to them later. Such a record of 'expressions of interest' in the products and services of the organisation are (if you keep them accurately) not only useful management information for the organisation: they also qualify as evidence of your competence in Element 23.2!

3.28 Finally, if it is you who first became aware of the non-availability of **information that is regularly sent to customers**, be sure that you do something about it. It may be your responsibility to re-order from the printers or you may need to notify somebody else. If you do not know your organisation's procedure, find out what it is.

Activity 7.7

You have recently started working in the sales office of R Feathertone Ltd, a company which manufactures telephone equipment.

Below is shown a product specification chart detailing the main features of the company's new range of answerphones. This is accompanied by notes (for internal use only) on some of the features. You also have a typed list of nationwide stockists of the old range (not shown) which has many handwritten amendments scrawled on it. All the products are brand new models and brochures are not yet back from the printers.

Product code	Description	Wall Mounting Facility	Digital Voice Prompt	Micro Cassette	Call Screening	Memo Facility	LCD/Digital Display	Remote Facility	Answer Only Option	2-Way Conversation Record	Day/Time Stamp	No. of Memories	Last No. Redial	PABX Compatible	Variable Ringer Volume	On-Hook Dialling	Hands Free Speech	Mute Facility	Ringer On/Off	Call Count	Price
AF 1	Basic		●		●	●						–							●		37.99
AF 2	Basic One	●	●		●	●		●				–									44.50
AF 3	Basic Plus	●	●	●	●	●		●			●	–							●		57.99
AF 4	Standard	●		●	●	●	●	●	●			–							●		69.00
AF 5	Deluxe	●			●	●		●				–							●		89.50
AF 6	Super	●			●	●		●				–							●		109.00
With Telephone																					
AF 7	Basic				●							10	●	●					●	●	49.50
AF 8	Basic One			●	●	●		●				10	●	●	●				●	●	58.50
AF 9	Basic Plus	●		●	●	●		●				10	●	●	●			●	●		69.50
AF 10	Standard		●	●	●	●		●			●	10	●		●				●	●	78.50
AF 11	Deluxe	●		●	●	●		●	●	●		13	●	●	●	●			●	●	89.50
AF 12	Super	●		●	●	●		●	●	●		20	●	●	●	●		●	●	●	109.00
AF 13	Super-deluxe	●	●		●	●	●	●		●	●	32	●	●	●	●	●	●	●	●	179.00

Notes

(a) **Connection**. The unit can only be connected to the exchange line via the new standard British Telecom plug and socket. Premises without this facility must first be converted by a British Telecom engineer.

(b) **Colour**. Units are two shades of the same colour with a darker base, keys and controls. The choices are grey, cream, green, red, blue, yellow.

(c) **Digital voice prompt**. When the unit is called up from another telephone and a special code number is dialled an electronic voice announces the number of messages received and instructs the user on the keys to press to hear the messages, rewind, change the outgoing message and so on.

(d) **Call screening**. If at home when receiving a call, the user can hear the message being left and choose whether or not to answer in person.

(e) **Memo facility.** The user may record a personal message by speaking into a microphone located on the control panel, for example if he wishes to comment on the messages received.

(f) **LCD/Digital display**. When the unit is not in use the display shows the time of day. When a number is being dialled the display shows which keys were pressed.

(g) **Remote facility**. The user can retrieve recorded messages from a remote location by ringing his machine and then pushing the keys for a special code number chosen by the user. More expensive models (Deluxe and above) allow the outgoing message to be re-recorded from a remote location.

(h) **Answer only option**. The unit can be set to answer calls but not record messages if desired (for example, if the user wishes to tell callers to contact him on another number).

(i) **Day/time stamp**. The unit tells you the time and date that messages were received (voice prompt models only).

(j) **PABX Compatible**. The unit can be used as a normal extension where the user operates in a building with its own switchboard. PABX stands for private automatic branch exchange, and allows direct dialling between extensions, call transfer between extensions and so on.

(k)   **Availability**. Stocked by all major department stores, electrical chains and telephone shops. See stockist list for full details.

You have received a number of enquiries which are shown below.

To ___Di Ling___

Date ___8.8.00___   Time ___12.45pm___

WHILE YOU WERE OUT

M ___iss Cook___

of ___Cook, Cook, Stove & Co, Solicitors___

Phone No. ___020-7234 5678___

TELEPHONED	✓	PLEASE CALL	✓
WAS IN TO SEE YOU		WILL CALL BACK	
WANTS TO SEE YOU		**URGENT**	
RETURNED YOUR CALL			

Message _____

_____ Wants answerphone

_____ -pls advise

Operator ___G. Mourning___

BPP
PUBLISHING

Mr L Keye
20 Pipe Street
Washaway
Cornwall

3 August 2000

Dear Sir

Help! I am a plumber and I came home from work tonight to find a message from my wife: 'Gone to Mabel's. Fed up being tied to telephone. Dinner in oven.'

I get plenty of work, mostly emergencies, but I can't afford one of those mobile phones so I advertise my home number and my wife takes the calls. I ring in to ask her where my next job is, but it's not much of a life for her.

Would one of your answerphones be any good? I hear they're quite cheap these days.

Please tell me what I need and where to get one.

Yours

Lee

Sue Parry
Management Consultant
10 Upmarket Way
Maidenhead
Berks MH2 3DW

Tel: 01987 654321

R. Feathertone Ltd
Industrial Estate
Ring's End, Nr Grantham
Lincs
GM2 4BR

4 August 2000

Dear Sir

Re: Answerphone

I should be grateful if you would let me know whether you can supply an answerphone that suits my lifestyle.

My work takes me all over the country and although I am always contactable by telephone I rarely know the number in advance. My present answerphone allows me to call it up and listen to messages received, but I often need to speak to my callers directly as a matter of urgency and obviously I do not always know when to ring my machine. I also receive complaints from my neighbour (whose work requires her to sleep during the day) about the constant noise of my telephone ringing.

If you can solve my problem, money is no object, although I would like to be offered a range of options. (Taupe, incidentally, would be ideal but I can be flexible about colour if need be.)

I look forward to hearing from you.

Yours faithfully

Sue Parry

Ms Sue Parry

Tasks

(a)   Study the product specification chart and notes and answer the following questions.

   (i)   Which models would you recommend to a customer who wanted to spend no more than £90 and needed a unit which was PABX compatible and offered an answer-only option.

   (ii)   Which models would you recommend to a customer who asked for 'as many features as possible for as little money as possible'.

   (iii)   Explain the following features, and give an example of circumstances in which they might be useful.

      (1)   Wall mounting facility
      (2)   Last number redial
      (3)   Hands free speech

BPP PUBLISHING

(b) You are going to return Miss Cook's call. Draft brief notes for your call, listing the questions you will need to ask to find out precisely what she needs. Do not rewrite the chart, but note any features you think may be particularly useful to this customer.

(c) Reply to Mr Keye's letter.

(d) Reply to Ms Parry's letter.

4 THE TELEPHONE

4.1 The telephone is probably the **most used item of office equipment**. There are bound to be many situations in which you find yourself having to communicate via the telephone with internal and external customers. Make sure that you consider the following guidelines before making telephone calls: they should make even the most 'awkward' telephone call much easier, and ensure that you promote a positive image of the department and organisation.

Making telephone calls

4.2 You can prepare quite extensively before you make a call.

(a) **Know what result you are aiming at**. What action or information will satisfy you, where and when must you get them? You might say 'I was just wondering...' to sound tactful, but make sure that you have done all your 'wondering' before you pick up the receiver.

(b) **Know whom you should be talking to**. If you have ever been left hanging on, or passed from extension to extension, until you found someone to deal with you, you will not have enjoyed the experience.

(c) **Know what you want to say, and the order and manner in which you want to say it.**

(i) A **checklist of points**, in logical/persuasive/tactful order, will be an invaluable reminder.

(ii) You might like to give yourself brief **'prompts'** as to tone and approach: 'NB. Sensitive point. Careful.' or 'Agreed at last meeting. Remind.'

(iii) Have all **relevant documents and reference material to hand** (together with your notes). Muttering 'Oh, sorry... hang on a minute... I'll just...' while scrabbling for the filing cabinet wastes time and irritates your listener.

(d) **Make sure you will not be interrupted, distracted or disturbed** once you have dialled.

4.3 Once you are through to the correct number **wait for a greeting and identification** from the answering party. If you are speaking to a switchboard operator or individual other than your 'target', **return the greeting**, introduce yourself by name and organisation, and state whom you wish to speak to (name, department and extension if known). 'Good afternoon, this is Miss Brown of Colours Ltd. I would like to speak to Mr E Black of the Accounts Department, please.' If you are through to your target's secretary, you may be asked to explain the nature of your call: do so **briefly**, and don't be afraid to say politely that it is a personal or confidential matter, if it is.

4.4   If the target recipient of your call is out or unavailable, carry out your strategy of:

(a)   **Speaking to someone else** who might be knowledgeable enough to help you

(b)   **Leaving a message with the secretary, or switchboard operator**. Make it a brief one, but dictate clearly all essential details of who you are, where you can be contacted, and what the main subject of your call was to be (tactfully, since this message will be open); state whether you wish to be called back

(c)   **Arranging to call back at a convenient time**, when it is anticipated that the target will be at his desk/available.

4.5   Once through to your target, remember the cost of the call and the time you are spending on it. Make it as satisfying as possible, in as brief a time as possible, consistent with courtesy.

(a)   **Greet the other person**. Prepare the ground by explaining the context of your call.

(b)   Remember that **the other person cannot see you**, to lip-read, judge your facial expression or see you nod your head. You will have to **speak clearly** so as to be audible, **spell out proper names and figures**, and **use your tone of voice** to convey friendliness, enthusiasm or firmness.

(c)   **Pace your message** so that the other person can refer to files or take notes. Check your own notes as you speak, and make fresh ones of any information you receive.

(d)   You may easily be misheard or misinterpreted over the telephone line, so you will have to **seek constant feedback**. If you are not receiving any signals, ask for some ('Have you got that?', 'Can you read that back?', 'Am I going too fast for you?', 'OK?')

(e)   **Close the call effectively**. Emphasise any action you require, and ask the other person to read back or otherwise confirm that he has understood the gist of your message, and your further expectations if any. Thank him politely for his time, concern or help: you may need his co-operation in the future.

(f)   **Don't slam down the receiver** - even if you are angry this just makes you seem like a petulant child. Don't comment or start talking to somebody else in the room before you have put down the receiver. You could destroy all your hard work if you express your real opinion of the other party while he is still on the line!

4.6   Above all, *never* be in too much of a hurry to say **'please'** and **'thank you'**.

Receiving telephone calls

4.7   As we mentioned previously, when you make a telephone call, you can prepare quite extensively before you make the call. Unfortunately, there is no such advantage when receiving telephone calls! Unless you anticipate receiving a certain call, you should study the following guidelines for receiving telephone calls.

4.8   It is very important that those who answer the telephones in an organisation should be **efficient, courteous** and **helpful**. A voice on the telephone may be the

first or only impression of the organisation that an outsider receives: remember that your smart appearance and elegant office cannot be seen over the telephone, and you will have to create the impression you make with your voice alone.

4.9 If you anticipate receiving calls, keep your **message pad, pen** and **appointments diary** handy, together with a **list of internal extensions**, in case you have to transfer a call.

4.10 If you are on a direct outside line you should always **answer the telephone in a formal manner**: don't get caught saying 'Yes. What?' because you think it might only be from someone in the office. **Greet the caller, identify your organisation, and the department if appropriate**: 'Good morning. Best's Garden Furniture, Accounts Department: can I help you?'

4.11 If the call has been routed through a switchboard, such a greeting (as in the previous paragraph) will already have been given, and you should **identify your department**, and **your own name** and **designation**: 'Accounts Department, John Cake speaking.'

4.12 **Identify and note the caller's name and organisation**. Then listen carefully to his message: it may require instant action or response. If he speaks too quickly, or if you do not catch something or are not sure that you have heard it properly, or if you simply do not understand, do not be shy to say so: a courteous interruption to ask for a repetition or spelling is helpful to the caller, providing feedback, and ensuring that his message is effective.

4.13 **Provide the caller with positive feedback.** Remember that a nod and a smile will go unnoticed: you will have to say: 'Yes, I am sure that will be fine', 'Yes, I have that'.

4.14 **Do not leave callers hanging on unnecessarily**, especially since they are paying for the call. If you do have to transfer them to another extension, leave the phone to refer to a file or make an enquiry on their behalf, keep them informed. They may prefer you to call them back later.

4.15 **Remember to speak clearly and with a certain formality**, and to keep your tone appropriately helpful, courteous and alert. It is all too easy to sound brusque when you intend to sound efficient, and the telephone is not so impersonal that you can afford to be rude with impunity.

4.16 **Co-operate with the caller.** If you can resolve the matter in the course of the call, for example by providing information, do so: you can then close the conversation with a polite word. If there are still matters to be resolved - further action to be taken or information to be sent to the caller by post - make sure that you are both clear as to what is required, what is to be done, and within what deadlines.

Activity 7.8

If you have not yet completed Activity 10.1(b) - or could use some more information about who your organisation's customer base is - now is the time to do the research: **by phone!** Gather the necessary information, make a written plan, and call someone in the marketing department.

(If your target adviser is not available, plan to have him or her call you back - so you can practise receiving calls as well!)

Telephone messages

4.17 During the call, **make concise notes of everything** that has been agreed, offered or requested. **Read these details back to the caller** at the end of the conversation, to make sure that you have got them down accurately. If you are answering a call for someone else, you may have to take a concise message on whatever form of message pad your organisation uses.

4.18 Do **make sure that you have the caller's name, telephone number and address** if you are likely to have to write to him. The ability to contact him again may well be the most important item of information in the message.

4.19 **Message pads**, such as the one below, obviously give you a 'head start'. You don't have to write out over and over again the basic information that in many cases will provide an adequate account of the call: 'returned your call', 'please call', 'will call back'.

4.20 The **name of the operator** (or whoever else takes the message) is vital, in case the recipient of the message has any queries.

4.21 The actual 'message space' on the pad is small - so your summarising and note-taking techniques will be particularly valuable.

To _____	
Date _____ Time _____	

WHILE YOU WERE OUT

M _____

of _____

Phone No. _____

TELEPHONED		PLEASE CALL	
WAS IN TO SEE YOU		WILL CALL BACK	
WANTS TO SEE YOU		**URGENT**	
RETURNED YOUR CALL			

Message _____
_____
_____
_____
_____

Operator _____

BPP PUBLISHING

4.22 When taking telephone messages, it is obviously important that you get down correctly details such as the **name and organisation of the caller**, a contact phone number, and any unfamiliar names or places that come into his message. Unless a name is very obvious, you should ask for it to be spelt out to you letter by letter.

4.23 Pass on a telephone message taken for someone else **immediately**. Act on your notes, or write them into your appointments/forward planning diary or files as soon as possible: actions, memoranda, letters of confirmation and future meetings depend on your keeping the details safe and to hand while they are relevant.

Activity 7.9

The following telephone conversation has just taken place.

PAUL: Accounts department, Paul Phillips speaking.

CALLER: Hello, could I speak to Jennifer please?

PAUL: I'm afraid she's out of the office at the moment, could I take a message?

CALLER: Oh. It's a bit complicated, are you ready? I agreed to meet her on the site in Bracknell at 10.30 on Thursday morning but I've just been speaking to the site manager and he tells me that there won't be an electricity supply from 9 o'clock until 11.30.

PAUL: That was this Thursday?

CALLER: Yes, that's right. Anyway, I think it would be better to see the site either on Thursday afternoon or else we could bring it forward to Wednesday. It all depends how Jennifer is fixed really.

PAUL: OK, I think I've got that. I'll let Jennifer know.

CALLER: Thanks ever so much. Bye

PAUL: Bye.

Required

(a)   Write a message for Paul's colleague, Jennifer.

(b)   Why is this not an effective piece of communication? (Your answer to part (a) should provide you with the answer.)

---

5   COLLABORATING AND NEGOTIATING

5.1 In many ways, **relationships with suppliers** are the same as those with colleagues, customers, visitors and other business contacts. As **interpersonal relationships** they require:

- Rapport and willingness to initiate and develop the relationship
- Cultivation, through regular contact and communication
- Courtesy, as a minimum condition of maintaining the relationship
- The use of influencing skills to achieve one's aims
- Co-operation in achieving the aims of both parties as far as possible
- Integrity and reliability, in order to build trust
- Conflict resolution or management
- Networking, to extend the circle of contact, communication and influence
- The projection of a positive image of oneself and one's organisation.

5.2 As **business relationships,** however, they raise a number of other issues.

   (a) They involve **dealings with other business organisations** which have their own aims and objectives which may or may not be in harmony with yours.

   (b) They involve dealings with **representatives of other business organisations,** who have a dual responsibility to you (as their client) and (primarily) to their employers.

   (c) They are governed by **legal terms and constraints,** expressed in contracts.

   (d) They are subject to **commercial and competitive pressures**: if one party is not satisfied, they can break the relationship.

5.3 We will look briefly at two aspects of business relationships: collaborating and negotiating.

Collaborating

> **KEY TERM**
>
> **Collaboration** simply means 'working with', but is used in the stronger sense of working *jointly* or sharing tasks and responsibility with another party.

5.4 There are **three main elements** to collaborating effectively with other business organisations and their representatives.

   - Contracts
   - Systems and procedures
   - Purpose

Contracts

5.5 Remember, when working with other organisations, it is helpful to exchange a contract, letter or purchase order which:

   - **Documents** in **writing** (even if only to confirm a verbal agreement)

   - **Defines the products/services** to be supplied, and the delivery schedule

   - **Defines the division of responsibility** between the parties

   - Confirms the negotiated **terms and conditions for payment**

5.6 A contract may set out **express terms,** or clearly stated terms. A contract also has **implied terms,** which are 'understood' from the context of the business relationship.

Activity 7.10

Get hold of a copy of the Terms and Conditions of any service supplier you may do business with. (Check the back of quotation stationery and the bottom of invoices. Use your research skills.) Note the main issues covered by contract terms and identify areas where your procedures and practices may need adjusting (if any) to comply more securely.

Systems and procedures

5.7 The procedures to be followed will be dictated by the particular task or project in hand. Be aware that simply following recommended procedures correctly and efficiently is a major element in working smoothly and successfully with other organisations, who have usually developed ways of working for a reason!

5.8 In general, however, a **systematic approach** to collaboration should include the following.

(a) **Clear and specific briefing on requirements**. Be clear what you want suppliers/collaborators to do for you. Objectives, schedules, budgets and job specifications make everyone's job easier.

(b) **Joint planning**. The brief sets out what you want to achieve: how you get there (together) is best decided collaboratively, since the other party has input to offer, and their own aims, procedures and constraints to take into account. Define clearly the scope and limit of everyone's activity, and establish how to implement any recommendations agreed on.

(c) **Negotiation of terms.** (This will be discussed in more detail below.)

(d) **Sharing of information and resources**. Helping others to help you requires the provision or availability of any information, materials and other resources they may require. (A designer working on the Annual Report and Accounts, for example, may require catalogues, existing corporate literature, corporate identity specifications, contacts with the company's printers and so on.)

(e) **On-going monitoring, checking and approval** of work at each stage (especially of complex projects). If this is not built into the procedure, initiate it yourself.

(f) **Exchanging feedback**. Developing on-going relationships requires mutual adjustment. Regular feedback meetings allow both parties to reinforce positive aspects, identify and solve problems and celebrate collaborative successes. Balance constructive criticism and complaints.

(g) **Paying debts.** Nothing sours a commercial relationship like non-payment or persistent late payment. Accounts departments may resist for cash-flow reasons, but be prepared to champion legitimate demands.

Purpose

5.9 Here, we are referring to more than the job specification or task objectives which govern the activity of a relationship. If you want to develop an effective collaboration, consider what it is for: what is the purpose of collaborating rather than doing the work yourself?

5.10 Your purpose in retaining financial, PR, legal, human resource or other consultancy services is to take advantage of the expertise, experience, contacts, facilities and synergy they offer. Your organisation is paying for specialist skills and objectivity and wide experience. It is only sensible to use them!

Negotiating

5.11 **Negotiating** is one of the key ways in which you can make your purchasing budget go further!

> ### KEY TERM
>
> **Negotiation** is, essentially, a **bargaining process**, through which commitments and compromises are reached, using the relative power of both parties.

5.12 The aim of negotiating is *not* to get the best position for yourself or your organisation at the expense of the other party (a **win-lose outcome**). This can cause resentment, under-motivated performance by the 'losing' collaborator, or even the breaking of the relationship.

5.13 Remember the 'win-win' approach (Chapter 5)? A basic **'win-win' approach to negotiating** is as follows.

Step 1	Map out, in advance, what the needs and fears of both parties are. This outlines the psychological and practical territory.
Step 2	**Define your desired outcome** and estimate the worst, realistic and best case scenarios. ('If I can pay £500, it would be ideal, but I'd settle for £600. Above £700, it's just not worth my while.') Start with the best case and leave room to fall back to the realistic case. Keep your goal in sight.
Step 3	**Look for mutual or trade-off benefits.** How might you both gain (for example, by getting a higher discount in return for prompt or direct-debit payment). What might be cheap for you to give that would be valuable for the other party to receive or vice versa?
Step 4	**Spell out the positive benefits** to the other party and support them in saying 'yes' to your proposals by making it as easy as possible. (Offer to supply information or help with follow-up tasks, for example.) Emphasise areas of agreement and common ground.
Step 5	**Overcome negativity** by asking questions such as: • **'What will make it work for you?'** • **'What would it take to make this possible?'**
Step 6	**Overcome side-tracks** by asking questions such as: 'How is this going to get us where we need/want to go?'
Step 7	**Be hard on the issue/problem but soft on the person.** This is not personal competition or antagonism: work together on problem solving (eg by using flip chart or paper to make shared notes). Show that you have heard the other person (by summarising their argument) before responding with your counter argument.
Step 8	**Be flexible.** A 'take it or leave it' approach breaks relationships. (However, saying 'no' repeatedly to sales people is a good way of finding out just how far below the list price they are prepared to go!) Make and invite, reasonable counter offers.
Step 9	**Be culturally sensitive.** Some markets thrive on 'haggling'. Some cultures engage in a lot of movement up and down the bargaining scale (eg Asian and Middle Eastern), while others do their homework and fix their prices.

Step 10	Take notes, so the accuracy of everyone's recollection of what was proposed and agreed can be checked.
Step 11	Summarise and confirm the details of your agreements to both parties (by memo, letter, contract) and acknowledge a mutually positive outcome.

5.14 **Experience, knowledge** and **expertise** count in negotiation: they add up to bargaining power, which is important even in a win-win approach. If there is someone in your department who has experience in a particular field (such as print or equipment buying), be prepared to let them handle negotiations for you.

Activity 7.11

Get together with fellow students (or friends) in pairs or teams to prepare and role-play a negotiation.

Scenario:

You want to go on holiday with the whole family to a coastal resort this summer. Your (role-play) partner wants to have some quiet time at home redecorating the bathroom, knowing that the two teenage (role-play) kids are keen to spend time with friends. These projects are important to both (or all four) of you. Negotiate! If you really can't find role-play partners, make notes on the possible strategies, win-win potential, and best-realistic-worst positions for all participants.

Key learning points

- **External customers** include customers/clients/consumers, suppliers and external agencies.

- Promoting a positive image of your department or organisation involves: awareness that you are a representative; integrity; professionalism; discretion; and good news spreading.

- Whatever type of visitor you are receiving, you should always be **polite, courteous** and display **good manners**.

- You may receive **routine** or **non-routine** enquires in your place of work; it is important that you are able to deal with them in the proper manner. Make sure that you are familiar with the guidelines covered in this chapter. Always use your common sense when dealing with visitors.

- **Confidentiality** should always be maintained where considered necessary. The affairs of your own organisation and its clients are confidential and should not be disclosed to others unless the circumstances are appropriate.

- The **telephone** is a vital piece of business equipment for dealing with people from outside the organisation. Make sure you familiarise yourself with the guidelines for **receiving and making calls** given in this chapter.

- Collaborative working with suppliers includes:

  - briefing
  - joint planning
  - negotiation of terms
  - sharing of information and resources
  - monitoring, checking and approval
  - feedback and
  - payment

- Negotiating is a bargaining process through which commitments and compromises are reached which are acceptable (and ideally beneficial) to both parties.

Quick quiz

1   List three dimensions of 'professionalism'.

2   What sort of information does a visitors' signing-in book usually record?

3   What are the guidelines that should be followed when dealing with external visitors?

4   What can you do in order to create a good impression when greeting visitors?

5   What can you do to protect the confidentiality of client details?

6   What aspects of a telephone call can you plan in advance?

7   What three factors determine collaborative working with suppliers?

8   Outline a 'win-win' approach to negotiating.

Answers to quick quiz

1   Courtesy, expertise, efficiency.

2   • Their name
    • The name and department of the person they have come to see
    • The purpose of their visit

3   See Paragraphs 2.5 - 2.6 for complete list.

4   Smile, make eye contact and shake hands with your visitor.

5   Don't discuss clients with other clients or third parties (external or internal). Use the 'need to know' principal. Beware casual gossip.

6   The purpose and results aimed for; whom you want/need to talk to; what you want to say and how; uninterrupted privacy to make the call.

7   Contracts; systems and procedures; purpose.

8   See paragraph 5.13 for a full outline.

8 Information

This chapter contains

1   Information in organisations

2   Data protection

3   Copyright

Learning objectives

On completion of this chapter you will be able to:

- Follow confidentiality and data protection requirements
- Consider the different types of documentation to be dealt with
- Outline the sources and provisions of relevant legislation

Performance criteria

(1)   New documentation and records and put into the filing system in line with organisational procedures

(2)   Item movements are monitored and recorded where necessary

(3)   Documentation and records are kept according to organisational and legal requirement

(4)   Out of date information is dealt with in accordance with organisational procedures

(5)   Opportunities for improving filing systems are identified and brought to the attention of the appropriate person

Range statement

1   **Documentation:** incoming correspondence; copies of outgoing correspondence; financial records

2   **System:** manual; computerised

3   **Legal requirements:** document retention; confidentiality

---

Knowledge and understanding

- Relevant legislation: copyright; data protection; equal opportunities (Element 23.2)

- The different types of documentation: incoming correspondence; copies of outgoing correspondence; financial records (Element 23.3)

- Sources of legal requirements: data protection; companies act (Element 23.3)

- Methods of classifying information: alphabetical, numerical, alphanumerical (Element 23.3)

- Sorting, handling and storing information (Element 23.3)

- The purpose of storing and retaining documents (Element 23.3)

- Organisational document retention policy (Element 23.3)

1 INFORMATION IN ORGANISATIONS

What is information?

KEY TERMS

- **Information** is anything that is communicated. It is made up of data - facts and figures and so on which are processed so that they are meaningful to the person who receives them.

- **Data** is a 'scientific' term for facts, figures, information and processing. Data are the raw materials for data processing.

1.1 It is important that you are able to distinguish clearly between these two terms. We shall demonstrate the distinction between these two terms by considering the following figures, which are examples of data.

1729468

1948327

2001452

Now here are two ways in which those (meaningless) figures can become information.

The following accounts are in excess of their credit limits:

Account no.

1729468
1948327
2001452

Fixed assets	£
Buildings	1,729,468
Plant and machinery	1,948,327
Fixtures and fittings	2,001,452
	5,679,247

1.2 **Information is the life blood of an organisation**, flowing through it and prompting actions and decisions: without information, no-one in an organisation could take a single effective action. As a simple example, giving an order to a subordinate is a flow of information: the manager or supervisor gathers data about a problem, 'processes' it to decide what needs to be done and then communicates his or her decision as an order to a subordinate.

Who needs information - and for what?

1.3 There is a constant **demand for information within the organisation**, particularly from managers, who may request information of the following kinds.

   (a) **Records of past and current transactions**, which must be stored pending confirmation, or for later analysis.

   (b) **Information about past trends and current operations** on which to base planning and decision-making. For example, the past rate at which raw materials were consumed by a production process would dictate the frequency and amount of stock orders in the future.

   (c) **Routine transaction information** on which to base current operations and decisions (for example, the information on a customer order dictates how many items, and of what sort, must be supplied from stock, and what delivery and payment arrangements should be made).

   (d) **Information about performance** to compare with plans, budgets and forecasts for the purposes of control (checking for and correcting errors and shortcomings).

1.4 **People and groups outside the organisation** who are entitled to information, include the following.

   (a) **Others involved in the business's transactions**: customers, suppliers, or sub-contractors, who require instructions, requests, contracts and so on.

   (b) Parties interested in the financial performance of the organisation: the owners (share-holders), **investors** and **creditors** (those to whom the firm owes money, such as banks).

   (c) **Outside agencies requiring information for surveys, or for their own activities**. The Department of Trade and Industry requires company accounts to be filed; returns have to be made to the Inland Revenue for the purposes of assessing tax and National Insurance contributions; Value Added Tax (VAT) is administered by the Excise authorities; and so on.

   (d) **Regulatory bodies**. Non-financial information has to be supplied on working practices to the Health and Safety Executive; on employees to the Training Commission and its agencies; on new building works to local government planning departments; and so on.

1.5 Information **exchanged on a more specific personal or interpersonal level** may include the following.

   (a) **Details relevant to enquiries or complaints** from clients, customers, colleagues or other parties, including introductions, explanations, apologies and answers to questions.

   (b) **Information supplied to the organisation about an employee:**

> • Which he supplies about himself in an interview, on a job application form or curriculum vitae; and
>
> • For the organisation's records.

(c) **Information supplied to employees about the organisation**, its activities and methods, and about their own place in the system. For example, an 'induction' course or training manual; a memorandum sent to members of staff with instructions, warnings, or encouragement; a staff meeting to discuss 'how things are going'.

1.6 In an Accounts Department, the main types of information which therefore require handling and storage (as discussed in Chapter 9) are as follows.

(a) **Incoming correspondence:** letters, e-mails, memos, reports and other documents directed from people outside the organisation and department to those within it. These need to be stored and managed for the purposes of action (reply, transaction), analysis, confirmation and so on.

(b) **Outgoing correspondence:** similar messages generated by the department and flowing outwards. Copies of these need to be stored and managed as evidence and confirmation of what has been sent.

(c) **Financial records** prepared or received in the course of transactions and reporting. These require storage and management for the purposes of planning and control, and to comply with the accountability requirements of external agencies (eg the DTI, the Inland Revenue, Customs and Excise) and legislation (eg the Companies Acts).

2 DATA PROTECTION

General confidentiality

2.1 Information flows through the organisation - but to **whom**, precisely, should it flow? In deciding who is an '**appropriate person**' to receive any given piece of information, you will need to consider the following matters.

Matter to consider	Reason
Who has asked for it, and what their **authority** within the organisation is	If your supervisor asks for information, you will need a good reason *not* to give it to her - such as it being marked 'strictly private' or 'for the Managing Director's eyes only'. If the receptionist asks for information, you will want to consider whether it is relevant to his area of authority: say, affecting security or customer service procedures.
Whether the information is classified in any way	'Sensitive' information will often be clearly identified as being 'confidential' or 'private' or 'limited access' or 'for authorised individuals only'. (If you ever come across such files, take the opportunity to practise working out who the authorised recipients of the information would be.)
Whether the information is personal and private	Sharing it would infringe someone else's privacy (or your own).

Matter to consider	Reason
Whether the information could be used for purposes detrimental to the organisation's business or personnel	We've already mentioned (in Chapter 2) the need not to disclose security procedures, legal dealings and new product plans, for example, but you might like to think about other categories of information that could be detrimental.

2.2 There may be established guidelines on any or all of the above in your organisation: now is the time to check! **Organisational policy** must be followed in this area.

Activity 8.1

Would you give the following items of information to the following people, if asked to do so? (Briefly explain why you would or would not, or what you would do.)

(a) The company's security guard asks for details of the visitors expected by your department that week.

(b) The company's security guard (a 'casual' worker, whom you do not know) asks for the home addresses of several people in your department.

(c) The Human Resources Manager asks you for details of how many (a) sick days, (b) absences and (c) late arrivals have occurred in your department in the last month.

(d) Your supervisor asks you for details of the latest Research and Development expenditure on new products.

(e) A caller, saying she is a financial journalist, asks you for details of the latest Research and Development expenditure on new products.

(f) A trade union representative asks you for any projections on staff numbers for the following year, with particular reference to any changes in labour requirements.

The Data Protection Act 1998

2.3 Especially with the advent of computer records systems, fears have arisen with regard to:

- Access to personal information by unauthorised parties

- The likelihood that an individual could be harmed by the existence of computerised data about him or her which was inaccurate or misleading, and which could be transferred to unauthorised third parties at high speed and little cost

- The possibility that personal information could be used for purposes other than those for which it was requested and disclosed.

The Data Protection Acts (first in 1984, replaced in 1998) address these concerns.

2.4 The legislation is an attempt to afford some measure of protection to the individual. It covers data about **individuals** – not corporate bodies – and data which are processed **mechanically** (which includes any 'equipment operated automatically in response to the instructions given for that purpose', not just computers) and **manually** (a new development in the 1998 Act) – as long as the

manually created records can be systematically used to access data about the individual.

KEY TERMS

Personal data are information about a living individual, including facts and expressions of opinion about him or her. Data about other organisations are not personal, unless they contain data about their members. The individual must be identifiable from the data, whether by name, or by code number (say, an employment number).

Data controllers (formally known as data users) are organisations or individuals who control the contents of files of personal data and the use of personal data which are processed (or intended to be processed) automatically.

2.5 Data controllers and computer bureaux have to register with the Data Protection Commissioner. Data controllers must limit the use of personal data to the uses which are registered, and must abide by Data Protection Principles (discussed below).

2.6 The 1998 Act establishes the following rights for data subjects.

(a) A data subject may seek compensation through the courts for damage and any associated distress caused by:

(i) the loss, destruction or unauthorised disclosure of data about himself or herself; or by

(ii) inaccurate data about himself or herself.

(b) A data subject may apply to the courts or to the Registrar for inaccurate data to be put right or even wiped off the file.

(c) A data subject may obtain access to personal data of which he or she is the subject.

(d) A data subject is entitled to know the purposes for which data is collected and processed, the recipients to whom it may be disclosed and (in some cases) the source of the data.

Data Protection Principles

(1) The information to be contained in personal data shall be obtained, and personal data shall be processed, fairly and lawfully. (In particular, information must not be obtained by deception.)

(2) Personal data shall be held only for one or more specified (registered) and lawful purposes.

(3) Personal data shall be adequate, relevant and not excessive in relation to its purpose or purposes.

(4) Personal data shall be accurate and, where necessary, kept up to date. ('Accurate' means correct and not misleading as to any matter of *fact*. An *opinion* cannot be challenged.)

(5) Personal data shall not be kept for longer than is necessary for its purpose or purposes.

> (6) An individual shall be entitled:
>
>   (i) to be informed by any data controller whether he/she holds personal data of which that individual is the subject;
>
>   (ii) to be informed of the purpose or purposes for which personal data is held;
>
>   (iii) to have access to any such data held by a data controller; and
>
>   (iv) where appropriate, to have such data corrected or erased.
>
> (7) Appropriate security measures shall be taken against unauthorised access to, or alteration, disclosure or destruction of, personal data and against accidental loss or destruction of personal data. The prime responsibility for creating and putting into practice a security policy rests with the data controller.
>
> (8) Data may not be exported outside the European Economic Area, except to countries where the rights of data subjects can be adequately protected.

2.7 There are some important **exemptions** from the Acts.

(a) **Unconditional exemptions**: personal data which are essential to national security, required to be made public by law, or concerned only with the data user's personal, family or household affairs;

(b) **Conditional exemptions**, including:

    (i) personal data held for payroll and pensions;

    (ii) data held by unincorporated members' clubs, relating only to club members; and

    (iii) data held only for distribution of articles or information to the data subjects (say, for mailshot advertising) and consisting only of their names and addresses or other particulars necessary for the distribution.

(c) **Exemptions from the 'subject access' provisions only**, including: data held for the prevention or detection of crime, or assessment or collection of tax; data to which legal professional privilege could be claimed (for example, that held by a solicitor); data held solely for statistical or research purposes.

(d) A **special exemption for word processing operations** performed only for the purpose of preparing the text of documents. If a manager writes reports on his employees for disclosure to third parties using his computer as a word processor, he will not as a result become a data user. If, however, he intends to use the stored data as a source of information about the individual and can extract the information automatically, he must register as a data user.

2.8 **The organisation will need to appoint a Data Protection Co-ordinator.** He/she will arrange registration and set up systems: to monitor compliance with the Principles; meet subject access requirements; and alert him/her to any changes in the organisation which may require amendment in the registered entry. The entry should be amended whenever there is a change in the nature or purpose of data being held and used. The organisation's staff should be informed of the Acts' implications and their rights as data subjects, as well as their duties as data users (if they work with computers).

Activity 8.2

Are the following examples permissible under the Acts, or not?

(a)   You demand your right to access any personal data held by the Inland Revenue on your tax affairs.

(b)   Your personnel file contains an appraisal report by your supervisor which states: 'In my opinion, [your name] appears to display a negative attitude towards supervision, which may account for recent disciplinary proceedings?' You do not, in fact, have a negative attitude towards supervision: the disciplinary proceedings were caused by factors outside your control. You demand compensation for loss caused to you (since you were not promoted, as expected, following appraisal) as a result of this inaccurate data.

(c)   You discover that your employee record contains a mention of a conviction for drink-driving – which you have never had. You had wondered why you were always refused access to the 'pool' car at work. You claim compensation for the loss caused as a result of this inaccurate data, and ask for it to be wiped from the file.

(d)   The Accounts Manager has compiled a recruitment file on a candidate for the position of his assistant. He hired a private investigation agency to search her home, access her bank records and tap her phone (all without her knowledge) in an effort to vet her character and circumstances, in the interest of the firm's security. The report is held on your database.

The Criminal Justice and Public Order Act 1994

2.9   This Act creates new offences in the field of data protection by amending Section 5 of the Data Protection Act 1984. The new offences are:

- Procuring the disclosure of computer-held information
- Selling computer-held information
- Offering to sell computer-held information.

This is relevant to accounts, because personal financial/taxation information could be quite valuable to other organisations for the purposes of credit control, product marketing and so on.

Data security measures

2.10   To refresh your memory of data security measures, see Chapter 2, paragraph 4.4.

3   COPYRIGHT

What is copyright law?

3.1   Copyright law is a highly specialised subject. In this section we shall therefore have a brief look at those parts which are of general interest, and any parts which could be considered useful knowledge in your day-to-day office work.

KEY TERM

The basic idea of **copyright** is that **the individual has an exclusive right to use his own work, and also has a right to stop others from exploiting that work.**

3.2 The Copyright, Designs and Patents Act 1988 covers the following types of 'work'.

- Original 'literary' works, which means books of all kinds (including this one that you are reading at the moment), short stories, poems, words of songs, articles and letters

- Dramatic works (plays, operas, etc)

- Musical works

- Artistic works such as paintings, drawings, photographs, pottery

- Sound recordings, films, broadcasts and cable programmes

- Computer programs

Copyright generally applies for a period of **70 years**.

3.3 **Copyright protection covers the form of an idea,** not the idea itself. For example, if you go on a course and pick up some new ideas from the lecturer about organising yourself at work, the lecturer cannot sue you for repeating those ideas to your colleagues. However, if the lecturer writes his/her ideas down in a book, the written version is protected by copyright and cannot be copied without his/her permission.

3.4 **There is no need to register copyright with any third party agency** (unlike patents). Where there is a strong likelihood that other people will try to exploit your work it is usual to mark it with the **international copyright symbol** © (see page (ii) of this book). This symbol warns other people that you are aware of your rights, that you will seek to protect them and that your permission is required for any commercial use of your work.

Photocopying

3.5 You can normally photocopy a few pages of someone else's work for **research** (either commercial or non-commercial) or **private study**. This is subject to the notion of '**fair dealing**'. It is not considered fair, for example, to make a copy of a *whole* book, or to copy extracts from a book to circulate to every member of a class of pupils. The use of photocopying for educational purposes is limited to 1% of a work in every three months, unless a licensing agreement has been entered into.

3.6 The author of this book, for example, photocopied a few pages of her colleague's copy of Kluwer's *Business Law Handbook* as an information source for this section. This was not an infringement of copyright because it was done for the purpose of commercial research.

Letters and other works written by you

3.7 If you write a **private** letter, you own the copyright in it. The person you send the letter to is not entitled to publish it without your permission (unless you write to somebody that normally publishes reader's letters, like a newspaper).

3.8 If you write a letter, a memo, a report or whatever in the course of your job you have created the letter for your employer, and **your employer owns the copyright**. The same applies to anything else you produce at work, unless you have an agreement to the contrary.

Activity 8.3

Does the law of copyright affect *you*? If so, in what ways?

Key learning points

- Information flow in an organisation includes:

    ○ Records of past and current transactions
    ○ Information about past trends and current operations
    ○ Routine transaction information
    ○ Information about performance/results

- Three basic types of documentation to be handled include:

    ○ Incoming correspondence
    ○ Outgoing correspondence
    ○ Financial records

- Care must be taken to ensure the confidentiality and security of information, and compliance with the Data Protection Acts and Criminal Justice and Public Order Act.

- Copyright law protects the rights of ownership of authors/creators of literary and dramatic works, musical and artistic works, broadcasts and computer programmes. There are constraints on what material can legally be reproduced without permission.

Quick quiz

1   What external agencies are entitled to information from the organisation?

2   What should you consider when deciding whether it is appropriate to pass on information?

3   What rights do data subjects have under the Data Protection Act 1984?

4   What is the copyright symbol, and what warning does it carry?

Answers to quick quiz

1   Other parties to transactions; parties interested in the financial performance of the organisation; outside agencies requiring information for their own activities; regulatory bodies.

2   Their authority to ask for and receive it; the classification or confidentiality of the information; the privacy of the subject of the information; the interests of the organisation's business and personnel.

3   Right to compensation for damages and distress caused by loss or inaccurate data; right to have inaccurate data corrected or removed; access to personal data.

4   ©. You are aware of your rights and will seek to protect them, and your permission must be sought for any commercial use of your work.

9 *Information storage and retrieval*

This chapter contains

1   Filing systems

2   Classifying, indexing and cross-referencing information

3   Storing documents securely

4   Creating, updating, and retaining files

5   Recording item movements

6   Computerised systems

Learning objectives

On completion of this chapter you will be able to:

- Put new information into the storage system, following organisational procedures

- Monitor record item movements where necssary

- Keep documents and records according to organisational and legal requirements

- Deal with out of date information in accordance with organisational procedures

- Identify opportunities to improve filing systems, and bring them to the attention of the appropriate person

- Outline methods of information classification

- Outline methods of sorting, handling and storing information

- Understand the purpose of storing and retaining documents

- Outline the organisation's document retention policy

Performance criteria

(1) New documentation and records and put into the filing system in line with organisational procedures

(2) Item movements are monitored and recorded where necessary

(3) Documentation and records are kept according to organisational and legal requirement

(4) Out of date information is dealt with in accordance with organisational procedures

(5) Opportunities for improving filing systems are identified and brought to the attention of the appropriate person

Range statement

1 **Documentation:** incoming correspondence; copies of outgoing correspondence; financial records

2 **System:** manual; computerised

3 **Legal requirements:** document retention; confidentiality

Knowledge and understanding

- Relevant legislation: copyright; data protection; equal opportunities (Element 23.2)

- The different types of documentation: incoming correspondence; copies of outgoing correspondence; financial records (Element 23.3)

- Sources of legal requirements: data protection; companies act (Element 23.3)

- Methods of classifying information: alphabetical, numerical, alphanumerical (Element 23.3)

- Sorting, handling and storing information (Element 23.3)

- The purpose of storing and retaining documents (Element 23.3)

- Organisational document retention policy (Element 23.3)

1 FILING SYSTEMS

1.1 The information source that you will use most frequently in practice is the paperwork generated by the activities of your own organisation. This is held in **files** and so we are now going to look at the characteristics of a **filing system**, and at how files are organised and stored.

1.2 This chapter should help you to deal with files in practice - getting hold of them, finding documents within them, putting new documents into them, opening new files, keeping track of files, and knowing when to thin them out or throw them away. We discuss **manual filing systems** first, but many of the principles of data storage and retrieval apply to computer documents as well as physical documents.

Information flow

1.3 Filing is an integral part of the process of **creating information** that will lead to an activity or decision of some kind. Creating and using information is not just a matter of processing input data to create output information (as outlined in Chapter 8). Other things happen in the information-creating process.

(a) **Copies of information** are made: documents are duplicated so that everyone who needs a copy gets one.

(b) Information has to be **sent to the people who need it**, and it has to be properly received by them.

(c) Not all information is needed straight away. Or if it is, it might be needed again later, for reference. This means that information has to be **filed away** somewhere, for a time that might range from a very brief period to years. The same item of information might be stored in several different files, once by each person or group who will want to use it again some time.

(d) Information on file will be needed again, sooner or later.

> **KEY TERM**
>
> **Information retrieval** is the term used to describe getting information out of file for use in further data processing.

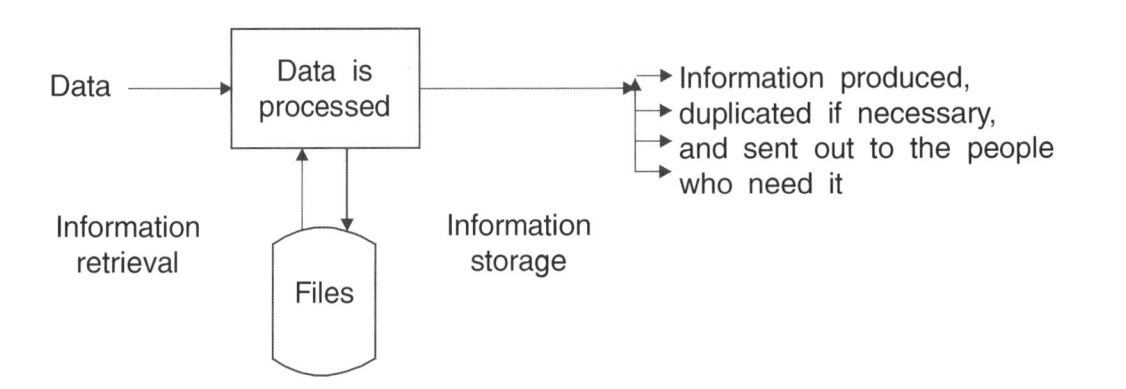

The features of a filing system

1.4 Information for business users takes many forms. Whatever form documents and recorded information take, if they are to be of any use, they must be maintained in such a way that:

(a) **Authorised people** (and only authorised people) can get to the information they require quickly and easily

(b) Information can be **added, updated and outdated** as necessary

(c) Information is **safe from fire, loss or handling damage** for as long as it is required (but not necessarily for ever)

(d) Accessibility, flexibility and security are achieved as **cheaply** as possible

Files

> **KEY TERM**
>
> A **file** is a collection of data records with similar characteristics.

1.5 **Examples of files**

- A sales or purchase ledger
- A cash book
- A price list
- A collection of letters, memos and other papers all relating to the same matter, usually kept within a single folder
- A collection of data records or documents in an electronic 'file' on computer disk or in a computer database

Activity 9.1

Apart from these basic records - grouped items of information - what other items of information might pass through organisations needing to be kept track of? Give at least five examples.

What makes a good filing system?

1.6 A **filing system** should:

- Contain all the information that users might want
- Be classified and indexed in such as way as to make it easy to find information quickly
- Be suited to the people who will use it
- Be reliable and secure
- Be flexible enough to allow for expansion
- Be cost-effective to install and maintain - there is no point spending more to hold information on file than the information is actually worth
- Allow users to retrieve information within an acceptable period of time

Activity 9.2

Your organisation has just received the following letter. List the details that are likely to be used when deciding where it should be filed. What other department would you send a copy of the letter to?

SANDIMANS LTD

72 High Street, Epsom

Surrey EP12 4AB

Your reference: Z/0335/MJD
Our reference: BRC/1249/871

Mr G Latchmore
Purchasing Department
Lightfoot & Co
7 West Broughton St
LONDON W12 9LM

Dear Mr Latchmore

Stationery supplies

I refer to your letter of 11 April 1996.

I am afraid that we are still unable to trace receipt of your payment of £473.20 in settlement of our invoice number 147829. I should be grateful if you would look into this and issue a fresh cheque if necessary.

Your sincerely

Mandy Sands

Mandy Sands

1.7 So, with all of this information floating around, how are we going to locate a particular item of information? We need to make sure that our information is held in an organised fashion, and that we have procedures in place which enable us to find what we are looking for quickly and easily. The next section of this chapter considers the ways in which we can track down the information that we are looking for.

2 CLASSIFYING, INDEXING AND CROSS-REFERENCING INFORMATION

Classifying information

2.1 When information is filed, it has to be filed in such a way that its **users know where it is and how to retrieve it** later when it is needed. This means having different files for different types of information, and then **holding each file in a particular order.** Information in an individual file might be divided into categories and then held in a particular order within each category.

> **KEY TERM**
>
> **Classification** is the process of grouping related items of information together into categories that reflect the relationship between them.

BPP PUBLISHING

2.2   **Ways in which information can be grouped together, or classified**

(a)   By **name** (for example correspondence relating to a particular person or company).

(b)   By **geography** (for example all documents relating to a particular country, area or city).

(c)   By **subject matter** (for example all documents relating to a particular contract, transaction or type of problem).

(d)   By **date** (for example all invoices for a certain month or year).

(e)   By **department** (for example profits or costs for each department or employees of each department).

2.3   Once broad classifications are established, the material can be **put into a sequence** which will make individual items easier to retrieve. Again there are various systems for arranging files.

(a)   **Alphabetical order** - for example customers listed in name order.

(b)   **Numerical order** - for example invoices listed in numerical order of invoice numbers.

(c)   **Alpha-numerical** (A1, A2, A3, B1, B2 and so on).

(d)   **Chronological order** - for example letters within a subject file listed by the date they were written.

2.4   These ways of subdividing and arranging data in a logical way within suitable categories make it possible to store, find and also **index** or **cross-reference** information efficiently (as we will discuss later in this section).

2.5   We shall now have a look at some of these systems for arranging information.

Alphabetical classification

2.6   The most common means of classification is **alphabetical**. In an alphabetical name system, items are filed according to the first and then each following letter of a person's or company's name (for example in the phone book). This sounds simple enough, and indeed it is most of the time, but there are some rules which must be followed .

2.7   The system works by **surname**. The hyphen is ignored in double-barrelled names. When surnames are the same, initials or first names are taken into account. All of this is illustrated below.

Dawson
Ullyott
Vivian
Watkins
Williams
Williams
Williamson
Winters, Douglas
Winters, George

2.8   **Initials.** Names made up of initials may come before whole-word names.

PBAB Parties Ltd
Party Time Ltd

2.9   **Prefixes** are included as part of the surname.

De Beauvoir
Le Bon
McVitee
Von Richthofen

2.10   Mc, Mac etc are all treated as if they were Mac, so:

McGraw
MacLaverty

and St is usually treated as Saint, so:

St Angela's Convent
Saint George's Chapel.

2.11   **Titles and common words.** Words such as 'Mr', 'Mrs', 'Sir', 'The', 'A' are ignored for filing purposes (or most names would be under M or T!) while departments, ministries, offices, local authorities and so on are filed under the key part of their name:

Stanwick, B (Mrs)	Bromley, London Borough of
Stock Exchange (The)	Fair Trading, Department of
Trend, N U (Prof)	Foreign Office
Finance, Ministry of	

2.12   **Businesses** with names like 'Phillip Smith Ltd', 'Frank Tilsley & Son' etc are sometimes listed under the first letter of the surname (as usual) but perhaps more often under the first letter of the whole name (P and F in the examples given).

2.13   **Numbers** which appear as names may also count as if they were spelled out as words:

84 Charing Cross Road (under 'E' for Eighty)
2001: A Space Odyssey (under 'T' for Two)
3i plc (under 'T' for Three).

2.14   You will find things arranged differently in some cases. Rules do vary from system to system. **Get to know the ones you have to work with in your organisation.**

2.15   The **alphabetical name system** is used, for example, in files of clients or customers, students, employees or members and also for index cards and cross-referencing (which we will come to a bit later). It is a simple to use and easily expandable system: there is a 'right' place for files, so they can simply be taken out or slotted in as necessary.

Numerical classification

2.16 **Numerical sequence** is natural where standard documents are concerned. Invoices, for example, are numbered: if one needs to be checked, the number need only be established (quoted by the enquirer, or looked up in the customer account perhaps) and can be easily found. This is known as a **numerical-sequential** system.

2.17 Numerical classification is very **flexible**. Unlike the alphabetical method, you do not have to decide how much filing space to allocate to each letter, wasting space if you are too generous and having to shuffle the whole system along if you are too 'mean'. With numerical order, you simply give a new file the next number and position in the system.

2.18 On the other hand, numbers may not be very meaningful in isolation. A strict **alphabetical index** also has to be kept, and also a **numerical file list** or **accession register**, in order to establish the file number to look for. It also means that there is little room for subdivisions for easier identification and retrieval, although blocks of numbers can be allotted to different departments, say.

Files   **Index**

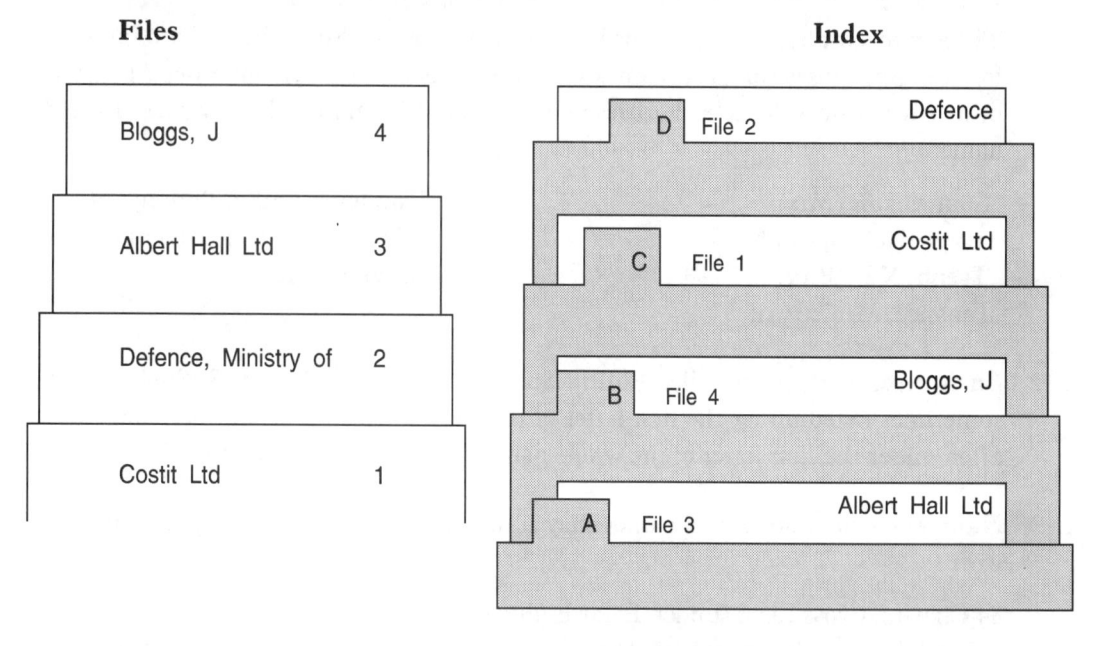

2.19 EXAMPLE: FILING

Numbers can be given a meaning to a limited extent. For example one of the leading UK Building Societies has account numbers constructed from three parts. A number in the form 7 - 666 - 55555 would indicate that this customer has a type 7 account (which pays such and such per cent interest and allows withdrawals with 60 days notice, say), that the account was opened at branch 666 (perhaps branches in the 600 range are in the Manchester region), and that it was account number 55555 opened at that branch, this being the number uniquely identifiable with a named customer. This type of coding is generally used in computer systems.

Alpha-numeric classification

2.20 In an **alpha-numeric system** files are given a reference consisting of **letters** and **numbers**. For example a letter received from Mr Blotson about the purchase of a flat in Mayfair might be given the reference BLO/8745/97/1. The system uses the first three letters of the correspondent's name and a number to distinguish him from anybody else called Blotson and/or to indicate that the subject matter is domestic property. The number 97 indicates that this correspondence began in 1997. The 1 shows that it is the first file which has anything to do with this subject. If Mr Blotson's property deal fell through but he then found another flat the correspondence relating to this would be kept in the separate but related file BLO/8745/97/2.

2.21 A system like this is most useful where there is a very large volume of correspondence on different but related topics. The Civil Service, for example, uses a system along these lines.

Other classifications

2.22 Using any of the above systems, bear in mind that you could group your files in any logical way. Common examples include:

(a) **Subject classification**, where all material relating to a particular subject (client, contract, project, product and so on) is kept together. (You just need to title your subjects thoughtfully, otherwise you end up with a lot of 'miscellaneous' items that do not fit your subject categories.)

(b) **Geographical classification**, which is useful for sales, import/export and similar activities that may be organised by region or territory.

2.23 Here is an example of geographical files, sub-classified by subject, in alphabetical order.

		Waders
DARTFORD BRIDGE		Ladders
		Torches
		Shovels
CHANNEL TUNNEL		

Activity 9.3

Listed below are details of 30 people who have written to your organisation.

	Name and address	Account	Date
1	Cottrell J, 5 Heathview Avenue, Bromley	-	2.6.93
2	Holden R, 27 Exning Road, Bexley	-	13.7.92
3	Williams J, 29 Gray Gardens, Dartford	100276	5.4.94
4	Bidwell D, 176 High Road, Dartford	-	16.5.95
5	Bexley J, 25 Romney Road, Orpington	400452	17.5.95
6	Maclean T, 1 Pitt Road, Orpington	400721	7.12.95
7	54321 Discos, 107 Warren Road, Bexley	300924	19.4.96
8	Dr J Crown, 20 Wimfred Street, Woolwich	-	1.1.93
9	Locke D, 22 Davis Street, Crayford	-	14.8.95
10	Sainton E, 15 Filmwell Close, Bromley	200516	3.5.96
11	Argent-Smith M, 17a Waterson Road, Bexley	-	7.8.96
12	Britton T, 81 Ward Avenue, Crayford	-	27.8.94
13	McLaughlin D, 80 Brookhill Road, Orpington	200435	4.3.94
14	Williams J A, 148 Godstow Road, Woolwich	-	6.6.96
15	O'Grady E, 40 Holborne Road, Sidcup	300989	4.4.91
16	Saint Francis Pet Shop, 14 Glenesh Road, Dartford	-	7.9.93
17	Emly P, 8 Faraday Avenue, Orpington	-	18.4.96
18	Harry Holden Ltd, 5 Clare Way, Bexley	100284	9.7.93
19	BRJ Plumbing, 132 Lodge Lane, Crayford	200223	25.11.95
20	Gisling B, 18 Dickens Avenue, Woolwich	-	6.3.96
21	Argentson S, 20 Porson Court, Dartford	400542	5.2.92
22	Kelsey L C, 58 Cudham Lane, Bromley	-	8.1.95
23	ILD Services Ltd, 4 Cobden Road, Orpington	200221	3.2.96
24	Van Saintby A, 69 Brookhill Close, Bromley	400693	5.2.96
25	Williams, John, 10 Buff Close, Dartford	-	2.12.95
26	Page W, 11 Leewood Place, Crayford	400442	9.7.93
27	Harrison P, Robinwood Drive, Dartford	101301	16.4.95
28	Briton N, 3 Chalet Close, Bexley	-	7.2.92
29	Richmond A, 9 Denham Close, Crayford	-	4.1.96
30	St Olave's Church, Church Way, Bromley	400371	21.2.95

Required

(a) Referring to the documents by number (1-30), in what order would they appear if they were filed in date order?

(b) Rearrange the names in alphabetical order, noting the reference number in brackets after the name.

(c) In what order would those correspondents with accounts appear, if they were filed in account number order?

(d) Again referring to the documents by number, identify another sensible way of classifying them, and arrange them in this order.

Indexing

2.24 **Direct access filing** describes a filing system in which you should be able to insert or find a document in the files simply through knowledge of the system used, without reference to a separate index: information filed alphabetically according to name, subject or geography, for example. This sort of system is also known as **self-indexing**.

2.25 **Indirect access filing** is where you will have to consult a **separate index** before attempting to find your file, usually because information has been given a numerical code or label and put in numerical order: how do you know what the numbers refer to?

> **KEY TERM**
>
> An **index** is something which makes it easier to locate information or records: like your index finger, it is a 'pointer' to where a particular item may be found.

2.26 Most information needs to be indexed. For example, if you have got a lot of books in your office, say 500, how would you know where to find a certain book?

If you simply numbered all the books on your shelves from 1 to 500, how would you remember what number you had given to the particular one you then wanted to take out (short of going through all the books each time to remind yourself)? You would have to write the numbers down in an **index**, together with the books' titles and authors (perhaps listed alphabetically), which would give you a sufficient idea of where to find the information you wanted.

2.27 An index may also be a **record in itself**, containing sufficient information to make further reference unnecessary. You might keep revision cards as an index to your study notes and texts; they would each contain a résumé of the topic, as well as give references to appropriate pages of your study notes and to other index cards on related topics.

Cross-referencing information

2.28 Whatever system or combination of systems is used, there will always be items of information that could be filed in **more than one place**, or will be needed in connection with **more than one enquiry**. If the problem is simply that a piece of correspondence refers to more than one matter, the solution is to place a duplicate in each of the relevant files. Other problems may be more complex.

> **KEY TERM**
>
> **Cross-referencing** is a system of referring the reader of one item of information to other related or relevant items.

2.29 EXAMPLE: CROSS-REFERENCING

Dedd Boring Ltd, a company which produces various machinery for mining operations, has over the years fulfilled several contracts for drill bits and air vents for (among other companies) mining firm Olking Coal Ltd. There has also been further correspondence with Mr U Wing, Olking's Chairman, on general matters connected with the business.

In connection with this one relationship, Dedd Boring may keep files as follows.

Index cards

(a)	Air vents (production, sales etc)	X-ref: see also file (c),(f).
(b)	Drill bits (production, sales etc)	X-ref: see also file (d),(e).
(c)	Olking Coal Ltd Air vents contract (3/X4)	X-ref: see also file (a),(d),(g).
(d)	Olking Coal Ltd Drill bits contract (8/X2)	X-ref: see also file (a),(c),(g).

    (e)   Olking Coal Ltd Drill bits contract (3/X6)   X-ref: see also file (b),(g).

    (f)   Wing, U - correspondence   X-ref: see also file (c),(d),(e).

    (g)   Other Company Ltd Air vents contract (6/X3)   X-ref: see also file (a).

A letter from Wing about maintenance services (for which there is no subject file) would go into (f), while one about the air vents and the latest drill bit contract would be duplicated and placed in files (c) and (e). The filing clerk meanwhile discovers that there is another contract file under 'Associated Olking Coal Ltd': this is actually the registered name of the company which has always been known (and refers to itself as) Olking Coal Ltd. He simply adds the appropriate cross-reference to the index cards.

In a real system the letters (a) to (g) would of course be replaced by the appropriate code, depending on the coding system that was in use.

2.30   You can also cross-reference documents within a file.

2.31   Learn as soon as possible to ensure that documents that you generate are properly cross-referenced to each other: this is often very important in accounting work. Cross referencing within files also gives you a useful sense of the **hierarchy** of information within files and the relationship between items of information: this is very useful for keeping **computer** file systems in order.

Activity 9.4

Suppose you are working on the section of a year-end accounts file that analyses fixed assets. The file is organised alpha-numerically so that each 'subject' (fixed assets, current assets, stock and so on) has its own letter of the alphabet. The letter for fixed assets is F. Fixed assets include the broad categories of land and buildings, plant and machinery, and fixtures and fittings. How might you cross reference the various items in this file?

---

3   STORING DOCUMENTS SECURELY

Keeping physical documents in good condition

3.1   It is vital that material containing information is stored in an appropriate location and that its condition does not deteriorate.

3.2   Documents containing information may be classified and indexed so that they are easily accessible, but unless they can be kept in **good condition**, with **economy of storage space and cost**, they will not fulfil our requirements for an effective and efficient filing system.

3.3   Most documents containing information will have to be placed in **folders** or **binders** before they can be housed in filing cabinets or other forms of storage. **Plastic folders** or **paper envelope (manila) folders** are the most common and cheapest methods. For larger volumes of information, there are **lever arch files** and **box files**. If information is to be kept for a long time but not referred to very frequently, then box files are useful. If they are to be referred to and updated more often, ring binders or lever arch files would provide security (there would be no loose bits of paper flying about) but also accessibility.

3.4 Punching holes in a document so that it can be placed in some form of ring binder also needs to be carefully done so that vital numbers or words are not affected, either by the holes themselves or because they are placed in such a way that the information is hidden in the central binding, as it were.

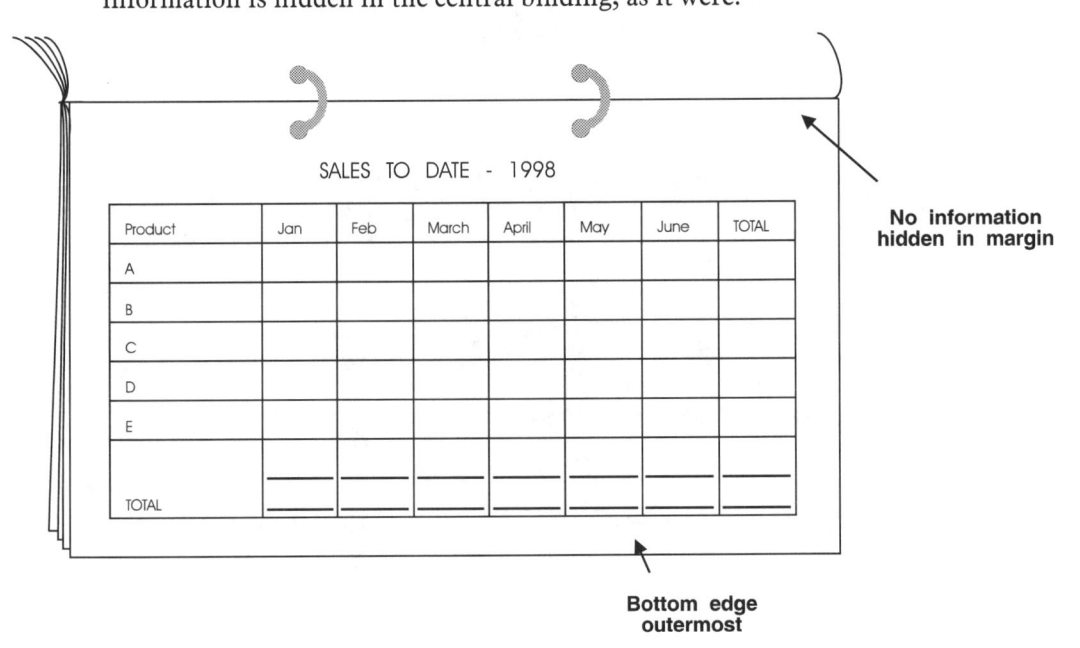

SALES TO DATE - 1998

Product	Jan	Feb	March	April	May	June	TOTAL
A							
B							
C							
D							
E							
TOTAL							

No information hidden in margin

Bottom edge outermost

3.5 Paper can very easily get screwed up, torn, stained, or otherwise damaged. This can result in its contents becoming difficult to read or even getting lost. For example tearing off the edge of a misaligned print-out could easily result in the final column of figures being thrown away.

Activity 9.5

Have a look around your office at work and look for examples of the different types of equipment that are used for storing and retrieving information.

Microfilm and microfiche

3.6 **Microfilming** is a particularly convenient means of information storage for saving space.

(a) Documents are photographed into a very much reduced ('micro') form. Microfilms are readable, but not to the unassisted naked eye, and a magnifying reading device (with a viewing screen) is needed by users. **Microfilm** is itself a **continuous strip** with images in frames along its length (like a photographic negative).

(b) Although there are now more up to date methods, some firms may still use this equipment.

Micro film

Micro fiche

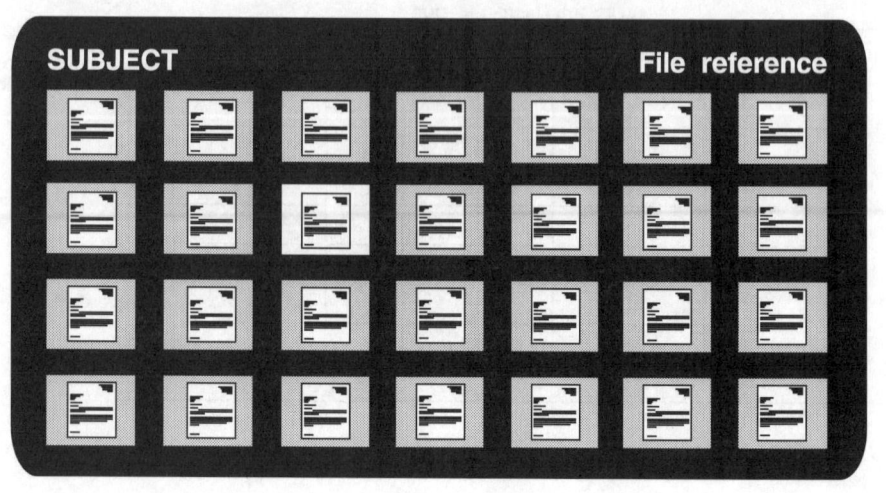

3.7 **Microfiche** consists of **separate sheets of film**, rather than a continuous strip. Microfiche is read by placing the fiche between two glass plates and moving a pointer (which is attached to the lens) across a grid.

3.8 Microfilm and microfiche need **special devices** in order to be read, updated or corrected. However, they do offer very space-saving, durable and secure information storage.

Document image processing (DIP)

3.9 DIP photographs documents onto a CD-ROM, and these photographs can be easily accessed.

File security and confidentiality

3.10 If files are **confidential** or **secret**, they will be 'classified', which means that access will be limited to authorised people. A list of classified files will be required and a policy must be drawn up stipulating **conditions of access** (for example who keeps the keys to the security cabinet, and whether files may be copied or taken out of the filing room) and specifying who has clearance to consult classified material.

3.11 You may sometimes find it frustrating that you have to go through a system to get access to such files. It may be that the information that you need does not seem particularly confidential or secret to you, and it may indeed not be out of context. This is no excuse to buck the system, however. If you really think a file should be declassified, mention it to someone in authority: you may be right or, if not, you should at least receive an explanation as to why the documents are confidential.

3.12 We discussed **data security** in Chapters 2 and 8: re-read any sections you need to. (Apart from anything else, this would be a useful practice of your ability to use **indexes** such as the one at the back of this Text, or the topic lists at the beginning of each chapter.)

Activity 9.6

Your manager is out of the office. He has phoned in and asked you to find a letter which is 'somewhere' on his desk and fax through a copy to him.

As you are searching for the letter you notice the following documents.

1   An electricity bill for £372.97 addressed to D Glover (your manager) at his home address.

2   A letter from a building society asking for a reference for one of your firm's clients.

3   A report entitled 'Potential Merger - Initial considerations'.

4   A mass of figures with your organisation's name at the head and the title 'Draft Budget'.

5   A staff appraisal report about you.

6   A thick sheaf of correspondence - the top sheet is signed 'Love, Nancy'.

7   A letter from P Glover asking for details about your organisation's services.

8   A *very* strongly worded letter of complaint from a Mrs Paribus.

9   A series of cuttings about your organisation from a trade journal.

10   A list of your organisation's directors with their addresses, telephone numbers and ages noted alongside.

Required

(a)   Identify which, if any, of these documents you think should be filed away confidentially. Give reasons.

(b)   Suppose that the letter that you had to fax was document 8 above. What would you do?

4   CREATING, UPDATING AND RETAINING FILES

Preparing documents for filing

4.1   When documents containing information have been received, acknowledged, acted upon or have otherwise fulfilled their immediate purpose, they are ready to be added to the storage system.

4.2   **Procedures to be followed when adding new information to the organisation's storage system**

(a)   The document containing the information is **indicated as being ready for filing** - perhaps initialled by the recipient or supervisor. This is a signal to the filing clerk that it is OK to go ahead and file it.

(b)   **Paper clips and binders are removed** leaving flat sheets for filing, and punched holes appropriate to the storage method are created so that documents can be inserted.

(c)   Documents are placed at **random in a filing tray**, or kept in rough order in a **concertina file**.

(d)   If the document is an internally generated one, it may have a **file reference** on it already (this will often be what the numbers and letters following 'Our reference ....' mean at the head of letters you receive). If not, a **reference number** will have to be determined.

(e)   The **reference number,** or **name** or **subject** of the file into which the document is to be inserted should be shown on the document.

(f) Batches of documents can then be **sorted** (by each name, subject and so on) and put into the appropriate filing sequence (chronological, numerical or whatever).

(g) Documents are **inserted in the appropriate place** in appropriate files. This process should be carried out daily at a set time, to avoid pile-ups and disorganisation.

Opening a new file

4.3 If there is no file existing for a document (that is, to avoid needless duplication, if the filing clerk is sure there is no existing file), a **new file** will be opened.

(a) In a centralised filing system, a **request** and **authorisation** for a new file to be opened. This is to check for duplication or misnaming of files.

(b) **Appropriate housing** for the document - a **folder** or **binder**, noting size, colour and so on as necessary. An extra pocket may have to be inserted in sequence for suspended files.

(c) **Identification**. This will mean writing the number or name on files or suspension pockets or on a suitable tag or label. Colour coding may also be used.

(d) **Adding** the new file name/number to the index, file list, and cross-referencing system.

4.4 The procedure will be much the same as when a file cannot hold any more documents, and a **continuation file** is needed. Simply mark the cover of the original file 'Volume 1' and add the range of dates its subject matter covers. Then open a new file marked 'Volume 2'.

Activity 9.7

What matters should you take account of when you are considering opening a new file for some documents in your possession?

Activity 9.8

The following is an extract from your organisation's permanent file on customer number 476/23/3.

Company:	Folworth Ltd
Address:	47 Bracewell Gardens London EC2
Directors:	Robin Folworth Margaret Foster Laurence Oldfield
Purchasing manager:	John Thornhill

You have just had a letter from this company which is shown below.

Your task is to update the permanent file as necessary.

FOLWORTH (Business Services) Ltd

Crichton Buildings
97 Lower Larkin Street   London   EC4A 8QT

D. Ashford
Sales Department
Bosley Products Ltd
Ducannon House
4-6 West Brook Road
LONDON W12 7LY

8 August 2000

Dear Mr Ashford

Account No. 476/23/3

I should be grateful for a reply to my letter of 30 July regarding the above account.

Yours sincerely

D. Simmonds
Purchasing Manager

Folworth (Business Services) Ltd, Registered Office:
Crichton Buildings, 97 Lower Larkin Street, London, EC4A 8QT

Registered in England, number 9987654

Directors:
R. Folworth, BA ACA; J. Crichton; M. Foster; L. Oldfield MA; T. Scott; J. Thornhill BSc

Retention policy

4.5   Files of data may be **temporary, permanent, active,** and **non-active.**

(a)   **Master files** and **reference files** are usually **permanent,** which means that they are never thrown away or scrapped. They will be **updated** from time to time, and so the information on the file might change, but the file itself will continue to exist.

(b)   A **temporary** or **transitory file** is one that is eventually scrapped. Many **transaction files** are held for a very short time, until the transaction records have been processed, but are then thrown away. Other transaction files are

permanent (for example a cash book) or are held for a considerable length of time before being scrapped.

(c) An **active file** is one that is frequently used, for example, sales invoice files relating to the current financial year, or correspondence files relating to current customers and suppliers.

(d) A **non-active file** is one that is no longer used on a day-to-day basis. For example, files that contain information relating to customers and suppliers who are no longer current, and purchase invoices relating to previous financial periods. **Semi-active files** are those that contain information that is still active, but are on their way to becoming inactive, for example, as a contract nears completion, it will not be used so frequently, but should be kept on hand for reference if so needed.

4.6 When information contained within files is no longer needed on a daily basis, it is not automatically thrown away (as you may be forgiven for thinking). It is generally dealt with in one of the following ways.

(a) **Microfilmed or microfiched** (as discussed earlier) for long-term storage

(b) Retained in its original form and stored elsewhere (this is generally known as **archiving**) for a certain period of time

(c) **Securely destroyed**

4.7 Imagine how distressed you would be if you needed to refer to a legal document that had been filed some years ago, and you found out that it had been thrown away by a filing clerk during the latest office spring-clean! (Alternatively, imagine trying to find an urgently needed current file, with *all* the paperwork of the organisation's history still in the active filing system!)

4.8 In order to streamline the system, information which is no longer current, but which may need to be referred to at some point in the future, should be given a revised **status**: no longer active, but semi-active; no longer semi-active, but non-active - in which case, a prime candidate for the **archive**!

> **KEY TERM**
>
> A **retention policy** sets down for how long different kinds of information are retained

4.9 **Retention periods** vary. Under **The Companies Acts**, documents concerned with the legal establishment of the organisation will have to be kept permanently, as will the annual accounts. Simple legal contracts will have to be kept for six years, and more important sealed ones for twelve. Other documents may be kept at the organisation's discretion but the principle overall is: if you think you might need it, for as long as you might need it - keep it!

4.10 **Some recommended retention periods**

Document	Years
Agreements	12
Balance sheets	30
Bank statements	6
Cheque counterfoils	1
Correspondence files	6
Credit notes	6
Customs and Excise VAT records	6
Delivery notes	1
Directors' reports	30
Expense claims	1
Insurance claims forms	6
Leases, expired	12
Licences for patents	30
Medical certificates	1
Patents, expired	12
Paying-in books	1
Powers of attorney	30
Prospectuses	30
Purchase orders	6
Quotations, out	6
Royalty ledgers	30
Sales invoices	6
Share applications	12
Specifications, product	6
Tax records	6

DEVOLVED ASSESSMENT ALERT

Try to find out what **your organisation's policy** is for the retention of documentation: it is part of the required background knowledge. 'Dealing with out of date information in accordance with organisational procedures' is likewise a performance criterion.

Activity 9.9

Dribble Ltd, a very small company, file their correspondence as follows.

(a) All incoming mail is placed on a 'current' file initially. It is usually actioned within a week, after which the correspondence is filed permanently.

(b) Business customers each have their own separate correspondence file.

(c) Correspondence with domestic customers is placed on a single file; only one file has been needed per year since the business started in 1944.

(d) Letters relevant to the latest year's accounts are filed in a file entitled 'Auditors'.

(e) There is also an extremely thick file entitled 'Miscellaneous 1959 -'.

This is the theory, and Derek Dribble, who founded the business, was an enthusiastic filer. His son, Dominic, however, sees himself as a dynamic entrepreneur and cannot be bothered with it. The current file has not been reviewed for several years and presently includes the following documents.

1   Letter from Miskimin Ltd dated 9.9.94 returning goods.

2   Undated letter from Jacksnares School concerning jumble sale.

3   Letter from London Borough of Greenwich dated 31.12.95 concerning Business Rates.

4   Letter dated 21.7.88 from Dribble Ltd to Mr T N Clipper requesting payment in advance. This has 'Pending - 28.7.88' written across it in red ink.

5   Letter dated 4.3.96 from A J Butterworth Esq requesting '2 × green spats (pair), 1 × red spats (pair)'.

6   Letter from Landlord notifying rent increase as from 1.9.92

7   Letter dated 26.5.86 from Hardman and Free Shoes Ltd ordering '20 pairs spats'.

8   Memo to 'all staff including secretaries' concerning the staff Christmas lunch. This is dated 3.12.93.

9   Letter from Jacksnares School dated 7.5.96 thanking Dribble Ltd for their 'generous donation but unfortunately returning goods unsold'.

10   Letter from Dudley Theatre Company dated 14.4.96 ordering '7 pairs of spats in white'.

11   Letter dated 14.2.96 from Major John Cummings asking for a brochure.

12   Letter dated 14.3.96 from Major John Cummings ordering '1 pair in a conservative colour'.

13   Letter from Miskimin Ltd dated 24.8.94 ordering '2 dozen pairs in white'.

14   Letter from Mr Howard P Wisebacker dated 17.2.90 congratulating Dribble Ltd on 'keeping up a fine old tradition'.

15   Letter dated 17.11.95 from Period Costumiers Ltd ordering '50 pairs, 10 in each colour'.

16   Letter from London Borough of Greenwich notifying dates of refuse collection as from 3.12.95.

17   Letter from Period Costumiers Ltd dated 12.1.96 ordering '50 pairs, 10 in each colour'.

18   Letter dated 15.3.96 from Mrs A J Butterworth returning goods.

19   Letter regarding insurance claim dated 19.4.89.

20   Memo to 'all staff' about summer outing in July 1996.

Task

It is November 1996. Which of these documents would you remove from the current file and where would you place them?

Do you have any suggestions for improving the system?

Deleting or destroying out-of-date information

4.11   Once information becomes **out-of-date,** it may be **deleted or destroyed**. Be aware that screwing up a piece of paper and throwing it in the bin is not destroying it. Even if information (particularly financial information) is out-of-date it may still be damaging if it falls into the wrong hands. Waste paper bins are the first place that the wrong eyes will look in!

4.12   Many organisations have **shredding devices** for such documents, or a system of disposal which involves **special confidential waste bags**. Find out what your organisation's system is and be sure to use it.

5 RECORDING ITEM MOVEMENTS

5.1 Once you have located the information you require in the filing system, you need to **gain access** to it. Other people need to do the same - perhaps at the same time, so it is vital that when files containing information are moved, someone is keeping track of them.

Obtaining files

5.2 A typical procedure for **withdrawing a file from storage** is to fill out a **file requisition slip**.

1

To: Central Filing
     Room 101

FILE REQUISITION SLIP

Please deliver the following file.

File reference: ☐☐☐ / ☐☐☐☐ / ☐☐ / ☐

Title: ....

Date required: ....

Deliver to: .... (Name)
                  .... (Department)
                  .... (Room number)

Signature: .... Date: ....
Authorisation: .... Date: ....

FILING DEPARTMENT USE

Reason for non-delivery

☐ File in use (see over)   ☐ Slip not authorised

☐ File destroyed   ☐ Restricted access

☐ Inadequate identification   ☐ Other (see over)

This example is part 1 of a two part document – part 2 would be kept in the filing department, showing who had the file.

5.3 The system may vary in many ways. You may need to send the letter down to the filing department with a note saying 'File please', or just ring them up giving them the details and letting them do the rest. You may be able to fetch the file for yourself once you have found out the reference number. All the documents may be filed within reach in your own office. Make sure you familiarise yourself with whatever *your* system is.

Keeping track of files

5.4 When a file is taken out of storage on loan, a record must be kept identifying the **file**, the **borrower** and the **dates of borrowing** and **return**. Details can be entered in a book: loans are recorded in **chronological order**, and all in one place, so the clerk can see at a glance what files are out or overdue.

5.5 If a particular file is needed but is absent from its place, however, the whole book might have to be checked to find its whereabouts: in such cases, there is advantage in a system of **cards or slips which can be inserted in the filing system itself**, in place of the file which is absent.

5.6 In a larger filing system, the clerk may keep a series of 'out' cards with headings as follows.

File identification	Date borrowed	By	Clerk	Date returned
L 193 / x	7 / 9	E.A.M.	*BL*	

Any card can then be completed and inserted in place when a file is lent out.

5.7 In a smaller system, a card may be kept with each file, so that only the **borrower** and **date** need be noted: if very few people have access to files, it may be possible to have colour-coded cards for each likely borrower, which could be inserted with no further details.

5.8   If more than one person needs to use the information, a file may be passed from hand to hand without being returned to the file registry each time and the lending records will get hopelessly out of date. Files can still be kept track of, however, if the passer-on **sends a memo** or **fills in a file passing slip** to the clerk: his own name, the file name, the date and the new holder of the file are sufficient to allow the clerk to update the 'out' records.

To: Central Filing
     Room 101

FILE MOVEMENTS

File reference: ☐☐☐ / ☐☐☐☐ / ☐☐ / ☐

Title: _____

This file was passed from: to:

Name: _____   Name: _____

Department: _____   Department: _____

Room no: _____   Room no: _____

Date: _____

5.9   If it is essential for a person to remove a document from a file, they will normally be expected to **photocopy and replace the original immediately**. If for some reason the document must be borrowed for a time, the same procedures apply as with an 'out' card. As well as borrower details, the document's identification details will be needed, including the **date, sender** and **subject of the document**. The **substitution note** is inserted into the file at the appropriate place, and should be signalled in some way, so that routine file checks will show when the file is still incomplete.

SUBSTITUTION NOTE

The following document has been
removed from the file

- Document no./date: _____

  Source: _____

  Subject: _____

  Reason for removal: _____

- _____

  Name: _____

  Date: _____

DOCUMENT REMOVED

Overdue files

5.10 Just as a public library sets a limit on the length of time you can keep a book you have borrowed (particularly if it is in high demand), so your organisation may only lend out files for a set period.

5.11 In any case, there will need to be a **follow-up system** to draw attention to files which have not been returned by the due date. Such a system may involve:

- A diary or calendar, in which due dates for the return of files are entered

- A diary file, with pockets for each day of the current month, in which pre-printed **follow-up slips** (filled in with the file and borrower details) are filed under their due date

5.12 When a file is identified as overdue, a **reminder** will be sent out, asking the borrower to return the file or to renew the lending period, if necessary.

Activity 9.10

Your name is Jane Taylor. You work in P division in room 17. You requisitioned the file on Ralph Atkins (ATK/3964/92/1: 'Ralph Atkins - correspondence') on 2 July and found it in your in-tray the following morning. You worked on the file until 6 July when you sent it, together with a series of draft letters, to your supervisor, Edith Patten in room 25. Mrs Patten took the file to a meeting with Mr Atkins at his home in Slough on 8 July. She was unable to return to the office that evening before travelling to Manchester for a two-day business trip. On 9 July she phoned in from Manchester to tell you what extra work needed to be done on the Atkins case and faxed through the complaining letters from Mr Atkins dated 14 March and 3 April. On Monday 13 July you collected the file from Mrs Patten when you got to work. Eddie Rogers in J Division (room 246) was now finishing off the work required. On 10 July you had passed to him all of the papers on the Atkins case that you had generated since you last had access to the file. Eddie Rogers finished working on the case on 16 July.

Required

Set out on the following pages are copies of all of the various documents comprising your organisation's file control system. Show what entries need to be made to record the movements described above.

REQUEST FOR NEW/CONTINUATION FILE

To: Central Filing
     Room 101

File title: -

Department: -

Continuation file? Yes/No

Previous volume
reference: □□□□ / □□□ / □

Related files
(use continuation
sheet if necessary) □□□ / □□□ / □
                     □□□ / □□□ / □
                     □□□ / □□□ / □

Initiated by: - - - - - - - - - - - -   Date: - - - - - - -

Authorised by: - - - - - - - - - - -   Date: - - - - - - -

FILING DEPARTMENT USE
NEW/CONTINUATION FILE

Reference: □□□ / □□□ / □

Title: -

Date issued: - - - - - - - - - - - - -

Cross-referencing actioned?   Yes/No   Clerk's initials: - - - -

---

REQUEST FOR NEW/CONTINUATION FILE

To: Central Filing
     Room 101

File title: -

Department: -

Continuation file? Yes/No

Previous volume
reference: □□□□ / □□□ / □

Related files
(use continuation
sheet if necessary) □□□ / □□□ / □
                     □□□ / □□□ / □
                     □□□ / □□□ / □

Initiated by: - - - - - - - - - - - -   Date: - - - - - - -

Authorised by: - - - - - - - - - - -   Date: - - - - - - -

FILING DEPARTMENT USE
NEW/CONTINUATION FILE

Reference: □□□ / □□□ / □

Title: -

Date issued: - - - - - - - - - - - - -

Cross-referencing actioned?   Yes/No   Clerk's initials: - - - -

FILE REQUISITION SLIP

To: Central Filing
Room 101

Please deliver the following file.

File reference: ☐☐☐☐ / ☐☐☐☐ / ☐☐☐ / ☐

Title: -

Date required: - - - - - - - - - - - - - - - - -

Deliver to: - - - - - - - - - - - - - - (Name)
- - - - - - - - - - - - - - (Department)
- - - - - - - - - - - - - - (Room number)

Signature: - - - - - - - - - - Date: - - - - -

Authorisation: - - - - - - - - Date: - - - - -

FILING DEPARTMENT USE

Reason for non-delivery

☐ File in use (see over)   ☐ Slip not authorised
☐ File destroyed   ☐ Restricted access
☐ Inadequate identification   ☐ Other (see over)

FILE REQUISITION SLIP

To: Central Filing
Room 101

Please deliver the following file.

File reference: ☐☐☐☐ / ☐☐☐☐ / ☐☐☐ / ☐

Title: -

Date required: - - - - - - - - - - - - - - - - -

Deliver to: - - - - - - - - - - - - - - (Name)
- - - - - - - - - - - - - - (Department)
- - - - - - - - - - - - - - (Room number)

Signature: - - - - - - - - - - Date: - - - - -

Authorisation: - - - - - - - - Date: - - - - -

FILING DEPARTMENT USE

Reason for non-delivery

☐ File in use (see over)   ☐ Slip not authorised
☐ File destroyed   ☐ Restricted access
☐ Inadequate identification   ☐ Other (see over)

REQUEST FOR NEW/CONTINUATION FILE

To: Central Filing
Room 101

File title: ----------------------

Department: ----------------------

Continuation file? Yes/No

Previous volume reference:

Related files
(use continuation
sheet if necessary)

Initiated by: ---------------------- Date: ----------

Authorised by: ---------------------- Date: ----------

FILING DEPARTMENT USE
NEW/CONTINUATION FILE

Reference:

Title: ----------------------

Date issued: ----------------------

Cross-referencing actioned?   Yes/No   Clerk's initials:

1

FILE REQUISITION SLIP

To: Central Filing
Room 101

Please deliver the following file.

File reference:

Title: ----------------------

Date required: ----------------------

Deliver to: ---------------------- (Name)

---------------------- (Department)

---------------------- (Room number)

Signature: ---------------------- Date: ----------

Authorisation: ---------------------- Date: ----------

FILING DEPARTMENT USE
Reason for non-delivery

☐ File in use (see over)   ☐ Slip not authorised

☐ File destroyed   ☐ Restricted access

☐ Inadequate identification   ☐ Other (see over)

To: Central Filing
    Room 101

FILE MOVEMENTS

File reference: ⬚⬚⬚ / ⬚⬚⬚⬚ / ⬚⬚ / ⬚

Title: _____

This file was passed from: to:

Name: _____   Name: _____

Department: _____   Department: _____

Room no: _____   Room no: _____

Date: _____

To: Central Filing
    Room 101

FILE MOVEMENTS

File reference: ⬚⬚⬚ / ⬚⬚⬚⬚ / ⬚⬚ / ⬚

Title: _____

This file was passed from: to:

Name: _____   Name: _____

Department: _____   Department: _____

Room no: _____   Room no: _____

Date: _____

BPP PUBLISHING

SUBSTITUTION NOTE

The following document has been
removed from the file

● Document no./date: _____

Source: _____

Subject: _____

Reason for removal: _____

● _____

Name: _____

Date: _____

DOCUMENT REMOVED

SUBSTITUTION NOTE

The following document has been
removed from the file

● Document no./date: _____

Source: _____

Subject: _____

Reason for removal: _____

● _____

Name: _____

Date: _____

DOCUMENT REMOVED

6   COMPUTERISED SYSTEMS

6.1   You will learn about computer files when you study Unit 20: *Working with Information Technology*. Most of the principles of manual storage and retrieval of information still apply in a computerised context: it is still important to develop good habits, **to be tidy, to keep things in good condition** and so on. The computer does take some of the hard work out of such tasks, but it is also important to be careful, especially about keeping copies of your work.

6.2   We shall describe a typical PC-based system using Windows software. If the previous sentence sounds like a foreign language to you we suggest you spend half an hour or so in a High Street shop like Dixons looking at the PC displays (if any of the machines are turned on - they usually are) and perhaps getting someone to give you a demonstration of the word-processing and spreadsheet packages.

PC file organisation

6.3   In a PC system, information is organised in a clear hierarchy:

- Drives; which contain
- Directories; which contain
- Files; which contain
- Documents.

6.4   Most PCs access four 'drives'.

- The **C drive**, which contains the **non-removable hard disk**

- The **A drive**, into which **floppy disks** can be put interchangeably

- The '**D' drive** for CD-ROMs (you need special equipment to create, as opposed to see, files on a CD-ROM)

- The '**server**' where, in a network, data is held on a central server computer

6.5   Within each drive you can have as many **directories** as you need. You might have one directory for **spreadsheets** and another directory for **word-processed (WP) documents**. Within each of the WP directories you might have **sub-directories** for letters, memos and reports. You can call the directories whatever you like. With older systems the name you choose had to be no more than eight letters or digits (or a combination of letters and digits) long. This restriction does not apply with Windows 95 and subsequent Windows packages.

6.6   Your 'letters' sub-directory could be arranged into further **sub-sub-directories** for different types of correspondence. The PC itself can sort and re-sort the files within a directory or sub-directory in various ways as often as you wish, at the touch of a button.

(a)   By **file name** (alphabetically or numerically)
(b)   By **date created** or **last updated**
(c)   By **size**

Storing data in PC files

6.7   When you open a new document 'page' in a PC system, the system will give it a working title like 'doc2.doc'. This means, quite simply, 'document number two', the second document that you have created during that working session. The three letters after the full stop are to tell the computer what type of document the file is: in this case, a word-processing document created with Microsoft Word software. Depending on the package you are using, a spreadsheet might have a three letter extension like 'xls' or 'wk4'. A diagram would have a different three letter extension again.

6.8 Names like doc2 are fine if you only have three or four files in total, but once it starts to grow, your collection of files will quickly become unmanageable unless you have a clearer method of identifying the specific file that you want. In the system we are describing the first part of the file name, before the full stop, can have up to eight letters or eight digits, or a combination of the two.

6.9 You should follow the system of file-naming prescribed by your organisation if there is one. If not, try to give the file a name that would enable someone else to find it quickly, say, when you are on holiday.

6.10 Information can also be recorded on **back-up files**.

(a) Such files are very important, since if the files held on the PC are stolen or damaged in any way, the information contained in them will not be lost. It is usual to store back-up files in secure places, such as fire-proof safes.

(b) For this reason it is good practice to store work files, not on your PC's 'C' drive but on the server as this is likely to have backup copies taken daily.

Moving PC files

6.11 Like physical documents, electronic files can be moved or copied to other people and locations. However, this is a much quicker, easier and more efficient process on computer: copies can be made instantly and sent almost instantly to locations on the other side of the world (if necessary).

(a) A file can be **saved onto a floppy disk** and sent to the other user for insertion into his or her PC: the file can then be opened and/or saved onto his or her PC and used as required. **Beware viruses.**

(b) A file can be **'attached' to an e-mail message** and sent to the other user's inbox. He or she can download, open, save and use the file. This is a very efficient (although not yet entirely secure) way of sending files around the world. **Beware viruses.**

(c) PCs linked to each other in a **network** may be able to access the same files, whether they are stored **centrally on a server** or possibly on local PCs.

6.12 Like physical documents, electronic files should be clearly marked if they are:

• Classified for limited access

• 'Read only': that is, the data must not be changed by multiple users, to avoid confusion.

Electronic files can be 'locked' appropriately and access denied to users who do not have the password clearance, or who try to alter data on a 'read only' file.

6.13 Difficulties still exist where multiple copies of a file have been circulated and updated or amended by different users. Moved files should be saved under

different names, so that the source file can be identified: even so, it may be difficult to keep track of exactly which version now has the most up-to-date information - or which copies have the most up-to-date version of any given item of information!

6.14 This problem is resolved by organising data in a **database,** as discussed below.

Deleting PC files

6.15 It is very easy to delete files from a disk or to write over files that you meant to save in their existing form. Most systems will ask you to **confirm** that you want to delete a file if you give the computer this instruction. If you have any doubt say no. If you want to free up space on your hard drive, **copy anything that you intend to delete onto a floppy disk** first, just in case you need it again later.

6.16 We shall not go into any further detail, partly because you really need to know more about computers first, but mainly because you should learn your organisation's own system. We are restricted here by the need to generalise.

6.17 However, as with manual filing systems, the golden rule is to get into good habits early on. Set some time aside to organise the files that you have created on disk each day. This is called '**housekeeping**'.

Activity 9.11

Identify the software used in your college or workplace.

(a) What procedures are followed for naming files?

(b) What procedures are in place for storing files (eg on tape or floppy disk, with daily backups)?

(c) How do you retrieve a file that is no longer stored on hard disk on one of your organisation's computers?

You will find it instructive to compare notes with colleagues or classmates who use different systems, or different procedures on the same system.

KEY TERM

A **database** is a comprehensive, structured collection or file of data which can be accessed by different users for different applications.

6.18 In theory, a database is simply a coherent structure for the storage and use of data. It involves the centralised storage of information, which provides:

- **Common data** for all users to share

- Avoidance of **data duplication** in files kept by different users

- **Consistency** in the organisation's use of data, and in the accuracy and up-to dateness of data accessed by different users, because all records are centrally maintained and updated

- **Flexibility** in the way in which shared data can be queried, analysed and formatted by individual users for specific purposes, without altering the store of data itself

6.19 Such a structure could be fulfilled by a centralised file registry or library, or a self-contained data record like a master index card file. In practice, however, large scale databases are created and stored on *computer* systems, using **database application packages**, such as Microsoft Access or Filemaker.

Data storage

6.20 Computer database packages allow data to be stored in a coherent structure, in one place.

(a) **Data** are the raw components of information: names, dates, item descriptions, prices, colours, addresses and so on.

(b) **Fields** are the labels given to types of data. (the user-friendly manual, Access for Dummies refers to them as '*places for your data to live*'.) A customer database, for example, might include fields such as: title (data = Mr), first name (data = Joseph), last name (data = Bloggs), Company (data = Anon Ltd), Address, Phone Number, Fax Number, Contact Type (data = customer), interests (data = widgets) and so on.

(c) **Records** are the collections of fields relevant to one entry. ('Access for Dummies' suggests '*all the homes on one block*'.) So all the above data fields for a particular customer (Mr Bloggs) make up one customer record.

(d) **Tables** (or database files) are collections of records that describe similar data. ('*...all the blocks in one neighbourhood*'.) All the customer records for a particular region or product may be stored in such a file.

(e) **Databases** (or catalogues) are collections of all the tables (and other formats which can be created from them) relating to a particular set of information. ('*A community of neighbourhoods*'.) So your customer database may include tables for various regions' customers, product customers, customer contacts and so on, plus various reports and queries that you use to access different types of information.

6.21 There are two basic kinds of database.

(a) A **flat file** system lumps all the data into single table databases, like a phone directory where names, addresses, phone numbers and fax numbers are stored in the same file.

(b) A **relational database system** allows greater flexibility and storage efficiency by splitting the data up into a number of tables, which can nevertheless be linked and integrated together. For example, one table may contain customer names and addresses/contact details, while others track sales transactions by outlet or product, and another, customers' payment histories.

6.22 **Flat systems** are easy to build and maintain, and are quite adequate for applications such as mailing lists, or membership databases. **Relational systems** integrate a wider range of business functions, for invoicing, accounting, inventory, marketing analysis and so on: they are, however, complicated to develop and use.

Data manipulation

6.23 Basic features of database packages allow you to do these tasks.

(a) **Find particular records**, using any data item you know.

(b) **Sort records alphabetically**, numerically or by date, in ascending or descending order.

(c) **Filter records**, so that you 'pull out' and view a selection of records based on specified criteria (all addresses in a certain postcode, for example, or all purchasers of a particular product).

(d) **Interrogate records**, generating the selection of records based on a complex set of criteria, from one or more linked tables. (For example, you might specify that you want all customer records where the field 'City' equals 'London' or 'Birmingham' AND where the field 'Product' equals 'Widget' AND where the field 'Purchase Date' is between 'Jan 99' and 'Jan 00'. The query would generate a table consisting of customers in London and Birmingham who purchased Widgets in 1999.)

(e) **Calculate and count** data entries. (For example, if you wanted to find out how many customers had purchased each product, you could run a query that asked the database to *group* the data by the field 'Product' and then *count* by field 'Customer ID' or 'Last Name': it would count the number of customer ID numbers or names linked to each product. You could also ask to 'sum' or add up all the values in a field: total number of purchases, or total purchase value.)

(f) **Format** selected data for a variety of uses, such as reports, forms, mailing labels, charts diagrams and so on.

6.24 If you are working with a database, it will probably be one that has already been created for you, using a particular software package. It is up to you to get to know how to use it, what the protocols are, and how your organisation wants its data structured and formatted.

6.25 If you want to know more, talk to IT experts in your organisation, or borrow the handbook to one of the popular database packages.

Activity 9.12

Find out what type(s) of database your organisation (or college) uses, and for what applications. If possible, get access to the database and browse through the index, directory or switchboard to see what databases/catalogues contain what database files or tables, queries, reports and forms, with what fields. If you can't get access to a database at work, try the local library, where you may find that the 'index card' system has been computerised as a database. Or use an Internet search engine or browser to interrogate some on-line databases. This is not really something you can learn from books - have a go!

Key learning points

- A **file** is a collection of data records with similar characteristics.

- Characteristics of a **'good'** filing system are as follows.

  ○ It should contain all the information you may need

  ○ The information should be found easily

  ○ It should be of a convenient size

  ○ It should be capable of expansion

  ○ It should be easily accessible

  ○ It should be stored under suitable conditions so that it won't get damaged or lose its information

- An **index** is something which makes it easier to locate information or records.

- **Cross-referencing** information is commonly carried out when items of information could be filed in more than one place, or could be needed in connection with more than one enquiry.

- The three main systems for **classifying information** are **alphabetical**, **numerical** and **alpha-numerical**.

- **Adding new information** to an information storage system involves the following.

  ○ Indicating that the information is ready for filing
  ○ Removing any paperclips or binders
  ○ Placing information in a filing tray or concertina file
  ○ Allocating a reference number if there is not already a file reference
  ○ Sorting batches of documents containing information
  ○ Inserting the documents into the appropriate place in appropriate files

- Information is usually **destroyed** by using shredding devices or by placing in confidential wastebags.

- In general, when information is no longer needed on a daily basis, it is retained in its original form and stored elsewhere; this is known as **archiving**.

- A **retention policy** is the amount of time decided on by an organisation for the holding of various types of information.

- Tracks must be kept of file movements. If files containing information are borrowed, a series of **out cards** may be used to keep tracks.

- Most of the principles of manual storage information systems also apply in **computerised systems**.

- A database is a comprehensive, structured collection of data which can be accessed by different users for different applications.

Quick quiz

1 What is a file?

2 List four systems used for arranging files.

3 What procedures might be followed when adding new information to a filing system?

4 How is information that is no longer needed on a regular basis dealt with?

5 What are classified files?

6 In organisations where there are a large number of files, how are file movements monitored and recorded correctly?

7 Why is it necessary to store back-up files?

8 What is the hierarchy of information in a database?

Answers to quick quiz

1 A collection of data records with similar characteristics.

2 Alphabetical order, numerical order, alpha-numerical, chronological order.

3 Indicate that document is ready for filing, remove any paperclips and binders, place documents at random in a filing tray, determine a reference number for the document if it does not already have one, determine into which file the document is to be inserted, sort batches of documents and insert into appropriate place in appropriate files.

4 • Microfilmed or microfiched
   • Archived
   • Destroyed

5 Confidential or secret.

6 The use of out cards which record the file reference, the date file was borrowed, who borrowed it, the name of the clerk who released the file and the date that the file was returned.

7 Information is stored in computer files, and if the computer is destroyed or stolen, the information is lost. It is therefore necessary to record this information on back-up files and to store such files in a secure place.

8 Databases contain tables, which contain records, which contain fields, which contain data.

Answers to activities

Answers to Chapter 1 activities

Activity 1.1

(a) At worst, a serious accident may render you **permanently unable to work**.

(b) **You may be forced to stay away from work for a considerable period**. Employers generally allow a period of weeks or months on full pay, perhaps followed by a further period on half pay. The period is probably not as long as you think - check your contract of employment. Thereafter you will only receive state benefits.

(c) Your career or training will be interrupted. You might miss a sitting of professional exams, putting you back six months!

Activity 1.2

You should have answered from your own workplace experience. Note that the issue of communication and awareness is crucial: the best safety policy in the world is no good unless people **know** about it!

Activity 1.3

(a) Temperature. The temperature must be 'reasonable' inside buildings during working hours. This means not less than 16° C where people are sitting down, or 13° C if they move about to do their work.

(b) Eating facilities must be provided unless the employees' workstations are suitable for rest or eating, as is normally the case for offices. You may have mentioned that surfaces should be kept clean.

(c) Room dimensions. Each person should have at least 11 cubic metres of space, ignoring any parts of rooms more than 3.1 metres above the floor or with a headroom of less than 2.0 metres.

(d) Lighting should be suitable and sufficient, and natural, if practicable. Windows should be clean and unobstructed.

(e) Ventilation. Air should be fresh or purified.

(f) Equipment. All equipment should be properly maintained. Special rules apply to certain items like VDUs.

(g) Sanitary conveniences must be suitable and sufficient. This means that they should be properly ventilated and lit, properly cleaned and separate for men and women. 'Sufficient' means that undue delay is avoided!

Activity 1.4

(*Tutorial note*. The main purpose of this activity is to encourage you to read the operating instructions for items of equipment.)

Frederick should be fully reassured that the laser beam cannot escape from the machine because it has protective housings and external covers. Then the use of the machine should be demonstrated to him, and he should be encouraged to use it himself.

The information about radio interference and telecommunication systems need not really concern Frederick, except that it provides further evidence that the manufacturers take health and safety seriously.

The warning regarding ozone emissions should be heeded: Frederick should be able to see that the laser printers have been positioned appropriately, that the room is properly ventilated, and that multiple laser printers are not being used simultaneously.

Activity 1.5

Your answer to this activity - a realistic assessment of the health and safety of your work area, together with any suggestions for improvement you may have been able to make - would make good documentary evidence of your competence in this element. You may wish to reformat your answer as a report for assessment - and action! - purposes.

Activity 1.6

The following are the most likely work-related causes.

(a)   Sitting at a desk/chair that is set at the wrong height for you. One or both should be adjusted if possible.

(b)   Using equipment in such a way or in such a position that it is placing unnatural strain on your back. The equipment should be repositioned as appropriate.

(c)   Lifting items when you are not accustomed to doing so, and lifting them incorrectly, taking the strain on your back rather than bending your knees and using your legs. You should learn how to lift heavy objects properly.

Of course, your backache may not be caused by your new job at all, and if none of the above apply you should consider whether any aspect of your life outside work is to blame (a new bed, a new sporting activity or the like.)

Activity 1.7

Rearranging the layout of the office might minimise people bumping into things (or each other), or making unnecessarily long journeys with heavy loads. The measures in paragraph 3.28 minimise the risk of eye strain (by providing natural light), back and muscular strain (by cutting down on lifting and carrying), and accidents (by avoiding some causes of stress and loss of concentration, and by keeping foods and liquids away from work and machinery where they might cause damage).

Activity 1.8

Another activity which required active research rather than theoretical knowledge: keep the notes of your findings as evidence of awareness!

Activity 1.9

Keep a careful note of:

(a)   whom you asked for the information, and how; and
(b)   the information gained.

Together, these may demonstrate not only your knowledge of stress control (an aspect of organisational health) but also your competence in 'asking the appropriate people for any information, advice and resources required'. (See Element 23.3.2.)

Activity 1.10

You should have spotted the following hazards

(a)   Heavy object on high shelf
(b)   Standing on swivel chair
(c)   Lifting heavy object incorrectly
(d)   Open drawers blocking passageway
(e)   Trailing wires
(f)   Electric bar fire
(g)   Smouldering cigarette unattended
(h)   Overfull waste bin
(i)   Overloaded socket
(j)   Carrying too many cups of hot liquid
(k)   Dangerous invoice 'spike'

If you think you can see others, you are probably right.

Activity 1.11

See Answer 1.8 above.

Answer 1.12

Accident book

	Full name, address and occupation of injured person (1)	Signature of injured person or other person making this entry* (2)	Date when entry made (3)	Date and time of accident (4)	Room/place in which accident happened (5)	Cause and nature of injury † (6)
1	Constantine Larousse 14 North Street Islington (Office Junior)	C Larousse	14/8/98	10.30 14/8/98	Rm 74	Tripped over trailing wire & bruised knees and elbows whilst carrying cups of coffee for fellow workers
2						
3	Marcus Davis 17 Albert Sq, Acton London W3 (Accounting Technician)	M Davis	=	=	=	Attempted to prevent injury to Constantine. Suffered minor scalding to chest from hot
4						coffee and punctured hand on letter spiker. Obtained first aid
5						
6						
7	Percy Lal 247 East Street Finchley	M Davis (as above)	=	=	=	Percy was standing on a chair trying to put a box on the shelf. It appears that he was
8						alarmed by the above incident, banged his head on the shelf, dropped the box and fell off the
9						chair. He has been taken to hospital.
10						

* If the entry is made by some person acting on behalf of the employee, the address and occupation of that person must also be given

† State clearly the work or process being performed at the time of the accident

Answers to Chapter 2 activities

Activity 2.1

(a) The receptionist's attention is overloaded. It would be easy, in the general to-and-fro, for an unauthorised person to get past her into the offices without the appropriate checks and procedures - whether intentionally or unintentionally. It might also be a temptation to let the couriers deliver direct to the offices - again, a risk if they are unescorted and unlogged. To minimise the risk, reception should - permanently, or on a temporary 'at need' basis - be manned by extra personnel: a 'back-up' reception person might be kept 'on call'.

(b) It is surprisingly quick work to slip through an open door, gather a bag, or armful of valuable items, and slip out again! It can be done - swiftly - right under the nose of unwary occupants, and in this case, there is added risk since the door and storerooms are (i) close together and (ii) out of the way of office traffic. A further risk exists of the door being forgotten at the end of the day, if it is not usually left unlocked. The only way to minimise this risk is *not* to open the back door, or to allow it to be opened on a security chain or with a security gate or grill.

(c) The risk is that the visitor is not *bona fide* - nobody has checked - and has been left alone and unobserved in the office, where he has unchallenged access to anything left lying around. Ways of minimising such a risk include: vetting such visitors at reception and giving proof (such as a visitor's card) that this has taken place; requiring visitors to wait at reception or in other open areas until the visitee is available; people who are expecting visitors warning others in the office and describing/naming the visitor so they can cross-check the visitor's identity informally - especially if the visitee might not be available; having someone escort and stay with a visitor at all times, tactfully; and, as a last resort, ensuring that the door to the supervisor's office is kept open, and the visitor is visible to staff until the supervisor's return.

Activity 2.2

Your answer will obviously depend on your choice of topic, your organisation's specific procedures, and your imagination and communication style. You may have chosen to outline the steps in the procedure (**without** simply copying them from the Procedures Manual!), or you may have opted for a reminder/warning poster such as (at its simplest) the following.

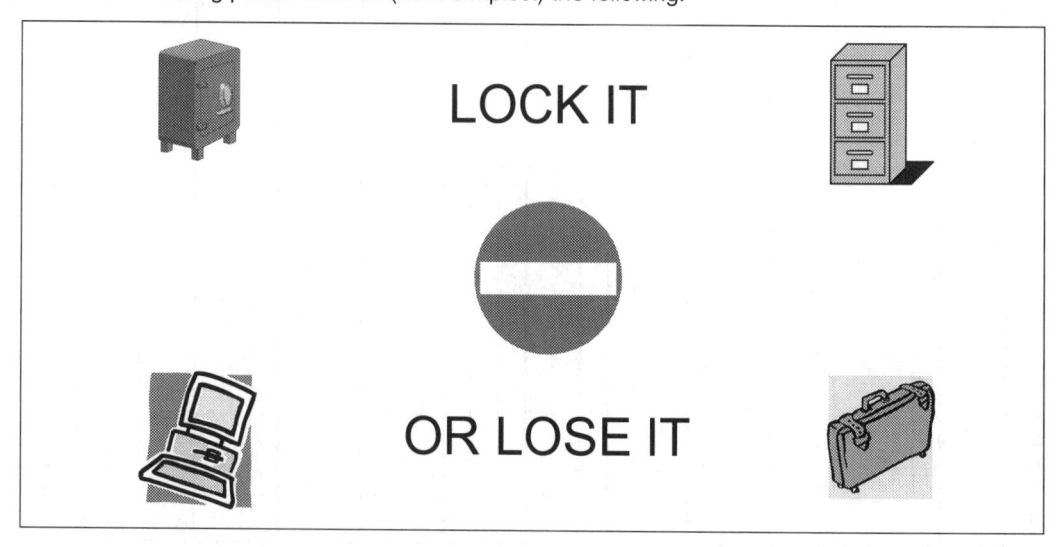

Activity 2.3

(a) The situation sounds very dubious: it is not usual for photocopiers to be repaired off-site. Here are some of the things that should be done.

    (i) Ask to see the men's identification.

    (ii) Under no circumstances allow them to take away the photocopier until you have established the facts. Get someone to keep an eye on them and make them a cup of tea. Don't let on that you are suspicious: say you are just going through the normal booking out procedures that have to be followed when assets are removed from the building and you'll get into trouble if you don't.

(iii)   Find out which company normally services the photocopier. Is this the company that the men claim to work for? You can start to be very suspicious if not.

(iv)   Telephone the company that the men claim to work for. Ask them to verify that the men do indeed work for them and they are responding to a call placed by someone in your organisation. Find out who in your organisation.

(v)   Telephone the person that called the men out and explain the situation. That person may then take responsibility for dealing with the situation.

(vi)   If the men do not work for the company they claim to work for, or if it does not exist, call the security department of your organisation, or the police if there is no security department. In fact if the men are thieves they would probably have made their escape by now, but you should still report the matter.

(b)   The reason is that your organisation *requires* all employees to *wear* their passes, and it is likely to have very strong grounds for doing so. Intruders will not stand out as people not wearing passes if bona fide personnel break the rules too.

If this matter is genuinely causing you distress, speak to your manager about it, or to another manager if your manager is one of the prime jokers. You could perhaps get another pass made up using your own, more presentable, photo, or at least get the issuer of passes to take a less unfortunate photo than the current one.

(c)   Simply see that the matter is reported at once to the MD. Assuming that you don't talk to the MD personally, make sure that the person to whom you give the message is reliable, and understands that you think the threats were serious. Your responsibility ends here, although the MD him or herself will probably want to check the facts with you directly, before taking further action.

(d)   If there is a telephone in the room notify firstly the first aid officer and secondly the security staff that help is needed and access for that help will have to be authorised. Stay with the injured person.

If you have to leave the room, leave it secure but accessible to authorised persons (ie don't run out leaving the keys locked inside!), get the help of the nearest available responsible member of staff and return to the injured person.

If it is left to you to authorise the entry of medical help when it arrives, make sure you see bona fide passes or documentation but don't cause undue delay.

(e)   Here are some of the issues. You may have thought of other matters.

(i)   The keys to the Deeds Room will probably be in the possession of certain nominated keyholders only. You will have to obtain the keys and perhaps have them booked out to you. The security of the Deeds Room will be your responsibility all the while the keys are in your possession.

(ii)   Procedures are likely to require the room to be kept locked at all times. You should not leave the door unlocked, even if you just have to pop out for a few moments.

(iii)   However, presumably (ii) means that the door should be kept locked while you are *inside*. This would be very dangerous, especially if the door were only able to be unlocked from the outside and there were no means of escape in an emergency. If this had not been thought about you ought to bring it to someone's notice. The Fire Service and your organisation's insurers would take a very dim view of this arrangement.

(iv)   No smoking rules will certainly apply. There may also be restrictions on food and drink.

(v)   There should be a telephone in the basement, in case of emergency.

(vi)   If someone else wants to enter the Deeds Room while you are inside and does not have their own key, you will need to be sure that they are who they say they are before you let them in.

(vii)   Would it not be better to do the work that you are required to do in your own office? Could the relevant files not be brought up to you?

(viii)   If (vii) is not possible, is the room properly equipped for the sort of work that you are going to do. Is there a desk and adequate lighting?

Answers to Chapter 3 activities

Activity 3.1

(a) (i)   The grapevine can be helpful in: spreading information that people need to know in order to do their jobs, which might overload formal communication systems; helping people to feel that they 'belong' in the organisation, which might increase their loyalty and commitment; facilitating the swapping of ideas between different departments and levels of the organisation (which might not be built into the formal system), leading to product/service innovation or problem-solving; by-passing 'blockages' in the formal system (eg two individuals who do not share information because of hostility or competition).

      (ii)   The grapevine can be unhelpful in: spreading inaccurate information in the form of gossip, which might be harmful (eg if it is negative about the organisation); by-passing formal channels of communication so that someone who needs the information in order to do his job is 'left out of the loop'; wasting time and energy passing information which nobody needs.

(b) (i)   Informal methods can be helpful in: getting things done swiftly (eg solving a customer's problem) where formal procedures are too slow or inflexible; encouraging employees to be flexible and creative in problem-solving (particularly when serving customers or clients); giving employees the satisfaction of using their initiative, which may enhance their morale (especially if such opportunities are rare in the formal system).

      (ii)   Informal methods can be unhelpful in: neglecting the detailed controls and safeguards deliberately built into formal procedures; undermining the consistency and standardisation of the output/service provided to all customers or clients.

Activity 3.2

(a) (i)   Delivering goods to suppliers   `4`

      (ii)   Preparing cheques for suppliers   `2`

      (iii)   Recording credit sales   `2`

      (iv)   Bank reconciliations   `2`

      (v)   Dealing with customers' enquiries   `3`

      (vi)   Negotiating discounts with suppliers   `1`

      (vii)   Calculating wages due to production staff   `2`

(b) (i)   The sales administrator (3) would need to tell the distribution manager (4) what goods to deliver to whom.

      (ii)   Cheque preparation would normally go ahead without further consultation unless for some reason the purchasing manager (1) gave instructions that a certain supplier should not be paid.

      (iii)   The accounts administrator (2) would record sales when told by the sales administrator (3) what sales had been made. (In some systems the recording of the sale might happen automatically, however.)

      (iv)   Bank reconciliations would be the task of the accounts administrator (2) alone, assuming proper records had been kept.

      (v)   The sales administrator (3) might need to communicate with the accounts administrator (2) if the enquiry were about payment for the goods, or with the distribution manager (4) if it were about delivery.

      (vi)   Discount negotiation would normally be the sole preserve of the purchasing manager (1), unless the time of payment was critical (for settlement discounts) in which case the accounts administrator (2) may need to be consulted.

(vii)   The factory supervisor (5) would need to provide the accounts administrator (2) with details of hours worked and so forth to enable wages to be calculated.

Activity 3.3 _____

(a)   *Functional structure*

In a functional structure, all similar activities are managed together, and so a summary accounting statement would bring together costs by function. Revenue would be aggregated in total.

	£'000	£'000
Total sales revenue		3,600
Production function	955	
Marketing function	450	
Finance and admin function	180	
Head office costs	150	
		(1,735)
Revenue less costs		1,865

(b)   *Product-divisional structure*

In a product-divisional structure, the accounting information is assessed by product.

	Yoricks	Ophelias	Total
	£	£	£
Sales revenue	2,500	1,100	3,600
Production costs	(675)	(280)	(955)
Marketing costs	(300)	(150)	(450)
Gross profit by product	1,525	670	2,195
Finance and admin			(180)
Head office			(150)
Revenue less costs			1,865

(c)   *Geographical structure*

	UK	Denmark	Total
	£	£	£
Sales	1,500	2,100	3,600
Costs: Production	(430)	(525)	(955)
Marketing	(170)	(280)	(450)
Finance and admin	(75)	(105)	(180)
Profit by country	825	1,190	2,015
Head office			(150)
Revenue less costs			1,865

Activities 3.4, 3.6, 3.7 _____

These activities relate solely to your specific organisation, job and selected tasks. There is no 'right' answer. We are asking you to expand your awareness of your own work role and practices: organisation charts, job descriptions and flow charts are useful technologies to help you think - perhaps in a fresh and clearer way - about what you do.

Activity 3.5 _____

Examples might include:

(a)   Logic of the task: routine task sequences such as petty cash systems or preparing invoices/ ledger balances/ management reports.

(b)   Law and regulation: data security measures, retention of financial records, drafting financial statements/tax computations, complying with health and safety provisions.

(c)   Policy: making (or defending) disciplinary complaints, non-discriminatory conduct, submitting leave requests, obeying smoking/alcohol rules.

(d)   Formal instruction: carrying out any task as requested by a team leader or manager.

241

(e)   Informal customs: taking smoking breaks 'out the back'; by-passing known blockages in the communication system; skipping certain forms or procedures accepted as redundant and so on.

Activity 3.8

Again your answer will be specific to you, so there can be no suggested solution.

Each of the statements is an *ideal* of work organisation. Wherever you have ticked the 'False' box you should have some kind of comment explaining why the ideal is not possible in the circumstances under which you work.

Where you have ticked a *false* box, is there anything you can do about it? For example, if you have said 'I sometimes miss deadlines because others do not deliver their input to me in time', is this really a problem of your relationship with others? If you said 'I am not always able to work on one task at a time until it is finished: sometimes there is a delay because I have to get information from elsewhere', is this the full story? Perhaps you do not plan out your work properly when you start.

This is an opportunity to reappraise the way you work. Take action on any suggestion that strikes you as being a more efficient way of working for you. You will soon begin to appreciate the time and effort saved by good personal organisation.

Activity 3.9

Note: Just our suggestion: The devising of the mnemonic was the point of the exercise.

Priority?
Relative consequences
Importance
Other people depend on it
Required for other tasks
Immediacy (urgency)
Time limits (deadlines0
Yes!

Activity 3.10

(a)   There are four reasons.

    (i)   Most of the work you do is not done in isolation. You rely on other people to provide you with certain information to get things done; when your work is finished you pass on the results to your colleagues or superiors or to customers and clients. Any delay on your part prevents other people from getting on with their work.

    (ii)   If you are late in producing a piece of work then you will tend to hurry it as the deadline draws near or passes, and its quality will suffer.

    (iii)   If you are late with one piece of work you will have less time to do your next piece of work. That too will be late or below standard.

    (iv)   You may get a reputation for unreliability.

(b)   The key points are as follows.

    (i)   Think through the entire task.
    (ii)   Plan how to achieve it in the time specified.
    (iii)   Arrange for any contribution needed from others to be available in plenty of time.
    (iv)   Monitor your progress.

Activity 3.11

Some suggestions, in addition to those mentioned in the text:

(a)   various specific stationery and forms (blank invoices, accident report forms etc etc);
(b)   furniture and accessories - desk, chair, filing cabinets, in-trays;
(c)   equipment: computer and accessories, calculator and so on.

Activity 3.12

You were asked to consider your own workspace. Be honest!

Answers to Chapter 4 activities

Activity 4.1

Your answers will be specific to your own job, of course, so no suggested solution can be provided.

You may well have found it difficult to say what the *single* most important thing that you do is. If so, it might be worth asking the opinion of your colleagues and your supervisor. You might be surprised at the way others perceive your job and role in the organisation.

If you do part (b) of the exercise properly and this is the first time you have thought about your job in this way you may well be able to see ways in which you can work more efficiently in the future - tasks that you can batch together, for example, or tasks which can best be started at the beginning of the day, or little tasks that interrupt the flow of your work and which could be left to the end of the day.

Activity 4.2

We would suggest that the first post should be read first (assuming that it arrives before Georgette starts work) in case it contains anything that needs to be attended to urgently. If the post has not arrived yet Georgette could get on with clearing the backlog of filing while waiting.

Once the post arrives, any item that can be dealt with quickly should be dealt with straight away - for example redirecting correspondence that is normally dealt with by someone else to that person. Other items will require information to be obtained which may cause some delay. At this point Georgette needs to take stock of work outstanding from earlier days and new work that has just arrived, and determine the priorities.

Chasing up replies should probably wait until after the second post has been received and read: some of the replies may have come in, in which case the effort will have been wasted.

The staff meeting needs to be worked around. It would be better not to start a lengthy task just after lunch if it is going to be interrupted by the meeting in half an hour's time. If possible Georgette should try to find out how long the meeting will last and how big a chunk it will take out of her normal day.

Here is a *suggested* schedule.

9am to 9.30   Get on with yesterday's filing until first post arrives.

9.30 to 10.00   Look through first post and identify priorities. Forward any items that will be dealt with by others.

10.00 to 1.00   Complete each task or progress it as far as possible according to priorities identified. File completed work as soon as it is completed rather than adding to yesterday's pile.

1.00 to 2.00   Lunch.

2.00 to 2.30   Read afternoon post and adjust priorities as necessary. Forward non-relevant items.

2.30 onwards   Attend meeting.

3.30 (say)   Chase up replies to previous correspondence.

4.00 to 5.00   Complete tasks as far as possible according to priorities identified.

5.00   Go home, if both yesterday's filing and all of today's filing is done. Stay a few minutes late to get this out of the way if not.

Activity 4.3

Just do it!

Activity 4.4

(a) Studying the manager's checklist shows that you don't need to worry about the ads: they are finished and sent off. Leaflet A is at the printers, and has been for 3 days: it still needs to be proofed and sent off before the 12th – a week to go. Leaflet B seems to be at the designers – with just over a week to go: it is clearly falling behind and will need watching: in particular, the photography seems to be held up and will have to be dealt with first.

(b) Checklists are particularly helpful in the event that you have to hand a task over to someone else for completion.

(c) You might have suggested shopping lists or things to do in general – or points to be covered in an essay (a very useful planning habit to get into!).

Activity 4.5

The example we have chosen is giving a dinner party.

(a) Brainstorming suggests the following: menu, date, time, people to invite, cooking, table decorations, contacting people, shopping, wines, setting table, shopping list.

(b) We now rearrange these ideas into activity order: people to invite, date, time, contact people, menu, wines, shopping list, shopping, table decorations, setting table, cooking.

(c) This information then converts to the precedence diagram below.

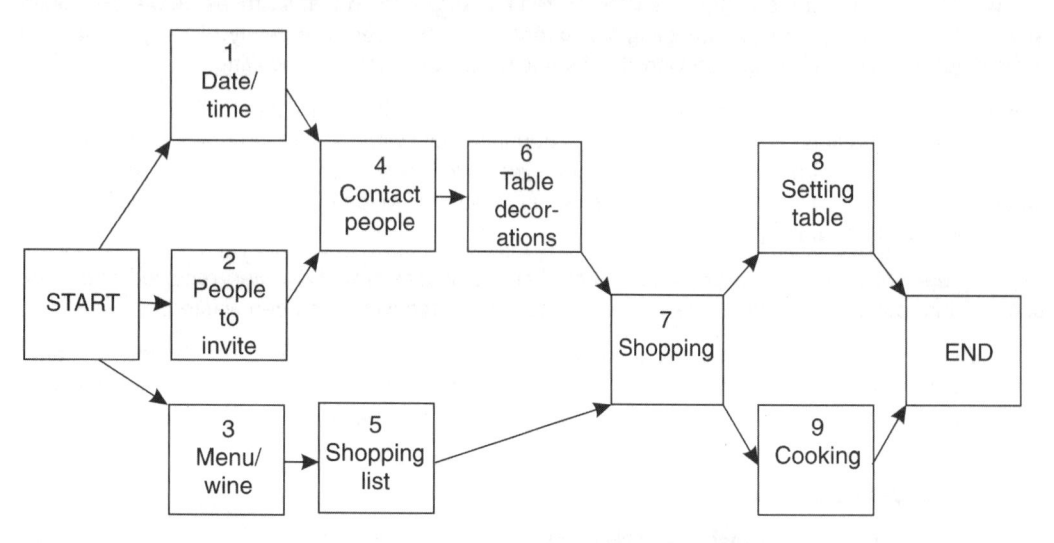

Activity 4.6

SATURDAY 3	WEDNESDAY 7
Request files	
SUNDAY 4	THURSDAY 8
Draft report	Approve report. Signature to report
MONDAY 5	FRIDAY 9
	Courier
TUESDAY 6	Week commencing 3 SEPTEMBER S S M T W T F ◯ 3 4 5 6 7 8 9
Type report	

Activity 4.7

On Monday you will have to check the situation on the Panthos account. It looks as though this is a slow paying customer and that legal action is being considered if payment has not been received by the 14th. It seems that your boss was due to have a meeting about this on Tuesday with the credit controller, but it may be worth bringing this forward, or at least contacting the credit controller to get the full story and find out exactly what you should do. You may not have the authority to institute legal action and the credit controller may wish to take over responsibility here.

There is also a new person joining the department on Monday, and she will need some induction. Having been new once yourself, you will have some idea of what is required, but you should check to see whether anything specific was planned: a tour of the department, a meeting with personnel staff, signing of forms and so on. This is an ongoing task, not just something that will take five minutes on Monday morning. Over the next few days you will frequently need to make sure that the new person is being 'looked after', given work to do, receiving on-the-job training and so on.

On Tuesday your boss was due to submit a report for Thursday's finance committee meeting. You will need to find out how near this is to completion as soon as possible. Was the deadline Tuesday morning or Tuesday last thing? Will *you* be able to complete the report or will you need help from others? Where do you have to send the report when it is finished? Does it usually have some kind of covering letter or memo?

On Tuesday afternoon Cynthia was due to conduct a staff appraisal with a member of staff called Julie. Assuming that it would not be appropriate for *you* to conduct the appraisal yourself, can this be delayed until after your boss's return to work? Or can another manager conduct it instead? Does a pay rise depend on the outcome of the appraisal? Note that Julie is going on holiday for two weeks starting on Friday: it may be demotivating to make her wait for her appraisal. You need to find out the background before making a decision and discussing the matter with Julie herself.

Note also that Cynthia was considering employing a temp in Julie's absence: the diary entry about this is on Friday, but you may have to decide whether a temp will be needed (and if so when and for how long) before then, to allow time to recruit one. This is another good reason for having a discussion with Julie early in the week, to find out what her current and anticipated workload is.

On Wednesday the only thing scheduled is a departmental meeting. What was this about? Will you be expected to lead it in Cynthia's absence? Do you have all the information you need to do so?

What else will you be doing on Wednesday? Who is doing your work while you are standing in for Cynthia?

On Thursday there is the finance committee meeting, for which the report was due on Tuesday. Are you expected to attend the meeting? Will you be expected to comment on the report?

On Friday Cynthia has made a note to herself which presumably means 'take home and read the details about one of the company's new products'. Do you know which new product(s) she had in mind, and why she particularly wanted to familiarise herself with the details over the weekend? Perhaps there is some kind of meeting about this or some work on the new product has to be submitted by next week. In other words you need to look ahead in the diary to see what is coming up: you cannot just take one week at a time.

Activity 4.8

(a)   The Gantt chart shows clearly that production is slightly behind schedule on Monday and Tuesday, spot on Wednesday, better than planned on Thursday, but well short on Friday.

(b)   It would be helpful to see how the cumulative production measured against the cumulative schedule, since daily comparisons are up and down.

(c)

Monday	Tuesday	Wednesday	Thursday	Friday
····►100	····►225	·····►375	·····►525	·····►675
➤ 75	➤175	➤ 325	➤ 505	➤580

(d)   It is easy to see that the final weekly total output is well down on schedule.

Activity 4.9

(a)

Day	Task (level)	Performed by (level)	Comments
Monday	Extraction (J)	Kathryn (I)	Junior staff not available
Tuesday	Extraction (J)	Kathryn (I)	
Wednesday	Analysis (S)	Kathryn (I)	Staff development, but takes all day
Thursday (Half)	Review	Alison (S)	Review of Wednesday's work
Thursday (Half)	Data entry (J)	Margaret (J)	After review, data entry can commence
Friday	Data entry (J)	Margaret (J)	-
Monday (Half)	Data entry (J)	Margaret (J)	-
Monday (Half)	Interpretation (S)	Alison (S)	-
Tuesday	Liaison (S)	Alison (S)	-
Wednesday	Correspondence (I)	Margaret (J)	Staff development, but task takes twice as long
Thursday	Correspondence (I)	Margaret (J)	-
Friday (Half)	Review	Kathryn (I)	-

(b)   Alison should speak to somebody in the production department to make sure that it will be possible to carry out the task that requires their input on the day planned and to make them aware of the overall deadlines so that they can organise any preparatory work that they need to do.

(c)   If Margaret is ill and is not back at work by Thursday, the whole job will be delayed. Alison should mention this matter to her section leader, who may be prepared to accept a revision of the final deadline or be able to arrange for help from another junior in the section.

Answers to Chapter 5 activities

Activity 5.1

This activity is intended to help you to think about your behaviour towards others at work. Look through your answers and consider whether you are satisfied that you behave in this way, think as you do, or that this is the situation that prevails. What can you do to change things? The biggest battle is recognising and accepting that there is a problem and being determined to do something about it. If you recognise a situation that used to apply to you but has now been resolved, how did it get resolved?

Activity 5.2

(a)   Touching someone, or standing very close to them, in a way taken to be sexually suggestive.

(b)   Derogatory comments about (most commonly) 'girls' or 'birds'.

(c)   Gender-related insults - like calling a woman a 'bitch' or a 'cow'.

(d)   Comments about appearance or dress that are sexually suggestive or offensive.

(e)   Sexual jokes and innuendoes.

Activity 5.3

Your answer will reflect your interpersonal activities on the day you chose: no two answers will be alike.

What could you learn from this data? You would expect technical/work-related conversations to dominate during work time, and friendly/courteous conversations during breaks. (If not, are you wasting the organisation's time? Or becoming a workaholic?)

You would expect to ask for advice and help sometimes, but not as a large proportion of your interactions. (If not, are you avoiding seeking help when you ought to do so? Or are you constantly in crisis, or asking for help needlessly?)

You would expect to receive some supportive and encouraging words occasionally. (If not, where can you get some?)

Activity 5.4

(a) Discussions regarding annual pay reviews involving managers and their subordinates should ideally be held in a private location, such as the manager's office or a private meeting room. Remuneration is a very sensitive issue in many organisations, and such information is generally considered to be confidential.

(b) Similarly, information regarding candidates for redundancy should be treated as confidential and dealt with sensitively. Such discussions should therefore be held in private locations.

(c) Many organisations have departmental Christmas parties, the location of which is usually discussed at length by the department's employees. Such discussions are very informal, and so may be held in the pub, in the office if it is open-plan or in a meeting room that is of sufficient size to house all staff involved.

(d) An appropriate location for holding discussions regarding plans for the new office location might be in the office if such discussions are to be held departmentally, or in a sufficiently large arena, if the whole organisation is to be involved. Such discussions are not deemed to be confidential, so the most appropriate location would really depend upon the number of staff involved, and whether additional equipment was required (such as an overhead projector or flip chart) for presenting the plans.

(e) Sales figures for the current year are likely to be discussed in a formal departmental meeting. The most appropriate location for such meetings is probably a meeting room. If the sales and marketing department were to remain in their office, it is likely that they would be interrupted by visitors from other departments and phone calls.

(f) Most discussions involving the personnel department are likely to involve confidential information. Depending on the number of staff involved in the recruitment process, such discussions would ideally be held in a private place, such as a meeting room or an individual office.

Activity 5.5

Just do it. What makes a team feel like a team? Perhaps a name, behavioural or dress norms, shared stories and successes (or heroic failures), 'badges' of some kind, its own space: there are many ways of building a team identity. As for the Belbin roles, you may have noticed that an individual can play more than one role, as required.

Activity 5.6

(a) Recreation helps the team to build informal relationships. In this case, the chosen activity also reminds them of their task, and may make them feel special, as part of the motor racing industry, by giving them a taste of what the end user of their product does.

(b) A team challenge pushes the group to consider its strengths and weaknesses, to find its natural leader, to co-operate and help each other in overcoming obstacles.

(c) This exercise creates an 'us' and 'them' challenge: perceiving the rival team as the enemy heightens the solidarity of the group.

(d) This exercise encourages the group to raise problems and conflicts freely, away from the normal environment of work, and also encourages brainstorming and the expression of team members' dreams for what the team can achieve in future.

Activity 5.7

(a) (i) **Win-lose**: one team member gets the window desk, and the other does not. (Result: broken relationships within the team.)

(ii) **Compromise**: the team members get the window desk on alternate days or weeks. (Result: half satisfied needs.)

(iii) **Win-win**: what do they want the window desk for? One may want the view, the other better lighting conditions. This offers options to be explored: how else could the lighting be improved, so that both team members get what they really want? (Result: at least, the positive intention to respect everyone's wishes equally, with benefits for team communication and creative problem-solving.)

(b) (i) **Win-lose**: one of you gets the file and the other doesn't.

(ii) **Compromise**: one of you gets the file now, and the other gets it later (although this has an element of win-lose, since the other has to work late or take it home).

(iii) **Win-win**: you photocopy the file and **both** take it, or one of your consults his or her boss and gets an extension of the deadline (since getting the job done in time is the real aim - not just getting the file). These kind of solutions are more likely to emerge if the parties believe they **can** both get what they want.

(c) (i) **Win-lose**: Manager A gets the computers, and Manager B has to upgrade her systems.

(ii) **Compromise**: Manager A will get some new computers, but keep the same old ones for continued data-sharing with Department B. Department B will also need to get some new computers, as a back-up measure.

(iii) **Win-win**: what does Manager A want the computers for, or to avoid? Quite possibly, she needs to use up her budget allocation for buying equipment before the end of the budgetary period: if not, she fears she will lose that budget allocation. However, that may not be the case, or there may be other equipment that could be more usefully purchased - in which case, there is no losing party.

Activity 5.8

Just do it! (And while you are at it, do the same exercise for other policies and procedures mentioned in paragraphs 2.11 - 2.19 of this chapter.)

Activity 5.9

(a) Senior management and shareholders, who expect the strategic objectives of the organisation to be met through effective and efficient accounting activity. Managers who expect accurate, up-to-date and focused management control reports, financial statements and so on.

(b) The various line departments of the organisation, to whom accounting is a 'staff' function. They expect clear and accurate budgets, forecasts and records of expenditure; payments made to their suppliers and invoices issued to customers on time; resources appropriately allocated and so on.

(c) The members of the organisation as a whole, who expect to be given information - and particularly 'good news' - by the organisation; to be able to feel pride in the organisation's image to the outside world, to identify with it; and to feel that the accounting function (among others) is 'getting it right' so that:

(i) their efforts in serving external customers are supported (and not undermined) by the image created by accounting communications and output;

(ii) their efforts are being properly reflected and communicated to management and the financial community via financial results.

Answers to Chapter 6 activities _____

Activity 6.1

Here are a few suggestions.

(a) **Sound**: your alarm clock bleeped at you telling you it was time to get up.

(b) **Speech**: you switched on the radio and somebody read out the news headlines to you.

(c) **Visual communication**: perhaps you watched breakfast TV and you saw a weather map which told you whether you needed to wear an overcoat or summer clothes.

(d) **Written communication**: maybe there was a message from your flatmate on the fridge ('Need more milk', 'Back late tonight'). Perhaps you had some letters. You may have glanced through a newspaper.

(e) **Numbers**: possibly you had to consult a train timetable which gave you an idea of when to leave home and whether you would be late.

Activity 6.2 _____

Positive feedback		Negative feedback	
1	Action taken as requested	1	No action taken or wrong action taken
2	Letter/memo/note confirming receipt of message and replying in an appropriate way	2	No written response where expected
3	Accurate reading back of message	3	Incorrect reading back of message
4	Statement: 'Yes, I've got that.'	4	Request for clarification or repetition
5	Smile, nod, murmur of agreement	5	Silence, blank look, frown etc

Activity 6.3

Scrooples & Co Ltd

93 Brindle Close, Bolton, Lancashire, BN2 9AJ
Telephone: 01101 222333 Fax: 01101 444555

Freda M Smethwick
8 Cornel Mansions
Mapesbury Avenue
Bolton
Lancashire. BL19 4PJ

4 August 2000

Dear Freda

Post of receptionist

We have now completed our selection procedure for the post of receptionist and sadly I have to tell you that your application has not been successful on this occasion.

I do hope that this will not be too much of a disappointment to you, and I would like to thank you for the interest that you have shown in Scrooples & Co.

With best wishes for your success in finding suitable employment.

Yours sincerely

Nora Scroople

Nora Scroople
Personnel Manager

Scrooples & Co Ltd
Directors: Nora M Scroople BA; Dora M Scroople ACA; Thora M Scroople
Registered office: 93 Brindle Close, Bolton, Lancashire BN2 9AJ.
Registered in England, Number 19191919.

Activity 6.4

---

10 November 2000

Dear Mr Bruce

Account: BTFASH

May we remind you that you have not yet settled our account for £1,445.00 due on 7 November 2000.

In case the invoice has gone astray, we enclose a copy statement of account and should be grateful if you would let us have your cheque in payment by return of post.

Yours sincerely

17 November 2000

Dear Mr Bruce

Account: BTFASH

We note that your accounts department has still not settled our account for £1,445.00. As you know, our conditions of sale include payment within thirty days of our invoice and I imagine the delay has occurred because this is your busiest trading season.

Nevertheless, this account was due on 7 November 2000 and we would very much appreciate settlement by return.

Yours sincerely

---

24 November 2000

Dear Mr Bruce

Account: BTFASH

We are surprised that we have received no reply from you to our letter of 17 November 2000 asking for payment of our account for £1,445.00.

In the circumstances we must suspend further delivery of goods and ask you to let us have your cheque by return of post.

Yours sincerely

---

1 December 2000

Dear Mr Bruce

Account: BTFASH

We are extremely concerned that you have not replied to our letters of 17 and 24 November 2000 regarding our outstanding account for £1,445.00 which was due on 7 November 2000. It is only because we value your goodwill that we have not referred the matter to our debt collectors. If, however, you do not settle the account within seven days, we shall reluctantly have to do so.

Yours sincerely

---

10 December 2000

Dear Mr Bruce

Account: BTFASH

Since we have received no reply from you to our letters of 17 and 24 November and 1 December 2000 we have reluctantly referred the matter to our debt collectors.

Yours sincerely

Activity 6.5

LETTERHEAD

S Wat Pora Esq
9 Blackheath Way
Greenwich
London SE10 2AL

10 August 2000

Dear Mr Wat Pora

Account no. 0139742

Thank you for your letter of 6 August 2000 regarding the above account.

I have looked into the matter that you raised and I am afraid that your letter of 27 June was indeed overlooked.

I apologise for this error. I have arranged for your account to be recredited with the sum of £25.50, the amount of the direct debit paid in July. I confirm that the direct debit instructions have now been cancelled.

Yours sincerely

N E Name

Clerk

Activity 6.6

Here is one suggestion: you may have laid your memo out in the form used by your organisation.

MEMO

To:	All staff	**Ref:** US/JBS/4
From:	Nora Scroople, Personnel Manager	**Date:** 4 August 2000
Subject:	Post of receptionist	

Please note that Laura M Scroople will be starting work with us on Monday next. I trust you will all make her very welcome.

Activity 6.7

> **MEMORANDUM**
>
> | | | | |
> |---|---|---|---|
> | **To:** | All staff in X Dept | **Ref:** STAT/1 | |
> | **From:** | Your name | **Date:** 24 September 2000 | |
>
> **Subject:** Stationery
>
> Please note that I am now responsible for ordering stationery for X Department.
>
> The normal procedure appears to have lapsed and as a gentle reminder I attach a copy of the standard stationery requisition form. I should be grateful if you would complete a form and pass it to me whenever you become aware that stocks of any item are running low.
>
> I shall ensure that there is always an ample supply of requisition forms and pens in the stationery cupboard.

Activity 6.8

The highlighters you ordered were not delivered. We suggest that you draft a letter of complaint as follows.

> # Letterhead
>
> William H Smythe
> Pens and Paper Ltd
> 31 Margin Alley
> North Hinchsey
>
> 10 June 20X6
>
> Dear Mr Smythe
>
> *Stationery order number 10573*
>
> I refer to the above order (a copy of which is enclosed) and to our telephone conversation last week.
>
> I am still awaiting receipt of the yellow highlighter pens which were omitted from your delivery on 17 May. These items are in constant demand and I have therefore placed an order with another supplier.
>
> I should be grateful if you would cancel the unfulfilled part of order no. 10573.
>
> Perhaps you would also let me know whether you expect to be able to supply yellow highlighters in the future.
>
> Yours sincerely
>
>
> Your name
>
> Stationery Buyer
>
> Enc

BPP PUBLISHING

Activity 6.9

This was a 'live interaction' activity. Your answer is: whatever results you heard and observed. (Do think about how successfully you listened and questioned: what might you do differently next time?)

Activity 6.10

The totals you should have got are as follows.

Product	T470	S332	V017	J979	B525	Z124
Total	7,520	2,355	5,760	1,510	6,725	4,375

Month	Total £'000
January	2,500
February	2,455
March	2,350
April	1,990
May	2,050
June	2,000
July	2,125
August	2,270
September	2,395
October	2,625
November	2,735
December	2,750
	28,245

> *Tutorial note.* We have laid out the answer like this to make you aware that it is more difficult to check information presented in one way against information presented in another. It would have been kinder of us if we had simply reproduced the table with totals. Note, also, how much more effectively the table uses space.

(a)

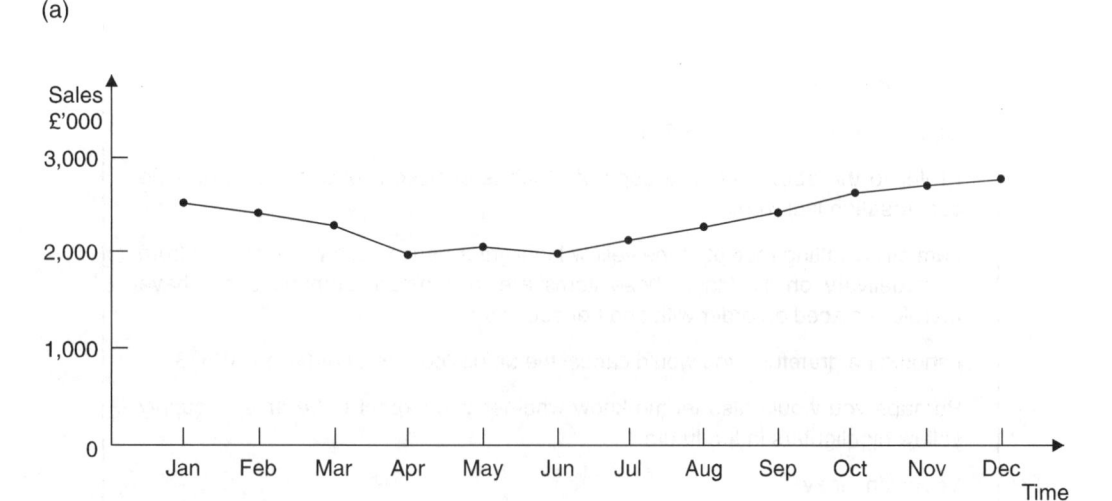

(b) We have divided our bar chart into segments for each product. Do not worry if you did not think of this, but notice how much more information you get if you present the information in this way.

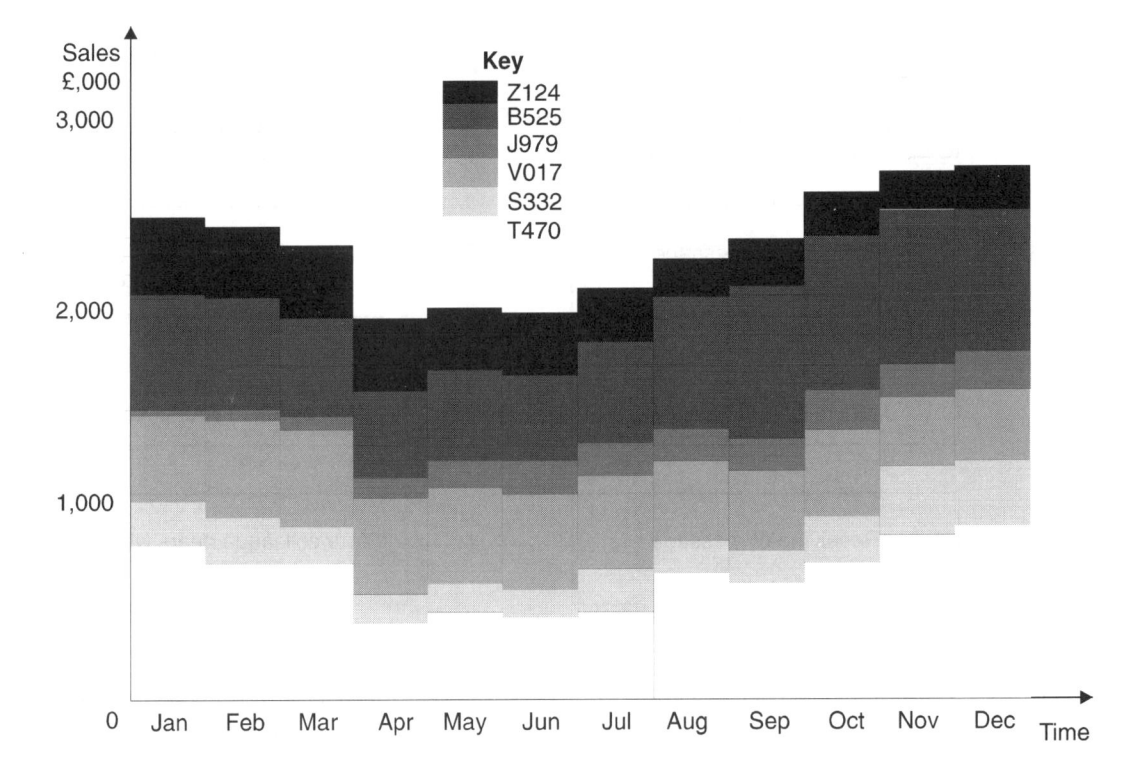

(c) We think that the share of total sales by product is the most appropriate information to show in pie-chart form. To arrive at the percentages for each segment divide the total for each product by the overall total and multiply by 100. To arrive at the number of degrees take the relevant percentage of 360°.

For example, T470: 7,520/28,245 × 100 = 27%; 27% × 360°= 96°

Total annual sales by product

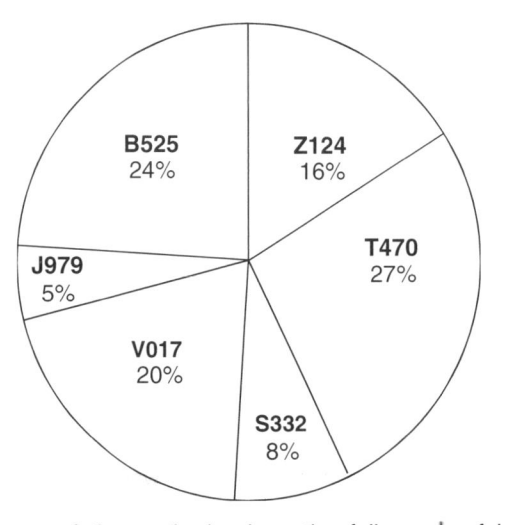

(d) We do not think that any of the methods show the full range of information completely effectively. The graph is perhaps the worst (individual lines for each product could have been plotted but the graph would have been very crowded). The bar chart is probably the best method.

In practice, of course, there is no reason why all four methods (including the table) should not be used.

BPP PUBLISHING

Activity 6.11

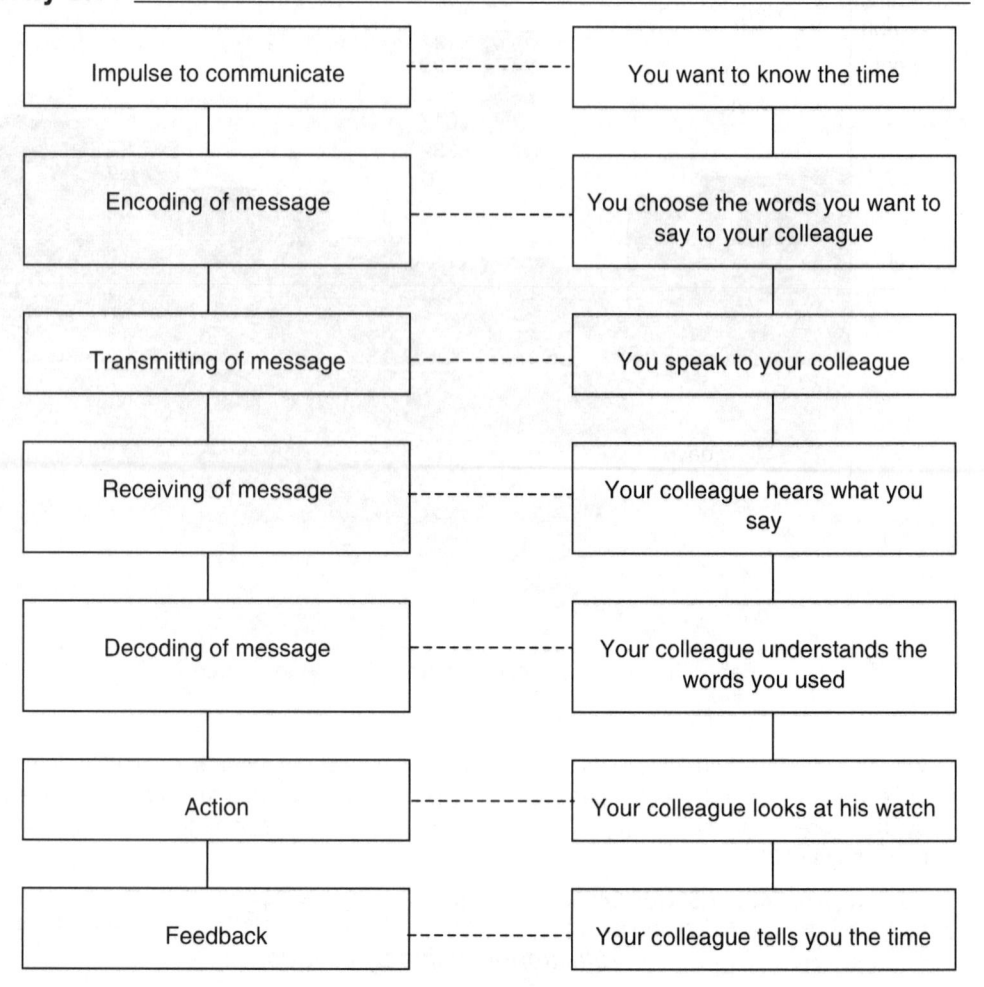

Impulse to communicate	- - - - - - - -	You want to know the time
Encoding of message	- - - - - - - -	You choose the words you want to say to your colleague
Transmitting of message	- - - - - - - -	You speak to your colleague
Receiving of message	- - - - - - - -	Your colleague hears what you say
Decoding of message	- - - - - - - -	Your colleague understands the words you used
Action	- - - - - - - -	Your colleague looks at his watch
Feedback	- - - - - - - -	Your colleague tells you the time

Activity 6.12

(a)   Anger or tenseness
(b)   Perplexity or thoughtfulness
(c)   Despair or exhaustion
(d)   A rather negative (tired? bored?) attempt to show attention
(e)   Impatience
(f)   Unease or coldness, even hostility
(g)   Relief, relaxation
(h)   Sadness, wistfulness
(i)   Surprise

Activity 6.13

(a)   The information is too detailed and complex. It would also be a very long and expensive telephone call.

(b)   This probably would be appropriate, provided you were sure that the person you were talking to was who he said he was, and that person was an appropriate person to receive the information. You would also need to stress that you were giving a draft figure.

(c)   The best way would probably be to put up a brief notice (giving details of the venue and time) where everyone would see. If the official notice board was generally ignored you could put your notice by the photocopier, or in the toilets. (Keeping quiet about your birthday is not an acceptable answer!)

(d)   In this case a memo 'to all staff' is probably the surest way. However, it might not be part of your office 'etiquette' for junior staff to send memos to more senior staff. In this case your message might have to be added to one being sent round by a more senior person.

(e) The answer depends on the precise circumstances. If there is a possibility that you will have to make extensive travel arrangements, it will probably be better to ring to get the information quickly. You might, however, want to avoid speaking to the person before the meeting, or they might be difficult to get hold of, in which case there is probably just enough time to write saying 'Please ring my secretary to tell her where the meeting will take place'.

Activity 6.14

Advantages of oral over written	Disadvantages of oral over written
• Swift/direct: no time lapse between send and receive	• 'Technical' and 'physical' noise can interfere
• Thoroughly interactive. (Note. Some written media - eg e-mail and network 'chat' facilities now have this advantage)	• Memory and perceptions not wholly trustworthy: written message provides confirmation and evidence of information exchanged, decision reached: more easily checked and referred to
• Instant feedback, including non-verbal cues: aids understanding	
• Ability to use non-verbal cues to reinforce message plus add persuasion, empathy etc	• Less time available to plan, choose words, consider implications: written better for legal proposals etc
• Flexibility good for sensitive interpersonal exchanges	• Opens you to persuasion or overruling by strong personalities or skilled persuaders: less time to appraise message 'off line'
	• Difficult to control the process where large numbers of people involved: written messages can be copied

Activity 6.15

Problems suggested by the statements made may be summed up as follows.

(a) A complete lack of tact and diplomacy. It may be that the manager is deliberately alerting 'S Simms' to the complaint by 'P Brown' but, of course, by putting the information on the noticeboard the whole department will be aware of it too.

(b) Here is someone from a specialist background talking in a jargon which will mean virtually nothing to the average recipient.

(c) At least the speaker has noticed Smith's body language! Even if the suggestion about fleas is an attempt to be facetious, the speaker appears to have misunderstood the nature of feedback: Smith is giving clear signals that (s)he is perplexed by the briefing.

(d) Technical 'noise', plus a further problem, which you may have spotted: the speaker has chosen an inappropriate medium, since he is not writing down the details which are clearly important and will require reference and confirmation later.

(e) A 463-page report to be read for the following day sounds like overload; (and since it's on 'communication', it sounds like a contradiction in terms!)

(f) Status differentials (real or imagined) are the principal source of difficulty here, the speaker evidently wishing to 'put down' the listeners and 'keep them in their place'. S(he) is potentially losing valuable contributions.

Activity 6.16

Communicating the situations given might best be done as follows.

(a)   Telephone, confirmed in writing (order form, letter).

(b)   Noticeboard or general meeting.

(c)   Face-to-face conversation. It would be a good idea to confirm the outcome of the meeting in writing so that records can be maintained.

(d)   Either telephone or face to face.

(e)   Face to face, supported by clear written notes. You can then use visual aids or gestures. This will give the opportunity for you to check the group's understanding. The notes will save the group having to memorise what you say.

Activity 6.17

(a)   Make sure that you and the person that you are communicating with are able to understand each other, that is to say, that you can communicate successfully in whatever language is suitable. Failing this, try to find somebody who can act as an interpreter for you.

(b)   If you are communicating with somebody who is not familiar with the technical language that you use in your organisation, make sure that you speak in simple 'layman' terms, omitting any fancy jargon which will only succeed in confusing the person that you are communicating with.

(c)   Make sure that you find somewhere quiet to talk with others. Printers and other people chatting can generally be avoided by finding a meeting room or quiet office in which to communicate with others.

(d)   Make sure that your writing is legible so that any messages written and subsequently transmitted may be done so successfully.

(e)   Speak clearly so that when you are communicating face-to-face or on the telephone, your message will be communicated successfully.

(f)   Make sure that you have the attention of the person that you are communicating with. If they appear disinterested, try to get them interested so that they will concentrate on the message that you are relaying. If they are too nervous or angry to listen, take time to help them calm down first.

(g)   Send the appropriate amount of information. Make sure that you pitch the volume just right so that all vital points are included and that any important items are not obscured.

(h)   Give constant feedback, and seek feedback to make sure that the recipient of your communication is understanding correctly.

(i)   Develop your communication skills, and give helpful feedback to others so that they can do the same.

Answers to Chapter 7 activities

Activity 7.1

(a)   **Inland Revenue**. There are a number of reports that must be sent to the Inland Revenue in relation to PAYE and National Insurance deductions.

(b)   **HM Customs & Excise**. Reports relating to Value Added Tax must be submitted to this body at regular intervals (monthly, quarterly and so on).

(c)   **Financial statements**. Every year a limited company must prepare these reports for submission to shareholders.

(d)   **Cashflow statements**. If a business has borrowings from the bank, the bank may wish to see proof that the business is generating income to pay interest on its loans. A bank may wish to see these reports on a regular basis.

Activity 7.2

Examples will relate to your own work, but might include:

(a)   answering an external line on your telephone or greeting a client visiting the Accounts Department;

(b)   a customer ringing to ask to whom a cheque should be made payable; an employee asking about salary arrangements;

(c)   a supplier ringing to chase late payment of an invoice; a customer complaining of a wrong amount invoiced; a manager or external agency querying errors on a report;

(d)   any of the above;

(e)   the swift correction of errors on reports; updating information supplied; checking that documents/payments received.

Activity 7.3

The point of the activity is the brainstorming exercise, but if you are stuck for ideas, see paragraph 1.9.

Activity 7.4

The following is just our suggestion, which may provide you with a more memorable way of remembering the issues involved.

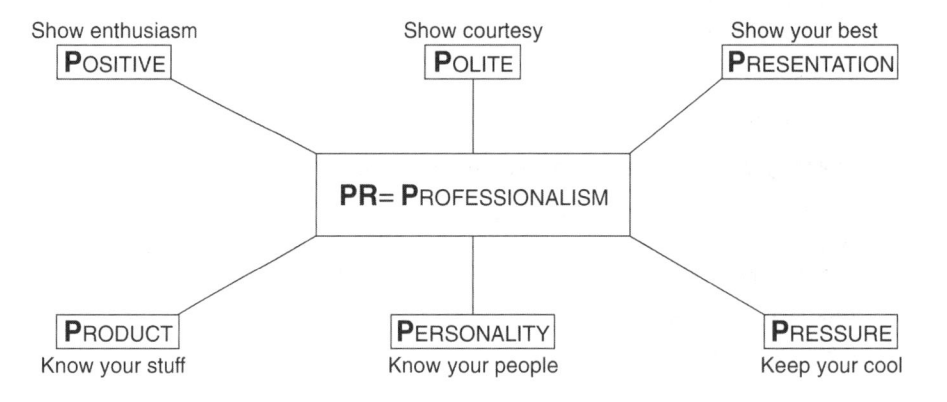

Activity 7.5

(a)   Peter (and the organisation generally) handle Mrs Weaver badly from start to finish.

(i)   Mrs Weaver is kept waiting for some while after the appointed time before she receives any attention. Even the receptionist is offhand with her.

(ii)   When he does arrive Peter does so in a very unbusinesslike manner. He does not greet Mrs Weaver by name. He does not apologise for being late. His comment about the magazine appears to be at the expense both of Mrs Weaver and the magazine (his trade's journal) itself.

(iii)   His tone of friendliness ('you can call me Peter') is belied by his complete lack of interest in Mrs Weaver's case.

(iv)   He is quite oblivious to any desire that Mrs Weaver may have for her business to be handled confidentially. He blurts out her financial problems in front of the receptionist.

(v)   He is most discourteous in not showing Mrs Weaver the way to the interview room. He should have let her go first and made some attempt to put her at her ease.

(vi)   He is more polite to the three juniors who appear to be wasting time than he has so far been to his customer. He becomes conspiratorial in referring to her, mysteriously, as 'an F104'. This tells Mrs Weaver that the organisation regards her as a number and that her case, however harrowing its circumstances may be, are about to be swallowed up by bureaucracy.

(vii) Peter's private joke with his colleagues may have nothing to do with Mrs Weaver, but by now she is likely to be feeling that, when the organisation is not being seriously inconvenienced by her, it regards her as a laughing matter.

(viii) Peter's joke at the expense of Mrs Weaver's name appears to be a corny attempt at a compliment. She has given no indication so far that either jokes or compliments are appropriate. The joke is not funny and the accompanying behaviour is quite out of place.

(ix) Once more Peter's lack of interest in the case is shown by his 'How can I help you?'. He is pulled up by Mrs Weaver's reply but then is 'saved by the bell'.

(x) He should not have accepted the telephone call - it could have been diverted to a colleague or he could have called back later.

(xi) As it is, it is quickly apparent to Mrs Weaver that she is far less valued as a customer than Peter's caller, who also appears to be a personal friend. The organisation's time and Mrs Weaver's is wasted by the discussion of the caller's domestic circumstances. Mrs Weaver will hardly be able to feel that her own affairs are being handled confidentially if Peter is prepared to have conversations about his friend's circumstances in front of her.

(xii) When Peter does at last get down to business he is very unsympathetic to Mrs Weaver's problem.

(xiii) Peter's change of tone when he realises that Mrs Weaver is far from penniless rings totally false. He is quite unable to cope with unexpected information.

(b) Your note should simply record what happened, so far as it concerns the organisation, and indicate any action taken or required.

Note for file

Meeting with Mrs Weaver, 10 September 2000

Mrs Weaver attended an interview to discuss her arrears problem with Peter Benton. She revealed that her husband had just received a redundancy settlement and paid off both the arrears and the outstanding amount of the loan.

She has been placed on the mailing list for high interest deposit accounts and financial planning advice.

Activity 7.6

You will gain by attending yourself, and so will your company and its clients.

(a) You can gain from the evening in a number of ways.

(i) You may learn more about the organisation you work for - about its overall aims and the way its various services are linked and complement each other. This will help you to do your job more effectively and alert you to opportunities for career development.

(ii) You will meet new people within your company and get to know others better.

(iii) You will meet new people in the shape of clients. This is valuable for its own sake, but you are also likely to find out more about how your clients use the services that your company offers. Again this will help you in your job of helping them.

(iv) Your manager will be impressed by your loyalty to the company.

(v) You will get a free meal! This is not entirely tongue in cheek. Your evening out with friends would have cost you money, and you would have eaten even if you had stayed in. The open evening therefore *saves* you money, perhaps as much overall as you would earn from a few hours overtime.

(b) Your company and clients will gain in the following ways.

   (i) Your company will have an employee who is more effective in his or her job and gives better service, as explained above.

   (ii) Your clients will be able to put a face to your name. They will feel more comfortable when dealing with you over the telephone (as you will with them).

   (iii) Your clients may be inclined to use your company's services *more* if they are dealing initially with a known quantity. This should be to the benefit of both parties.

Activity 7.7

(a)   (i) The Deluxe model with telephone is the only one which is suitable.

   (ii) Count the dots! You would really need to ask for a price range in this case, but you would probably end up selling one of the following.

Basic Plus with phone	11 features	£69.50
Standard with phone	11 features	£78.50
Deluxe with phone	14 features	£89.50

   (iii) (1) 'Wall mounting facility' means simply that the unit can, if desired, be mounted on a wall rather than resting on a flat surface. This would be a useful feature where the prospective buyer was concerned that the unit should not take up valuable desk or shelf space.

       (2) 'Last number redial' means that by pressing a single key the unit will automatically redial the same sequence of numbers as the last sequence dialled. This is very useful when a call is made but the line is engaged because it saves looking up the number again and pressing keys. So long as the sequence was entered properly on the previous occasion, it also avoids dialling errors.

       (3) 'Hands free speech' means that the user does not have to hold the receiver to his ear and mouth to carry on a conversation, he can simply speak as normal. The machine picks up his voice and relays the caller's voice over a loudspeaker. This is useful where the caller needs to move about the room as he is speaking, to leaf through many documents, or to write down notes.

(b) Your notes should have included the points on the following page. Note that the order in which the first few questions are asked is important. Did you think of our first question at all?

BPP PUBLISHING

Notes for call to Miss Cook - 020 7234 5678

Business or domestic?

BT socket fitted?

Business   Domestic

PABX?   With or without phone?

No   Yes

With or without
phone?   Price range?

Any particular features sought?
(NB. All or most have:
Call screening
Memo facility
Remote facility
Ringer on/off etc. (if phone)
Last no. redial
Call count

Go through chart if customer not forthcoming

Useful for Solicitor: 2 way record,
lots of memories, hands free, mute facility

Don't forget colour!

(c)

R. Feathertone Ltd
Industrial Estate, Ring's End, Nr Grantham
Lincolnshire GM2 4BR

Mr L. Keye
20 Pipe St
Washaway
Cornwall

5 August 2000

Dear Mr Keye

<u>Answerphone</u>

Thank you for your letter of 3 August 2000.

We offer a wide range of answerphones, some of which are like simple tape recorders while others are combined with a telephone and have many features.

I think that what you need is a fairly basic machine which has no telephone of its own but which allows you to dial in and listen to messages that you have received. At the lower end of the price scale we have the Basic One model which costs £44.50 and the Basic Plus model which costs £57.99.

It occurs to me that it might be useful to you to know precisely when your callers ring, since you deal mainly with emergencies. In this case the more expensive Basic Plus model would be more suitable because it has an electronic voice which announces the time and date of the messages that are left when you dial in to listen to them.

I am afraid that I am not able to send you a brochure illustrating our products at present, but they are available from all major department stores, electrical chains and telephone shops. I believe that your nearest large town is Bodmin, where there is a branch of Dicksons which stocks our full range.

I do hope that you will purchase one of our machines.

Please do not hesitate to contact me if I can be of any further assistance.

Yours sincerely

Diana Ling
Diana Ling
Sales Department

(d)

R. Feathertone Ltd

Industrial Estate, Ring's End, Nr Grantham
Lincolnshire GM2 4BR

Ms S. Parry
Management Consultant
10 Upmarket Way
Maidenhead
Berks MH2 3DW

5 August 2000

Dear Ms Parry

Answerphone

Thank you for your letter of 4 August 2000.

I think we can offer a solution to your problem. As I understand it you need a machine which allows you to do the following.

1. Change the outgoing message regularly from a distant location, so that you can let callers know the number on which you can be contacted directly.
2. Prevent callers from leaving messages themselves, since you may then not get the message in time.
3. Turn off the `ringer' when you are away from home.

If this is correct, I can recommend either of two models: the Deluxe unit, which costs £89.50 and the Super, which costs £109.00. The Super model allows 20 numbers to be stored in its memory while the Deluxe allows 13 numbers. The Super also has a mute facility, allowing you to speak without your caller hearing what you say.

As for the colour, our units are in two shades of the same colour with a darker base, keys and controls. The choices are grey, cream, green, red, blue and yellow. The grey model may suit your decor particularly well but of course this is entirely up to you.

I am afraid that I am unable to send you a brochure at present, but our products can be purchased from all major department stores, so hopefully you will be able to inspect them at first hand at some point on your travels.

I hope that you do decide to purchase one of our machines: I am sure that our Deluxe and Super models are perfect for your needs.

Please do not hesitate to contact me if you need any further assistance.

Yours sincerely

Diana Ling
Diana Ling
Sales Department

Activity 7.8

Just do it! Keep any notes you made in preparation for the call(s), any messages received *and* the notes of information received about the customer base: all good documentary evidence of background knowledge and performance for this Element.

Activity 7.9

(a) A brief message as follows is all that is necessary.

'A man/woman rang concerning your meeting at the Bracknell site on Thursday at 10.30. There will be no electricity supply at this time and he suggests that the meeting is rearranged for either Wednesday or Thursday afternoon.'

(b) As soon as you started to write your message you should have realised that Paul did not take the person's name or number. The caller was at fault too, for not volunteering it, but he or she may have assumed that Paul had been told by the switchboard who was calling.

The exchange would have been far more effective all round (and much shorter) if the caller had simply asked if Jennifer could be told to ring him or her as soon as possible regarding their meeting on Thursday.

In fact, the two speakers do not even agree on what further action is to be taken - is Jennifer to ring back or will the caller ring again later?

Activity 7.10

Just do it! If you feel you need to improve your working methods in order to comply with your supplier's Terms & Conditions, write a recommendation to your supervisor. Good performance evidence for Elements 23.1 and 23.2!

Activity 7.11

Again, just do it. It's fun!

Answers to Chapter 8 activities

Activity 8.1

(a) Yes: this is information necessary to the security of the premises (although the 'details' given would not include personal information).

(b) No: home addresses might be used for purposes detrimental to the employees (for example, robbery or kidnap), especially since the guard is a casual and unknown worker. If he persists in his enquiry, it may be advisable to report the matter.

(c) Yes: this is a legitimate request backed by organisational authority. (Note that you were asked for numbers, not personal details, so you need have no doubts about privacy or 'whistleblowing' on absentee colleagues.)

(d) Yes: this is another legitimate request from someone in a position of authority (provided that the R&D information was not flagged as 'classified', in which case authorisation may be required).

(e) No: this is likely to be sensitive information integral to the organisation's competitive advantage. Even if the caller *is* a journalist (and you have no way of knowing: she may be a competitor's R&D manager ...), she has no right to this information, and should be politely refused.

(f) No: although trade unions will have to be informed in due course of proposed changes which affect their members' employment, it is not up to individual (junior) members of the organisation to precipitate this process! This is another type of information that may be detrimental to the organisation (its bargaining position in regard to redundancies, for instance).

Activity 8.2

(a)   No: this is an exemption from the 'subject access' provisions.

(b)   No: an opinion cannot be challenged on these grounds.

(c)   Yes: this is your right.

(d)   No: data must be obtained 'fairly and lawfully'.

Activity 8.3

The law of copyright affects you if you use a photocopier. You should bear in mind the notion of 'fair dealing'. It is normally not a problem, however, if you need to photocopy a few pages of someone else's work for the purpose of research (commercial or non-commercial) or private study. Likewise there is no problem if you are simply photocopying internally generated documents or suppliers' invoices and the like.

You own the copyright in any private writing that you do, or any computer program that you might develop for private reasons. If you produce anything in the course of your work that is subject to the law of copyright (letters, reports, spreadsheets etc) your employer owns the copyright unless you have an agreement to the contrary.

Answers to Chapter 9 activities

Activity 9.1

Here are just a few of the items that might cross your desk

- Letters, memos, telegrams, telexes, emails.
- Notes of phone calls and meetings.
- Reports.
- Advertising material and press cuttings.
- Mailing lists.
- Important/routine addresses and phone numbers.
- Machinery documents such as guarantees or service logs.
- Legal documents such as contracts, property deeds or insurance policies.

Activity 9.2

You should have noted the following details.

Our (Lightfoot & Co's) reference:	Z/0335/MJD
Department:	Purchasing
Supplier name:	Sandimans Ltd
Previous correspondence:	11 April 1996
Resent correspondence:	4 May 1996
Subject:	Stationery (invoice 147829)

It is most unlikely that details like the geographical source of the letter or the name of its writer would be needed for filing purposes.

The accounts department should be sent a copy so that they can chase up the cheque that has not been received.

Activity 9.3

(a)   The order would be: 15, 21, 28, 2, 8, 1, 18 and 26, 16, 13, 3, 12, 22, 30, 27, 4, 5, 9, 19, 25, 6, 29, 23, 24, 20, 17, 7, 10, 14, 11.

A good approach would have been to highlight all the documents of the same year in the same colour, thereby breaking down the task into more manageable portions.

(b)   54321 Discos (7)
Argent-Smith M (11)
Argentson S (21)
Bexley J (5)
Bidwell D (4)
Briton N (28)
Britton T (12)
BRJ Plumbing (19)
Cottrell J (1)
Crown Dr J (8)
Emly P (17)
Gisling B (20)
Harrison P (27)
Harry Holden Ltd (18)
Holden R (2)
ILD Services Ltd (23)
Kelsey L C (22)
Locke D (9)
McLaughlin D (13)
Maclean T (6)
O'Grady E (15)
Page W (26)
Richmond A (29)
Saint Francis Pet Shop (16)
Sainton E (10)
St Olave's Church (30)
Van Saintby A (24)
Williams J (3)
Williams J A (14)
Williams John (25)

(**Note**. Slight variations are possible, for example with the treatment of numbers and initials, depending upon the policy of the organisation.)

(c)   The order would be: 3, 18, 27, 23, 19, 13, 10, 7, 15, 30, 26, 5, 21, 24, 6.

(d)   Geographical classification by towns gives the following results.

Bexley:	2, 7, 11, 18, 28
Bromley:	1, 10, 22, 24, 30
Crayford:	9, 12, 19, 26, 29
Dartford:	3, 4, 16, 21, 25, 27
Orpington:	5, 6, 13, 17, 23
Sidcup:	15
Woolwich:	8, 14, 20

Activity 9.4

At the front of section F you could have a document F1 that summarises fixed assets by broad category - land and buildings, plant and machinery, fixtures and fittings, say. Each figure on this front sheet could then be cross-referenced to a later sheet that contained a more detailed break-down of how the figure was made up: F2 for land and buildings, say, F3 for plant and machinery, F4 for fixtures and fittings. Figures on the sheet numbered F2 might be broken down further on other sheets numbered F2(a) or F2(1) and so on.

Activity 9.5 _____

You were asked for relevant examples from your own workplace. Consider in-trays and pigeon-holes, computers, message boards etc as well as various forms of filing boxes, cabinets etc.

Activity 9.6 _____

(a) There is room for some flexibility in answers here - what follows is very much a suggestion.

    1   The bill is not confidential if Mr Glover chooses not to keep it so. It is nothing to do with your organisation anyway.

    2   Not confidential. The reference that was given might be, but this is not mentioned.

    3   This is probably very confidential: public knowledge of merger proposals could affect the outcome of the negotiations.

    4   This may or may not be confidential depending upon your own organisation's policy. The general view is that budgeting should be done with the involvement of staff, so we are inclined to say that this is not, on the face of it, a confidential document.

    5   This is obviously a highly personal document: it should be filed away in your personnel file.

    6   This is probably not confidential. The familiarity of the signature is most likely to be due to the length of time your manager and 'Nancy' have been dealing with each other. If not, your manager is not ashamed of it and what business is it of yours anyway?

    7   There is nothing confidential about this: the surname is irrelevant.

    8   Mrs Paribus's letter is probably not particularly confidential although the nature of her complaint might make it so. To preserve the reputation of your organisation it might be better to shut it away in a file to stop cleaners, caterers or other external parties reading it.

    9   This material is published: it is clearly not confidential.

    10   There is no reason why personal details of directors should be confidential. If the list or an item on it had a heading or note such as 'Do not disclose to anyone below the level of Senior Manager', however, your manager should be ensuring that it does not fall into the wrong hands.

    To summarise, documents 3 and 5 are definitely confidential, and documents 2, 7 and 9 are definitely not. The remainder may or may not be confidential depending on the circumstances, and whose point of view you are considering the matter from.

(b) The danger here is that your fax will be collected by someone other than your manager. Its contents seem as if they might be damaging to your organisation in the wrong hands. You should therefore ring your manager and discuss the problem with him. The best solution is probably for him to stand over the receiving fax machine until your fax is received.

Activity 9.7 _____

A good deal of thought needs to go into the opening of new files.

(a) Is there already a file for this purpose?

(b) What other files are related to this purpose? In other words, what cross-referencing needs to be done?

(c) Are the documents to be filed of an unusual size or material, requiring special storage facilities?

(d) Are the documents confidential?

(e) Will the documents be needed by you frequently, so that a personal or departmental file would be more appropriate than a central one?

(f) What title should be given to the file to make it clear to all potential users what it contains?

(g) How should documents be arranged within the file?

You may have thought of other points in addition to the above. Point (a) is the most important.

Activity 9.8

The updated file should show the following information.

Company:	Folworth (Business Services) Ltd
Address:	Crichton Buildings 97 Lower Larkin Street London EC4A 8QT
Directors:	Robin Folworth BA ACA J.................... Crichton Margaret Foster Laurence Oldfield MA T........................ Scott John Thornhill BSc
Purchasing manager:	D Simmonds

Note that space has been left to fill in the new directors' first names.

Activity 9.9

Business Customers' Files	Domestic customers' files	Auditors' file	Miscellaneous file
13, 1	5, 18	3	2, 9
7	11, 12		14
10			
15, 17			

(a) Given its date, document 3 is likely to be relevant to the current year, 1996.

(b) Document 4 may as well be thrown away.

(c) Document 6 should be placed on the auditors' file for 1992.

(d) Documents 8 and 20 can be thrown away, or kept with personnel records, perhaps in a file for 'staff entertainment'.

(e) Document 16 could most appropriately be given to whoever is responsible for cleaning or pinned up on a noticeboard.

(f) Document 19 could be thrown away, or else put in the auditors' file for 1989.

It would be sensible to close the old 'miscellaneous' file and either start a new one or else have a file for 'unusual orders', especially as the product is somewhat unusual.

Maintaining a single file for domestic orders seems sensible as these are likely to be 'one-off' purchases. However, it would be helpful if this were arranged alphabetically so that related documents (for example 5 and 18) could be quickly matched.

Activity 9.10

Rather unkindly, we gave you far more forms than you needed as 'distractors'. The substitution notes are not needed, for example, because nothing is actually removed from the file. There is no need to record the physical movements of the file while it is in Mrs Patten's possession. You should realise that it is not necessary to know the precise location of every piece of paper on a file at every minute. The name of the person holding the file is usually sufficient. You certainly should not have opened a new file.

To: Central Filing
      Room 101

FILE MOVEMENTS

File reference: | A | 7 | K | / | 3 | 9 | 6 | 4 | / | 9 | 2 | / | 1 |

Title: _Ralph Atkins - correspondence_

This file was passed from: to:
Name: _Jane Taylor_   Name: _Edith Patten_
Department: _P Division_   Department: _P Division_
Room no: _17_   Room no: _25_

Date: _6.7.98_

To: Central Filing
      Room 101

FILE MOVEMENTS

File reference: | A | 7 | K | / | 3 | 9 | 6 | 4 | / | 9 | 2 | / | 1 |

Title: _Ralph Atkins - correspondence_

This file was passed from: to:
Name: _Jane Taylor_   Name: _Edith Patten_
Department: _P Division_   Department: _P Division_
Room no: _25_   Room no: _246_

Date: _13 July 2000_

1

To: Central Filing
    Room 101

FILE REQUISITION SLIP

Please deliver the following file.

File reference: | A | 7 | K | / | 3 | 9 | 6 | 4 | / | 9 | 2 | / | 1 |

Title: _Ralph Atkins - correspondence_

Date required: _2 July_

Deliver to: _Jane Taylor_ (Name)

P Division (Department)

_17_ (Room number)

Signature: _J Taylor_   Date: _2.7.00_

Authorisation: _E Patten_   Date: _2.7.00_

FILING DEPARTMENT USE

Reason for non-delivery

☐ File in use (see over)   ☐ Slip not authorised

☐ File destroyed   ☐ Restricted access

☐ Inadequate identification   ☐ Other (see over)

Activity 9.11 & 9.12

You were asked to explore your *own* most relevant computerised filing system and database.

Part C
Practice devolved assessments

Note to Tutors

Competence in the health, safety and security unit is probably best assessed by observation in the workplace. Hopefully you will not be presented with evidence of incompetence in the classroom!

However, in order to ensure that students have ample practice material, practice devolved assessment 1 has been devised so that it can be completed independently of any specific workplace.

For practice devolved assessment 2 prior warning will have to be given of tasks 1, 2, 3, 7 and 10 to allow students the opportunity to return to their workplace and collect the necessary information.

Practice devolved assessment 3 covers some elements of Unit 23. This is also best dealt with by workplace evidence, but the material can help provide a useful focus.

Performance criteria

The following performance criteria are covered in this Devolved Assessment

Element 22.1 Monitor and maintain health and safety within the workplace

1   Existing or potential hazards are put right if authorised

2   Hazards outside own authority to put right are promptly and accurately reported to the appropriate person

3   Actions taken in dealing with emergencies conform to organisational requirements

4   Emergencies are reported and recorded accurately, completely and legibly in accordance with established procedures

5   Work practices are in accordance with organisational requirements

6   Working conditions which do not conform to organisational requirements are promptly and accurately reported to the appropriate person

7   Organising of own work area minimises risk to self and others

Element 22.2 Monitor and maintain the security of the workplace

1   Organisational security procedures are carried out correctly

2   Security risks are correctly identified

3   Identified security risks are put right or reported promptly to the appropriate person

4   Identified breaches of security are dealt with in accordance with organisational procedures

Notes on completing the Assessment

This Assessment is designed to test your ability to meet all of the performance criteria for Unit 22, as listed above.

You should attempt each of tasks 1 to 10. All the data needed is provided within each task.

You are allowed 3 hours to complete your work.

Correcting fluid may be used but should be used in moderation. Errors should be crossed out neatly and clearly. You should write in black ink not in pencil.

A full solution to this Assessment is provided on page 313.

Do not turn to the suggested solution until you have completed all parts of the Assessment.

Task 1

What are your legal responsibilities as an employee with regard to health and safety at work?

Task 2

List as many ways as you can think of in which *you* can ensure that your working conditions are safe and secure.

Task 3

(a) You have to bind twenty copies of a report which are needed for a meeting that is due to start very shortly. Your boss points out to you that this can be done much more quickly if the binding machine is operated without the safety guard in place.

What should you do?

(b) You are loading up a computer printer with paper and your hair (which is very long) gets caught in the machine. There is nobody else in the computer room.

What should you do?

(c) You are visiting a client and you need to do some copying. There is only an ancient machine and you begin to feel light-headed, because it seems to give off fumes.

What should you do?

(d) You are still at the client's, photocopying. The quality starts to get very poor and the machine indicates that it needs toner. You notice a packet on a nearby shelf and decide to top up the machine yourself, since you regularly do this on your own work premises. As you pick up the packet it splits open and your hands and arms are covered in toner.

What should you do?

Task 4

Reproduced below are extracts from the General Guidance leaflet that should be contained in every first aid box. Read the extracts and then answer the questions that follow.

NOTE: TAKE CARE NOT TO BECOME A CASUALTY YOURSELF WHILE ADMINISTERING FIRST AID.

USE PROTECTIVE CLOTHING AND EQUIPMENT WHERE NECESSARY.

TREATMENT POSITION

Casualties should be seated or lying down when being treated, as appropriate.

Advice on treatment

If you need help send for it immediately. If an ambulance is needed, arrangements should be made for it to be directed to the scene without delay.

Priorities in first aid

(1)   BREATHING

[NOT SHOWN IN THIS EXTRACT]

(2)   UNCONSCIOUSNESS

[NOT SHOWN IN THIS EXTRACT]

(3)   SEVERE BLEEDING

Control by direct pressure (using fingers and thumb) on the bleeding point. Apply a dressing. Raising the bleeding limb (unless it is broken) will help reduce the flow of blood.

OTHER CONDITIONS

(4)   SUSPECTED BROKEN BONES

Do not move the casualty unless he is in a position which exposes him to immediate danger.

(5)   BURNS

BURNS AND SCALDS

Do not remove clothing sticking to the burns or scalds or burst blisters. If burns and scalds are small, flush with plenty of clean cool water before applying a sterilised dressing. If burns are large or deep, wash your hands, apply a dry sterile dressing and send to hospital.

CHEMICAL BURNS

Avoid contaminating yourself with the chemical.

Remove any contaminated clothing which is not stuck to the skin. Flush with plenty of clean, cool water for 10-15 minutes. Apply a sterilised dressing to exposed, damaged skin and send to hospital.

(6)   EYES

Loose foreign bodies in the eye: Wash out eye with clean, cool water.

Chemical in the eye: Wash out the open eye continuously with clean, cool water for 10-15 minutes.

People with eye injuries should be sent to hospital with the eye covered with an eye pad.

(7)   ELECTRIC SHOCK

Do not touch the casualty until the current is switched off. If the current cannot be switched off, stand on some dry insulating material and use a wooden or plastic implement to free the casualty from the electrical source. If breathing has stopped start mouth to mouth breathing and continue until casualty starts to breathe by himself or until professional help arrives.

---

(8)   GASSING

Use suitable protective equipment.

Move casualty to fresh air.

If breathing has stopped, start mouth to mouth breathing and continue until casualty starts to breathe by himself or until professional help arrives. Send to hospital with a note of the gas involved.

(9)   MINOR INJURIES

Casualties with minor injuries of a sort they would attend to themselves if at home may wash their hands and apply a small sterilised dressing from the first-aid box.

(10)   RECORD KEEPING

An entry of each case dealt with must be made in the accident book.

(11)   FIRST-AID MATERIALS

Articles used from the first-aid box should be replaced as soon as possible.

Tasks

(a)   You get a bit of grit in your eye. What should be done?

(b)   A courier falls down the main stairs just as lunchtime begins, when the traffic on the stairs is heaviest. She thinks she has broken her leg. What should be done?

(c)   A company's first aid box contains (amongst other things) a bottle of aspirin, a pair of nail scissors, a corkscrew, a ball of string, an 'eye pad', seven extra large wound dressings, some hand cream, a bottle of Optrex with an eye bath, a tube of Savlon and a bottle of TCP.

What should be done about this, if anything?

(d)   At the office Christmas Party the managing director inhales most of the contents of a helium-filled balloon and gives a speech in a squeaky voice. A minute or two later the managing director seems to be behaving and speaking quite normally. What should you do?

(e)   There is a small fire in your waste-paper bin and your shirt sleeve is burnt as you attempt (successfully) to put out the fire. What should you do?

(f)   You have just cut your finger at work and it is bleeding a little. This happened through your own carelessness and if you had done this at home you would just have ignored the wound and let the blood clot.

What should you do?

(g)   How should you free a casualty from an electrical source?

Task 5

Peter Spratt is a new manager in your department who started on Monday 3 April 19X6. He is very enthusiastic in everything that he does and rarely sits still. On his first afternoon he was striding past the kitchen as Helen Bruce emerged carrying two cups of coffee. Her right hand is still bandaged, because she was quite badly scalded.

The next day, fairly late in the morning, you heard a clatter and a muffled shout. About five minutes later Peter Spratt hopped into your office carrying a large bundle of rather battered looking files. He grimaced as he put his weight on both feet and seeing your concern he told you that he had just 'popped upstairs' and had 'had a bit of a spill'. You suggested calling the first-aid officer. He refused at first but you notice that his ankle is bandaged and that he is limping for the next few days.

By the following Thursday he appears to be fully recovered. As you were coming down the corridor that morning to do some photocopying you saw that he was crouching in front of the photocopier apparently trying to remove something. Rachel Preston was standing by holding a bundle of papers. There was a sudden flash and a loud noise and Peter Spratt was slumped motionless against the opposite wall. You ran up, switched off the machine and pulled the plug from the wall. It seemed to be safe. You told Rachel to stand back but to remain with Peter Spratt while you got help. You phoned the first aid officer and then returned to the scene to await his arrival. You also phoned Mr Tompkins, the office manager and informed him that there appeared to be a problem with the photocopier. Your name is David Gardner.

Tasks

(a)   Complete the entries in your firm's accident book that would have been made by Helen Bruce, Peter Spratt, Rachel Preston and you. Use your imagination to supply any details that you have not yet been given.

(b)   Imagine that you are the firm's safety officer Xavier Dent. In the light of the above write a memo to all staff including any reminders that you think need to be made and indicating any action that will be taken.

(c)   Write the safety officer's entry or entries in the accident book.

Pages from the firm's accident book are shown on the following pages.

Date	Name	Details of accident (include time, place and names of any witnesses)

TO BE COMPLETED BY THE INJURED PARTY OR A WITNESS

First aid treatment	Report to HSE	Preventative action taken

TO BE COMPLETED BY FIRST AID OFFICER

TO BE COMPLETED BY SAFETY OFFICER

TO BE COMPLETED BY
SAFETY OFFICER

TO BE COMPLETED BY
FIRST AID OFFICER

First aid treatment	Report to HSE	Preventative action taken

TO BE COMPLETED BY THE INJURED PARTY
OR A WITNESS

Date	Name	Details of accident (include time, place and names of any witnesses)

	Report to HSE	TO BE COMPLETED BY SAFETY OFFICER
		Preventative action taken

TO BE COMPLETED BY FIRST AID OFFICER

First aid treatment	

TO BE COMPLETED BY THE INJURED PARTY OR A WITNESS

Date	Name	Details of accident (include time, place and names of any witnesses)

Task 6

Now adopt the role of Peter Spratt. You want to set out your version of the photocopier accident and you decide to write a letter while you are recovering. You have often removed jammed paper from photocopiers before and you were familiar with this model. You woke up in hospital and knew nothing about the accident.

Write Peter Spratt's letter to his company, Duckley Ltd, Canardly Walk, London EC4A 9XJ. You may (for the purposes of this task) make up any further details that you feel are necessary.

Task 7

Knowing of your interest in health, safety and security matters, Xavier Dent has asked you to help with the investigation into the accident.

You are asked to complete as much of the form shown below as you can. If there are any details that you are unsure of write 'to be determined', but try to avoid this if you can. If you make any assumptions, note them in the comments column.

ACCIDENT INVESTIGATION QUESTIONNAIRE

Name of injured person	
Date and time of accident	
Name of investigator	
Date of investigation	

Accident type

Exposure to explosion		Contact with electricity or electrical discharge	
Exposure to fire		Exposure to/contact with harmful substance	
Injured by animal		Contact with moving machinery	
Struck by vehicle		Injured while handling lifting or carrying	
Drowning or asphyxiation		Trapped by something collapsing or overturning	
Fall from height		Slip, trip or fall on same level	
Struck by moving object		Struck against something fixed or stationery	

Brief details of accident

Possible causes: please give, in order of importance, the code references of up to 5 possible causes (see the attached code sheet)

1 ....   2 ....   3 ....   4 ....   5 ....

BPP PUBLISHING

DETAILED ENQUIRY			
	YES	NO	COMMENTS
Was the person injured carrying out a task that was part of their normal duties?			
Was the person injured involved in an activity associated with work?			
Was the person's immediate supervisor present in the area at the time of the accident?			
If 'NO' state the location of the supervisor at the time and any specific instructions given by the supervisor prior to leaving the area.			
Was the accident reported immediately?			
If 'NO' state why there was a delay and how long the delay was.			
To whom was the accident reported?			
Has the task being performed been covered by a risk assessment?			
Was the injured person specifically warned of the hazards of the task?			
Was the person injured instructed to carry out the task?			
Was the task carried out in accordance with normal practice?			
Was the task within the capability of the person injured?			
Was the person injured familiar with the type of plant/equipment/tools etc?			
Had the person injured been trained to carry out the task safely?			

	YES	NO	COMMENTS
Was the task carried out by prescribed method?			
Was protective clothing being worn?			
Were any of the person's senses obscured/nullified which could have been a contributory factor?			
Were plant/equipment/premises in normal condition?			
Were guards/protective devices operating effectively?			
Were warning notices displayed warning persons of hazards or to use protective clothing?			
Was there a failure of service, component, plant or machinery?			
Is there a system for monitoring that procedures/instructions are followed?			

Did any of the following environmental factors contribute to the accident?

Rain	Snow	Ice	Fog	Cold
Humidity	Fumes	Gas	Vapour	Noise
Restricted space	Confined space	Uneven/unlevel surface	Condition of ground/floor	Radiation

POSSIBLE CAUSES OF ACCIDENTS			
GENERAL		214	Personal protective equipment not provided or failed
000	No reasonably practicable precautions available	215	Weather conditions
ORGANISATIONAL FACTORS		216	Other (give details)
101	Inadequate training or instruction		**EMPLOYEE OR OTHER PERSON'S CONTRIBUTION**
101	Inadequate supervision	301	Loss of concentration
102	Inadequate standard of maintenance	302	Defeating safety devices
103	Inadequate traffic control system	303	Guarding device provided but not used
104	Other (give details)	304	Using obviously defective equipment
PHYSICAL FACTORS		305	Improper use of equipment including interference with equipment
201	Guarding devices failed	306	Failure to comply with or misinterpretation of instructions
202	Guarding devices inadequate	307	Failure to use available personal protective equipment
203	Guarding devices removed	308	Failure to give necessary warning to others
204	Electrical hardware fault (unearthed, uninsulated, overloaded, uncovered short, etc)	309	Recklessly going into hazardous situation
205	Instrumentation fault	310	Employee judgement error
206	Structural or physical aspects of premises	311	Assault
207	Poor housekeeping	312	Horseplay
208	Poor control of toxic substances	313	Working under the effect of alcohol or drugs
209	Poor control of flammable substances	314	Using unsafe or dangerous methods of handling or lifting
210	Inadequate standard of design	315	Riding or standing in an unsafe position
211	Inadequate standard of installation	316	Arson, burglary, vandalism
212	Illumination/heat/noise	317	Medical or physical condition of significance
213	Poor stacking or storage	318	Other

Task 8

'Health and safety is often seen as just being bureaucratic, and there is a reluctance to change familiar ways of working. There is also an element of male pride in being able to lift a heavy load. Many men do not like using equipment to move things when colleagues are not doing so. But employees have a responsibility for their own safety and are required to get a lifting aid if they need one.'

Safety Officer, DHL

Imagine that you are the junior member (male or female) of a team of staff that is about to visit a client's offices in Bristol on Monday for the following two weeks, travelling by train. Your organisation is based in central Manchester. You joined very recently and this is your first away job.

The deputy team leader tells you that the junior member has the honour of carrying the bulk of the files and papers needed for the job. Towards the end of Friday you are presented with two pilot cases (extra-large briefcases) and a carrier bag, all filled to capacity. You are told you should take them home with you at the weekend (you travel to work by public transport) and bring them with you to the station first thing on Monday morning.

You can lift the three bags, but they are very heavy. It is not going to be easy.

In the light of this scenario and the quotation preceding it, what practical options do you have and what are the likely consequences?

Task 9

According to Gee's *Essential Facts on Premises, Health and Safety*, there are three methods of protection from the consequences of a breach of security:

(a) defence;
(b) detection;
(c) deterrence.

Explain what you understand these three 'Ds' to involve for a typical organisation.

Task 10

At about a quarter to six one evening you are one of the few people left at work. You have stayed behind to take delivery of a package which is being sent over by courier from a client's building. You are waiting in the reception area.

The courier arrives, rings the buzzer in your entrance lobby and is admitted. He hands you the package, you sign for it and he leaves.

Less than a minute later the buzzer rings again. It is the courier, who tells you that his mountain bike has gone missing.

Apparently he had brought the bike through the main doors of your building and left it, unlocked, in the entrance lobby. There had been another person in the lobby who seemed to be tending to the plants by the door. The courier had left his bike unattended for no more than 30 seconds.

Your building is separate to the main building on your site where the security guards are located. You take the courier over to the main building and ask to speak to one of the guards to see whether they can shed any light on the matter. You also reassure the courier that the theft will have been captured on video since there is a camera overlooking the car park beside your building.

A new security shift begins at 6 o'clock and you find that you have to wait until then before you can speak to one of the guards. He tells you that, so far as he is aware, the theft had not been noticed and no suspicious characters had been reported.

Unfortunately the video had been switched off at 5.45 to rewind the tape, and had not been turned on again until just after 6 o'clock.

The security guard is reluctant to take any further action (he confides in you that he sees no reason to, since the courier is not a member of your organisation), but eventually you persuade him to let you watch the last few minutes of the tape that was switched off to see if you can at least spot the person who had been hovering in your entrance lobby. However it transpires that the camera points at the car park and any activity around the main entrance to your building cannot be seen.

Tasks

(a) Draw a diagram to illustrate the above scenario.

(b) Write a memo to the Office and Premises Administration Manager pointing out any aspects of security that you feel need to be tightened up.

Your name is Carol Hunter and the Office and Premises Administration Manager is called Eleanor Merton. You may embellish the scenario with any further details that you need to draw your diagram and write your memo or, if you like, you can substitute details that apply in the case of your own organisation.

2 Practice devolved assessment Portfolio

Performance criteria

The following performance criteria are covered in this Assignment

Element 22.1 Monitor and maintain health and safety within the workplace

1   Existing or potential hazards are put right if authorised

2   Hazards outside own authority to put right are promptly and accurately reported to the appropriate person

3   Actions taken in dealing with emergencies conform to organisational requirements

4   Emergencies are reported and recorded accurately, completely and legibly in accordance with established procedures

5   Work practices are in accordance with organisational requirements

6   Working conditions which do not conform to organisational requirements are promptly and accurately reported to the appropriate person

7   Organising of own work area minimises risk to self and others

Element 22.2 Monitor and maintain the security of the workplace

1   Organisational security procedures are carried out correctly

2   Security risks are correctly identified

3   Identified security risks are put right or reported promptly to the appropriate person

4   Identified breaches of security are dealt with in accordance with organisational procedures

Notes on completing the Assessment

This Assessment is designed to test your ability to meet all of the performance criteria for Unit 22, as listed above.

You should attempt each of tasks 1 to 13. All the data needed is provided within each task.

Tasks 1, 2, 3, 7 and 10 should be completed in the workplace and the evidence collected should be handed in to your tutor.

Spend no more than 2 hours completing the remaining tasks.

Correcting fluid may be used but should be used in moderation. Errors should be crossed out neatly and clearly. You should write in black ink, not in pencil.

Full solutions to Tasks 4-6, 8, 9 and 11-13 of this Assessment and suggestions about the solutions for the remaining tasks are provided on page 325.

Task 1

he Health and Safety Executive issue a guide entitled 'Five Steps to Risk Assessment'. This is mainly intended for employers but you can also use it to assess the risks to yourself in your work environment.

Complete the sections (adapted from the HSE guide) below. If you think you will need more room photocopy the pages and write on the back.

1 Look for the hazards

Look only for hazards which you could reasonably expect to result in significant harm under the conditions in your workplace. Here are some examples, but they are only a guide: other or different hazards may exist in your work environment.

Slipping/tripping hazards	Electricity
Fire	Dust
Chemicals	Fumes
Moving parts of machinery	Manual handling
Work at height	Noise
Ejection of material	Poor lighting
Pressure systems	Low temperature
Vehicles	

List hazards here

2 Who might be harmed?

Health and safety is about thinking about others as well as yourself. There is no need to list individuals by name – just think about groups of people doing similar work or who may be affected, for example:

Office staff   Operators
Maintenance personnel   Cleaners
Contractors   Members of the public
People sharing your workplace

Think especially about staff with disabilities, inexperienced staff, visitors and lone workers.

List groups of people who are especially at risk for the significant hazards which you have identified

3　　Is the risk adequately controlled?

Have precautions already been taken against the risks from the hazards you listed? For example are you provided with adequate information, instruction and training? Do the precautions meet the standards set by a legal requirement, comply with a recognised industry standard, represent good practice and reduce risk as far as is reasonably practicable?

If so, then the risks are adequately controlled, but you need to indicate the precautions that are in place. Refer to procedures, manuals, company rules and so on giving this information.

List existing controls here or note where the information may be found

4   What further action is necessary to control the risk?

What more could be done for those risks which you found were not adequately controlled?

You will need to give priority to those risks which affect large numbers of people and/or could result in serious harm. Apply the principles below when taking further action, if possible in the following order.

Remove the risk completely

Try a less risky option

Prevent access to the hazard (eg by guarding)

Organise work to reduce exposure to the hazard

Issue personal protective equipment

Provide welfare facilities (eg washing facilities for removal of contamination and first-aid)

List the risks which are not adequately controlled and the action you will take where it is reasonably practicable to do more. You are entitled to take cost (money, resources and time) into account, unless the risk is high.

5   Review the above assessment from time to time and revise it if necessary.

Task 2

(a) Draw a diagram showing the following.

(i) The layout of your office.

(ii) The route to the fire exit which you should use in an emergency.

(iii) The location of the nearest fire extinguishers, and the next nearest.

(iv) The location of the first aid box or cupboard.

(b) Annotate your diagram with the following information.

(i) The name, location and telephone number of the person responsible for first aid.

(ii) The name and number of the person to ring in case of emergency.

(iii) The location of your 'assembly point' in an emergency.

(c) Draw a bird's eye view of your own immediate work area - your desk and the area around it. Draw in any equipment that you keep on the desk and any cables that run up to it. Show your route to any filing cabinets or items of office equipment that you use regularly.

Mark on your drawing any potential hazards in your work area.

(d) Obtain the instruction manuals for all items of equipment that you use regularly and look through them for safety instructions. (These may come under headings like 'Warning', or 'Do's and Don'ts' or 'Fault finding', since manufacturers often reluctant to admit that their goods might be unsafe. Obtain copies of the relevant pages and include them in your portfolio.

(e) Collect as much of the following as you can. Tick the box when you are satisfied that you have the evidence.

(i) Details of hazards or emergencies that you have identified at work (tick if
you have completed Task 1). ☐

(ii) Copies of any reports that you have made about these hazards, emergencies
or accidents. ☐

(iii) Details of any hazards at work that you have put right. ☐

(iv) A note of when you last took part in a fire drill or other evacuation
procedure, and what you were required to do. ☐

(v) A copy of the relevant pages of your organisation's procedures manual (or similar) that explain the health and safety procedures to be followed. You should highlight those points that set out your responsibilities with regard to identifying, reporting and putting right hazards, and dealing with accidents and emergencies. ☐

Task 3

Collect as much of the following information as you can. Tick the box when you are satisfied that you have the evidence.

(a)   Make a list giving details of all the security procedures that you are personally responsible for at work - ensuring that equipment is secure, locking your desk drawer, keeping the keys to a filing cabinet, or whatever.

(b)   Obtain a copy of any official manual that exists in your organisation detailing security procedures that affect your work (this will include things like showing passes, obtaining entry to secure areas and so on).

(c)   Prepare a record of any security risks in your organisation that that you have identified and/or dealt with in some way. This should include a description of the incident and copies of any reports or memos that you may have written.

(d)   Prepare a record of any breaches of security that you have dealt with. Again include a description and copies of any appropriate original documents.

Task 4

What, in your own opinion and experience, are the main health, safety and security risks facing staff who work in an *accounts* department (in other words, how risky is it to be an accountant rather than, say, a production worker)?

Task 5

You are a sales ledger assistant and most of your day is spent using a computer. Describe what *you* can do to make your workstation a safe and healthy working environment.

Task 6

What goes on in your head at work is at least as important as what goes on in or happens to your body. Psychological pressures are probably the biggest dangers faced by accountants.

The following paragraphs are adapted from the Health and Safety Executive's leaflet on Mental Health at Work.

> The workplace can be a stimulating and supportive environment and have a positive effect on mental health, but adverse situations can have a negative effect. Thus there is a great value in employers instituting an effective occupational health policy which routinely includes consideration of mental health aspects. Apart from reduction in personal distress for individuals, an effective policy will have positive benefits for the whole organisation.
>
> It has been estimated that 30-40% of all sickness absence from work is attributable to some form of mental or emotional disturbance. Organisational factors such as change, the design of the workplace, and approaches to management play a part. Some of the main *individual* work and domestic factors are as follows.
>
> (a)   Over promotion or resentment at failure to be promoted
> (b)   Too much or too little work
> (c)   Relocation, change in work environment or of colleagues
> (d)   Change in the nature of work or style of management
> (e)   Role conflict or ambiguity (not knowing what is expected of you or how you fit in)
> (f)   Irregular or long hours
> (g)   Lack of autonomy (not being able to decide for yourself how best to do a job)
> (h)   Family illness or bereavement
> (i)   Marital or family problems
> (j)   Financial difficulties
> (k)   Moving house
> (l)   Injury or illness which interferes with the quality of life.

People do not always, or even usually, realise that they have a problem. Early signs may include a sense of apprehension, sleep disturbance, impaired concentration and short term memory, change in appetite, lack of energy, indecisiveness or irritability. More severe signs may include spontaneous weeping, a sense of hopelessness or excessive alcohol or drug consumption.

Feelings of inability to cope and physical symptoms may occasionally prompt the seeking of assistance before anyone else realises there is a problem. Alternatively colleagues or supervisors may notice changes in patterns of behaviour such as:

(a) unusual irritability, resentment of advice and constructive criticism;
(b) becoming withdrawn and unsociable;
(c) unusual absenteeism or poor timekeeeping;
(d) overworking and failure to delegate;
(e) impaired performance;
(f) changes in appetite, personal appearance, habits and behaviour;
(g) increasing use of coffee, cigarettes, alcohol and drugs;
(h) accident proneness;
(i) unexpected difficulty with training and examinations.

You would be unusual if you have not suffered from some of these symptoms and problems yourself at some time.

Try to think back to a difficult period and describe (not necessarily in this order):

(a) the circumstances that you think caused your problems;
(b) how your work was affected;
(c) how your colleagues were affected, if at all;
(d) how the problem was solved;
(e) what you feel your organisation should have done in the circumstances;
(f) what your own responsibilities were.

Task 7

You can find out the answers to the following questions by inspecting a first-aid box. Ask permission before you do this and wash your hands first. Inspect it in its usual location – don't walk off with it for hours – and take care not to damage or tamper with the contents.

(a) What are the standard minimum contents of a first-aid box?

(b) What does the box that you are inspecting actually contain? Does it conform to the minimum requirements. Does it breach the requirements in any way.

(c) What action should you take in the light of your answer to (b)?

Task 8

According to a recent crime survey there are 35,000 incidents of workplace violence every year, three-quarters of which are assaults on staff by members of the public.

If you were in a position that regularly required you to deal with members of the public in situations that could potentially become unpleasant, what would you do to protect yourself and what would you expect your employer to do?

Concentrate on *interview* situations (for example working in a benefit office), not situations that are prone to crime of other sorts such as (armed) robbery.

Task 9

What are the implications of the following?

A. N Employee

CONTRACT OF EMPLOYMENT (extracts)

During the period of your employment with the company and thereafter you shall keep secret the affairs of the company. At the termination of your employment for whatever reason you shall surrender to the company all files, records, documents and information belonging to or in the possession of the company in whatever form which shall include all electronically recorded information.

...

During the period of your employment the company reserves the right to conduct a search of your person and your personal belongings on your departure from the company's premises and in your presence any place on the company's premises where you may keep personal possessions. The search shall be undertaken by trained staff of the same sex.

NOTICE

DUE TO THE NATURE OF THE COMPANY'S ACTIVITIES, THE COMPANY RESERVES THE RIGHT TO SEARCH EMPLOYEES AND VISITORS ON DEPARTURE FROM THE PREMISES.

IF YOU ARE NOT PREPARED TO BE SEARCHED,

DO NOT

ENTER THE PREMISES

Searches are conducted by members of the same sex who are fully trained in search procedures.

Task 10

Read the article from a magazine reproduced below, and then carry out the tasks listed afterwards.

Caffeine may be a significant factor in work-related stress. It raises the levels of two of the key stress hormones, adrenaline and cortisol. People drink it for its initial 'pick-me-up" qualities but it has after effects such as lower blood sugar levels, which in turn lead to an inability to concentrate, poor decision making, irritability, nervousness, forgetfulness and fatigue, (these are the same symptoms that make people drink caffeine in the first place!)

Caffeine also accentuates the symptoms of pre-menstrual syndrome, causes diarrhoea and brings on insomnia.

Coffee contains the highest amount of caffeine (between 80 to 300 milligrammes per cup, depending on the type of coffee); tea contains between 50 and 100 milligrammes

per cup; cola between 43 and 65 milligrammes per can. A large bar of chocolate can contain 60 milligrammes. It is reckoned to be wise to limit caffeine intake to between 200 and 250 milligrammes per day.

Tea was recently the subject of an international conference. The tea plant is rich in a chemical found in fruits and vegetables called polyphenols, that may help prevent heart disease and cancer. Research in the Netherlands, for example, has shown that men whose diets are richest in polyphenols have the lowest risk of having a heart attack. These men got 61% of their polyphenols from black tea. Similarly Japanese who drink more than 10 cups of green tea a day have lower rates of stomach cancer and of lung cancer (despite being heavy smokers).

(a) Based on the above article and any personal views or knowledge you may have, draw up a notice that could be put up in the kitchen or by the drinks machine at work to encourage better liquid refreshment habits.

(b) Keep a 'caffeine diary' for yourself for a typical week. You should note down how many cups of tea or coffee, cans of cola and bars of chocolate you have each day (both at home and at work) and then work out your daily average.

(c) If you can, encourage some of your colleagues at work to do exercise (b) at the same time as you.

(d) If you or your colleagues think you are exceeding the recommended maximum daily intake of caffeine, try reducing your consumption for a few days. Do you notice any benefits?

Task 11

Some organisations run incentive schemes to encourage safety in the workplace, for example having a prize draw when so many weeks of accident-free work have been achieved.

Devise such a scheme for your own workplace. Your scheme should include the following elements.

(a) Safety 'targets' to be aimed at.
(b) Incentives to encourage *all* workers to participate.
(c) Rules about what would give rise to incentives not being awarded.

Task 12

The three documents shown below were received by your company. What should be done in response to them?

Cinders Fire Protection Ltd

CFP

Certificate of Inspection

Customer address

Khan & Co

Jemimah Road

Stevenage

Herts

Date _14/1/X2_

Contract No. _____

Serviced		Recharge/Spares	12084
Fire/Intruder Alarm		Supplied: - 41 × Security tags	
Emergency Lighting		5 × Series 2000 clips	
Fire Protection System		6 × O Rings	
Water Extinguisher	26	Water extinguisher on 5th floor rear stairs condemned - corroded base (unfit for service last visit)	
Carbon Dioxide	6		
Dry Powder			
Foam		Recharged on site:-	
Hose Reels	8	1 × 9 litre water 6th floor main stairs	
B.C.F.	5	1 × 9 litre water ground floor end building (Breton House)	
F/Blankets			
Misc.			
TOTAL	45		

Recommendations:- Replace condemned water extinguisher on 5th floor rear stairs.

Serviced in Accordance with BS 5306: Part 3: 1985

Routine inspection by the user.

It is recommended that regular inspection of all extinguishers, spare gas cartridges and replacement charges should be carried out by the user or the user's representative at intervals, to make sure that appliances are in their proper position and have not been discharged, or lost pressure. The frequency of inspection should not be less than quarterly, and preferably at least monthly.

Engineer's Signature _Joe Bloggs_   **Customer's Signature** _I Khan_

Cinders Fire Protection Ltd

SITE REPORT 51935 **CFP**

Site Address	**Customer address**
Khan & Co	
Jemimah Road	
Stevenage	
Herts	

SERVICE ☑ INSTALLATION ☐ CALLOUT ☐

				TYPE OF SYSTEM	
	DATE	13/4/X6		FIRE ALARM SYSTEM	☑
QUARTERLY ☐	ARRIVAL TIME	7.20		HALON SYSTEM	☐
6 MONTHLY ☑	DEPART TIME			INTRUDER ALARM	☐
				DOOR ACCESS	☐
ANNUAL ☐	TRAVEL			EMERGENCY LIGHTING	☑
	TOTAL			OTHER	☐

REMARKS:- Tested and serviced fire alarm and emergency lighting. Fire alarm was found to be in good working order but found two emergency lights faulty : 5th floor rear room, 4th floor front lobby.

All servicing carried out in accordance with British Standard regulations.

PARTS USED:- Have replaced main ground floor supply fuse 60a MBC as when switching main switch, parts of an old fuse board left inside main switch shorted out. Main supply cupboard is in a poor state of repair.

	TYPE	TESTED
CALLPOINTS	KAC	✓
IONISATION	APPOLLO	✓
OPTICAL		
HEAT	" "	✓
SOUNDERS	BELLS	✓

CONTROL TYPE	
NO. OF ZONES	

UNITS TESTED AND OPERATING CORRECTLY

ALL WORK COMPLETED	☐
FURTHER VISIT REQUIRED	☑

Engineer's Signature _Joe Bloggs_   **Customer's Signature** _I Khan_

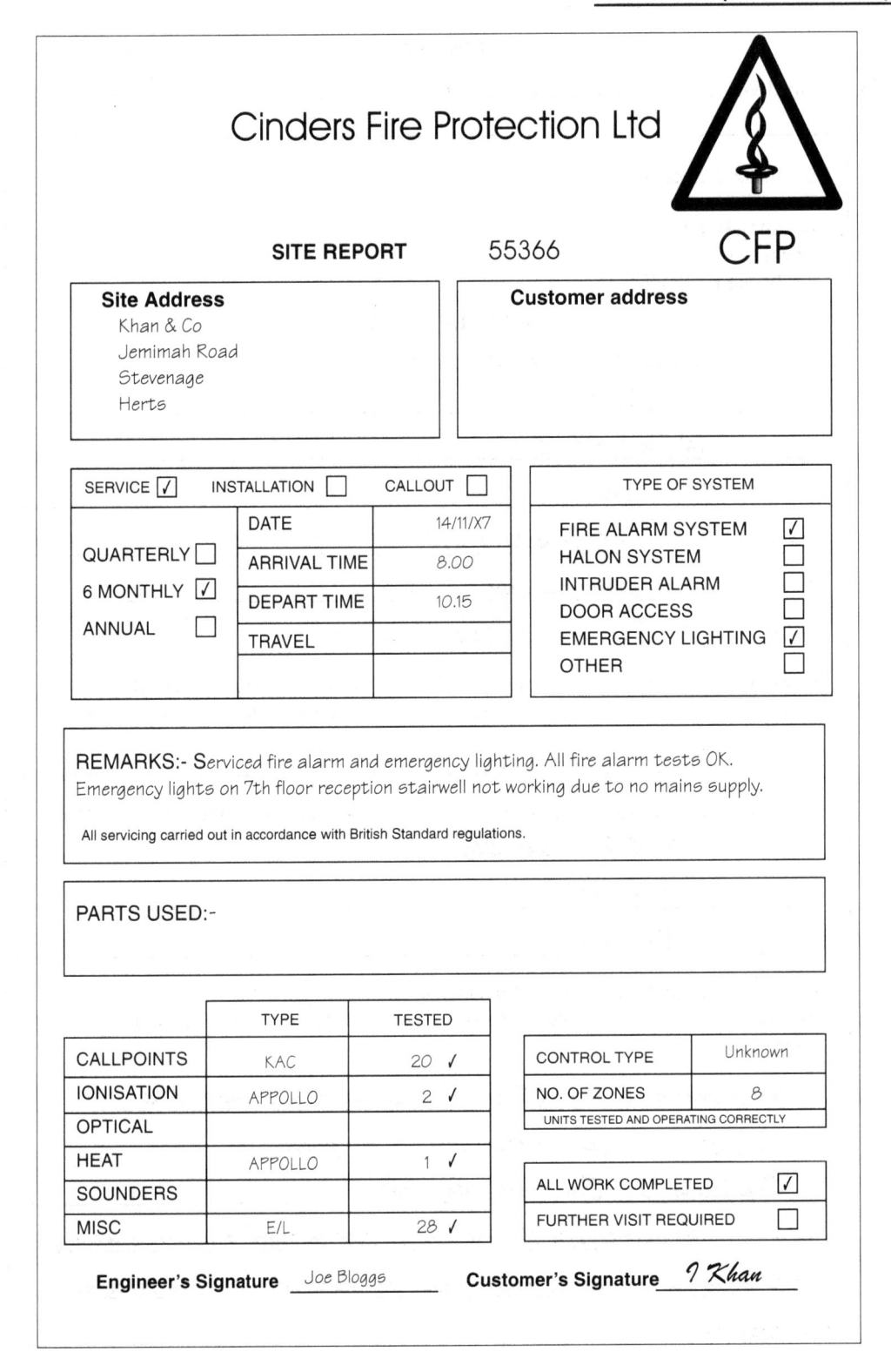

Cinders Fire Protection Ltd

CFP

SITE REPORT   55366

Site Address
Khan & Co
Jemimah Road
Stevenage
Herts

Customer address

SERVICE ☑	INSTALLATION ☐	CALLOUT ☐

QUARTERLY ☐	DATE	14/11/X7
	ARRIVAL TIME	8.00
6 MONTHLY ☑	DEPART TIME	10.15
ANNUAL ☐	TRAVEL	

TYPE OF SYSTEM	
FIRE ALARM SYSTEM	☑
HALON SYSTEM	☐
INTRUDER ALARM	☐
DOOR ACCESS	☐
EMERGENCY LIGHTING	☑
OTHER	☐

REMARKS:- Serviced fire alarm and emergency lighting. All fire alarm tests OK.
Emergency lights on 7th floor reception stairwell not working due to no mains supply.

All servicing carried out in accordance with British Standard regulations.

PARTS USED:-

	TYPE	TESTED
CALLPOINTS	KAC	20 ✓
IONISATION	APPOLLO	2 ✓
OPTICAL		
HEAT	APPOLLO	1 ✓
SOUNDERS		
MISC	E/L	28 ✓

CONTROL TYPE	Unknown
NO. OF ZONES	8

UNITS TESTED AND OPERATING CORRECTLY

ALL WORK COMPLETED	☑
FURTHER VISIT REQUIRED	☐

Engineer's Signature   *Joe Bloggs*   **Customer's Signature**   *I Khan*

Task 13

What should you do if you see a machine with the following notice attached?

Downstown Local Authority
Town Hall
Rossney Road
Downstown
Keithshire KT23 2WE

PROHIBITION NOTICE

Health and Safety at Work etc Act 1974, sections 22, 23 and 24

To _____ *Mr J West* _____

_____ *14 Back Street* _____

_____ *Downstown* _____

Trading as _____ *D G Practices Ltd* _____

?. _____ *Firmin Limpar* _____

one of _____ *The Environmental Health Officers* _____

of the Environmental Health Department, Town Hall, Rossney Road, Downstown
hereby give you notice that I am of the opinion that the following activities, namely

_____ *The operation of a paper shredding machine* _____

which are ~~being carried on by you/about to be carried on by you~~/under your control at

_____ *D G Practices Ltd* _____

_____ *Back Street* _____

_____ *Downstown* _____

involve or will involve a risk/ ~~an imminent risk~~, of serious personal injury. I am further of the opinion that the said matters involve contraventions of the following statutory provisions:

_____ *The Provision & Use of Work Equipment Regulations 1992* ___

_____ *Regulation 11 – Dangerous parts of machinery* _____

_____ *Regulation 16 – Emergency stop controls* _____

because _____ *the operator of the machine is able to touch dangerous moving parts while the machine is working and the emergency stop control is not functioning*

and I hereby direct that the said activities shall not be carried on by you or under your control immediately/ ~~after~~
unless the said contraventions in the schedule, which forms part of this notice, have been remedied.

Signature *F Limpar*   Date *2 February 1998*

Being an inspector appointed by an instrument in writing made pursuant to Section 19 of the said Act and entitled to issue this notice.

Performance criteria

The following performance criteria are covered in this Assignment

Element 23.1 Plan and Organise Own Work

1   Routine and unexpected tasks are identified and prioritised according to organisational procedures

2   Appropriate planning aids are used to plan and monitor work

3   Where priorities change, work plans are changed accordingly

4   Anticipated difficulties in meeting deadlines are promptly reported to the appropriate person

5   Assistance is asked for, where necessary, to meet specific demands and deadlines

Element 23.2 Establish and Maintain Working Relationships

1   Information is provided to internal and external customers in line with routine requirements and one-off requests

2   The appropriate people are asked for any information, advice and resources that are required

3   Commitments to others are met within agreed timescales

4   Communication methods are appropriate to the individual situation

5   Any communication difficulties are acknowledged and action is taken to resolve them

6   Opportunities are taken to promote the image of the department and organisation to internal and external customers

7   Confidentiality and data protection requirements are strictly followed

Element 23.3 Maintain Accounting Files and Records

1   New documentation and records are put into the filing system in line with organisational procedures

2   Item movements are monitored and recorded where necessary

3   Documentation and records are kept according to organisational and legal requirements

4   Out-of-date information is dealt with in accordance with organisational procedures

303

5   Opportunities for improving filing systems are identified and brought to the attention of the appropriate person

Notes on completing the Assessment

This Assessment is designed to test your ability to meet all of the performance criteria for Unit 22, as listed above.

You should attempt each of tasks 1 to 10. All the data needed is provided within each task.

You are allowed 3 hours to complete your work.

Correcting fluid may be used but should be used in moderation. Errors should be crossed out neatly and clearly. You should write in black ink, not in pencil.

A full solution to this Assessment is provided on page 325

Do not turn to the suggested solution until you have completed all parts of the Assessment.

The situation

You work as a trainee Accounting Technician for Staniland & Roberts, a firm of Accountants. In addition to the work you perform related to your accounting training, you also assist with general practice administration.

The firm's details are as follows:

Staniland & Roberts (Accountants)
40-42 Maypole Street, Sandsend, SS1 DXX
Tel: 01749 221720,
Fax: 01749 217400

E-mail: mail@stanilandroberts.co.uk

Task 1

You have been assigned the responsibility for maintaining the petty cash system in the Staniland & Roberts office. The imprest is set at £500 and is replenished monthly.

Prepare:

(a)   a checklist of the tasks you will perform on an ongoing basis. Divide the task into daily, weekly and monthly tasks;

(b)   an action plan for how you will set up an on-going schedule to remind you of these tasks and when they should be performed.

Task 2

Paul Santorini, a new junior colleague in your section, appears to be highly stressed by the workload he has been assigned, although he seems highly competent at the technical aspects of the work.

At first, when non-routine tasks got added to his routine workload from time to time, he would do them immediately - often missing deadlines on routine but important tasks. When your supervisor, Gina Sawhala, pointed this out to him, he started performing the

occasional non-routine tasks after all the routine tasks for the day or week were complete – often missing deadlines on important non-routine tasks. Gina noted this also, suggesting that Paul needs to settle into the pace of the workflow in the office.

You now notice that Paul has taken to staying behind to put in extra hours so that all deadlines are met. However, you also notice that he is getting tired, irritable and slightly withdrawn in his relationships in the office.

What is the problem and what (if anything) should you do about this? Prepare brief notes for yourself, outlining the strategy you will follow and what (if anything) you will say to any of the people involved.

Task 3

You receive the following communication from one of the senior partners, Ray Staniland.

MEMORANDUM

To: [Your Name]   **Date:** 25 April 2001
From: Ray Staniland   **Ref:** RS/yn/0401

Subject: Jones & Co

Louise Hartley, one of your fellow Accounting Technicians in our organisation, recently analysed the time spent to date by various members of staff on Jones & Co's year-end work.

The hours worked by each grade of staff involved in the work were as follows.

Grade	Hours
Senior Partner	36
Partner	9
Senior	36
Semi Senior	54
Accounting Technician	45

I'd like to present this data to the Partners' Meeting on Wednesday 1 May. Could you please format the information in some appropriate way, to show the distribution of hours worked by each grade of staff?

If you need any more information, please e-mail me.

Prepare:

(a)   the e-mail you will send (if applicable) requesting any further information you may need. Ray Staniland's address on the firm's network is rstaniland@infonet

(b)   the formatted information requested by Ray Staniland. (You may invent the answers to any questions you have put to him in your e-mail, if they influence your presentation.)

Data for Tasks 4 - 6

It is now Thursday 2 May 2001, and you have received the minutes from the Partners' Meeting, which include the following notes.

MINUTES OF PARTNERS' MEETING
Wednesday 1 May 2001

...

3   The 'Where Next for the EMU?' Seminar

It was agreed that this seminar by held for clients on Monday 15 July 2001 at 6.30 pm. All clients will be notified of the event.

4   Petty cash

Ray Staniland noted that some staff are not signing petty cash vouchers when requesting cash and that others are not providing adequate receipts. A memo explaining the correct procedure to adopt when requesting petty cash will be circulated to all staff.

...

You may complete Tasks 4 – 6 in any order you choose. Indicate in your answer the order of priority you allocated to each task, and why.

Task 4

Prepare:

(a)   a standard letter to all of Staniland & Roberts' clients, inviting them to attend the seminar, including some convenient method for them to reply;

(b)   a message or messages requesting further information (if any) you will require in order to do this.

Task 5

Prepare a memo to all staff, describing the correct procedure to follow when requesting petty cash. Explain that vouchers for expenditure up to £10 must be authorised by David Jones, and that those in excess of £10 must be authorised by the office manager.

Task 6

Prepare a checklist of the procedures you will adopt for receiving visitors to the seminar outlined in the notes of the partners' meeting.

Task 7

Staniland & Roberts has been monitoring telephone conversations in the workplace in order to appraise and improve the standard of client communication.

One day, a colleague hands you the following typescript, laughing. "Look at this," he says. "This is a call from Joanne Doe – you know, our new Compliance Officer? – before she joined the firm. Apparently, Clara got hauled over the coals by Mr Armstrong! I just think it's funny: imagine the look on her face when she found out the call had been recorded!"

TRANSCRIPT

Lines

1	Jenny Kramm (operator):	Can I help you?
2	Caller:	This is Joanne Doe. Can I speak to Mr Armstrong in Personnel, please?
3	[Silence: clicking and buzzing noises]	
4	Clara Lau (Personnel Secretary):	Hello, Mr Doe? I'm sorry, Mr Armstrong is not available. Can I help?
5	Caller:	It's Mrs Doe, actually. I have an interview with Mr Armstrong at 3 pm today. Can I change it to tomorrow?
6	Clara Lau:	One moment please. [Lengthy pause] I think Mr Armstrong might be able to manage 3 pm tomorrow. Will that suit you?
7	Caller:	Yes. Unless something comes up at work…
8	Clara Lau:	Right, Ms Doe. Mr Armstrong will see you then. Goodbye.
9	Caller:	Oh. OK. Thank you. Goodbye.

(a) Using the line numbers for reference, list any ways in which you think this communication was not well handled.

(b) What confidentiality issues (if any) are raised by this whole incident?

Task 8

You have received the followed memorandum.

MEMORANDUM

To: [Your Name]	**Date:** 15 June 2001
From: Ray Staniland	**Ref:** RS/yn/0601

Subject: Payroll records: security issues

I was most concerned recently to find that, when I needed some staffing records for a client's enquiry, the information was not on the correct file.

Such records are of a most sensitive nature and so I would like you to design a form for requisitioning clients' payroll records from store. Once we have introduced such a mechanism, it will be possible to track information at any time and to tighten the security procedures for handling such records.

If you need any guidance on this and/or need to discuss your ideas, please feel free to come and see me.

Prepare a draft design for a form for requisitioning clients' payroll records, for discussion with Mr Staniland.

Task 9

The following is an extract from Staniland & Roberts' permanent file on one of its regular suppliers of office products and services.

Company:	Folworth Ltd
Address:	47 Bracewell Gardens, Sandsend SS4 LP3
Directors:	Robin Folworth Margaret Foster Laurence Oldfield
Sales Manager:	John Thornhill

You have just received the following letter.

FOLWORTH (Business Services) Ltd

Crichton Buildings
97 Lower Larkin Street   London   EC4A 8QT

Staniland & Roberts (Accountants)
42 - 44 Maypole Street
Sandsend SS1 DXX

Your ref: Po97345   8 August 2000

Dear Sir or Madam

Statement: 54692

I should be grateful for a reply to my letter of 15 May regarding the above account.

Yours sincerely

D. Simmonds
Purchasing Manager

Folworth (Business Services) Ltd, Registered Office:
Crichton Buildings, 97 Lower Larkin Street, London, EC4A 8QT

Registered in England, number 9987654

Directors:
R. Folworth, BA ACA; J. Crichton; M. Foster; L. Oldfield MA; T. Scott; J. Thornhill BSc

(a)   Show how you would update the permanent file (if required).

(b)   Where will you 'put' this letter:

(i)   Now?
(ii) When you have updated the master record?

(c)   Staniland & Roberts uses a chronological filing system for correspondence, within an alphabetical system for clients and suppliers. Purchase orders are duplicated and filed separately under a numerical system. Indicate how you would deal with Mr or Ms Simmonds' letter in the light of this.

Task 10

Your supervisor, Gina Sawhala, is out of the office at a conference for a couple of days. She has phoned in and asked you to find a letter from a Mrs Paribus which is 'somewhere' on her desk and fax through a copy to her, as she wants to draft a reply as soon as possible.

1   As you are searching for the letter, you notice the following documents on Gina's desk.

2   An electricity bill for £372.97 addressed to Ms Sawhala at her home address

3   A letter from a building society asking for a reference for one of your firm's clients

4   A report entitled 'Potential Redundancies: Initial Considerations'

5   A very strongly worded complaint about S & R's performance from a Mrs Paribus

6   A series of cuttings about your organisation from a trade journal

7   A file of correspondence from a supplier that has subsequently gone out of business

8   A file of Gina's expenses claims for the year 1998

9   A file of sales invoices from the year 1996

10   A memo to all staff about the Christmas Party in 1999

11   An urgent telephone message from a client, requesting that Gina call back today

(a)   State what you will do about Gina's request.

(b)   State what you will do with the other documents on Gina's desk.

(c)   State what you would recommend that Gina do with any documents on her desk that you have not dealt with.

Solutions to
practice
devolved assessments

SOLUTION TO PRACTICE DEVOLVED ASSESSMENT 1: SAFE AND SOUND

Task 1

You have a general legal (and moral) duty to behave like a responsible person (not harm people, not set light to buildings and so on). Under the Health and Safety at Work Act 1974 you are obliged to do the following.

(a)   Take reasonable care to avoid injury to yourself and others.

(b)   Co-operate with your employers to help them comply with their statutory obligations.

Under the Management of Health and Safety at Work Regulations 1992 you have further responsibilities.

(a)   You must use all equipment, safety devices, etc, provided by the employer properly and in accordance with the instructions and training received.

(b)   You must inform your employer, or another employee with specific responsibility for health and safety, of any perceived shortcoming in safety arrangements or any serious and immediate dangers to health and safety.

Task 2

Here are some suggestions. You probably have others.

(a)   Use equipment properly (don't attempt to do things like repairs unless you are properly trained to do so)

(b)   Don't tamper recklessly with the electrical supply to equipment.

(c)   Take care with inflammables and toxic things like aerosols and chemicals.

(d)   Don't put liquids on or near equipment. Clean up spilled liquids immediately.

(e)   Be careful with things designed to cut or puncture paper.

(f)   Don't wear clothes or jewellery that are likely to lead to accidents: things that dangle are the worst!

(g)   Follow the guidelines for working with VDUs: *adjust* your adjustable chair, use the blinds, take breaks and so on.

(h)   Take care when moving about: look where you are going, be aware that there may be someone on the other side of the door or just round the corner.

(i)   Make sure that your own work area is free of hazards such as obstructions that people could trip over, open drawers, hidden sharp implements, dangerous or unhygienic rubbish and so on.

(j)   If you smoke don't cause fires: don't throw lighted cigarettes or matches into rubbish bins.

(k)   Don't get intoxicated during working hours.

(l)   Store things safely: heavy objects low down, lighter ones higher up. Don't stand on chairs that have wheels to reach high objects: use proper steps.

(m)   Take care when lifting things: don't try to lift more than you can manage; bend at the knees and so on.

(n)   Lock up things that are meant to be kept locked up.

(o)   Carry and show your identification as required. Don't lend it to anyone else.

(p)   Don't reveal passwords or combinations to unauthorised people.

(q)   Follow organisational procedures for health safety and security.

(r)   Report hazards and breaches of security promptly.

Task 3

(a)   You may have said that in practice you would have used the machine without the safety guard to avoid earning the disapproval or ridicule of your boss. If so, we hope you would be very careful. The only correct answer is that you would not compromise your own well-being by operating the machine unsafely and your boss should not expect you to do so.

(b)   The first thing you should do is switch off the printer at the wall if possible, but if you cannot reach then at least turn off the switch on the machine. You can then make tentative attempts to free yourself but you should not risk damaging yourself or the machine, so be gentle. If this fails, get help. If there is a telephone at hand, use that. Otherwise, you may have to shout for help or even wait for somebody to come. You may, unfortunately, have to cut your hair if it cannot be freed.

One thing that you may have forgotten is to *report* the accident: others should be warned to tie their hair back if they are carrying out the same task and/or the machine should be adapted so that this cannot happen again.

(c)   Leave the room for a while and get some fresh air. When you feel better go back and open a window if possible to make sure that there is proper ventilation. Finally be sure to point the matter out to whoever is responsible for the photocopier - it may have a fault. If you don't start feeling better, see the first-aid officer.

(d)   In the first place you should not have attempted do-it-yourself maintenance on a machine that is not familiar and not your responsibility. Given that you did, however, you should now do the following.

   (i)   Read (what is left of) the packet: it should give instructions telling you what to do if the contents come into contact with your skin.

   (ii)   Follow the instructions and remove the chemical immediately.

   (iii) Report the matter to whoever is responsible for the machine, even though you may feel guilty for interfering. They should see to it that the mess is cleared up immediately.

Task 4

This is an easy task because you are given all the answers. The purpose is to make you read the leaflet.

In general, any accident should be noted in the accident book.

(a)   Wash out your eye with clean, cool water.

(b)   Do not move the courier. Find some way of ensuring that people using the stairs have to go around the casualty (perhaps by blocking off one half of the stairs) or that they go another way entirely.

(c)   The only items on this list that are part of the standard minimum contents are the eye pad and the extra large wound dressings. All of the others should be removed. Report the matter to the person in charge of the box.

Individuals can, of course, carry aspirin, hand cream and so on around with them or keep them in their desk drawer, but they should not be administered to others as first aid.

(d)   Nothing, but don't try this yourself. If the MD later seems to be having breathing difficulties he should be moved to the fresh air until he is better or until professional help arrives.

(e)   If *you* are burnt (and not just your clothing) be careful not to remove clothing sticking to the burns, flush with plenty of clean cool water if the burns are small and then apply a sterilised dressing. If burns are large or deep, wash your hands, apply a dry sterile dressing and go to hospital.

(f)   You should wash the wound. Then do what you would do at home: either ignore it or put a plaster on it if it merits it. Health and safety at work is important, but don't get things out of proportion.

(g) Turn off the current. If you can't do this stand on some dry insulating material and use a wooden or plastic implement.

Task 5

(a)

TO BE COMPLETED BY THE INJURED PARTY OR A WITNESS			TO BE COMPLETED BY FIRST AID OFFICER	TO BE COMPLETED BY SAFETY OFFICER	
Date	Name	Details of accident (include time, place and names of any witnesses)	First aid treatment	Report to HSE	Preventative action taken
3.4.X6	H. Bruce	3.20pm on 3rd floor kitchen. Spilt boiling coffee on right hand. Knocked into by Mr Spratt who was walking past. Witness: Mr Spratt			Isolated incident - no action taken
4.4.X6	P. Spratt	Twisted ankle running upstairs at about 11am - dropped files, attempted to catch them and fell headlong. No witness. On 4th floor landing.			I spoke informally to Mr Spratt who is hobbling and now realises the danger of running about the building.
13.4.X6	David Gardner (Witness)	10.47am. 3rd floor corridor by photocopier. Mr Spratt had his hand in the body of the photocopier and was red-faced because he was trying to pull something out. There was a flash and a loud bang and Mr Spratt was thrown backwards, I switched off the photocopier and phoned the First Aid Officer. Rachael Preston remained with Mr Spratt while I did so.			Memo issued to all staff re running and interfering with equipment. Safety lectures arranged for all staff.

		TO BE COMPLETED BY FIRST AID OFFICER		TO BE COMPLETED BY SAFETY OFFICER
		First aid treatment	Report to HSE	Preventative action taken

TO BE COMPLETED BY THE INJURED PARTY OR A WITNESS

Date	Name	Details of accident (include time, place and names of any witnesses)		
13.4.X6	R. Preston (Witness)	10.40. 3rd floor. The photocopier jammed while I was using it. Mr Spratt came running past and I asked him for help. He pressed a few buttons and then opened the machine and started feeling abour for the jammed paper. He thought he had found it and tugged but there was a loud bang and a flash and he fell backwards. He seemed to be unconscious, I stayed with Mr Spratt while Mr Gardner called the First Aid Officer. I did not touch him or move him, and he did not speak or move. I left when the First Aid Officer arrived.		

(b)

MEMORANDUM

To: All staff   Date: 14 April 20X6

From: Xavier Dent, Safety Officer

Subject: Safety in the workplace

No doubt you have all heard about the accident to Mr Spratt on the 3rd floor last Thursday.

I am glad to report that Mr Spratt is now resting at home and is not seriously hurt. He expects to be back at work in a few days.

This was one of a spate of accidents that have been occurring in the office in the last few months and I feel that it is time for some well-meant reminders.

(i)   Do not dawdle as you go about your work but there is no need to run, particularly when going up or down stairs, when passing dooorways, or turning blind corners.

(ii)   Electrical equipment in the office should be handled with care. Do not attempt to deal even with minor problems unless you have read the appropriate instruction manual; all faults should be reported immediately to Mr Tompkins, the office manager, who will willingly and promptly deal with them.

(iii)   All staff will be required to attend a brief lecture on health and safety in the office. These will be held each afternoon from next Monday and 30 staff may attend at any one time. I append a draft rota to cover all departments. Perhaps managers will let me know if they require any amendments.

(c)   The safety officer's entries in the accident book are shown in the right hand column of the book (on the previous pages).

Task 6

Peter and Mary Spratt
'Mari Celeste'
19 Duncan Drive
Epsom, Surrey

X E Dent Esq
Safety Officer
Duckley Ltd
Canardly Walk
London EC4A 9XJ

15th April 20X6

Dear Mr Dent,

Accident involving photocopier

I gather you spoke to my wife on the telephone earlier. As I believe she told you, not too much harm seems to have been caused by my accident yesterday although I still feel rather shaky and I am resting in bed at home.

For the record I should like to set down my understanding of what happened.

At about 10.30 am on 13 April I was walking down the third floor corridor in the direction of my office. I passed a young lady whom I believe is called Rachel. She appeared to be having difficulty with the photocopier. I am not sure what the model is but there was an identical one in my previous office and I frequently removed jammed paper from that one without coming to any harm.

I opened up the front of the photocopier and I could see the offending sheet inside. It was difficult to reach but not impossible and I started to tug at it.

I have no idea what happened after this. I woke up in hospital on Thursday afternoon. I was kept in 'for observation' and treated for shock, but was allowed to come home on Thursday evening.

So far as I am aware my actions were not dangerous in themselves. I am of the opinion that the photocopier is faulty. I trust that you will be having it inspected by a service engineer at the earliest opportunity.

Thank you again for your concern and please could you also thank anyone who gave assistance while I was unconscious. I hope I will be fit enough to return to work early next week.

Yours sincerely,

Peter Spratt

Peter Spratt

Task 7

Your answer will depend in part on your answers to previous tasks. Here is our suggestion. Yours should be consistent with any assumptions you made for tasks 5 and 6.

ACCIDENT INVESTIGATION QUESTIONNAIRE		
Name of injured person	MR PETER SPRATT	
Date and time of accident	10 40 - 10 50 THURSDAY 13TH APRIL	
Name of investigator	YOUR NAME	
Date of investigation	14TH APRIL 19X6	

Accident type

Exposure to explosion	?	Contact with electricity or electrical discharge	✓
Exposure to fire		Exposure to/contact with harmful substance	
Injured by animal		Contact with moving machinery	
Struck by vehicle		Injured while handling lifting or carrying	
Drowning or asphyxiation		Trapped by something collapsing or overturning	
Fall from height		Slip, trip or fall on same level	
Struck by moving object		Struck against something fixed or stationery	

Brief details of accident

MR SPRATT WAS ATTEMPTING TO REMOVE A PAPER JAM FROM THE PHOTOCOPIER AND APPEARS TO HAVE RECEIVED AN ELECTRIC

SHOCK. HE WAS HOSPITALISED BRIEFLY AND IS NOW RECOVERING AT HOME.

Possible causes: please give, in order of importance, the code references of up to 5 possible causes (see the attached code sheet)

1 305   2 309   3 204   4 201   5 101
....

			DETAILED ENQUIRY
	YES	**NO**	**COMMENTS**
Was the person injured carrying out a task that was part of their normal duties?		✓	MR TOMPKINS, THE OFFICE MANAGER, IS RESPONSIBLE FOR THE PHOTOCOPIER.
Was the person injured involved in an activity associated with work?	✓		APPEARS TO HAVE BEEN ASSISTING RACHEL PRESTON, WHO WAS PHOTOCOPYING PAPERS.
Was the person's immediate supervisor present in the area at the time of the accident?			NOT KNOWN.
If 'NO' state the location of the supervisor at the time and any specific instructions given by the supervisor prior to leaving the area.			-
Was the accident reported immediately?	✓		
If 'NO' state why there was a delay and how long the delay was.			-
To whom was the accident reported?	FIRST AID OFFICER, OFFICE MANAGER		
Has the task being performed been covered by a risk assessment?			NOT KNOWN. REFER TO SAFETY OFFICER.
Was the injured person specifically warned of the hazards of the task?			NOT KNOWN. UNLIKELY.
Was the person injured instructed to carry out the task?		✓	HE WAS VOLUNTARILY ASSISTING RACHEL PRESTON. NORMAL PROCEDURE IS TO CALL THE OFFICE MANAGER.
Was the task carried out in accordance with normal practice?		✓	SEE PREVIOUS ANSWER.
Was the task within the capability of the person injured?	✓		IN PRACTICE PAPER JAMS CAN NORMALLY BE REMOVED BY STAFF.
Was the person injured familiar with the type of plant/equipment/tools etc?	✓		IDENTICAL EQUIPMENT WAS USED IN HIS PREVIOUS JOB.
Had the person injured been trained to carry out the task safely?			NOT KNOWN IF TRAINED. HE CLAIMS TO HAVE REMOVED PAPER JAMS SAFELY IN THE PAST.

	YES	NO	COMMENTS
Was the task carried out by prescribed method?			*NOT KNOWN.*
Was protective clothing being worn?		✓	
Were any of the person's senses obscured/nullified which could have been a contributory factor?			*NOT KNOWN.*
Were plant/equipment/premises in normal condition?			*NOT KNOWN. HOWEVER MR TOMPKINS HAD TO CALL IN THE MAINTENANCE ENGINEER.*
Were guards/protective devices operating effectively?			*NOT KNOWN. SEE PREVIOUS ANSWER.*
Were warning notices displayed warning persons of hazards or to use protective clothing?			*THE PHOTOCOPIER HAS WARNING STICKERS DRAWING ATTENTION TO THE PRESENCE OF ELECTRICITY, BUT THESE ARE NOT PROMINENT.*
Was there a failure of service, component, plant or machinery?			*NOT KNOWN*
Is there a system for monitoring that procedures/instructions are followed?			*REFER TO SAFETY OFFICER, XAVIER DENT.*

Did any of the following environmental factors contribute to the accident?

Rain	Snow	Ice	Fog	Cold
Humidity	Fumes	Gas	Vapour	Noise
Restricted space *POSSIBLY* ✓	Confined space *POSSIBLY* ✓	Uneven/unlevel surface	Condition of ground/floor	Radiation

Task 8

Hopefully this won't happen to you, but the scenario is drawn from genuine experiences.

It seems as if you are likely to strain a muscle if you attempt to do what is being asked of you. However, if you refuse to carry the bags you risk being labelled a 'wimp' and incurring the displeasure of your seniors. You are unlikely to win many friends if you complain to someone at a higher level that you are being picked on. If you simply give in and manage as best you can you will be seen as a soft touch.

This is a human relations problem really, but one that directly impinges on your health and safety. If you do yourself a serious injury you won't be able to travel to Bristol in any case.

Forget pride (male or female). Common sense is far rarer and far more admirable than physical strength. What you need to do in this situation is be assertive.

BPP
PUBLISHING

First reason with the person asking you to carry the bags. Explain as a simple fact that you are not physically able to do so. Do not accept arguments to the contrary, but suggest alternatives. ('I can't carry all of these, they're too heavy, so why don't we ...').

(a)   You could ask to be allowed to claim taxi fares home this evening and to the station on Monday morning. This is probably more attractive than travelling by public transport, so you would be turning the situation to your advantage – brain over brawn!

(b)   You could suggest that the load be spread amongst team members more evenly.

(c)   You could suggest that some of the papers be left in the office: if they are not all needed on Day 1 they could be taken to Bristol later on, or perhaps sent by post.

(d)   If you get nowhere with these suggestions you have little option but to speak to the team leader (who hopefully will have the maturity and authority to insist on option (b)).

Task 9

(a)   Defence means things like locked doors and cabinets, security passes, indelible markings on assets, computer passwords, procedures for visitors, and the security conscious actions of staff.

(b)   Detection is what happens if somebody manages to get through the defences (alarms ringing, security guards being called, searches being carried out of people leaving the building and so on).

(c)   Deterrence is the combination of defences and detection systems: if people know that these exist they will not be tempted to try and break through the defences in the first place.

Task 10

(a)   The main elements included in your diagram should be shown below. You have probably drawn something that looks similar to the place where you work, which is fine.

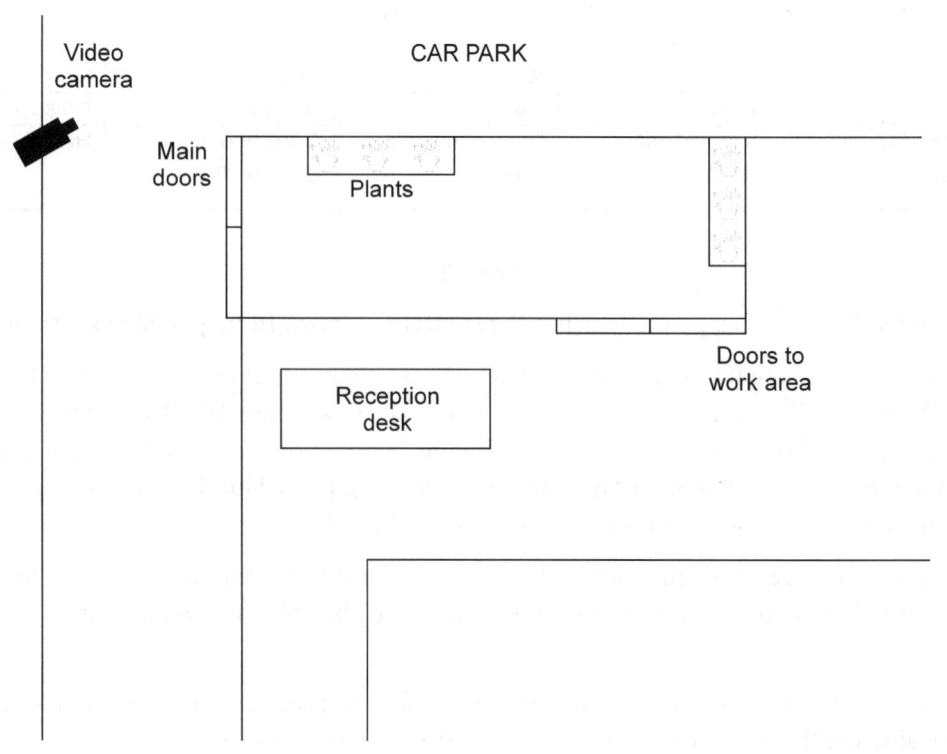

(b)

MEMO

To: Eleanor Martin
From: Carol Hunter
Subject: Security   Date: 2   June
20X6

As you are possibly aware, one of our courier's bikes was stolen from these premises yesterday evening. The courier admits that he did not lock his bike before leaving it unattended but the incident also shows up one or two problems in our own security procedures.

(i)   A person was loitering in our entrance lobby after office hours. It is not known who this person was, how he got on to the premises, or what he was doing or intending to do. The only thing that is reasonably certain is that he left on the courier's bike!

(ii)   It appears that there were no security guards on duty at all between 5.45pm and 6pm.

(iii) The video camera overlooking our building is pointed at the car park. This is perhaps the most vulnerable area, but it means that security guards are totally unable to keep surveillance over the entrance to our building. Another camera, or a camera that sweeps from side to side is surely needed.

(iv)   The video was, in any case, switched off when the incident occurred 'to rewind the tape'. Would it not be preferable to have at least two tapes and keep the video running constantly? The current procedure leaves us in the position where we have no visual evidence of any incidents that occur between certain times.

(v)   Our security staff do not feel that they have any responsibility for the property of visitors to our premises. This may be the legal position but it is a highly anti-social attitude. I cannot see any reason for security staff to make a distinction and I am sure that all of our visitors, major customers and delivery people alike, would like to feel that they can visit us without placing themselves or their belongings at risk.

SOLUTION TO DEVOLVED ASSESSMENT 2: PORTFOLIO

Task 1

The answers will be specific to your own job and organisation so no solution is provided.

Task 2

(a)   and (b)

Obviously we do not know what your place of work looks like, but here is a diagram that shows what we had in mind. We suggest you keep a copy of your own version near at hand at work. Draw a fresh one if you change offices or if any of the information changes.

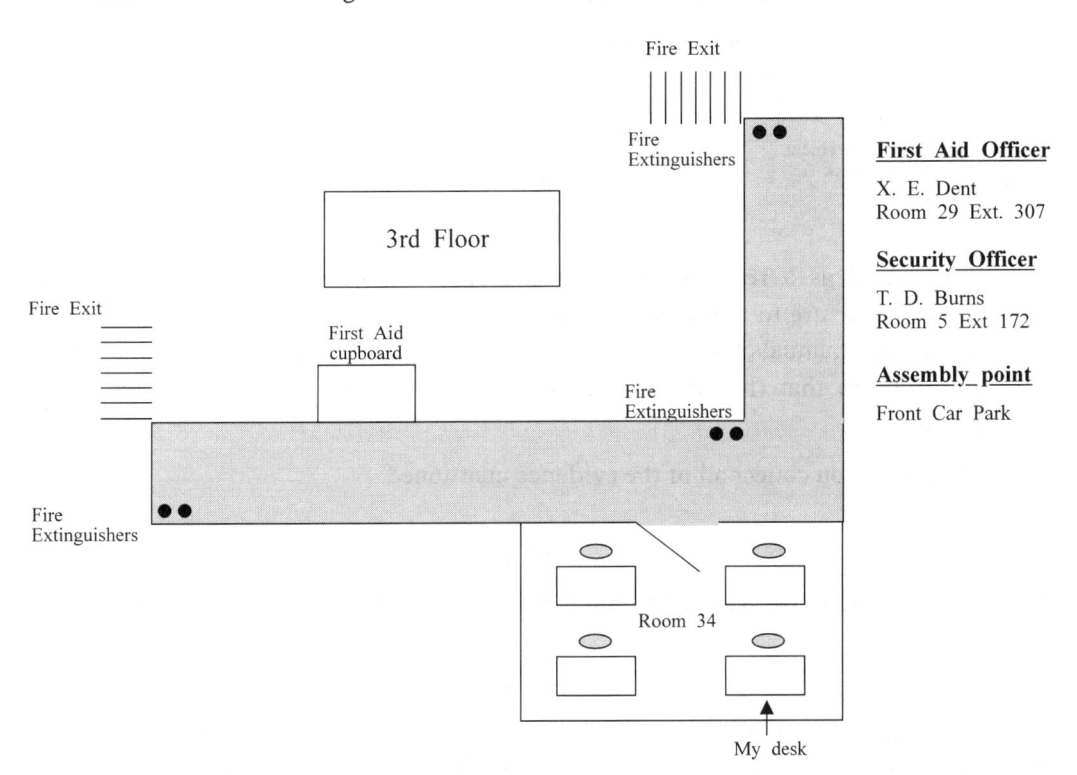

(c)   Again we cannot draw your work area, but the diagram on the next page is what we had in mind.

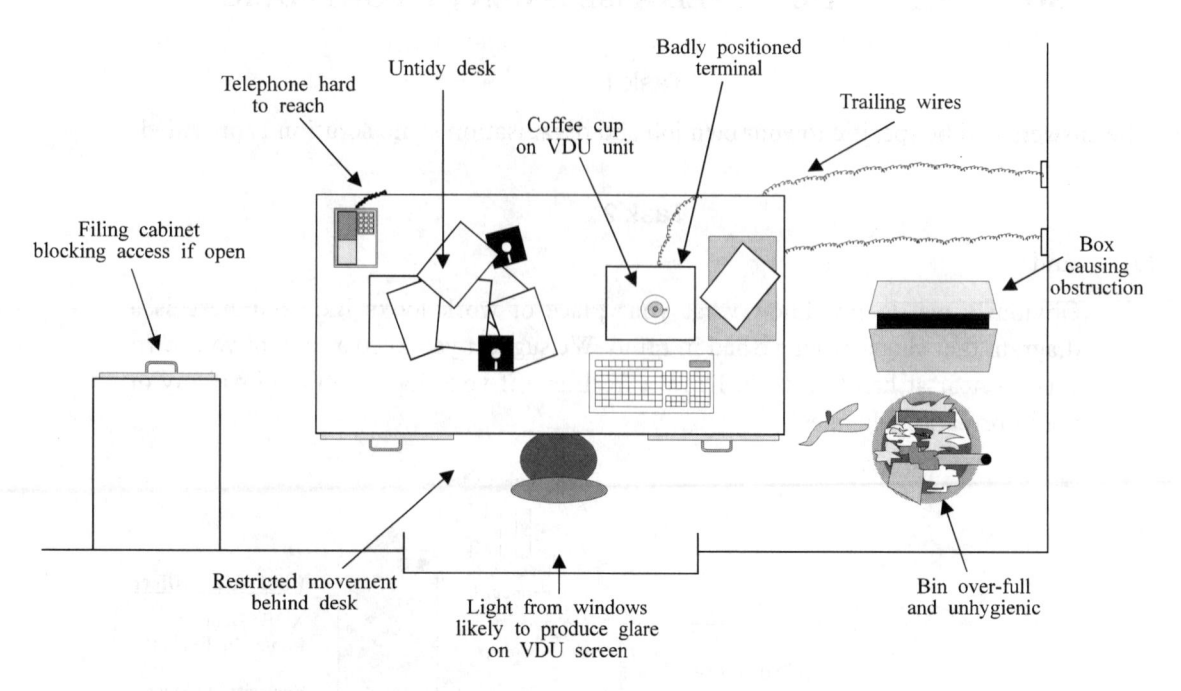

Telephone hard to reach

Untidy desk

Badly positioned terminal

Coffee cup on VDU unit

Trailing wires

Filing cabinet blocking access if open

Box causing obstruction

Restricted movement behind desk

Light from windows likely to produce glare on VDU screen

Bin over-full and unhygienic

(d) If you find as a result of this exercise that you have been using equipment wrongly, be sure to mend your ways. Items like scissors or staplers will not have instruction manuals but do not forget that they can be dangerous if they are used for purposes that they are not intended for, or even if they are just left lying around.

(e) Make sure you collect all of the evidence mentioned.

Task 3

Make sure that you have collected as much as possible of the evidence mentioned.

Task 4

We ask for your own opinion which will of course be influenced by your experiences. During the author's time in practice the main *health* problems were as follows, in order of seriousness.

(a) Stress
(b) Tiredness
(c) Smoking and drinking (excess caffeine or alcohol or both)
(d) Lack of exercise
(e) Eye strain due to close figure work, VDU perils and so on (RSI, perhaps).
(f) Building-related problems such as poor ventilation, bad lighting, bad seating, etc.
(g) Minor office perils such as paper cuts
(h) Perils due to employee carelessness – bumping into others and the like

You might also have included travelling, harassment (sexual or otherwise) and a variety of other ailments related to sedentary work, such as weight problems or back pain.

Regarding security, accountants may be amongst the most at risk since they guard highly desirable assets such as cash and information.

Task 5

The HSE leaflet *Working with VDUs* has the following suggestions.

(a) Adjust your chair and VDU to find the most comfortable position for your work. As a broad guide, your arms should be approximately horizontal and your eyes at the same height as the top of the VDU casing.

(b) Make sure there is enough space underneath your desk to move your legs freely. Move any obstacles such as boxes or equipment.

(c) Avoid excess pressure on the backs of your legs and knees. A footrest, particularly for smaller users, may be helpful.

(d) Don't sit in the same position for long periods. Make sure you change your posture as often as practicable. Some movement is desirable, but avoid repeat stretching movements.

(e) Adjust your keyboard and screen to get a good keying and viewing position. A space in front of the keyboard is sometimes helpful for resting the hands and wrists while not keying.

(f) Don't bend your hands up at the wrist when keying. Try to keep a soft touch on the keys and don't overstretch your fingers. Good keyboard technique is important.

(g) Try different layouts of keyboard, screen and document holder to find the best arrangement for you.

(h) Make sure you have enough workspace to take whatever documents you need. A document holder may help you to avoid awkward neck movements.

(i) Arrange your desk and screen so that bright lights are not reflected in the screen. You shouldn't be directly facing windows or bright lights. Adjust curtains or blinds to prevent unwanted light.

(j) Make sure the characters on your screen are sharply focused and can be read easily. They shouldn't flicker or move.

(k) Make sure there are no layers of dirt, grime or finger marks on the screen.

(l) Use the brightness control on the screen to suit the lighting conditions in the room.

Task 6

Your answer will be specific to your own circumstances. Here is a fictional example of the sort of thing we had in mind.

(a) I experienced psychological problems at a time when there had been a number of changes in my personal circumstances.

    (i) My closest friend got married and left the area.

    (ii) A number of staff at work with whom I had had an extremely good relationship left to go to other jobs. I failed to make a serious effort to get to know their replacements.

    (iii) I was faced with the possibility of having to find £2,000 at short notice to pay off a debt.

(iv)   There was a temporary change in the management of the firm: my normal boss was sent on a secondment and I became directly responsible to my boss's boss.

(b)   The uncertainty of my new social 'role' at work and the curtailment of social activities at home led to my becoming withdrawn and unsociable. I worked extremely long hours in the office and often took work home and continued in the evenings and at weekends.

The quality of my work did not suffer at all: in some ways I have never produced work of higher quality. However, I was working very inefficiently, often making false starts or following red herrings rather than concentrating on the matter in hand. This meant that work was often not finished by the deadline.

(c)   My colleagues were undoubtedly affected by my problems. No action was taken to encourage me to meet deadlines, but a number of pieces of work were reallocated. At the time I felt no guilt about this, since in the past I had often helped out colleagues who were struggling to meet deadlines. In retrospect it is true to say that the work was not reallocated fairly by my temporary boss and, of course, it should not have had to be reallocated at all. My behaviour and its consequences was resented amongst my colleagues.

(d)   The solution to the problem came about more by accident than design.

(i)   I had a series of arguments with both colleagues and my temporary boss, during which the above came to light.

(ii)   My social life at home improved as I moved into a new circle.

(iii)   I took some time off work simply to relax. I came to terms with the fact that some of the criticisms that had been made of me were justified and that I was harming myself, my colleagues and my organisation by my attitude to work.

(e)   Since the circumstances giving rise to the problems were largely personal, there is a limit to what could have been expected of the firm. The HSE leaflet advises that managers should be on the look out for indications of possible problems and includes the following general guidance.

> Intervention may simply consist of a timely, sympathetic enquiry regarding general health. When made by an acceptable person this may prevent distress from becoming a mental health problem. At this stage reassurance about job security and the confidentiality of discussion of personal problems is essential. It always helps to listen to what distressed people have to say.

In my situation the deadlines missed and the necessity to reallocate work were clear signs that all was not well. If this had been noticed by my employer action could have been a combination of sympathy and understanding together with closer than usual monitoring of my efficiency, and steps to ensure that I took account of the impact of my performance on others as well as myself.

(f)   My responsibilities were to attempt not to allow personal difficulties to intrude upon my work (or at least to explain to my employer that all was not well) and in particular to work harder at relationships and consider the consequences of my actions for others.

Task 7

(a) Standard minimum contents are as follows. These will probably be listed on the lid of the box.

1 Guidance leaflet on first aid
20 Sterile adhesive dressings 'airstrip'
– Sterile adhesive dressings 'elastoplast'
2 Sterile eye pad with bandage no. 16
6 Triangular bandage B.P. 90cm × 127cm
6 Safety pins
6 Sterile wound dressing medium no. 8
2 Sterile wound dressing large no. 9
3 Sterile wound dressing extra large no. 3
1 Person in charge notice, self-adhesive (this may be stuck up somewhere rather than in the box)

(b) The box inspected at BPP Publishing was missing the plasters ('because people keep using them', according to the person in charge of the box!) and only had 4 safety pins and a paper clip. It had more than the minimum contents of some of the dressings. During the inspection the person in charge dropped the box on her foot!

(c) The discrepancies should be reported to the person in charge of the box who should rectify them (for example replace the missing plasters and safety pins and remove the paper clip). There is, of course, no reason why a box should not contain more than the minimum number of standard items.

Task 8

To protect yourself you could take measures such as the following.

(a) Follow organisational guidelines about personal safety and security to the letter.

(b) Avoid doing things that might provoke people. These could include, for example, being insensitive (wearing a £500 Armani suit to work when you spend much of the day dealing with people living in poverty, say); descending to abusive language if people start swearing at you; allowing yourself to be distracted by telephone calls or other demands on your attention that make the person you are dealing with feel that he or she is not being taken seriously; being inconsistent or showing favouritism (bending the rules for one customer but not for the next).

If you can think of more specific things that would upset the people you deal with in your job, be sure to note them down.

(c) Don't take unnecessary risks. If a customer asks you out for a drink, say, refuse if you are at all unsure of them. If you are tempted to agree, meet in a public place, make sure someone knows you are going, don't give them personal information like your address and phone number until you are sure of them.

(d) Seek assistance from colleagues or security staff if an interviewee starts to become threatening.

(e) Don't be violent or aggressive in manner towards your customer: an obvious point, but worth making.

Your employer could take the following measures.

(a) Provide you with training in dealing with difficult situations.

(b)   Provide you with protection by arranging the working environment in such a way that it would be physically difficult to assault you. The obvious example is the counters and screens in banks and post offices. Modern systems have armour plated screens that are not normally on view but which can rise up and seal off staff from the public area in less than a second.

(c)   Not place you in situations that are likely to lead to aggression. One example would be abandoning petty bureaucratic rules that just annoy people. Another would be providing whatever it is that people are paying for to the required standard (assaults on public transport staff, for example, may ultimately be due to the failure of the public transport managers to provide a good service).

Neither of these answers is exhaustive. You may well have thought of other examples form personal experience.

If you really are in this situation you may be interested to know that the Suzy Lamplugh Trust has produced a *Guide to Personal Safety at Work* which gives advice on developing confidence, assessing and reducing risks, dealing with aggression and physical attack, and travelling safely outside the workplace.

Task 9

The contract of employment contains a confidentiality clause. If you do not keep the affairs of the company secret you are in breach of contract.

In practice this is unlikely to mean that you have to clam up even if your partner asks what sort of a day you have had at work. However the clause would certainly operate if it were discovered that you had leaked internal information to somebody that could misuse it for their own advantage and/or to the detriment of the company.

This contract also requires that if you leave the company you must surrender any of the company's records that are in your possession and anybody else's records that you have on behalf of your company, for example the cash book of a client that you were working on. This is quite a common position for an accountant working for a firm of accountants to be in, so you may well have a clause like this in your own contract.

The second clause in the contract entitles the company to search you, your bag and your locker and so on. The company has no general right to do this unless there is such a clause in your contract.

As for the notice, if it is displayed prominently, so that people entering the building can see it, it entitles the company to search anyone entering or leaving the premises. The notice alone would not give the employer the right to search an employee's locker.

Task 10

(a)   You may have seen an article in the newspaper a while ago that showed the effects on spiders' web-spinning abilities of various drugs. Caffeine came off worse than marijuana and speed, leaving spiders incapable of spinning anything better than a few threads strung together at random. Only sleeping pills did worse than caffeine, because the spiders dropped off before they got started.

Here is a possible notice based on the article reproduced in the question.

DO YOU NEED THAT CUP OF COFFEE?

Medical research shows that the effects of caffeine are ....

an inability to concentrate

poor decision making

irritability

nervousness

forgetfulness

fatigue

insomnia

In some people caffeine causes an accentuation of pre-menstrual syndrome and diarrhoea.

Fancy a cup of ...... water?

Parts (b), (c), and (d) will have answers specific to you.

If it is of any interest, the author of this task, a confirmed caffeine addict, tried this experiment, noticed only withdrawal symptoms and gave up. However, in many ways this merely confirms the findings of the research: poor decision making, inability to concentrate (on giving up coffee) etc!

Task 11

An example of a real scheme will allow you to judge how good your answer was. This is taken from a work environment far more likely to encounter safety problems than the average accounts office, but it illustrates the principles.

On the construction site of its new research centre Glaxo, the pharmaceuticals company, had a scheme whereby prizes such as a car were raffled as rewards for safe working. The safety record of the site was ten times better than the national average.

(a) The target was a million man-hours without losing time through serious injury: this took about three months. (Time without injury targets are sensible: the time will depend on the number of workers.) There were also monthly league tables measuring things such as safe working systems, and attitudes amongst different parts of the workforce.

(b) Once this was achieved a prize draw was held at a feast to which the whole workforce was invited, underlining the importance attached to safety by management and allaying suspicions that the draw might be a fix.

(c) Everyone currently on the workforce had an equal chance of winning, even if they had only been employed for a few weeks. This meant that short-term workers had the same incentive to work safely as others. Other companies with more stable workforces have schemes allowing individuals to build up safety merit points that can be exchanged for gifts of varying value like holidays and store vouchers.

(d) The main prize was a car and there were six runners up prizes of £4,000 each. Obviously the size of the prize would depend on the size of the organisation. There were also daily spot prizes of £10: these were awarded by safety personnel to any worker who was observed carrying out their duties with a high regard to safety or taking steps to remove some potential hazard (eg reporting a hazard). There was also a monthly quiz with prizes worth up to £100.

(e)   The rules were strictly applied. Even a relatively trivial accident could result in the clock being set back to zero. This happened for example when a worker had to take more than three days off work after tripping on some steps on his way to the toilet. Some distinction clearly has to be made between absences due to things that happen at work and those due to things that happen outside work.

Task 12

The first document is a fire extinguisher inspection report. The extinguisher on the fifth floor rear stairs needs to be replaced (in fact it should have been replaced following the previous visit). The document is dated 19X2. A further inspection is long overdue. It would probably be worth looking at the extinguishers in your own area for any obvious signs of faults and reporting them if you find any. This may not be particularly easy to do, since you are unlikely to be trained to do so, but if you see something leaking or obviously damaged, or if you pick up an extinguisher and it feels empty this should certainly be mentioned.

The second two documents are a fire alarm and emergency lighting test reports. The first (13.4.X6) suggests that two emergency lights need to be repaired: presumably this is why the 'further visit required' box is ticked, since nothing seems to have been done on this visit. The main supply cupboard also seems to need repairs.

The final document suggests that the 7th floor emergency lighting needs repairs and perhaps calls into further question the safety of the mains supply.

Task 13

You should not under any circumstances operate the paper shredding machine, even if instructed to do so.

There is not a great deal that you as an employee can do about this - in practice you are not likely to have access to such documents and we are not suggesting that you should spy on your employer. It is your duty to report any possible hazards though, so if it is ages since the last fire drill and the alarms are never tested, it is worth pointing this out to whoever is responsible. If you use a PC or some other electrical equipment, has it ever been tested for electrical safety?

You should draw the notice to the attention of anyone you see operating the machine and any other colleagues *likely* to try to use the machine.

SOLUTION TO DEVOLVED ASSESSMENT 3: EFFICIENT AND EFFECTIVE

Task 1

Checklist of tasks associated with responsibility for petty cash ☑

Daily

☐ Issue petty cash only when requests are supported by an authorised petty cash voucher and valid receipt

☐ Write up the Petty Cash Records

Weekly

☐ Balance and reconcile actual cash to the Petty Cash Record

Monthly

☐ Balance and reconcile actual cash to the petty cash records

☐ Reimburse the imprest, requesting a cheque for the appropriate amount of cash

Action plan for scheduling and follow-up

1   Enter weekly task in Desk Diary for Friday afternoon, each week

2   Enter monthly tasks in Desk Diary on appropriate month-end date, each month

3   Set up reminders on PC, using Outlook Scheduling facility, for each daily/weekly/monthly recurring task

4   Add Petty Cash to standing To Do List each morning

5   If any tasks are carried over to later days (because of non-routine demands), enter into Desk Diary on appropriate day

Task 2

The problem

PS is technically competent: tasks are not necessarily taking longer than they should. His problem appears to be in coping with the intervention of non-routine demands: ie a problem of effective prioritising of workload.

Secondary problem now arising: symptoms of stress from long hours and inability to control conflicting demands.

PS needs coaching in prioritising skills.

Other issues

GS has pointed out the symptoms (missed deadlines) to PS – but may not have correctly diagnosed the problem. Communication/authority issue: can I give PS informal help (as colleague to colleague) or would this be perceived as usurping GS's authority? If I consult with GS first, would this be perceived as criticism of PS and/or criticism of GS's handling of the situation? What is the best way to maintain working relationships with both individuals, while acting to solve the problem?

If help and advice are given to PS, it needs to be tactful and constructive: he knows he is struggling and is bound to feel insecure about it – especially in his current stressed state.

Action plan

1   Initial one-to-one informal approach to PS (perhaps during a break, or outside work). Empathise first (difficulties of conflicting demands, long hours), before attempting to 'fix': check PS's understanding of the problem. Tactful offer of informal (and confidential) help.

2   If offer accepted, give PS some notes on prioritising. (Written form allows him to assess in own time and away from office: not highly visible to others.)

3   Discuss notes with PS when he has time to read them: offer to clarify, explain, demonstrate.

4   Suggest that it might be helpful for him to discuss the situation with GS – now that he is beginning to understand it better. It may be possible for work time to be allocated to coaching or training, or for re-allocation of workload (if genuinely excessive).

5   Suggest strongly that whenever PS realises that he will be unable to meet a deadline, it is important for him to inform GS, so help can be given or plans adjusted.

6   If situation fails to improve, urge PS to discuss situation with GS for his own health and the effectiveness of his work. If situation deteriorates, consider approaching GS – in strict confidence – to explain that there may be a problem.

Task 2

Notes on task scheduling and prioritising

Ways of determining the order of tasks:

(a)   Important or 'high priority' tasks (routine or non-routine) to be done first – especially if urgent.

(b)   Urgent tasks - with 'least slack time' or closest deadline – to be done first unless relatively unimportant.

(c)   Routine tasks can be done according to arrival time (first come, first served), most nearly finished, shortest queue at next operation and so on.

A task is high priority if:

(a)   it has to be completed by a deadline **and**
(b)   other tasks depend on it; or
(c)   other people depend on it; or
(d)   it is important in terms of benefits, consequences and so on.

Routine priorities should be planned and scheduled: however, flexibility is required for non-routine demands. Relative priorities should constantly be monitored.

Task 3

E-mail text

From: yname@infonet
To: rstaniland@infonet
Cc:
Subject: Re Jones & Co

Three quick questions about the information you requested in your memo of 25 April re the presentation of the Jones & Co staff hours for the Partners' Meeting.

1   What format will you wish to use for your presentation: overhead, Powerpoint presentation, printed report?

2   My suggestion is to use a pie chart, as the clearest visual presentation of the data: will this suit you?

3   Will you require the chart prior to the meeting, in order to approve the format or merge with other documentation? Would Monday 29 April be suitable?

Thanks.

Workings

Grade	Hours	Proportion of hours	Degrees
Senior partner	36	0.20	72
Partner	9	0.05	18
Senior	36	0.20	72
Semi senior	54	0.30	108
Accounting technician	45	0.25	90
	180	1.00	360

Slide:

Staff hours worked on Jones & co year-end

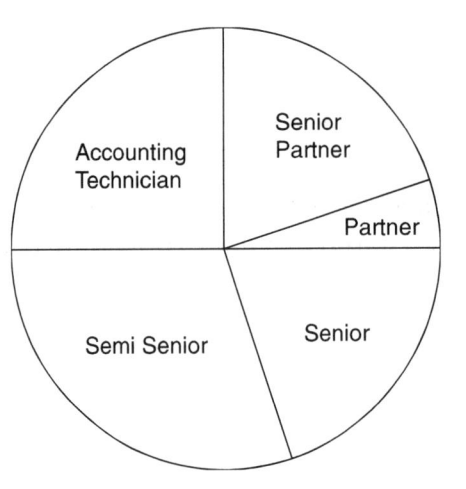

BPP
PUBLISHING

Key

Grade	*Hours*	*Proportion of hours*
Senior partner	36	20%
Partner	9	5%
Senior	36	20%
Semi senior	54	30%
Accounting technician	45	25%
Total	180	

Task 4

Of Tasks 4-6, this comes second in order of priority: it is important (since it involves client communication and plenty of notice must be given), however it is a longer task – and, since the lead time is quite long, arguably a less urgent task – than Task 5. Within Task 4, the asking of the questions clearly comes – logically – before the drafting of the letter.

E-mail text

From:	yname@infonet
To:	rstaniland@infonet
Cc:	
Subject:	Where Next for the EMU?' Seminar: Invitation to Clients

I have been given the task of drafting the letter to clients inviting them to the Seminar. I would like to be able to include as much information as possible to facilitate their decision to attend, and the Minutes of the Partners' Meeting did not go into detail as to the arrangements. Could you please let me know, at your earliest convenience:

1   The proposed venue for the Seminar (and whether this has been confirmed, or you would like me to contact the venue to make the arrangements)

2   What the purpose and nature of the proceedings will be (including whether refreshments will be provided)

If someone else in the office has been handling these details, please just forward this message to him or her.

Thanks.

PS. I intend to format the invitation letter for 'mail merging' from our client database, so that it is personally addressed. I trust that this meets with your approval.

STANILAND & ROBERTS

Accountants
40-42 Maypole Street, Sandsend, SS1 DXX
Tel: 01749 221720   Fax: 01749 217400
E-mail: mail@stanilandroberts.co.uk

[client name]   [date]
[client organisation]
[client address]

Dear [client greeting]

As you are aware, doing business within the European Economic Area has presented many challenges in recent years. In particular, much speculation has surrounded the role and impact of European Monetary Union on trade and employment practices in the UK.

We have decided to explore this issue in our Year 2001 Seminar: 'Where Next for the EMU?'

'Where Next for the EMU?' Seminar

Date: Monday 15 July 2001
Time: 6.30 for 7.00 pm
Venue: The Early of Whitby Hotel, Sandsend

Light refreshments will be provided.

If you wish to attend this special seminar, please complete the tear-off slip below and return it to me by post or fax (no later than 8 July, please).

Many clients have told us that they found our Year 2000 'Millennium Bug' Seminar both helpful and enjoyable. We hope that you will be able to attend this year, and look forward to seeing you on the 15 July.

Yours sincerely

Your Name
Accounting Technician

✂ -

To: Your Name, Staniland & Roberts, 40-42 Maypole Street, Sandsend, SS1 DXX
Or FAX: 01749 217400

Staniland & Roberts 2001 Seminar: 'Where Next for the EMU?'

15 July 2001, 6.20 pm

From: [client name]   of   [client organisation]

★ I wish to attend the Seminar
★ I am unable to attend the Seminar   ★ Delete as applicable

Task 5

Of Tasks 4-6, this comes first in order of priority: it is rendered urgent by the fact that rectifies a serious failing in office procedure that has already come to the attention of the senior partner: at the same time, it is not time-consuming to do, so it will not impact greatly on the task sequence, despite its high impact.

MEMORANDUM

To: All Staff   **Date:** 2 May 2001
From: [Your Name]   **Ref:** YN/staff/0501

Subject: Petty Cash

Ray Staniland has asked me to draw to your attention the standard procedure to be followed when requesting petty cash.

Please ensure that all requests for petty cash are supported by:
*   An authorised petty cash voucher and
*   A valid receipt.

Expenditure up to £10 must be authorised by David Jones.

Expenditure in excess of £10 must be authorised by the office manager.

This system is for our convenience as well as efficient and secure cash management. Please, let's all adhere to the correct procedures in future.

Task 6

Of Tasks 4-6, this comes third in order of priority: it will not be required for some time.

Checklist for welcoming seminar participants

1 week ahead

☐   Confirm Hotel to set up appropriate Welcome signage and signposts to seminar room

☐   Confirm Hotel to supply appropriate catering staff to serve light refreshments

☐   Prepare list of RSVP'd participants, identification labels and seminar pack (seminar notes, note paper, feedback form)

☐   Allocate welcome/registration duties and brief staff

On the day

☐   Set up a Registration Area in the lobby of the seminar room

On the evening

☐   Welcome participants, sign them in, hand out identification labels and seminar packs

☐   Staff on 'traffic control' and enquiries: direct participants to cloak rooms, seating and so on

☐ Introduce key clients (where required) to partners 'mingling' over refreshments

☐ Member of staff to remain on duty in lobby to welcome latecomers

Task 7

(a) Line 1. The operator does not give the name of the organisation.

Line 2. The operator does not reply to the caller's request: for all the caller knows, she has been cut off.

Line 4. Clara and the operator have failed to communicate or feedback clearly, with the result that Clara misaddresses Mrs Doe (and does so again in Line 8).

Line 4. Clara has not been announced by the operator, and does not identify herself.

Line 6. Clara does not inform Mrs Doe what she is going to do: she merely leaves the line. Her response is also inadequate: 'might' is not a firm foundation for a meeting.

Line 8 and 10. Clara fails to notice feedback suggesting uncertainty and hesitation from Mrs Doe in line 7 and line 9: she should have checked that the solution was genuinely acceptable or offered alternatives. Mrs Doe did not give a definite answer – but did not expect to be summarily cut off without further discussion or alternatives.

All of the above is compounded (in retrospect) by the fact that the caller is a potential high-level member of the firm: the telephone practices have failed to create a positive impression of the firm as a potential employer.

(b) There are two different confidentiality issues here.

1 Staniland & Roberts may be legally construed as invading the privacy of staff and callers by monitoring phone calls without their knowledge or formal consent.

2 The 'leak' of the transcript of this call to a member of staff (presumably, circulating round the office) is a breach of customary confidentiality in regard to disciplinary matters. The transcript was presumably used in a formal or informal disciplinary interview between Clara and Mr Armstrong: it should not have gone beyond that context, unless Clara expressly consented to its use as a training case study (unlikely).

Task 8

PAYROLL UNIT

File requisition form

Please issue the following record from store:

Client name:...

Client file no:...

Date:...

Signature:...

Authorised by:...

Reason for request:...

....

....

....

....

Task 9

(a) The updated file should show the following information.

Company:	Folworth (Business Services) Ltd
Address:	Crichton Buildings 97 Lower Larkin Street Sandsend SS3 DB4
Directors:	Robin Folworth BA ACA J..... Crichton [space left to insert new directors' names when known] Margaret Foster Laurence Oldfield MA T.... Scott [as above] John Thornhill BSc [full name known as previous Sales Manager
Sales Manager:	D.... Simmonds

(b) This letter will be put:

(i) into your 'action' tray, as it requires short-term follow-up action in the updating of the master record; and, once this is done

(ii) back into your 'action' tray to await your attention in locating the previous correspondence and replying to Mr or Ms Simmonds - or into the pigeonhole of another person who may already be aware of the matter and/or have specific responsibility for the follow-up action (if this is not you): the purchasing officer, perhaps.

(c) Your first action will be to try and locate the alleged letter of 15 May. You would do this by looking for Folworth in the alphabetical suppliers files, under F, and then looking through the chronologically filed correspondence (somewhere near the front – or back – where the most recent correspondence is) for May 15.

You will also check the Purchase Order file, numerically, for Purchase Order PO97345 (which was given as the S & R reference in Simmonds' current letter).

You could also check the Statements Received or Payable files for the Statement mentioned in the letter.

Armed with any or all of the above documents, you should be able to reply to Mr or Ms Simmonds – or at least to telephone him or her to make enquiries, armed with a least some of the references cited.

Task 10

(a) The danger is that your fax will be collected or seen by someone other than Gina at the conference centre. Its contents seem as if they might be damaging to the reputation of your department and/or organisation if they fall into outside hands, causing severe embarrassment. In addition, Mrs Paribus may not appreciate her personal details, inevitably contained in the letter, from being sent outside the office by such open means. You should contact Gina by telephone at the conference centre and discuss the problem with her: she may be able to stand over the centre's fax machine to ensure immediate receipt of the letter. You should also ensure that the words 'Private and Confidential' are prominently displayed on the fax header sheet.

(b) Apart from the letter from Mrs Paribus (document 4), you do not have authority or permission to do *anything* with the other documents on Gina's desk. Given that you could not help reading them as you searched the desk (which you were authorised to do), you may however notice the urgent telephone message from the client (document 10) which will be received too late *unless* you do something. It may be worth mentioning this to Gina in the same phone call as the one to arrange the confidential fax: she may instruct you to handle the matter or inform the caller that Gina will not be available and route the matter elsewhere.

(c) There are some confidentiality issues and some retention issues in the question of what should be done with all these documents and files. It may be that they are only on Gina's desk because they are related to some matter with which she is currently dealing: in which case they should stay where they are (perhaps a little more tidily arranged) until they are not longer required. It may be, however, that Gina is not very good at distinguishing between active, semi-active and non-active files, and/or is not aware of S & R's retention policy or legal requirements. In this light, you might make notes as follows.

1   A personal bill is irrelevant to you and the organisation. It might be thought of as confidential – but not if Gina does not choose to make it so. (You may suggest to her that details such as her home address should not be quite so open to passing strangers, however.)

2   The letter from the building society may be confidential if it contains personal or financial details about the client, in which case it should be flagged 'confidential'. (The reference itself would certainly be confidential.) If the reference has been written, the letter should be filed in the client's correspondence file: if not, it should go in the 'action' tray.

3   This is likely to be highly confidential – and specifically not to be seen by junior staff prior to formal consultation on defined proposals. It should be securely kept in Gina's personal files – assuming *she* is entitled to have a copy. (As a member of the junior staff, and perhaps of a relevant union or staff association, the mere sight of this report may put you in a moral dilemma.)

4   Once faxed to Gina, the letter from Mrs Paribus should be filed in the correspondence files or Gina's 'action' tray (to check that she has indeed followed up, on her return).

5   The cuttings are published material, in the public domain: they are clearly not confidential. The only issue will be whether they are active, semi-active or suitable for the archives – which will depend on the specific use Gina has for them.

6   Some of the ex-supplier's correspondence may now be redundant and/or past the recommended retention period of 6 years. Some may still be within the retention period laid down by S & R's policy – and some may even be regarded as active or semi-active (for example, if Gina is researching trends in prices or product specifications over time): correspondence should be sorted and re-filed accordingly.

7   Expenses claims have a recommended retention period of 1 year: these may now be destroyed (unless S & R's policy dictates otherwise, for archival or management information purposes).

8   Sales invoices have a recommended retention policy of 6 years: these are still current, but unless they have an immediate purpose, they should be in the archives.

9   This is of passing interest, and may safely be destroyed (unless a single archive copy is kept as a 'template', and this is that copy, in which case it should be in the archive).

10   This needs immediate attention, as outlined in (b) above.

List of Key Terms and Index

These are the terms which we have identified throughout the text as being KEY TERMS. You should make sure that you can define what these terms mean; go back to the pages highlighted here if you need to check.

BPP
PUBLISHING

See overleaf for information on other
BPP products and how to order

AAT Order

To BPP Publishing Ltd, Aldine Place, London W12 8AW
Tel: 020 8740 2211. Fax: 020 8740 1184
E-mail: Publishing@bpp.com Web:www.bpp.com

Mr/Mrs/Ms (Full name) _____

Daytime delivery address _____

Postcode _____

Daytime Tel _____

E-mail _____

	5/01 Texts	6/01 Kits	Special offer	5/01 Passcards	Tapes
FOUNDATION (ALL £9.95)					
Unit 1 Recording Income and Receipts	☐	☐	All		
Unit 2 Making and Recording Payments	☐	☐	Foundation		
Unit 3 Ledger Balances and Initial Trial Balance	☐	☐	Texts and	£4.95 ☐	£10.00 ☐
Unit 4 Supplying Information for Mgmt Control	☐	☐	Kits		
Unit 20 Working with Information Technology	☐	☐	(£80)		
Unit 22/23 Healthy Workplace & Personal Effectiveness	☐	☐	☐		
INTERMEDIATE (ALL £9.95)		8/01 Kits			
Unit 5 Financial Records and Accounts	☐	☐	All	£4.95 ☐	£10.00 ☐
Unit 6 Cost Information	☐	☐	Inter'te Texts	£4.95 ☐	£10.00 ☐
Unit 7 Reports and Returns	☐	☐	and Kits (£65)		
Unit 21 Using Information Technology	☐	☐	☐		
TECHNICIAN (ALL £9.95)					
Unit 8/9 Core Managing Costs and Allocating Resources	☐	☐	Set of 12	£4.95 ☐	£10.00 ☐
Unit 10 Core Managing Accounting Systems	☐	☐	Technician	£4.95 ☐	£10.00 ☐
Unit 11 Option Financial Statements (A/c Practice)	☐	☐	Texts/Kits		
Unit 12 Option Financial Statements (Central Govnmt)	☐	☐	(Please		
Unit 15 Option Cash Management and Credit Control	☐	☐	specify titles		
Unit 16 Option Evaluating Activities	☐	☐	required)		
Unit 17 Option Implementing Auditing Procedures	☐	☐	(£100)		
Unit 18 Option Business Tax (FA01)(8/01 Text)	☐	☐	☐		
Unit 19 Option Personal Tax (FA 01)(8/01 Text)	☐	☐			
TECHNICIAN 2000 (ALL £9.95)					
Unit 18 Option Business Tax FA00 (8/00 Text & Kit)	☐	☐			
Unit 19 Option Personal Tax FA00 (8/00 Text & Kit)	☐	☐			
SUBTOTAL	£	£	£	£	£

TOTAL FOR PRODUCTS

£ _____

POSTAGE & PACKING

Texts/Kits

	First	Each extra
UK (max £10)	£2.00	£2.00
Europe*	£4.00	£2.00
Rest of world	£20.00	£10.00 £

Passcards/Tapes

	First	Each extra
UK	£2.00	£1.00
Europe*	£2.50	£1.00
Rest of world	£15.00	£8.00 £

Grand Total (Cheques to *BPP Publishing*) I enclose
a cheque for (incl. Postage)   £ _____

Or charge to Access/Visa/Switch

Card Number ☐☐☐☐ ☐☐☐☐ ☐☐☐☐ ☐☐☐☐

Expiry date _____   Start Date _____

Issue Number (Switch Only) _____

Signature _____

We aim to deliver to all UK addresses inside 5 working days; a signature will be required. Orders to all EU addresses should be delivered within 6 working days. All other orders to overseas addresses should be delivered within 8 working days. * Europe includes the Republic of Ireland and the Channel Islands.

REVIEW FORM & FREE PRIZE DRAW

All original review forms from the entire BPP range, completed with genuine comments, will be entered into one of two draws on 31 January 2002 and 31 July 2002. The names on the first four forms picked out on each occasion will be sent a cheque for £50.

Name: _____   Address: _____

_____

_____

How have you used this Interactive Text?
(Tick one box only)

☐ Home study (book only)

☐ On a course: college _____

☐ With 'correspondence' package

☐ Other _____

Why did you decide to purchase this Interactive Text? *(Tick one box only)*

☐ Have used BPP Texts in the past

☐ Recommendation by friend/colleague

☐ Recommendation by a lecturer at college

☐ Saw advertising

☐ Other _____

During the past six months do you recall seeing/receiving any of the following?
(Tick as many boxes as are relevant)

☐ Our advertisement in *Accounting Technician* magazine

☐ Our advertisement in *Pass*

☐ Our brochure with a letter through the post

Which (if any) aspects of our advertising do you find useful?
(Tick as many boxes as are relevant)

☐ Prices and publication dates of new editions

☐ Information on Interactive Text content

☐ Facility to order books off-the-page

☐ None of the above

Have you used the companion Assessment Kit for this subject?   ☐ Yes   ☐ No

Your ratings, comments and suggestions would be appreciated on the following areas

	Very useful	Useful	Not useful
Introductory section (How to use this Interactive Text etc)	☐	☐	☐
Chapter topic lists	☐	☐	☐
Chapter learning objectives	☐	☐	☐
Key terms	☐	☐	☐
Assessment alerts	☐	☐	☐
Examples	☐	☐	☐
Activities and answers	☐	☐	☐
Key learning points	☐	☐	☐
Quick quizzes and answers	☐	☐	☐
List of key terms and index	☐	☐	☐
Icons	☐	☐	☐

	Excellent	Good	Adequate	Poor
Overall opinion of this Text	☐	☐	☐	☐

Do you intend to continue using BPP Interactive Texts/Assessment Kits? ☐ Yes ☐ No

Please note any further comments and suggestions/errors on the reverse of this page.

Please return to: Nick Weller, BPP Publishing Ltd, FREEPOST, London, W12 8BR

REVIEW FORM & FREE PRIZE DRAW (continued)

Please note any further comments and suggestions/errors below

FREE PRIZE DRAW RULES

1   Closing date for 31 January 2002 draw is 31 December 2001. Closing date for 31 July 2002 draw is 30 June 2002.

2   Restricted to entries with UK and Eire addresses only. BPP employees, their families and business associates are excluded.

3   No purchase necessary. Entry forms are available upon request from BPP Publishing. No more than one entry per title, per person. Draw restricted to persons aged 16 and over.

4   Winners will be notified by post and receive their cheques not later than 6 weeks after the relevant draw date.

5   The decision of the promoter in all matters is final and binding. No correspondence will be entered into.